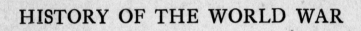

HISTORY OF THE WORLD WAR

Walter
E.
Gaultney
Corporal

Joseph Cummings Chase GERMANY
1919

THE DOUGHBOY

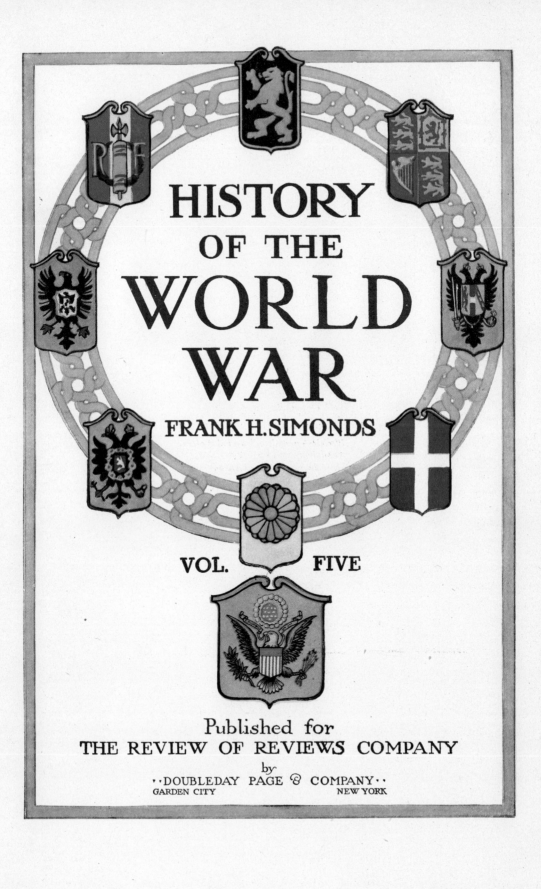

HISTORY
OF THE
WORLD
WAR

FRANK H. SIMONDS

VOL. FIVE

Published for
THE REVIEW OF REVIEWS COMPANY
by
·· DOUBLEDAY PAGE & COMPANY ··
GARDEN CITY   NEW YORK

CONTENTS

PART I

CHAPTER I

THE FINAL PHASE

CHAPTER II

PICARDY—THE KAISER'S BATTLE

CHAPTER VI

AMERICA FROM CANTIGNY TO ST. MIHIEL

CHAPTER VII

FOCH MANŒUVRES

CHAPTER VIII

ST. MIHIEL

CHAPTER XI

THE ARMISTICE

CHAPTER XII

THE OTHER FRONTS

CONCLUSION

CONTENTS

PART II

I

LIST OF ILLUSTRATIONS

LIST OF MAPS

PART ONE
HISTORY OF THE WORLD WAR
BY
FRANK H. SIMONDS

CHAPTER ONE

THE FINAL PHASE

I
THE LAST CAMPAIGN

The last campaign of the World War was a fitting climax to a struggle which had endured already for more than three years and had surpassed all previous contests recorded in human history. In the final phase more than six millions of men, representing seven nations, fought for 235 days on a front of 250 miles from the North Sea to the Moselle, from the outer defences of Metz to the ruins of Nieuport. And the struggle was not limited to the west front. While Germany met her ancient foes in decisive contest on the battlefields of France, Italian armies first repulsed then crushed the Austrians on the Piave; Serbian, Greek, French, British, and Italian troops fought Bulgarians in Albania and Macedonia, and British troops overwhelmed the Turk on the Plain of Armageddon. Two continents furnished the battlefields, and five, reckoning Australia, supplied the combatants.

But it was the issue of contest in France which decided the fate of the world and the question of victory and defeat in the great struggle. And in this contest, which French historians already regard as a single engagement and describe as the "Battle of France," all the previous western campaigns were repeated on a hugely increased scale. When the Germans crushed the British Fifth Army in March, 1918, they swept forward over all the territory which had been gained and lost in the First Battle of the Somme and the subsequent "Hindenburg" Retreat.

When in April German effort turned north, it was on the fields of Flanders, the scene of the three great struggles about Ypres, that one more tremendous battle was fought. In April, before the war drifted northward, too, the German storm once more reached the foot of Vimy Ridge. In May, when Ludendorff faced southward, a new conflict

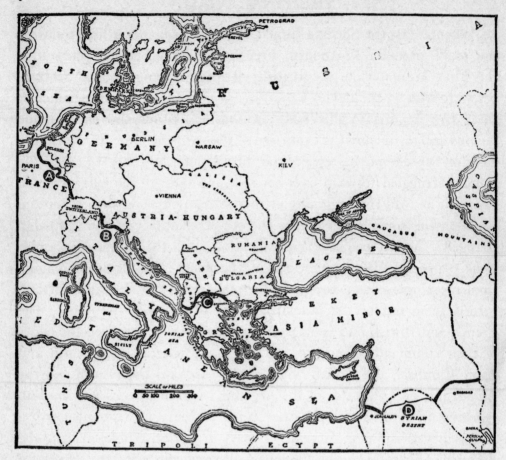

THE FOUR FRONTS

A—Western Front.   B—Italian Front.   C—Macedonian Front.   D—Eastern Front.

broke out upon the battlefields on the Craonne Plateau, where Kluck had checked the French and British advance from the Marne in 1914, where Ludendorff had broken the Nivelle offensive in 1917.

In July the last German attack stormed at the lines held by the French in Champagne, since the first great offensive, that of September, 1915, and in the same hour passed the Marne at the towns where the armies of Bülow and Kluck had crossed and recrossed that stream in the days of the First Battle of the Marne.   Indeed, the Second Battle of the Marne in July, 1918, was in so many respects a replica of the First in September, 1914, that history affords no parallel more striking.

When at last the tide had turned, the Allied advance in July followed the roads used by Maunoury, French, and Franchet d'Esperey after the First Marne, while the British victories of August and September were won on the fields of the First Somme, and the battle names of these two months recalled with glorious exactitude the places made famous and terrible by the campaign of two years before. In the closing days of September, moreover, the first American army to enter the conflict struggled forward over the hills and through the villages which had seen in 1916 the beginning of the German offensive before Verdun.

With the coming of October the whole character of the campaign changed. At last one saw the realization of all the various and ambitious plans for Allied operations in the past. The British, emerging from the Ypres salient, swept the Germans from the Belgian coast and turned them out of the industrial cities of the French north. The French and British on the sides of the Noyon salient realized the hopes of their commanders in 1916 and 1917, and entered St. Quentin and Laon, Cambrai, and Douai. Still to the eastward the French and the Americans, on either side of the Argonne between Rheims and Verdun, repeated on a widened front the attack of Joffre in September, 1915, and achieved supreme success. Lastly, in the St. Mihiel salient, the American First Army in its initial engagement put into successful operation the plans of the French in the winter of 1914-15 and, by abolishing the salient, closed the gap in the eastern armour of France.

Flanders, Artois, Picardy, Ile-de-France, Champagne, and Lorraine were, in their turn, scenes of new contests whose extent of front surpassed the limits of ancient provinces, whose circumstances recalled the history of previous campaigns, and disclosed in success the purposes and plans of Allied commanders, which had been in the past imperfectly realized or totally wrecked. And as a final dramatic detail, when at last the Armistice came, King Albert was approaching his capital at the head of a Belgian army; Canadian troops had entered Mons, where British participation in the struggle had begun; French armies were in Sedan, the town for ever associated with the French disasters of 1870; and a Franco-American offensive was just about to break out to the east of Metz, over the ground which had seen the first French dash into the "Lost Provinces" and the opening reverse at Morhange.

Nor was the drama alone splendid in its magnitude. Every element of suspense, surprise, intensity was present to hold the attention of the world, neutral and engaged alike; and so terrible was the ordeal that, the moment of victory once passed, conqueror and conquered alike sank back exhausted by a strain beyond that which had ever before been placed upon the millions in line, and behind the line, who constituted nations at war.

For history, moreover—which has attached to the Hundred Days of Napoleon a lasting significance as affording a standard of measurement for the rise and fall of one of the world's great figures—there must be hardly less meaning in the span of Ludendorff, longer by twenty days only, which saw the greatest of German military leaders three times on the edge of supreme victory and, on the final day, overtaken by swift defeat, ordering a second retreat from the Marne; and this retreat, in barely more than another hundred days, would end in surrender after decisive defeat, which alone prevented the supreme disaster of a Waterloo twentyfold magnified.

Since Napoleon fell, no soldier had known such intoxicating success as came to Ludendorff in March, in April, and again in May; while between March 26th and November 11th, Foch—first in defeat prepared by his predecessors, and then in victory organized by his own genius—wrote the most brilliant and far-shining page in all military history, and earned the right to rank as a soldier with the great Emperor, who had been his model.

In less than eight months, the finest army in size, equipment, and training ever put into the field by a civilized nation was transformed—after initial victories which had no parallel in this or any other war, after conquests of ground, captures of guns, harvestings of prisoners unequalled in all the past campaigns of the war—into a broken and beaten host, incapable of warding off the final blow, defeated beyond hope of recovery, still retaining a semblance of its ancient courage and in parts a shadow of its traditional discipline, but incapable of checking its pursuers, of maintaining its positions, of long postponing that ultimate disaster, already prepared, when an armistice—incomprehensible even to the beaten army, by reason of the completeness of the surrender—saved the conquered from the otherwise inescapable rout.

II. THE TWO PHASES

In this final campaign there are two distinct phases, which in turn fall into three divisions. There is first the German phase, the period beginning with March 21st and ending on July 18th, within which the Germans seek desperately and magnificently to win a decision in three great offensives: that delivered against the British alone, on March 21st, and continued in the April attack which carried the battlefront from Picardy to Artois and Flanders; that of May 27th against the French and British on the Chemin des Dames, which was extended to the heights north of Compiègne, in the early days of June; and finally, that of July 15th, between Rheims and the Argonne and between the Mountain of Rheims and Château-Thierry, which, failing, was totally transformed by Foch's deadly counter-offensive of July 18th.

The Allied phase, between July 18th and November 11th, displays a similar threefold division. It opens with the stroke between the Aisne and the Marne on July 18th, which lives as the Second Battle of the Marne and gained for the Allies the initiative. It continues with the Second Battle of the Somme, delivered on August 8th, Ludendorff's "black day for Germany," in which the British army had its full revenge for the still recent past. It reaches its climax on September 26th and the successive days, in which the Allies break the Hindenburg Line and begin the march to victory, which ends only with the Armistice.

Nor can one be blind to the political as well as the military aspects of this brief but astounding period. When the campaign opened, Germany, by her forty-odd months of success, had created an empire overpassing even that of Napoleon at the zenith of his career. German will was supreme from Schleswig-Holstein to Palestine. Belgium, Poland, northern France and the Ukraine, Serbia and the Baltic Provinces, Roumania and eastern Venetia paid tribute to German power and saw behind the Austrians, Bulgars, Turks, and Hungarians, who in certain places replaced the German master, the sustaining force of the true conqueror.

Eight months later William II and his family had fled Germany; the ancient dynasties of every German state, the youthful heir of the Hapsburgs, the alien Czar of Bulgaria were fugitives. The "cascade of thrones" had come, and the sole sovereigns left in Europe ruled over neutral states or survived the storm because they had been loyal members of the victorious alliance. Before the year ended, French armies were on the left bank of the Rhine; Poland had risen from her ashes; Roumanian armies awaited only the appointed hour, no longer distant, when they should enter Budapest. In Berlin Germans killed Germans, as Frenchmen had slain Frenchmen in Paris after the disasters of the Terrible Year. Of all the mighty Middle Europe, intact on March 21st, nothing but fragments were left. Germany was a republic, at least in name; the Hapsburg Empire was a memory; Alsace-Lorraine had reëntered the French frontiers; Constantinople was under the guns of an Allied fleet. Of the most colossal national dream in all history there was left nothing but wreckage strewn over three continents, while the German fleet, which had insolently challenged British mastery of the blue water, had come captive to British waters, hauled down its battle ensign, and lay helpless at anchor against the hour when it should be ignominiously scuttled by its crew.

III.   THE GERMAN OPPORTUNITY

Turning now to the military aspects, what were the conditions under which this supreme battle was joined? What was the advantages, resources, necessities of the two contending forces: of Ludendorff, who had now become the supreme master of the fate of Germany; of the Allies, who in the hour of disaster at last transferred the reins to the firm hands of that great soldier who was to save a cause, a continent, the world, from the fatal consequences of German success.

Looking first at the German side, it is clear that the enemy possessed these advantages: They outnumbered the Allies, counting 205 divisions against 177. They had the initiative, the power to strike when and where they chose, since the Allies had resigned the offensive. They possessed an army more highly trained for the task in hand and, for the moment, better engined. They had devised a method of attack, destined temporarily to transform the very character of the struggle, and they had successfully applied this method in Russia, in Italy, and in Flanders in the closing months of 1917. Finally, they had in Ludendorff a great commander, certainly the greatest German military genius of the war, who was capable of exacting the last ounce from that German machine which he had in part built up, and, for the rest, had become a final expression of the Prussian military tradition. And Ludendorff as master, through this unity of command, added a supreme advantage to all the others in his hands.

Behind the lines, too, the Germans profited by a far better morale. The collapse of Russia, made permanent to the German mind by the Treaty of Brest-Litovsk; the defeat of Italy at Caporetto; the recognition of the opportunity and the belief in the man who led the German armies, had combined to reanimate German spirits, reawaken all the hopes and expectations of August, 1914, before the Marne, and of February, 1916, before Verdun. Once more the German people were confident of victory, supreme victory, and world hegemony after victory. Army and people expected triumph, and, to achieve it, were capable of unprecedented effort during that period in which the faith survived.

On the other hand, time was no longer an ally of the German. Ludendorff's position was exactly analogous to that of Napoleon when the French Emperor returned from Elba. Since the submarine had failed to close the seas, a time must be expected when American troops would begin to arrive in great numbers. As the problem of Napoleon was to dispose of the armies of Wellington and Blücher in Belgium before those of Russia and Austria could arrive in Lorraine, Ludendorff must destroy the British and the French before the American millions became effective. In 1918, as in 1815, victory might be expected to preclude the possibility of the arrival of the enemy's reinforcements.

It was essential, too, that the success should not be delayed. The first blow must be decisive, if the confidence of the German people was

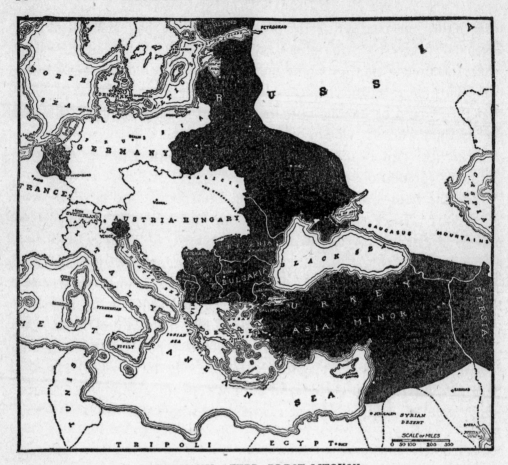

GERMANY AFTER BREST-LITOVSK

Solid black shows Turkish and conquered territory in German hands at the beginning of the campaign of 1918

to endure.   After the experiences of the First Marne and Verdun, delay might spell a fatal decline in civilian morale.   Even the hint of another campaign like that before Verdun, the mere suggestion of a check after that first forward rush, which could be calculated upon in advance as the irreducible minimum of profit of any great offensive, would prove a signal for dangerous depression, while the smallest semblance of defeat would not alone banish German hope but would infallibly entail Bulgarian, Turkish, and even Austrian desertion or collapse.

Here, too, were all the elements of the first campaign of the war. Then the French had avoided ruin in the opening defeats, parried the fatal blow, survived until the Russian pressure had compelled the Germans to give over the offensive in the west and turn to the east, where for three years they would find occupation, would discover a task compelling them to concentrate so much of their effort in saving Austria that they would be unable, save for the brief Verdun interlude, to seek the decision where it alone could be found, namely in the west. But this time the Americans would ultimately play the Russian rôle, and Germany's present opportunity was palpably her last chance.

For the hour which was now come Ludendorff had laboured for three years. His victories in the east from Tannenberg to Tarnopol, his patient labour against the Russian, his moments of agony, when Roumania suddenly thrust in, during the British attack at Arras, throughout the long summer of 1917, had been rewarded. The war on two fronts was over; his hands were free to deal with the western enemies. He could choose the point of attack, be sure of superior numbers at the decisive point; he had three months in which to achieve victory without too much apprehension on the American score. On the whole, it was more than he could have expected and as much as any soldier could hope. Small wonder he turned a deaf ear to those who suggested negotiation in advance of attack.

IV. THE ALLIED CASE

What, by contrast, was the situation of the Allies? Opposing 177 divisions to 205, they not only confessed inferiority of numbers, but their smaller forces served under divided leadership. The largest single element—the French, counting 99 divisions—had, in Petain, a splendid chief, who had brought them out of the slough of despond of the previous years; restored discipline, confidence, morale; overcome the consequences of the defeat of April, 1917, and the blunders of Nivelle. But the army had already passed its maximum of strength; the losses of four terrible campaigns could only in part be made good, and the moment was at hand when it would be impossible to replace wastage. Yet in strength and in spirit, and even more in mechanical equipment, the French army was formidable—equal, division for division, to the German.

It was different with the British army.   Its 58 divisions had not been kept up to proper strength.   Reinforcements, replacements, had been denied by reason of the mistaken policy of Lloyd George, who had decided that victory on the west front—and defeat as well—were impossible, and had consented to the transfer of divisions to the east. In March, 1918, the British army was weaker by 180,000 bayonets than it had been a year earlier.   The strength of divisions had been reduced by breaking up three battalions in each to reinforce the balance, and this makeshift had contributed alike to disorganize and to discourage.

Not only had political influence withheld the necessary replacements, but it had also consented to the extension of the line.   The result was that fewer British troops were on the front; and these necessarily held an extended line more thinly.   In addition, taking over the line had not been followed by the proper fortification of the new positions.   The time and the labour were lacking and on the new sector, between the Somme and the Oise, the British Fifth Army, dangerously extended, was without proper support lines against the possible emergency which might come.

In addition to this the confidence of the army had been shaken. The terrible losses in Flanders in the previous year, the unmistakable blundering of their commanders, coupled with failure of replacements to come and the weakness disclosed to the soldiers themselves by the extension of the lines, combined to create a situation which might be dangerous, as dangerous as the French situation after the initial defeat in April of the previous year.

The French army was then, relatively, in admirable condition; that of the British was less good.   As to the Belgians, they maintained twelve divisions on their own front, admirable divisions but lacking in replacements.   Two Portuguese divisions of doubtful value—which was to prove less than doubtful in the later crisis—completed the European troops of the Allies, and their colonial contingents, as well.   As to the Americans, four partially trained divisions were actually in France when the campaign opened.   But the first of these divisions was not available for combat use before late April, and the next two to engage went into the furnace as late as June 1st, when the second great German offensive had almost reached its term.

It was still true that in eventual reserves the Allies were stronger than their foes, even with America out of the reckoning. Thus the French counted 682,000; the British, 764,000; the Belgians, 30,000; a total of 1,476,000 against 1,082,000 for the Germans. But the Allied reserves were scattered, a large fraction locked up in Britain, and the result was to be that three months were to pass before the balance of numbers actually engaged was in favour of the Allies; and this would come only when America was able to engage divisions which were still in the United States when the battle began.

At the moment when the first attack was launched, on March 21st, the actual battle strength of the Allies—that is, the troops actually in line or in regular formations behind the line—was in favour to that of the Germans by upward of 300,000. Again, while the German troops were concentrated against the selected front, the Allied were still scattered; the reserves were subject to the command of at least two different general staffs, each of which was, in the nature of things, bound to view the situation of the other through its own glasses.

As to the American contribution, in eleven months of actual participation in the struggle the United States had as late as the end of February sent but six divisions—of which only four were even partially trained—and there was as yet no hint that the pace could or would be accelerated. Therefore the German might conclude that he would have, until the decision had been achieved, a homogeneous army under a single commander assured of superior numbers.

V. THE DIRECTION OF ATTACK

Even with inferior numbers Foch—as yet nothing but a sort of military adviser at the Versailles Conference of military representatives, charged to "coördinate" the movements of the two great Allied armies—had advised attack. But he had been overruled. Lloyd George was satisfied that the Flanders experiment of 1917 had proved what the

Somme adventure of 1916 had suggested: that an Allied offensive could not bring success, given the existing conditions of warfare.

In the same way George had decided, the views of Haig and Petain tending to confirm him, that a German success was equally impossible, since the German had no greater advantage of numbers or machinery than the Allies had possessed when they attacked at the Aisne and in Flanders in the previous year. But Haig, agreeing with George as to the wisdom of the defensive, had protested vainly against the folly of a defensive which did not envisage adequate numbers to maintain the lines.

Since Foch's suggestion had been overruled and the Allies had adopted a policy of waiting until America could arrive, that is of resigning all hope of a victory in 1918, Ludendorff acquired the initiative without even having to fight for it—that initiative which the Germans had lost on the west front, when the Allied attack at the Somme in July and August, 1916, had compelled Falkenhayn to abandon the Verdun attack.

Having the initiative, his problem was which to strike, the British or the French, since—despite the foolish conjectures of the winter of 1917–18—it was necessary for Ludendorff to strike, if a decisive victory was to be achieved and a truly German peace attained. Obviously, his choice must be to attack the British, because the British army was weak in numbers, as a consequence of the failure of George to furnish replacements, perilously placed because of an extension of line, unwarranted in view of the effectives available, and at a lower ebb of spirits than at any time before or after, during the whole war.

By contrast, the British civilian morale was, on the whole, the strongest among the European allies, and unless the British army were defeated decisively there was little chance of arriving at a peace which would even measurably satisfy the German expectations of March, 1918. But if Ludendorff could strike the British army—defeat it, separate it from the French, drive it back to the edge of the sea, exhausting French reserves wasted in a vain effort to save the British—then he might expect, even in advance of a final blow, that France would surrender.

Ludendorff's objective then was the British army, just as the younger Moltke's objective had been the French army in the Marne campaign of 1914. The geographical ends which he pursued were of relatively minor importance. Before July, that is until the surprising success at the Chemin des Dames led him to his fatal attack upon the French, his purpose was steadily to smash the British army. In his original plan he had contemplated, after an attack upon the French at the Chemin des Dames, to return to the northern field and finish the task begun in March and pushed well toward completion in April.

To use the familiar comparison, just as Napoleon set out to crush first the Prussian and then the British armies in the Waterloo campaign, Ludendorff set out to smash the British and then, if necessary, the French, in his last campaign. And just as the great Emperor heavily defeated the Prussians at Ligny, Ludendorff even more severely defeated the British in the fighting of April and May. But he did not actually crush them, just as Napoleon failed to dispose permanently of Blücher's Prussians. Nor was he able to put the French out, when he turned against them. Then he was in turn overwhelmed by the British and the French, reinforced by the Americans, as Napoleon was routed by the British reinforced by the Prussians at Waterloo. But one campaign lasted seven days; the other, seven months.

We see, then, that Ludendorff had the advantage of numbers, of the offensive; that he wisely selected the weaker army to attack; that his strategy was Napoleonic. He had one further advantage, which was of almost incalculable value, namely a new and revolutionary system of attack, the efficacy of which was not even suspected by his foes; that method of attack which, after nearly four years, was to restore the element of surprise and, for the moment, bring back the old war of movement, after producing that actual break through, so long sought and hitherto never realized, on a grand scale since the war of trenches had begun in November, 1914, in the deadlock in Flanders.

VI. LUDENDORFF

Because this gigantic campaign was, on the military side, after the first tragic week, a duel between soldiers, between Ludendorff and Foch, it is necessary to look for a moment at the men, themselves, the men who played a rôle hardly paralleled in history, since Napoleon, who was conquered at last—not by a greater military genius but by a combination of circumstances, political even more than military, and, even after defeat, lived—and lives—as the supreme military genius of his own age.

Oddly enough, while the personality and the history of Foch are easily discoverable—are revealed alike by his own actions, his written and spoken words, and by the endless tributes coming from all who knew him, whether in the days of preparation or in the period of his greatness —Ludendorff remains, in a measure, a man of mystery. His own heavy volume setting forth his recollections of the war helps but little to explain or even to animate the solid, rather brutal, but enormously virile portrait supplied by all German military photographs.

Erich Ludendorff was born at Kruszezewnia in the Prussian province of Posen won for the Hohenzollerns as a result of the partition of Poland, on April 9, 1865. He was a product, not of the "junker" nobility, but of the small Prussian bourgeosie. He was the first of his name to choose the army as a career, although his father had been a reserve officer in the Prussian cavalry and had served in the wars of 1866 and 1870. His mother was a Swede, a circumstance explaining his retirement to Sweden following German defeat and revolution. His family had few resources to aid him in acquiring education. Poor, like Napoleon, Ludendorff at the very outset of his life dedicated himself to a consuming ambition; but it was not a personal ambition, rather it was a religion, the religion of his country. German greatness he saw attainable only through the army and the navy. His task was military, and to it he devoted his life, the life of a Spartan. With the modern Germany, its excesses, its display of wealth, its exaggeration of the trappings of military life, and its gross imitation of British manners and industrial objectives he had neither sympathy nor patience. He was an "old" German; even his master the Kaiser could enlist his loyalty but could not command his approval.

In 1904 this soldier, already marked for his intelligence, his devotion to work, went to the General Staff. The fruit of his labour was the later demand of the German army for a gigantic appropriation, an enormous expansion, which preceded by only a brief time the coming of the war, drove France to the three-year service, and constituted one of the last of the interminable warnings.

Ludendorff's first service in the war was brilliant. The attack upon Liége having led to confusion and preliminary failure, he put himself at the head of a small detachment, penetrated the city, seized the citadel, restored the situation. It was a deed reminiscent of the "Little Corporal" at the bridge of Lodi, but it was a single instance of battlefield audacity and courage. Almost immediately he was caught up and transported to the east, where he became the brains of the Hindenburg legend.

The relation between the two men was not unknown in German military history. Gneisenau had played the same part for old Blücher, and the famous marshal had acknowledged it once in London, where he wagered that he was the only man in the drawing room who could kiss his own head, and won the wager by bestowing a sound smack upon Gneisenau's forehead. At first the true mission of Ludendorff was not generally appreciated. The legend grew about Hindenburg and, as it grew, expressed itself in the preposterous wooden statue with its ridiculous nails; but in the end fact outran fiction, and Ludendorff emerged.

In the east his daring won Tannenberg, and but for Austrian blundering he might have conquered Poland in 1914. In the end Austrian necessities compelled a modification of his plans and he delivered the great blow at the Dunajec in 1915, which was the beginning of the Russian collapse. But in 1916 the German offensive at Verdun and the Allied attack at the Somme deprived him of the men to finish the Russian task; and the Russian offensive of June, in Galicia, and the Roumanian eruption of August gave him anxious hours.

Even in 1917, when at last he and Hindenburg had come west, he was unable at once to take the offensive. His first decision was expressed in the famous Hindenburg Retreat, which enabled the Germans to block all the Allied efforts in the west until Russia was finally reduced to chaos and Roumania conquered. In this period Ludendorff consented to the launching of the submarine campaign because he accepted, with reservations as to time, the forecasts of the naval branch. He did not reckon the American intervention as dangerous; he expected to win the war by an offensive in the west in 1918, if the submarine did not bring a decision before, and he did not dream of the arrival of American masses. This was his supreme miscalculation, but the real blame must rest with the navy.

In the debate over the submarine his voice was decisive, and he gave it for the blockade unhesitatingly. He was unmoved when military necessities involved the destruction of two French provinces in 1917; he was no more considerate of rights or of humanity when the same necessity entailed a policy of marine murder. He dealt with both questions as one might deal with an arithmetical calculation.

In 1918, when he delivered his opening blow, he had been more frequently victorious than any other real or nominal commander-in-chief in the war. He had planned greater battles and brought off more complete successes. He had engineered the crushing of Serbia, Roumania, Russia; the victory over Italy had been won under his direct supervision. His mastery of the German war machine was unquestioned; his power was almost as great as that of Napoleon, and he used it for political quite as much as for military ends, when political circumstances had a bearing upon military conditions. The civil government of Germany, the Chancellor, and even the Emperor, were unable to thwart him.

Reading the man's own account of himself, one recognizes that he was prepared for everything except failure; that he considered everything except the strategy and the moral force of his opponent. His eyes were turned inward, not outward; his memoirs contain hardly a passing reference to his opponents—to Foch, to Haig, to Pershing. When his own offensives failed, he showed himself bewildered; then he attempted to lay the blame, first upon certain units in the army, which failed to accomplish their duty, then upon the civil government and the civilian morale. If his strategy failed it was not because he had met a master; if his armies were defeated it was not because they showed themselves inferior to Allied armies, which had not collapsed in the spring disasters.

When the first defeats came, Ludendorff was seized with a panic and promptly demanded that the government make peace. After August 8th he lost his own nerve, and his official statements shocked the German people, already shaken by the outward appearance of defeat. But even in this crisis he could not believe that the real defeat was the army's, he sought a civilian explanation. When at the last his Emperor accepted his resignation, after rebuking his general for an excess of zeal, Ludendorff retired, still unshaken in his faith in the system which he typified, still incapable of finding any real explanation for the impossible: the defeat and proximate rout of the German army.

A certain genuine sincerity there is about the man Ludendorff in the midst of all the deliberate and the unconscious inveracity of his own memoirs, a measure of arresting simplicity. The man gave his whole life, his great talents, everything to the cause he adopted. He was not unworthy of the great trust, for no selfish aspiration interfered with his service to his country. If he was brutal—and he was brutal—it was inherent brutality, the spirit which he had acquired, which had been born in him, perhaps, as a sharer in the Prussian tradition. But once his faith is shaken by defeat, his gods upset, his religion confounded, the great man becomes unmistakably a very little man; he crumples up with the system, the same weaknesses appear in both.

But in March, 1918, in all the vast German Empire, in all the subject provinces and allied races there was none to question his will. The Kaiser was a pale shade. The Chancellor was without power. Hindenburg was little more than a colossal figurehead, which bowed assent to Ludendorff's words. Personal ambition he had none, he was not a mere cringing courtier, he could take a firm hand with the Kaiser or the Crown Prince, but not as a soldier of fortune, merely as a servant of his country's greatness, as he conceived it.

Grim, silent, heavy handed and, after a fashion, heavy minded—almost a gloomy fanatic—his whole life a deliberate sacrifice to the ideal of his service and his country, Ludendorff was the embodiment of the greatness of Germany, as well as an illustration of her weakness. He would crush, he believed in force, he had little sympathy, and no remorse. He was the architect of the Hindenburg Retreat, which transformed two provinces of France into a desert. As a man, as a thinker, as a soldier, he was inferior to Foch, but he was the greatest soldier Germany had produced during the war, and he came within two steps of victory. Foch would one day describe the German army as an express locomotive in the hands of a stage-coach driver—but to the present writer he affirmed emphatically that Ludendorff was the best German leader of the World War.

Count Czernin, Foreign Minister of the Hapsburg Empire in the latter days of the war, supplies, in his own memoirs, an admirable picture of Ludendorff. A really trained and able statesman, the Austrian tremendously admires Ludendorff the soldier but bemoans his political limitations, which were those of the German military caste. They could not realize—he points out shrewdly—that a nation might die of military victories which were indecisive, and that unlimited securities for negotiation in the shape of conquered provinces were valueless if the enemy were neither willing nor compelled to redeem them at the German price. The great Moltke was equally dangerous but he had a Bismarck to control him, and Czernin laments the absence of a Bismarck, of a statesman capable of restraining the Ludendorff caste and of seeing beyond the battle map. When Czernin wanted to negotiate, when he proposed the cession of Alsace-Lorraine, the German generals were more amused than angry—victory seemed to them so inevitable. When the generals were at last ready to negotiate, their defeat in battle was so complete that diplomacy could accomplish nothing.

Czernin, like all other critics of Ludendorff, save the German, emphasizes beyond all else the blind, arrogant pride of the man, and sees in this, not so much an individual trait as the ultimate expression of the same characteristic in the whole German-Prussian military caste. Bismarck, in his own memoirs, more than once complains of the same thing. Of Foch one feels that he was a great man, above and beyond all systems; of Ludendorff, that he was the greatest exponent of one system, formidable beyond doubt, but possessing certain dangerous limitations; and the limitations as well as the virtues of the system were

expressed in Ludendorff with equal exaggeration. The more one analyzes German military operations, the more completely this blindness—
due to pride, to overweening confidence—discloses itself, the neglect
of the actual factors in the situation and the blind reliance upon an
estimate based upon a sense of superiority, an assurance rising to a
total ignoring of the other side of the barbed-wire entanglements. Like
the younger Moltke in 1914, Ludendorff assumed that the enemy had
been conquered by his blows and having made the assumption, acted
upon it to the ruin of his army and his country. The same misconcep-
tion underlies the First Marne, Verdun, and the Second Marne. With
Foch, victory was a faith, but with Ludendorff, a superstition. The
difference is capital.

VII. FOCH

No greater contrast to Ludendorff—physically, intellectually, morally—can be supplied than by the figure of Foch. Ludendorff had in-
herited the tradition of a victorious army. Foch began his service in an
army recently defeated; he saw Metz, which he knew as French, torn
from the Fatherland. For France everything, the army first of all, was
to be remade. Foch undertook, with his contemporaries, to return to
the Napoleonic tradition, to find in the history of 1870 the causes of
defeat, and in the strategy of the great Emperor the principles which
would show the way to victory.

The result was the First Battle of the Marne, where the French
military school definitely vanquished the German. It could not follow up
success with adequate exploitation because numbers were lacking, but
the answer had been found, and Foch was a conspicuous factor in
delivering the answer. Ludendorff had begun at Liége by victory;
Foch began before Nancy by saving a beaten French army, defeated at
Morhange. At the Marne he delivered the most brilliant and compelling counter-stroke.

Sent north, he coördinated British, French, and Belgian armies and
saved Calais. The genius of that splendid campaign was his, although the
glory is shared by British and French armies, by Belgian, too. In 1915

he directed the offensive in Artois which fell short of success. He was hardly more fortunate at the Somme in 1916, and, as a consequence, suffered temporary disgrace. But he kept to his work. After Nivelle fell, he was called to new tasks; when Caporetto came, he was sent to advise the Italians.

Before the war he had been a marked man among soldiers. As head of the École de Guerre his teachings had inspired many. He had also been a frank and uncompromising Catholic, a circumstance which more than once injured his professional prospects. But beyond all else he was a soldier who had taught abstract principles magnificently and tested each of the precepts on the battlefield adequately.

"A lost battle is a battle someone accepts as lost," he had asserted in the past. After August 8th, Ludendorff proved the truth of this assertion, but after Picardy, Flanders, the Chemin des Dames, Foch conceded nothing. "Tell Lloyd George that I still prefer my side to Ludendorff's," he told a friend of the British Prime Minister, recalling the fact that, after the April disaster, he had made a statement, to which he held, when the Chemin des Dames had been lost and Paris was in danger.

Ludendorff, save for the moment at Liége, was an office soldier: he provided armies with plans and with orders. But Foch was something more; his personality expressed itself in contact with his subordinates, and in critical hours he ran from place to place and his presence was an unfailing inspiration. The soul of the man Foch comes out of his deeds and his words alike, and it is possible to perceive how it animated those about him. Exactly this spiritual element is lacking in Ludendorff, and the lack of it makes him impersonal in victory and almost insignificant in defeat.

We have, then, in this tremendous duel, the clash of two great military ideas, the French and the German, for the higher strategy is all Ludendorff and Foch. And in this clash the victory of the French is not only incontestable but in the end simply explicable. We have also the struggle between two minds and two moral natures, and the triumph of the higher mind and the finer moral nature is not less unmistakable.

For Americans it is an interesting circumstance that the two chief figures in the last campaign of the World War were separated by approximately the same years which lay between Grant and Lee in the Civil War. Foch was born at Tarbes, in the Pyrenees, on October 2, 1851, and was thus a "meridional" like Joffre who came from the eastern Pyrenees. His family, like that of Ludendorff, was respectable rather than distinguished. His mother's father had fought with distinction under Napoleon, and his own family had cherished an admiration for the great Emperor, which was disclosed in the fact that one of his father's several names was Napoleon—a circumstance interesting in view of the fact that the future marshal was to prove one of the greatest admirers of Napoleon and, as a student of his campaigns, to discover and revive for France the secrets of system which explained Napoleonic victories.

The story of Foch's career in the French army is little significant now, save as its study reveals the development of the man. Worth recalling, however, is the anecdote—told by his biographer, Raymond Recouly—of the meeting between Foch and Clemenceau in 1908, during the "Tiger's" first ministry, when he sent for Foch to offer him the direction of the École de Guerre.

"But, Mr. President," expostulated Foch, "I'm afraid you don't know the whole truth about me. Do you know that I have a brother who is a Jesuit?"

"I don't care a damn," retorted Clemenceau. "You will teach military science—not religion—and you will make a good director of the college; and that is all I care about."

A significant interview, this, when one recalls the bitterness against the Church in France at that time. And, as director of the École de Guerre, Foch did much to prepare the French high command for war; for the war he always believed inevitable. From this post Foch went out a General of Division in 1911. At the École he met General Weygand, later to serve him as faithfully as Berthier served Napoleon, from the Grand Couronén to the interview at Rethondes.

Reading the teachings of Foch, his lectures, it becomes clear that, while penetrating the system of Napoleon, he had equally accurately appraised the strength and the limitations of the German method. His analyses of the German campaigns of 1870 disclose a prescient grasp of the methods actually employed in 1914–1918. The weakness before Metz revealed the same misconceptions of the true situation of the enemy—which, had a Napoleon or a Foch commanded Bazaine's army, would infallibly have ruined German prospects in 1870—turn up again; and Foch foresees them before they arrive: at the Marne, at the Yser, finally, and for ever memorably, at the Second Battle of the Marne.

General Pershing, on his return from Europe, characterized Foch as "a great strategist." But he was something far more: he was a great and an accurate psychologist, not merely at headquarters, in the calm of study, but in the heat of battle. Recall his message to Joffre, after four days of defeat and retreat at the Marne:

"My centre is giving way, my right is retiring, impossible to manœuvre, the situation is excellent, I shall attack."

And attack he did, moving a division across all his rear, putting it in at sunset, and producing that moral effect which won the day—giving just that little added weight which, like the proverbial straw, broke the camel's back.

But, as Recouly points out, his statement: "the situation is excellent," was not bravado, only the result of an accurate appraisal of the enemy's situation. The fury of the attack directed against him, as he told his staff, disclosed the bad turn things were taking for the Germans elsewhere. When in November, 1914, the Prussian Guard was broken at Ypres, he remarked, forthwith: "We shall have a long period of quiet in the west now." The calm lasted, so far as German offensives were concerned, until February, 1916, when the attack on Verdun began.

In a word, one of the salient details in Foch's strategy was his psychology, which enabled him to get at what his enemy was actually thinking, and to act upon this knowledge, while Ludendorff and his predecessors decided on what the enemy *must* think, and then acted on this assumption, which, on the western front, was almost without exception inaccurate. At La Fère-Champenoise Foch knew that the Germans had their last reserves in and that the hour of decision had arrived. At the Second Marne Ludendorff reasoned that the previous offensives had exhausted French reserves and on this conclusion went to defeat, when French and American reserves intervened.

As one examines the German campaigns, the three great western offensives in 1914, 1916, and 1918, a single characteristic tends more and more clearly to detach itself. There is the same magnificent preparation—the same wise, skilful, scientific upbuilding of a tremendous instrument—an accurate appraisal of the weak points in the enemy's armour. All being ready and marvellously ready, the machine is set in motion. It strikes, and the first impact is tremendous, the first results colossal; but thereafter the machine, in some unaccountable fashion, seems slowly to run down, like a child's electric toy. Its movements become uncertain, its direction indistinct; presently it comes to a dead halt or even recoils. Just at the moment when the Allied publics see utter ruin in plain view and the German people are celebrating victory without limit, something happens, almost miraculously—and some people still believe the First Marne a miracle.

There is a phrase of Foch's, descriptive of German methods in 1870, which admirably sums this up:

"Does not that prove," he asks, "that if a tool is too heavy for the worker's hand, it will either slip through his fingers or pull him over?"

Now, by contrast, when Foch becomes master of the military forces of the Allies, when the great stress due to the necessity to parry the enemy's first blows has passed, one sees his method put into operation. Could anything be more totally different? Instead of a machine complete at the hour of joining battle, his machine seems to grow with the battle—develop, expand, take on new vitality and strength. When Ludendorff struck one saw ruin imminent and colossal; in Foch's offensive the actual victory comes almost as a surprise, the separate steps are so imperceptible. Of Napoleon's method, Clausewitz had written:

In Napoleon's battles a veil seems to cover the tediousness inseparable from taking up positions and carrying out the first movements, but once that is lifted, one always sees the decisive attack by masses of men filling the scene with tragic fury.

In Foch's phrase, the separate attacks of the Germans in 1918 were all "dammed." A dike was stretched across their front, the torrent of water rolled madly against the dike, but somehow the barrier just managed to hold. There is by contrast little to suggest a flood about Foch's attack, the tide rises steadily, the volume of water grows visibly but evenly. The German lines are not suddenly breached at one critical point, rather the water seems to rise regularly until it overflows all along the German dike—not at one place, but at a score; and no temporary barrier can restrain the flood, because there is not one critical point.

All this belongs, perhaps, rather to the examination of the actual conflict than to a discussion of Foch; and yet, to understand the man, it is essential to recognize the method, the thought, quite as much as the will. Ludendorff, like Moltke and Falkenhayn, attempts to snatch a victory from a careless or incautious enemy, imperfectly prepared, inadequately fortified, but possessing enormous latent resources, possessing adequate reserves; and each attempt fails. Foch—patiently, deliberately—prepares his victory. Ludendorff opens the campaign with the blow that was to win the war; Foch's last blow was suspended by the Armistice. Ludendorff's three attacks, in Picardy, in Flanders, and at the Chemin des Dames, dislocated fractions of the Allied front, but only *seriatim*. On November 11th, all the German front, from Holland to the Vosges, was staggering back. Every army was beaten, all reserves were exhausted.

To dismiss this achievement as the result of the operations of a "great strategist" is to deal too brusquely with one of the greatest circumstances in all military history. To see in the contribution of the British, the American, or the French armies, the explanation of victory is to miss the whole truth. Each of these armies performed miracles, given their resources, but all three were but the bricks, the mortar, and the stones, in which the genius of Foch wrought. And not even at the end was Foch's machine more imposing than that with which Luden-dorff opened the campaign.

VIII. HUTIER'S TACTIC

In all war the essential condition of victory has been and remains the concentration of superior numbers at the decisive point. To achieve this the necessary condition has always been secrecy which in turn produces surprise. The great victories of history have thus been achieved. In the opening phases of the World War the same end had been sought. The first German attack upon France had, as its underlying conception, the sending of an overwhelming force through Belgium to arrive on the western flank of Anglo-French armies before a counter-concentration could be achieved. Joffre's answer had been a retreat until—in turn, and without German foreknowledge—an army had been concentrated on the German flank before Paris.

When the war was transformed into a trench conflict, the element of surprise was not at first abandoned on either side. In the first Allied offensive, French's ill-starred venture at Neuve-Chapelle was success-ful in achieving surprise because he was able secretly to concentrate over-whelmingly superior artillery at a selected point, and this artillery literally swept away German defences. For hours the road to Lille had been open, but he had so mishandled his infantry that the opportunity passed.

In Artois there had been a similar opportunity in May, which had not been realized. But by September of this same year, 1915, the Germans by organizing in depth were beginning to guard against sur-prise and the great French offensive of September 25th in Champagne, in part a surprise, penetrated two of the three German defence systems only to be checked at the third, which could not be destroyed by the preliminary artillery preparation.

When the Germans attacked at Verdun, the following February, they were even more successful in bringing off a surprise, but their attack was upon so narrow a front that, after swift and considerable preliminary advances, they were held up by the enfilading fire delivered from the unbroken sections of the French line on either side of the wedge they had driven into it. Before they could break down the sides of this wedge, the advantage of surprise was gone; the French had achieved a sufficient counter-concentration of men and guns, and the battle became a siege.

At the Somme in July, 1916, the British laid aside all pretense at surprise and sought to achieve a rupture by the intensity of artillery preparation and the prolongation of the bombardment over many days. Partly through the inexperience of their artillery—for they were still a new army just entering their first great battle—the preparation fell short of the expectation, and the initial assaults of the infantry won only limited gains at prohibitive costs. As the battle continued the artillery practice improved but there was no further chance of surprise, and the Germans multiplied their defences behind the sector attacked as the chance of a break through disappeared. This was the Verdun lesson over again.

In 1917, Nivelle endeavoured to change the method. He did not hope to bring off a surprise, but he did expect, by widening the front assailed—by employing Petain's artillery method, which on a narrow front at Verdun had achieved splendid results in the preceding October and December—to destroy German defences on a front so wide that it would not be possible for the Germans to hold up the victors by enfilading fire, as at Verdun. The effort failed; first, because the Germans, knowing where the attack was coming, were able to make an adequate counter-concentration of men and guns; and, secondly, because Nivelle lacked the artillery to make adequate preparation for his infantry.

Finally, in Flanders, in the late summer and autumn, Haig tried a grand offensive, on a front somewhat smaller than Nivelle's but far wider than that of the Germans at Verdun or of the British at the Somme. But he, too, ignored the element of surprise, and the Germans met the first onslaught with a new defensive tactic, an organization in depth, a prodigal use of concrete machine-gun emplacements, and a concentration of infantry reserves behind the front menaced and beyond the range of the artillery preparation. German reserves, counter-attacking when the enemy infantry had won through the first zone of German defence, got beyond its own artillery barrages and, become disorganized by its own efforts and exhausted by its losses, sufficed to hold up and even to throw back the British.

Thanks to this tactic—developed by Ludendorff himself when he came west in 1916—the first British attacks in Flanders were transformed into dismal failures. Later the British were able to improve upon their own methods, but by this time the Germans were able to match division against division. Moreover, the experience in Flanders confirmed all previous lessons by demonstrating that the very volume and power of artillery preparation for attack almost eliminated hope of successful infantry attack by the fashion in which it turned the country which had been shelled into an impenetrable tangle of impassable shell craters and morasses.

But in the closing hours of the campaign of 1917 the tanks at Cambrai suddenly achieved one of the few real surprises of the war. Transported to the front before Cambrai secretly as was possible, launched after nothing more than a brief preliminary artillery preparation and accompanied by barrages, they cut the way through German defence systems, and the infantry following in their wake were able to advance over a country which had not been torn to pieces by weeks of artillery practice.

The Cambrai offensive failed because there were lacking infantry reserves to exploit the initial success and because the handling of the tanks was not equally good at all points. Moreover, the type of tank employed, because of its size, proved too vulnerable to artillery fire, and too slow and unwieldy, while the tank suffered from lack of accompanying field artillery. Nevertheless, the lessons of Cambrai were to revolutionize the tactics of both armies, and the chief lesson was the demonstration that surprise could be attained, and it had already been proven that without surprise a real success was unthinkable. Therefore the Allies, against the time when they should regain the offensive, undertook to expand the tank attack and began the construction of smaller and swifter tanks and studied the coördination of tanks with their artillery course as with their infantry. In the end, the tactic developed as a consequence broke the German resistance, smashed the Hindenburg Line, and made victory possible. But this was only after many long months of waiting.

The Germans on their side were equally impressed by the Cambrai episode. But Ludendorff did not accept the tank. To be sure, Germany lacked the materials out of which to construct both submarines and tanks, but Ludendorff was convinced by the Cambrai experience that in the end tank attacks could be checked as were those at Cambrai. He did not foresee the eventual expansion of the tank tactic, and he concentrated his attention on improving a German method which should similarly restore the element of surprise, but without making the same demand upon German factories and labour for mechanical equipment. It seems fair to say that Ludendorff totally underestimated the value of the tank, but it is not less accurate to say that he lacked the material to construct tanks in the necessary numbers.

Ludendorff's method was known then and will probably live as the Hutier tactic, deriving its name from the general who first used it, in the taking of Riga in the autumn of 1917. Against the Russians the trial was little more than an experiment recalling the warfare of the grand manœuvres of peace times, since the Russians were too disorganized to offer serious resistance to any attack. The same method was employed in part against the Italians at Caporetto, with supreme success, but once more the low morale and disorganization of the Italians in part seemed to explain success and to blind Allied observers to the efficacy of the tactic. Finally, Marwitz used it against the British in the second phase of Cambrai, bringing off a swinging success after an undeniable surprise. And with these experiences in mind Ludendorff devoted the winter months to improving the system, training the officers and men in it, and gathering up the necessary material to make victory sure.

IX. FOCH'S DESCRIPTION

The most satisfying definition of this Hutier tactic is found in a communication addressed by Foch to his subordinates on June 16, 1918, at the moment when the successful answer was in the process of formulation. Remembering that at the outset it practically transformed the character of the fighting, and that it was not until July 15th—nearly four months after it was first employed on a colossal scale—that an answer was found, its value can be fully appreciated. In sum, it represented the fruits of almost four years of study of the lessons of the war by the best brains of Germany, and it almost won the war for its authors. Foch's definition was as follows:

The German method of attack is characterized by surprise, violence, rapidity of execution, manœuvre, and the extreme depth of penetration sought.

I. The surprise is obtained by the brevity of the artillery preparation (three to four hours) and by the transport to the place of attack of units to be engaged at the very last moment, the marches to the front of the troops to be used being made by night and on foot.

Up to the night which precedes the attack there is not the slightest change in the customary appearance of the front; quiet reigns and the usual formations are in line.

The attack always takes place just at daybreak, the infantry being preceded by a barrage consisting of a strong proportion of smoke shells. As a result of the cloud effect thus produced, our infantry and our artillery only perceive the enemy when he is within a few metres of them.

II. The violence is achieved by the intensity of the bombardment, all calibres and every sort of shell being employed simultaneously on a depth of four or five kilometres [between two and a half and three miles] and by the attack of masses of infantry which, during the artillery preparation, assemble at from 700 to a thousand feet before the first lines to be taken.

After the first lines are taken it lengthens out and spreads out, the units in advance aiming as quickly as possible at successive objectives, which have been indicated for them in advance, without having any preoccupation for their own flanks or for cleaning up in their rear, to which task other units are assigned.

The designation of these successive objectives does not imply any halt at any of them, but merely provides landmarks showing the direction to be followed.

III. During the forward movement the infantry is protected by a rolling barrage of artillery, then by the light artillery and *mienenwerfer*, which accompany it. It also makes free use of its own rifle fire and of its machine guns.

If an infantry unit encounters an obstacle which it cannot take by its own strength, it halts and is immediately passed by units which support it, and these are charged with the task of taking the strong point which remains by enveloping it.

IV. The Germans generally employ their best troops in the centre of the attacking front in such a fashion as to give themselves every chance of obtaining a rapid and profound advance in the centre.

The manœuvre consists, first, in enlarging rapidly the breach thus opened, and then in attacking on the flanks of this breach.

V. The penetration in depth is obtained by the rapid and resolute march of the troops upon predetermined objectives situated far within the enemy's lines. It has for its consequence a prompt disorganization of any defence not completely organized by taking from it the essential points of organization, which are its predetermined objectives.

If, in reading the narrative of the successive German offensives, this simple analysis of Ludendorff's method is kept in mind, the seeming confusion will be eliminated. And if, in addition, the fact is recalled that for many months the best troops in the German army had been undergoing training in this method while the Allied troops had no effective preparation to meet the tactic and the Allied High Command no adequate appreciation of its character, the events of March, April, and May will be clearly understood, and the magnitude of Foch's achievement in finding an adequate answer, while the battle was in progress and going steadily against him, will be properly appraised.

But even before the answer was found the Hutier tactic failed to achieve a decision. Actual open warfare was not restored. A colossal break through, unprecedented in the history of the World War, was achieved. Prisoners were captured by the tens of thousands, guns by the thousands, material in amounts incalculable; advances were made in extent hitherto unparalleled on the western front since the opening days of the war. But in the end the Hutier tactic failed, because it too completely disregarded the human factor.

In each decisive phase of an offensive the Germans reached the point where a slight further success meant supreme victory, too weary to deliver the "knockout blow," while the stricken Allies were just able, by something approaching a miracle, to get up reserves to close the breach. German strategy and tactics were alike comprehended in the delivery of the original blow, in delivering it as a surprise, in multiplying the pounds of weight behind it. It was the strategy of the steam hammer, but if the hammer did not crush—if it did not crush immediately, completely, and permanently—then there must be delay, pause, a wait until it could be again raised, prepared, directed against a new obstacle. This delay carried ultimate doom.

There is, moreover, in this circumstance, a truth which it is essential to recognize, for in it lies the key of all the warfare of positions, of all the struggle on the western front from the Battle of the Yser onward. The Hutier tactic revived the element of surprise by its method of concentration, in addition it aimed at and achieved the paralysis of the enemy forces on the front to be attacked, by directing the artillery preparation as much at the human as the material elements in the defence. By the use of gas, by the use of smoke screens, in a multitude of ways, it crushed the capacity for resistance of the elements in line at the point of attack.

Where it failed ultimately was in the fact that it did not and could not prevent the arrival behind the imperilled sector of Allied reserves before the rupture had become irremediable. Behind the whole western front was an admirable network of railways; therefore, just as long as Foch had reserves, he could get them up to the battlefield in time! In the Battle of Picardy the margin was shadowy, but the reserves did arrive in time. The Germans had been able to do the same thing in Flanders and at the Somme, the French at Verdun.

A successful break through had to be preceded by a series of operations which had resulted in the exhaustion of the enemy reserves. This was what Ludendorff strove for when he had failed to bring off the decisive rupture in Picardy. But his successive blows in Flanders and at the Chemin des Dames were too widely separated in point of time. French and British armies had time to refit and recover from their strain. They were ready when the Germans were rested and reorganized and the same units met in each attack, while the steady flow of American divisions to France presently transferred the advantage of numbers from the German to the Allies.

Foch, when he took the offensive, sought to exhaust the German reserves in advance of the decisive thrust by exerting steady pressure on all fronts. At the end he had 100 divisions in reserve and the Germans not more than fifteen. Thus his offensive in Lorraine, planned for November 14th, had it taken place, would have been successful beyond limit, because there were no German reserves left to dam the flood, once there had been a rupture of the front.

The Battle of France in 1918 was beyond all else a battle between two systems of war, between the German machine and the French brain. Foch was no more supremely the embodiment of the military genius of France than was Ludendorff of Germany. By contrast with these two soldiers all others were less significant figures: Petain, Haig, Pershing on the one side, and the brilliant array of German subordinates on the other. They obeyed orders, they did well or ill what was planned for them, but this was the limit of their contribution.

And of the two men, Ludendorff was the perfect example of the doctrine of Force, of the gospel of Might which crushes and rends all in its pathway, of the German idea which had now challenged the world to yield or perish, while Foch was the equally complete exponent of the intelligence which masters even force and represents the ultimate achievement of civilization itself. All that brute strength, fortified by mechanical skill, could do, Ludendorff did. His failure represented something more than the triumph of French military brains over German, it represented the failure of the whole German conception of mechanically armed barbarism against western civilization. The issue of the conflict was the vindication of the faith to which the western democracies hold.

To see in this mighty conflict of millions of men, of a score of armies, only a military drama—the play of strategies and tactics, the success of generals because of their skill, or the failure of other commanders because of their mistakes—is to miss the reality which underlies the surface glitter. In the campaign of 1918, Germany had a better chance of supreme victory than any one of her prophets and high priests could have hoped for. For three months all the advantages lay with her. Her failure is one of the few great human facts emerging from the chaos which men call history. It was a failure as significant as that of the effort to chain men's faith in the wars of the Reformation or deny men's equality before the law in the wars of the French Revolution. Something more than generals, armies, races met upon the battlefield. The contest was between ideas, and the triumph of the western idea was not an accident of generalship or numbers; it was a revelation of the superiority of the idea, disclosed in its capacity to conquer brute force fortified to the maximum of physical resources.

CHAPTER TWO

PICARDY—THE KAISER'S BATTLE

I

LUDENDORFF'S PURPOSE

The refusal of the Allied civil and military authorities to consider any offensive operation, such as Foch had advised, automatically bestowed the initiative upon Ludendorff. In his memoirs the German commander tells the world that he considered three possible theatres of operations: the Flanders sector, between Lens and Ypres; the Verdun sector, on either side of the hills actually covering the town; and the Scarpe-Oise sector, mainly included within the boundaries of the old French province of Picardy.

He rejected the Verdun sector completely because the hilly character of the country promised difficulties in the exploitation of any victory, and, though he does not say this, unquestionably because Verdun had an unpleasant sound in German ears and anything but supreme success there would instantly set afloat a wave of pessimism, by recalling the terrible disappointments of the previous offensive. He had, further, very special reasons, easily recognizable now, for preferring to attack the British.

He postponed any Flanders effort, while preparing for it as a later possibility, because the condition of the country, the lowness of the ground, and the certainty of mud in the early spring would necessitate putting off operations until mid-April, a thing highly undesirable in view of the eventual arrival of American troops in France. His own narrative indicates that the time circumstance was decisive in influencing him to attack in Picardy.

Having decided to attack there, his first concern was to choose a time, and he fixed upon March 21st—an early date when one recalls the fact that the French offensive of 1917, launched on April 16th, nearly a

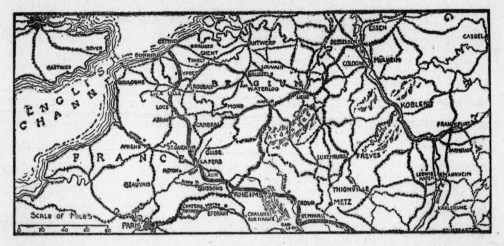

THE WESTERN FRONT

Note the railroad network enabling the Germans to strike with equal ease anywhere between Ypres and Verdun

month later, was fatally compromised by weather conditions. But Ludendorff felt that he could not wait, and as it turned out he was favoured by an almost phenomenal stretch of good weather, while the spring was one of the driest in history.

In choosing the Picardy sector extending from Fontaine-les-Croisilles right down to the Oise opposite La Fère, the German soldier had unerringly hit upon the weakest point in the Allied front. Here the British and French armies made junction, on the south side of the Oise: and the point of junction of two armies, and particularly of two armies belonging to different races and speaking different tongues, is notoriously a danger point.

But to this natural weakness others were added. The larger portion of this selected front the British had but recently taken over from the French against the judgment of British High Command. The troops in the new area mainly comprised the British Fifth Army, commanded by Gough. This army had suffered terribly in the Flanders contest, where Gough's leadership had been such as to shake the confidence of his soldiers. The divisions had a high percentage of replacements, that is of still-untrained troops. And in addition, like all British armies, it had for three years been constantly on the offensive and had not been allowed time to permit training in the defensive, a circumstance emphasized by Haig in his own reports.

Again, this vital sector was the worst protected in fixed defences. It had been newly taken over from the French, who had not devoted much time to fortification, since, during their occupancy, the Allied armies had been on the offensive. A single good system of defence faced the Germans, but behind this first system a second and a third line had not been more than sketched. The explanation is not in the main to be found in carelessness. The Fifth Army had barely time to reconstruct its forward system before the blow fell, and there was lacking labour to perform the task, since British man-power, outside of the army, was totally occupied in maintaining the navy, the merchant fleet, and the necessary industries.

Even worse was the situation in the matter of numbers. Haig felt, not unnaturally, that the vital sectors for him were those covering Calais and Boulogne; that is, his sea bases. A push of twenty-five miles toward the Channel from the Flanders front would bring the harbours of both towns under German fire, compel a sweeping retirement out of the Ypres salient and back upon the coast, where he would have to fight with his back to the sea. By contrast he had far more elbow room to the south, where his front was twice as far from the sea. Moreover, while at the north he would be for long necessarily dependent upon his own reserves, the French could be expected to reinforce Gough promptly, if he were heavily attacked.

The result was that the sector between the Oise and the Cambrai salient covered by Gough's army was most thinly held. Gough, with fourteen divisions of infantry and three of cavalry, occupied a front of forty-two miles, Gouzeaucourt to Barisis south of the Oise and near La Fère. Byng's Third Army to the north held twenty-seven miles, with fifteen divisions. So weak was Gough, in fact, that he did not feel able to hold all his front in force, and from the point where his line touched the Oise below St. Quentin to the right bank, facing La Fère, he relied upon the river as a barrier and did no more than maintain detached posts. As it turned out, this was a fatal circumstance, for in the spring of 1918 the river was so low that the Germans were able to cross the stream and overwhelm the British posts.

Finally, from the very outset it was plain that two totally different problems occupied the British and French commanders, Haig and Petain. Haig felt that in any circumstance he must cover his communications with Great Britain, must guard Calais and Boulogne. Petain's chief duty must be to cover Paris. But the British Fifth Army was actually covering the Oise route to the French capital. If it collapsed before French supports arrived, the road to Paris would be open.

Even the safety of Paris could hardly tempt Haig to employ his last reserves in supporting Gough when such a course might lead eventually to opening his southern flank and to weakening his own armies so fatally that, without closing the road to Paris, he would have uncovered the way to the Channel. At a certain point, then, it is clear that the purposes of Haig and Petain would inevitably diverge, and, if there were no commander-in-chief, each would follow his own necessities with results which might be fatal.

Exactly this did happen before the battle was a week old, on March 26th, the most critical day of all, and very nearly resulted in supreme disaster. The selection of Foch as commander-in-chief at the last minute of the eleventh hour alone prevented this terrible catastrophe. Established in the supreme command, Foch restored a community of strategical and tactical purpose, accelerated the pace of French reserves coming from Petain, fixed Haig in his positions, and thus avoided a complete severance of British and French armies with its necessarily fatal consequences.

A similar difference of opinion had, it will be recalled, occurred at a critical moment during the great retreat in the days of the first Marne campaign. Joffre had asked French to stay in line behind the Oise during the period when Lanzerac was counter-attacking at Guise. But despite Joffre's entreaty, Sir John had retired out of line altogether, leaving a gap in the Allied front which compelled a resumption of the retreat. Still again, when Joffre was ready to seek decisive action at the Marne and had ordered a general attack, French was reluctant to agree, considered a further retirement behind the Seine, and finally did comply with Joffre's request with very great tardiness.

The French Government and High Command had been so disturbed by this refusal of French to coördinate his movements with those of Joffre that Kitchener had been summoned from London; but despite his advice, French insisted upon freedom of decision, pointing to his orders which called upon him at all hazards to preserve his army, the single military reservoir on which the British had to depend for the making of their new army. Thus, all through the Marne campaign, while Joffre was seeking decisive action, French was authorized to coöperate only in so far as such coöperation did not risk the destruction of Britain's only field force.

Foch had faced a similar problem when he undertook to coördinate British and French operations in Flanders in the Battle of the Yser a few months later. There was one critical moment when Sir John French had actually ordered the British to retire out of the Ypres salient—a course which would have spelled ruin to the Allied cause, since the Germans would have reached Calais and thus the Channel coast. Foch surmounted this crisis; French recalled his decision after a memorable conference, but the peril still persisted, since, except during the ill-starred Nivelle period, the two armies acted independently. In 1918, it should be said, Haig had far more justification for his conclusion to follow his own line of action than had French four years earlier. But both at the Yser and in Picardy such a policy, had it prevailed, would have spelled disaster, exactly as it had led to evil consequences in the Marne operation.

II. LUDENDORFF'S OBJECTIVE

The main and obvious objective of Ludendorff was the whole British army, which he undertook to crush by one or more attacks, with the purpose of breaking the British will for war, the determination to continue the struggle which was still unshaken in the British people. Aside from this larger purpose, his strategy was comprehended in the following purposes:

He planned to employ some sixty-four divisions at once, 750,000 men, between the Scarpe and the Oise in a brutal and terrific attack, nourished by other divisions after the battle opened. This attack might be expected to accomplish a complete break through, and this break through would separate the British and the French armies.

The weight of the blow was to be delivered on either side of the Cambrai salient by the Seventeenth and Second armies, while the Eighteenth was to operate farther south. The three armies were commanded by Below, Marwitz, and Hutier, respectively. Ludendorff calculated that the two northern armies would smash the British line— roll it up north of the Somme and away from the French.

Meanwhile the Eighteenth Army, pushing through the British front on either side of St. Quentin, would drive southwestward. Its purpose would be to some extent determined by the success or failure of the efforts to the north, but it might, in certain circumstances, pursue the double objective of striking at Amiens, the vital centre of Anglo-French communications, and of opening the road to Paris down the Oise Valley by taking the Lassigny Heights southwest of Noyon or by turning them by way of Montdidier.

As the event turned out, neither the Seventeenth nor the Second Army realized more than a small portion of the expectations of Ludendorff. All of the Seventeenth and the fraction of the Second which faced Byng's British Third Army were held—forced to make a slow advance at terrific costs. By contrast, the Eighteenth made a clean break through, routed the British Fifth Army, and thereafter began a swift and terrifying advance both toward Amiens and Montdidier, while Ludendorff, modifying his plans, threw all his reserves to the Hutier army.

Ludendorff's strategic purpose, then, was to destroy the British army; to do it, if possible, by a single blow, but failing this, to isolate the British from the French army and prepare the way for a second blow against the British. On the subject of his own plans, Ludendorff has written as follows:

The centre attack (that on the Picardy front) seemed to lack any definite limit. This could be remedied by directing the main effort on the area between Arras and Péronne toward the coast. If this blow succeeded, the strategic result might indeed be enormous, as we should cut the bulk of the English army from the French and crowd it up with its back to the sea.

I favoured the centre attack; but I was influenced by the time factor and by tactical considerations, first among them being the weakness of the enemy. Whether this weakness would continue I could not know.

After determining the divisions and other forces available for the attack, it was decided to strike between Croisilles, southeast of Arras, and Moeuvres, and omitting the Cambrai salient between Villers-Guislain and the Oise, south of St. Quentin. It was to be supported on its left by a subsidiary attack from La Fère.

The Seventeenth Army, therefore, had to make the attack on the line Croisilles-Moeuvres; the Second and Eighteenth, that between Villers-Guislain and La Fère. In this operation the Seventeenth and Second were to take the weight off each other in turn and, with their inner wings, cut off the enemy holding the Cambrai salient, afterward pushing through between Croisilles and Péronne. This advance was to be protected on the south flank by the Eighteenth Army in combination with the extreme left wing of the Second. The strength and equipment of these armies were adapted to their tasks.

For the decisive operation the Seventeenth and Second armies were to remain under the orders of the Army Group of Crown Prince Rupprecht. The Eighteenth Army joined that of the German Crown Prince.

III. THE BATTLEFIELD

The front on which Ludendorff elected to attack was some sixty-five miles in extent and lacked any such striking circumstance as the Vimy Ridge or the Craonne Plateau. Beginning at Fontaine-les-Croisilles, the British line ran east and then south, first on the slope and then across the crest of a bare plateau between the Scarpe and the Oise rivers, a central knot of hills in which rise both the Somme and the Scheldt rivers. In its easterly trend the British line lay along the downward slope of the plateau and was crossed by two little streams, the Sensée and the Cojeul, which descend into the Scarpe in the Douai Plain. When it turned southward, having circled the high ground southwest of Cambrai seized in the 1917 battle, the British front approached but did not quite touch the Somme-Scheldt Canal, connecting St. Quentin with Cambrai. As a consequence, both banks of the canal were in German hands and the canal was not an obstacle to German advance.

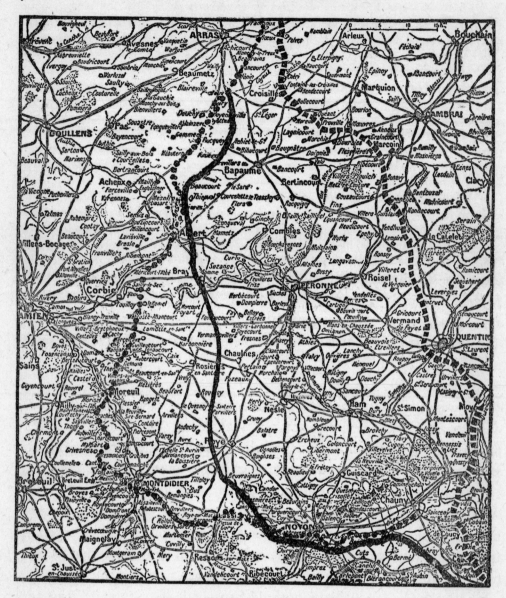

THE BATTLEFIELD OF PICARDY

Right-hand broken line shows the front on which Ludendorff attacked on March 21st. Solid line shows the front of July, 1916, before the Battle of the Somme. Left-hand dotted line shows the front reached by Ludendorff in the Battle of Picardy.

Circling around St. Quentin, which was less than a mile from the British front, the line inclined southeastward until it touched the Oise near Moy, and then ran behind this stream to the great bend near La

Fère. There it crossed the stream and made junction with the French lines west of the St. Gobain Forest, which remained in German hands. Save for the stretch behind the Oise, the British front was without natural protection, and the Oise barrier was to prove fatally inconsiderable. In addition, the country was devoid of woodland, in striking contrast to the regions south of the Oise and of the Aisne, where the forests of Compiègne and Villers-Cotterets were formidable military obstacles.

If the Germans should succeed in breaking through the defence system of the British between Fontaine-les-Croisilles and La Fère, there was no fully-organized line of artificial defences to be stormed. North of the Somme at Péronne, there was, too, no natural obstacle of any sort until the assailants had passed over all of the old battlefield of the Somme and arrived at the swamps into which the Ancre Brook had expanded after the bombardments of the 1916 campaign. As a consequence of the destructions of the Hindenburg Retreat the country was too destitute of all natural cover; villages, farms, even orchards, all had been methodically razed.

It was true that the tiny Tortille Brook, coming due south and entering the Somme below Péronne, did offer a suggestion of an obstacle, but it was inconsiderable and played no part in the conflict. From Péronne southward, as far as Ham, the Somme offered a natural barrier stretched straight across the pathway of advance of the Eighteenth Army, and this obstacle was prolonged to the Oise, behind the British battle positions, by the Crozat Canal. Ludendorff in his plan had taken cognizance of this natural defence line, and had therefore directed his main effort north of Péronne, where, once the British battle positions were broken, he would have nothing to impede him until he reached the Ancre.

Unfortunately for the British, however, the unusually dry winter had lowered the Somme, so that the stream, inconsiderable in all but flood seasons, constituted nothing like a serious barrier, while the completeness of the collapse of their thin line behind the Oise—similarly due to the low water in that stream—enabled the Germans to push westward and cross the Crozat Canal and the Somme at Ham, before the British could make good this line or destroy the bridges.

Once the line of the Somme was gone, the British had no real line of defence based on a natural obstacle until they had reached the west bank of the tiny Avre, which—after its juncture with its insignificant tributary, the Trois Doms, a mere brook—flows north from Montdidier to the Somme, which it enters just east of Amiens. Moreover, when the Germans reached the east bank of the Avre they would be within three or four miles of the all-important Paris-Calais railway, coming up to Amiens from Paris, and could cut it by their artillery fire as they cut the Paris-Verdun railway in the offensive of 1916. Likewise they would, by taking them under their artillery fire, abolish all the railway lines which at Amiens bound the British to the French and permitted the free interchange of reinforcements.

Again; from the great bend at La Fère to the hills near Noyon the Oise flows from east to west, parallel to the Somme after that stream turns west from Péronne, and momentarily the German advance could be canalized between the two rivers; beyond Noyon the Oise turns south, away from the Somme, and the corridor thus begins to widen. If the Germans could take Noyon and the hills southeast, in which stood Lassigny—hills which are vividly described in the local name of "Little Switzerland"—they would open the Oise road to Paris by way of Compiègne. Even if they were temporarily checked in these hills they might flow westward and then southward around them, having taken Montdidier, and thus open both the Compiègne and the Creil routes to Paris, down which Sir John French had retired behind the Oise in the far-off Mons campaign.

A collapse of the British defence systems, then, would clear the way for a German advance north of the Somme, where it makes its big bend at Péronne, as far west as the Ancre. South of the Somme there would be the Somme and Crozat Canal barriers. These passed, the Germans would have a clear road to the Avre; and if they reached the Avre they would cut the Paris-Calais railway and menace Amiens at the north and Paris—less immediately, but not less clearly—to the south.

If they were not checked on the line of the Avre, then the rupture between the British and French armies would be complete and permanent; the British armies would be crowded northward and in upon the coast—the French armies flung back upon Paris. If the line of the Ancre collapsed, either together with that of the Avre or before it, the result would be the same, so far as the isolation of the two enemy armies was concerned, but the profit for the Germans would be greater, because Gough's army would be cut off from the British, thus weakening the chief enemy more severely. As a consequence, his area of operations would be more circumscribed and the Somme would offer the Germans a good defensive barrier against the French during the period in which they were driving the British into the sea.

The mission of the British Fifth Army was to hold on until French reserves could arrive. If it could hold on, either at its battle system or at the Somme, the German gain would be unimportant; but a defence of ninety-six hours was essential, to enable the French to get up. If British resistance were broken before the French came, then the disaster might be without limit. As far as Gough was concerned he could rely only on the French for reserves. Byng, on the contrary, might look to Haig for support. In addition Byng had considerable reserves of his own, seven out of fifteen divisions in his army, but Gough had only three in fourteen, because the greater length of his front required more men to garrison.

To understand the Battle of Picardy, the greatest single contest of the whole war, a simple figure may suffice. Striking at the point of junction between the British and French armies, the Germans rushed in like a flood breaking through a dike. Owing to the measurable failure north of the Somme the flood was promptly restricted between the parallel rivers, the Somme and the Oise, as far westward as Noyon and the Lassigny Hills, and it was in a sense canalized. But beyond the point where the courses of these streams diverge, and save for the insignificant Avre obstacle, there was nothing to prevent the flood from spreading to the right and to the left, to the north and to the south, and swirling behind both the British and French lines, thus engulfing

Amiens and the Lassigny Hills, covering the roads to Paris, and also extending to the sea below Abbeville. The effort to prevent the flood from sweeping over the Avre barrier, to block the mouth of the corridor between the Oise and the Somme, comprehends the whole problem of British and French effort between March 21st and April 4th, and Foch's success in doing this was actually as great a contribution to ultimate victory as Joffre's manœuvre at the Marne nearly four years earlier.

A single other circumstance requires notice. Since the German occupied the centre of a great half circle, extending from Verdun to Ypres, he could direct his attack from the centre outward, wherever he chose. Not until the very last moment, when his reserves were almost at the battle front, would his purpose be unmistakable. Up to that hour his enemy could believe that he meant to strike in Champagne or in Picardy, in Artois or in Flanders. Moreover, by making preparations both before the British and the French front, he could compel each commander to retain his own reserves, against expected attack.

Thus, in March, 1918, both Petain and Haig expected attack. Before both Ludendorff had made extensive preparations. In this situation Haig, who was satisfied that the blow would fall south of Arras, although he did not foresee its magnitude or extent, would naturally have declined to send reserves to Petain, even had he possessed them. Petain, expecting a thrust on the Chemin-des-Dames front, where the enemy had made those preparations which enabled him to strike in May, disposed of his reserves to meet the blow he foresaw.

The result was an inevitable delay in the arrival in Picardy of French reserves, mainly concentrated to meet an attack in Champagne, while the absence of a general reserve in the British army, as a consequence of the Georgian estimate of the military outlook, terribly complicated the situation. Haig was right and Petain wrong as to the point of assault, but two months later Foch was wrong and Petain right; a blow did fall with deadly consequences upon the Chemin-des-Dames front, where Petain had expected it in March. For Ludendorff, the value of the initiative was vastly enhanced by having the equally great advantage due to his occupation of the central position.

IV. THE FIRST PHASE

On March 21st, shortly before four o'clock in the morning, the German artillery opened on the whole front from Arras to La Fère. It was the greatest artillery overture in history to the most colossal battle this planet had ever known. At that hour more than three quarters of a million men, the best troops of the German army—selected with utmost care, trained over many months and brought to the front by secret marches at night and on foot from camps fifty and even a hundred miles from the line—lay in the shelter trenches just behind the German line, awaiting the moment when the artillery should switch from its preparation to that barrage fire which was to cover their great advance.

Thus began Michael's Day, to give it the name the Germans selected in expectation of victory. For many days hundreds of thousands of German troops had been moving toward this designated front. "All Germany is on the march," one German officer had exclaimed, exultantly, and even with a degree of awe as he saw the enormous human tide rolling toward the front. "The chimes of Easter will sound peace," the German Crown Prince had boasted, forgetting his equally confident forecast two years before, when the attack upon Verdun had opened.

A month before, Ludendorff had told the Kaiser that though the battle would be hard the victory would be attained. Now he had moved his headquarters forward to Avesnes, to be nearer the scene of action, and the Kaiser had come in his special train and settled beside his great captain. Two huge armies, those of Below and Hutier, had taken position on either side of that of Marwitz, hitherto holding the sector. Sixty-four divisions were now to fall upon the twenty-nine of Byng and Gough, but unequally, since forty would strike the fourteen of the latter. And of this mighty concentration the British had no adequate warning. Before the battle ended, moreover, the Germans would employ no less than eighty-nine divisions.

Haig expected an attack on March 21st, he expected it astride the Bapaume-Cambrai road, that is on Byng's front. Both Byng and Gough had warned their troops, but as far as Gough was concerned, he had no other resource, nor is there anything to suggest that he had the smallest hint of the magnitude of the impending blow. Thus at the weakest point in the British line at the decisive hour, Ludendorff had accomplished a secret concentration of unparalleled strength. What was left now was the putting of everything to the touch.

On the subject of this supreme effort to win a decision, Ludendorff's narrative is extremely interesting: "That the attack in the west would be one of the most difficult operations in history, I was perfectly sure, and I did not hide the fact." This is the burden of his comment. It was the "biggest task in history" he says at another point, and at the outset of the assault, his view was: "What we would achieve—whether we should break through and start a war of movement or whether our effort would remain a sortie on a large scale—was uncertain, like everything in war."

The bombardment lasted five hours, and in that time more shells were consumed than in the whole Franco-Prussian War. The morning had been foggy and the smoke shells increased the density of the pall that hung over all the front. Toward the end of the terrible storm the Germans began to employ gas shells in great quantities and of various sorts, paralyzing the defence, forcing the artillerymen to don gas masks, and thus greatly reducing their effectiveness.

At exactly 9:40 A.M. the guns switched to a rolling barrage and the great attack began. Beyond the narrow "No man's land" the Germans entered the forward system of British defence. This system had been modelled upon the similar zone in which the Germans had received the British attacks in Flanders in the previous year. It was thinly held; not a continuous trench line but a series of strong points furnished with machine guns and designed to give a cross fire, and thus stop a hostile rush.

The fog and the smoke produced by the gas shells combined to destroy all visibility. The Germans were upon the strong points before the defenders were able to discover their advance. The efficacy of the cross fire was equally destroyed. All along the front the defensive zone was submerged with little or no really effective resistance and the German masses arrived with incredible speed at the battle positions themselves.

Thereafter the rate of German progress was unequal; in the main greater as one looked from north to south, that is before Gough's army rather than Byng's; but by the end of the day the British battle position had been reached everywhere on the front assailed, and in at least three places it had been actually penetrated. Moreover, the attack had been so swift that very large numbers of the forward troops had been submerged and captured or killed. Still, on the night of March 21st the situation did not yet appear critical and the official statements issued by the British led the world to believe that the German attack had been decisively held.

On the following morning, however, still aided by fog, the Germans began to disclose the real extent of their purpose. To the north they opened a breach in Gough's lines, west of St. Quentin and in the valley of the little Omignon Brook, which led to the Somme above Péronne. Thus they penetrated the third and last British position and entered the open country beyond. Meantime, two divisions belonging to the German Seventh Army had crossed the Oise near La Fère and swept through the thinly held line of posts on the west bank, had reached and passed the Crozat Canal, and taken Fargniers. Worst of all, Gough had used up all of his own reserves and French reinforcements were only just beginning to trickle up. Instead of holding out for ninety-six hours the British line, the larger part of Gough's front, had collapsed in less than forty-eight, while French reserves were a whole day late in getting off.

By the 23rd the Germans were across the Somme at Ham, while to the south the Crozat Canal had been permanently lost. To the north of Ham they had passed the Somme at several points and the last barrier, natural or artificial, west of the Avre was thus abolished. Gough's army was beginning to dissolve. It was still maintaining some sort of cohesion to the north, astride the Somme, although a dangerous gap had opened between it and Byng's Third Army, but to the south there was only a confused mass of men, fighting in groups, in handfuls—fighting magnificently but tossed upon the German flood like chips on an in-coming wave.   A gap was thus opening between the British and French armies and the road to Paris by the Oise Valley was beginning to be in danger.

The main hope of salvation to the south lay henceforth in the speed and strength of the French troops, which were already on their way in large numbers and beginning to intervene in small units.   Still the gap continued to widen; by March 25th the Germans were back in Noyon and the danger of losing the Lassigny Hills, the last considerable barrier on the road to Paris, was acute.   Only north of the Somme was the situation improving.   There the British had been driven straight across the old Somme battlefield but were beginning to take root behind the Ancre; would, in fact, hold fast—with minor fluctuations on the line coinciding with that front from which they had attacked on July 1, 1916 —although Albert and its knot o roads would be lost presently by an unlucky blunder.

South of the Somme, on the contrary, the situation was everywhere approaching a crisis.   Ludendorff, feeling himself checked in the north by Byng's forces—for Byng had now assumed command of all of Gough's troops north of the river—multiplied his efforts toward Noyon, toward Montdidier, and last of all toward Amiens.   Added to all else was the fact that Haig, now becoming acutely apprehensive for his own army, was beginning to draw his troops back in such fashion as would preclude all chance of closing the gap between the two armies, between the French and the British.   Lack of unified command now threatened to produce the supreme disaster, which Ludendorff concedes he expected on this day, March 25th.

V. FOCH IS CALLED

In this crisis, and on the following morning, British and French military and civil authorities met in solemn conference in the little town of Doullens, north of Amiens and back of the Arras front.   Haig and Petain were there, as were Poincaré and Clemenceau.   Lord Milner represented Lloyd George for Great Britain.   At two o'clock in the afternoon, the day and hour for ever memorable, Clemenceau and Milner, in the name of the French and British governments and with the approval of Petain and Haig, signed their names to the following document:

General Foch is charged by the British and French governments with coördinating the action of the Allied Armies on the western front. For this purpose he will come to an understanding with the generals-in-chief, who are requested to furnish him with all necessary information.

A halting, lame, almost pitiful commission to give a general literally called upon to save the world at a supreme crisis and in the presence of an unparalleled defeat, threatening hourly to become a disaster utterly irrevocable. But such as it was, Foch could use it; and the way he would use it would in a few weeks shame the givers into the extension of power which was necessary, if the war were first to be saved and later won. Meantime, Foch undertook the task.

And what a task it was! Between the Lassigny Hills and Bray-sur-Somme the flood of German divisions was ever swirling forward and ever increasing in volume. British divisions, already in ribbons, were tending away from the French, drawn by Haig's anxieties, by their own instinctive drift, toward their own armies. Above all, the German troops were approaching the Avre and the Trois Doms; were drawing near to Montdidier, which would fall the next day; were approaching the Paris-Calais railway, the life-line of Franco-British coöperation. They already seemed about to break out of the sides of the Somme-Oise corridor and thus to engulf Amiens and Montdidier and realize their terrible purpose and separate the British and French armies.

What was Foch's first objective? Unmistakably to prevent the separation of the two armies, to cover Amiens and Paris at one time, by bridling the flood, by constructing a dike across the front of the tidal wave, to make good the line of the Avre. This is the first, the single, the all-compelling task of Foch.

To fill the gap Foch can henceforth depend only on French troops. All available British reserves are required north of the Somme. It will require much effort to persuade Haig to permit his stricken divisions south of the river to hang on the necessary time, for time will still be required to get up the French divisions, flowing to the danger-point in a flood of horizon blue. Everyone must dig in, hold on, die—but not yield an inch. Joffre's order to his troops on the eve of the First Marne is again the word of command.

"Hold the enemy where he is. We can't afford to lose a single metre more of French soil!" This is Foch's first word to Petain. He will accomplish miracles, literally miracles, in hastening the reinforcements; but now, before they can arrive, he will demand miracles of the weary, defeated, stricken troops, who still fight back, after a week of this agony.

The French historian, Louis Madelin—clearest expositor of this crisis as of the First Marne campaign, whose facts I have frequently followed here—records the first twenty-four hours of Foch's activities thus:

One hour after his investiture he "runs" to Dury and sees Gough. Settles him at last, by putting his hands upon his shoulders, very energetically. "Make your Eighteenth Corps hold at all costs on its present front. Make your Nineteenth Corps hold at all costs on its front. Wait until you are relieved before you withdraw a single man or retire a single step!"

At Dury he sees also Barthélemy, chief of staff of Fayolle, who now commands the two French armies, those of Humbert and of Debeney, which are struggling to fill the yawning gap. For him he writes a short note, its tone unmistakable: "At all hazards maintain the position of the British army south of the Somme, then as quickly as possible relieve all British troops south of the Somme!"

Having telephoned to Debeney, he decides to join him at Maignelay. "Hold at all costs, where you find yourself, preserving your junction with the British." He reappears at Paris, at ten o'clock that night; writes a letter to Petain, indicating his first ideas; sets out for Clermont, where he sees Humbert and Fayolle. For them the same message, always the same message—"Hold where you are. Organize solidly. Demand of the troops their maximum effort. Make their commanders realize their responsibilities." By noon the next day he is back at Dury, where it is still necessary to hold Gough; and from Gough's headquarters he "runs" to Byng's.

Recall that Foch is sixty-seven; he was seventeen on that far-off evil day when he first saw the German invader in Metz; that he has been in nearly all of the great crises of the war since the Marne; that France held him exhausted a whole year before this March; and the magnitude of the merely physical exertion can be appraised. But the moral overpasses the physical; his spirit is in some mysterious manner almost immediately communicated throughout the whole Allied host. In the presence of defeat he does not recognize that he is beaten; he will not accept this battle as lost; his mood is that of Napoleon at Marengo.

Months later—the victory won, the war over—Foch will say to his friend, André de Maricourt:

> When, at an historic moment, a clear vision is given to a man, and when he finds as a consequence that this clear vision has directed operations having enormous results in a formidable conflict—and I think that I had that clear vision at the Marne, at the Yser, and on March 26, 1918—I believe that it comes from a Providence in whose hands the man is but an instrument and the victory is directed from above by a higher, by a Divine Will.

VI.   THE FLOOD IS DAMMED

March 26th is the decisive day. The course of events is oddly analogous to that at Verdun two years earlier. Then Falkenhayn attacked on February 21st, and on February 26th began to feel himself checked. But Foch has evil days before him still. The great gap between the British and the French is still open; in truth, there is a series of gaps, his line is still "dotted" rather than solid. On this day the Germans are crossing the Avre and mounting the eastern slope of the narrow plateau between the Avre and the Paris-Calais railway. On this plateau and at Cantigny, American troops, the 1st Division, will a few weeks hence do a heroic deed far-shining and fraught with grave consequences.

If only Gough will stick; if Haig will recall his decision to take his fragments north of the Somme; if Foch can hold the two corners of what has become the Somme salient, the Noyon and the Amiens corners, he will somehow contrive to stretch a dike between them. Again Ludendorff feels himself checked. He has already—he complains of it in his memoirs—been compelled to change his plans once, because of the failure of the forces north of the Somme. Exactly two months later an unexpectedly complete victory will lead him to a second change of plans in mid-battle, this time fatal. He has turned all his attention to the Somme-Oise front and, despite the capture of Montdidier on March 27th, he already senses the fact that the Noyon "corner", the Lassigny Hills, will hold.

Wherefore he turns north, storms against the line from the bend of the Avre to the Somme.   Amiens has become his final objective the next day, and he attacks in tremendous force north of the Somme all the way to Arras and to Vimy beyond.   This is the beginning of an effort to escape from the effects of the canalizing of his thrust between the Somme and the Oise.   It is an effort to break down the northern "corner" of the new Somme salient.   We shall see exactly the same manœuvre, partially successful this time in the Battle of the Lys, when Messines and Kemmel are taken.   We shall see the same effort in May, a failure on that occasion, when Ludendorff has broken through between Soissons and Rheims and endeavours to break down the Soissons "corner" of the new salient.

This offensive of March 28th is a particularly costly thing for the Germans, repulsed both before Byng's Third Army and Horne's First. Two days later Ludendorff makes his second great effort south of the Somme.   He has now abandoned the Montdidier thrust.   Amiens has become his last objective, but the thrust is parried.

The 31st is Easter Sunday, whose chimes, in the forecast of the German Crown Prince, were to sound peace.   But instead, as Madelin heard Fayolle promise Mangin two days earlier, the Allies sing "halleluiah" in Amiens Cathedral, although the German shells are now falling on that noble pile, seeking to repeat their achievement in vandalism at Rheims, but failing, failing utterly—a thing for which the whole world will be grateful.

April 4th and 5th see the last convulsions, attacks south and then north of the river Somme—the final effort, as Haig says, to prevent the new Allied front from stabilizing, to avoid a return to the war of positions, to escape a repetition of the Verdun check.   But these actions, in which he staked so much, prove "indecisive" as Ludendorff later reports. He cannot break the Amiens corner, he cannot extend the dislocation of the British front north of the Somme.   On the contrary, he suffers such heavy losses on the ground where the British won the Battle of Arras, just a year before, on Easter Monday, that he abandons all further idea of breaking through between the Somme and the La Bassée Canal, although he will try for Amiens by Villers-Bretonneux on April 24th, making a brief effort at the point where Sandeman Carey performed his great feat. Momentarily successful—thanks to tanks, here used by the Germans for the first time—this effort will be broken by the Australians. The battle has become one of exhaustion and on April 5th Ludendorff breaks it off.

Madelin saw Foch in the closing hours of the battle and his description of the interview is striking. He writes:

I saw General Foch at this period at Beauvais, in the hall of the Hotel de Ville, where he was camping rather than established. There was nothing like the stir one would expect to find about a chief of such importance. A handful of officers worked under the direction of General Weygand, the faithful chief of staff of the Grand-Couronné de Nancy, who had followed the great soldier everywhere, seconding him in an invaluable fashion, and had now hurried thither to resume his rôle as the good right arm. No apparatus; the least German colonel would have had ten times the racket.

The General himself, I found again, just as I had always found him, in his gray-blue uniform, moving about on legs which are a trifle short and strongly bowed as a result of horseback riding, his strong head crowned with short locks and furrowed and bronzed by war. His glance was clear, just a trifle malicious under his wrinkled eyelids, his shaggy gray moustache yellowed with tobacco and—that mouth which could in so few minutes assume so many different expressions of utmost vigour and of ironical good humour!

His gestures are still marvellously quick, prodigiously expressive. His hand as usual emphasized and supplemented his words. I found him calm and just a little bantering, but wholly without conceit. He led me to that map on which in various colours the dying battle was writing itself. He explained the phases to me and then— "There, that is over. What was the problem? To check at all costs," and he made a gesture with his arms which separated slowly. Instantly the "pocket" was dug before my eyes. "Next, to hold fast. That is now," and he plunged both arms to the ground with a gesture which would have stopped the universe.

"And finally, that will be later, *that!*" and his arms opened again and he brought his fists together to smash the reckless adventurer. I have related the circumstances. To-day it seems as if it had been arranged then just as it was going to be one day, but on a day a little further off than he thought then.

In fact, as Madelin points out, Foch was already prepared with his plan for an attack on the Somme side of the new salient by April 8th, but on the next day Ludendorff's attack in Flanders intervened. Foch would have to wait but this attack would come on August 8th, Germany's "black day" in Ludendorff's calendar. Still, on April 4th,

Foch could tell the Allied correspondents that the flood was "dammed"; and he could add, talking to General Maurice, "Ludendorff will probably try again, but he won't get through." That trial on April 5th was the last convulsion of the Battle of Picardy.

VII. THE RESPONSIBILITY

The Battle of Picardy was the worst British defeat in history. Gough, commanding the Fifth Army, was recalled. But the British army believed, and believes, that the responsibility was with the civilians, with Lloyd George. Haig showed his conviction in his subsequent reports. Buchan makes the same assertion, qualifying it with a concession as to Gough's failure in Flanders. Maurice, after he has left the army as a consequence of a dispute with Lloyd George over this question, writes:

Had the Government taken in time the measures which it had been urged to take, the reduction of two cavalry divisions and of more than one hundred infantry battalions might have been avoided, and both Gough and Byng might have had sufficient men to have enabled them to hold their battle positions against all attacks, while Haig's reserves might have been increased by at least two divisions.

Gough's statement is contained in the following letter written to an American friend in December, 1919:

Without inflicting upon you a long description of the battle I think I am fully justified in claiming that the British Fifth Army saved Europe and our Cause in that desperate week's struggle which began at dawn on 21st, March, 1918, and that no troops ever fought against such tremendous odds with more courage, skill, and tenacity.

Some few facts may tend to enlighten you on what the real work of the Fifth Army was, and may interest you.

The Fifth Army knew well that the attack was coming and all were in their places on that fateful morning.

The Germans threw two armies against the British Fifth Army, making a total of forty-eight divisions. The British Third Army, on our left, had nineteen divisions and was only required to hold a front of twenty-eight and one half miles, as compared with the forty-two and a half miles held by the Fifth Army. The Germans attacked the Third Army on the 21st of March with only eighteen divisions and the Third Army could place on the front attacked eight and one half divisions—nearly three times the number of men with which the Fifth Army was forced to hold similar frontage.

Yet the Fifth Army lost no more in depth along its front than did the Third Army on the 21st of March.

By the 24th, the right and centre of the Third Army was broken through by the German attack, though the Fifth Army line, still retiring and fighting, remained intact. This forced the Third Army to fall back behind the Ancre, a distance of six miles, behind the left wing of the Fifth Army.

Sir Arthur Conan Doyle, a historian of the war of reputation and reliability, states that the losses of the Third Army, though not exposed to anything like the same weight of attack, amounted to 70,000 men, while the Fifth Army's loss only came to 50,000. Therefore, the greatest proportion of losses cannot be laid at the door of the Fifth Army.

Knowing the facts, which have been concealed to a great extent from the knowledge of my countrymen and of our allies, I can feel a justifiable pride in the fighting and handling of the Fifth Army, under my command, though, for reasons which I do not desire to enter into, I was certainly made a scapegoat of, as Colonel Archer-Shee pointed out.

Gough's claim for his army is sharply contradicted by Ludendorff, who held Byng solely responsible for the failure to achieve a complete rupture of the Allied front. The French are rather more severe in their criticism of Gough than are his fellow-countrymen. Yet, as in the case of Ian Hamilton at Gallipoli, whatever mistakes the soldier made, the civilian government had made the fatal blunders in advance.

All things considered, Picardy was Lloyd George's defeat, as Gallipoli had been Winston Churchill's. Foch will have his own difficulties many months later, when he desires to make his final attack, that upon the Hindenburg Line, and Lloyd George holds back. Fortunately, Foch had the decisive aid of Pershing and the uncompromising approval of Haig, who had most at stake and justified his judgment by breaking the Hindenburg Line a few days later, aided by two of Pershing's divisions.

For the rest, the controversy—for controversy there is and will be—need not detain us here, although Gough's fate is reminiscent of that of a British admiral in a far-off century, who was hanged to "encourage the others," as the French said.

VIII. THE RESULT

It remains to appraise the value of the German offensive—of the Kaiser's Battle, as the Germans had proudly named it in advance. The battlefield success had been prodigious. There had been a break through on a front of nearly thirty miles; the extreme penetration had been more than sixty miles. One British army had been in part routed, and in the main destroyed. It would never again appear as an army and its commander was recalled in something approximating disgrace. The loss of ground had been unequalled in the history of the war of positions on the western front. In ten days all the territory gained by the British and French in six months of battle at the Somme in 1916—and, as a consequence, of the Hindenburg Retreat in 1917—had been abandoned.

The Germans were back at Noyon. Clemenceau's critics could now taunt him with precisely the fact with which he had taunted his predecessors from August, 1914, to March, 1917. They were westward of their old Somme line. They were within range of Amiens, and their guns commanded the Paris-Calais railway, which was thus closed to traffic. They gravely hindered, if they did not actually prohibit, the use of all the railway lines centring about Amiens and serving the Allied army. They had captured an enormous number of cannon, vast depots of material, hospitals, railway rolling-stock—a booty hitherto unsurpassed on the western front in the whole war.

Of prisoners Ludendorff counted 90,000. In captured and missing, the British alone had lost more than 75,000, including 2,392 officers and 72,968 men. Their killed for March exceeded 20,000, their wounded were in excess of 84,000. The ten days of battle from March 21st to 31st had cost them in killed and wounded approximately as much as the American operations from September 12th to November 11th, that is, in the St. Mihiel and Meuse-Argonne operations, would cost Pershing's army. Killed, wounded, and captured or missing, the British loss for March amounted to 175,000 officers and men, a number as large as Bazaine had surrendered at Metz, and equal to the combined strength of the armies of Meade and Lee at Gettysburg. Counting the loss of the French, Ludendorff's first blow had thus cost the Allies a quarter of a million of men. It had crippled their communications and, by lengthening the battle line, had increased the difficulties of the Allies since they possessed inferior numbers. It had further made a deep draft upon French reserves rushed up to save the British army and to restore the connection between the two armies.

By contrast, Ludendorff, despite very heavy losses, had realized none of his larger purposes. He had not crushed the British by a single blow. He had not separated them from the French. In his own memoirs he confesses that the hope of March 24th and 25th had not been realized, and concedes that at the close of the gigantic operation the future was obscure and the tactical and strategic outlook unpromising.

What was the cause of the German failure? For failure it was, in the larger sense. It seems to be discoverable in the fact that German strength was worn out before decisive results could be obtained. The great German mass arrived at the Avre, as on the battlefield of the First Marne, exhausted. It had outrun its artillery and used up its provisions; victorious, it was incapable of exploiting the success, of realizing the fruits of its labours. Once more, as at the Marne, German High Command had calculated the mechanical elements of the problem accurately, but had neglected the human factor completely.

Despite the enormous expansion of the front ruptured; despite an immediate progress seven times as great as at Verdun, the actual circumstances had been the same: the armies of Humbert and Debeney commanded by Fayolle, like Petain's immortal army at Verdun, had arrived in time to restore "a delicate situation" and the previous deadlock again prevailed. It reappeared so completely that Ludendorff broke off the engagement rather than run the risk of further repetition of the Verdun experience.

In point of fact, the Allies had lived through the worst crisis of the whole war; their danger would never again be as great although it might seem even more acute in succeeding weeks.

On the human side, the great conflict presents a picture of heroism and of devotion beyond the power of the historian to describe. If the cohesion of the British Fifth Army was largely destroyed in the first days, the isolated groups which survived fought to the end with courage and devotion unequalled. Day after day, unrested and unfed, the British fragments stolidly, doggedly fought on. Through the long moonlight nights, so favourable to the foe who had timed his attack to gain advantage of a full moon, these beaten men dragged themselves to new positions and at daybreak resumed the conflict.

Nor was the French contribution less splendid. Fayolle, Humbert, Debeney—these are names famous for ever in French history. The first French troops to arrive flung themselves into the furnace without artillery support; made of themselves willing sacrifices in the hope, not entirely vain, of gaining a few hours for the reserves which were coming up behind, and seeking to take root before the German masses arrived.

In the end victor and vanquished alike were exhausted. German divisions advanced, British troops retreated with dragging footsteps— fell asleep by the roads in the midst of the battle. Not even the retreat from Mons brought to British soldiers exhaustion like that of the first week of the March offensive.

Memorable, too, amidst the crowd of unforgettable incidents is the exploit of Sandeman Carey, in command of a force of fortune gathered from all ranks and conditions, like that forlorn hope of cooks and hostlers assembled by Sir John French at the crisis of the First Battle of Ypres, and including a detachment of the Sixth Engineers, U. S. A., Companies B., D., and Headquarters, which renders heroic service and wins deserved praise from Haig. With this "scratch" force Carey barred the road to German advance; not only held the gate, but, by a despairing counter-attack, actually threw the enemy back. Haig will have special and generous words of praise for these engineers later. Equally daring and devoted was the service of British and French aviators who, from the air, checked German divisions, paralyzed German transport, and thus gained time.

In this battle fell Lieutenant Colonel Raynal C. Bolling, the first American officer of rank to give his life in the war. Surprised while reconnoitring the German advance, he was killed, pistol in hand, defending himself to the last. In the circumstances of his death there was a reminiscence of the equally untimely fate of Colonel Ellsworth in the first days of the Civil War. In both cases a brilliant officer marked for greater services was cut down before his real work had more than begun.

IX. THE MORAL EFFECT

The military consequences of the Battle of Picardy were disappointing to Ludendorff. He had experienced precisely the same discomfiture that Falkenhayn had endured before Verdun. After ten days he had arrived at the position of his predecessor when Douaumont had fallen but French reserves had arrived. And, with Falkenhayn's experience in mind, he had escaped another Verdun siege by breaking off the battle. But if the military effect was relatively inconsiderable, it was far otherwise with the moral, and by one of the strange coincidences of war, the publics of both victor and vanquished nations were at least equally shaken by the results of the contest.

For the British the greatest disaster in their military history came as a shock unforeseen and incomprehensible. The nation believed in the "standing luck of the British army." In centuries of fighting history, no considerable British army had known anything approximating the reverse which had befallen Gough's army. The nation had believed that, once it was able to organize its man-power, equip the masses called suddenly from the factories to the battlefield its armies would equal, surpass, the German.

Army and nation had felt a sense of actual superiority at the close of the Somme, and even the failures and losses of the Passchendaele contest had not shaken the faith or the confidence of the civil population. From the public the fact was long hidden that the defeat was due primarily to the civil government, not the military command—that Lloyd George, by refusing the replacements and reinforcements needed by Haig and compelling an extension of the line, had prepared the way for Ludendorff. Thus defeat on such a huge scale was totally inconceivable, and inexplicable.

As the news of the onrush of the German flood reached Britain, the wave of depression was immense, the disillusionment was complete. The British public for the first time began clearly to appreciate the fact that the war might be utterly lost: indeed, in the last days of March defeat seemed imminent, and the impression strengthened when the disaster in Picardy was followed by the defeat in Flanders, and Haig himself was driven to the public declaration that his men were fighting "with their backs to the wall."   At no time in British history—not in the days of Napoleon, of Louis XIV, of Philip of Spain—had the peril to England seemed so great.

In France there was hardly less stupefaction.   Suddenly, down all the roads leading to Paris from Soissons and Amiens there began to run those tragic columns of refugees, almost forgotten since the evil days at the outset of the war.   Literally by thousands, with practically nothing left of their household goods, these refugees flocked southward, while the German flood swept over that devastated area ravaged by the Hindenburg Retreat—in which the returned natives had begun a work of restoration—then passed the limits of this region, leaped the old Somme front, and broke out in fertile lands hitherto unravaged.

For Paris the enormous despair was increased by a new German menace.   With the opening of the offensive Paris itself was bombarded by the notorious "*Grosse Bertha*"—a great gun mounted upon a hill at Crépy-en-Laonnois, more than seventy-five miles from Paris and on the road between Laon and La Fère.   At first the idea that it was shell fire from a fixed battery within German lines seemed unbelievable.   The Parisians looked to the air, and then suspected some concealed gun within French lines.

But the German guns—there were several presently—were soon discovered and the arrival of their shells became immediately a detail in Parisian life.   On Good Friday a shell falling on the roof of St. Gervais killed many women and children gathered in the church.   But despite the long continuance of the bombardment and the multiplication of air raids, far more fatal to life and property than the "*Grosse Bertha*," the aggregate damage was inconsiderable.   Even on the moral side the effect was below German hopes.   Neither the morale of France nor that of Paris was broken.

Depressed the French people were.   There was no mistaking the bitterness with which they saw Amiens subjected to the bombardments which had already destroyed Soissons, Arras, and Rheims, while they traced on the map new portions of French soil occupied by the barbarian or ravaged by new battles.   But the spirit of Clemenceau prevailed and Ludendorff was forced later to confess, with unmistakable surprise, that the first battle of the new campaign, so far from breaking the Allied will to fight, stiffened it.

Even in the United States the news of the disaster produced a profound impression.   On the first Sunday when the German onrush was at its height daily newspapers published hourly editions in many towns and every possible source of news was eagerly besieged.   In a sense the war became real as it had never been real before.   Moreover, there was an instant recognition throughout the nation that the British defeat and the French losses in restoring the front entailed real American sacrifices.   The nation read of Pershing's dramatic gesture, in offering all he had to Foch without condition, made at the crisis of the battle, with ungrudging approval.   And it now began to perceive that its rôle in the struggle was destined to be active beyond all earlier expectations.

As for the Germans, the first news, the reports of the opening successes, excited unlimited enthusiasm.   It was again as it had been in the first days of the war, in the initial week of Verdun.   But when the lines began to settle down again; when the map showed nothing but a huge pocket driven between Amiens and the Oise; when Easter did not bring peace, but exactly the same check which had in the end extinguished hope at the Marne and at Verdun, German morale began to decline.

Nor were the later successes in Flanders and on the Chemin des Dames sufficient to revive the drooping spirits.   The German army knew at once of the failure in Picardy and of the enormous cost in men. The German soldier had nerved himself for one supreme effort which should bring peace.   He had set out for victory as he had taken the road for Paris and then for Calais in 1914.   He had arrived after prodigious efforts only at new trench lines.   He was checked, and he recognized the check.

In the Battle of Picardy, the German soldiers did all that was humanly conceivable, more perhaps.   We shall perceive, and Ludendorff has testified, that in each succeeding battle his troops fought less well, even in victory, until with the change of the tide there began to appear fatal failures of German soldiers to perform what was expected of them. And of all this decline the cause may be found in the Battle of Picardy. The German soldier knew that there he had given his best, done his utmost; that he had been tested to the limit and had failed to bring off the promised victory. Tactically a victory, strategically a check, Picardy, the Kaiser's Battle, was thus on the moral side almost a disaster for the victor, while for the vanquished it proved the defeat which was to make ultimate victory possible.

THE FIGHTING JUST BEFORE THE AMERICANS GOT DOWN TO BUSINESS

TO THE RESCUE
A French infantry regiment pushing forward to the assistance of the hard-pressed British during the German offensive in March, 1918

FRENCH MACHINE GUNNERS IN ACTION
Pouring a deadly fire into the Germans

1. THE ROADS OF FRANCE

Motor transport carrying troops to the front

THE MARK OF THE GERMAN "420"

This picture shows a shell hole made by a shot from a German 420 gun. An automobile diving into i accidentally does not quite fill it. Imagine what happened when a shell from this same gun dropped into church full of worshippers

2. THE ROADS OF FRANCE

At the railhead. Artillery being brought up

THE RESULT OF A DIRECT HIT

All that was left of a motor truck after a shell struck it

By C. R. W. Nevinson

3. THE ROADS OF FRANCE

Infantry men marching through a ruined village on the way to the front line trenches.   A bit of camouflage
showing in the centre of the picture

British Official

AT WORK ON THE TRENCHES

The picture shows clearly the rugged nature of the Italian country.

4   THE ROADS OF FRANCE

Through No Man's Land.   Abandoned barbed wire in the foreground

AN ARTILLERY OBSERVATION POST

On the British front.   The effectiveness of the shooting could be observed from a post like this and telephoned back to the guns

PHOTOGRAPHY IN THE WAR ZONE

© *Underwood & Underwood*

This is a French photographic section at work. The dark room is sandbagged for protection

AN ANZAC RESTING UNDER DIFFICULTIES

British Official

Amid the débris of war and the mud of Flanders a soldier rested when he could

WHAT THE GERMANS LEFT BEHIND THEM

A glimpse of the principal street in Combles, in the Somme area, after the Germans had been driven out

REFUGEES FLEEING BEFORE THE GERMANS

A common sight in France during a German offensive

THE BARRICADE

British Tommies and French lancers awaiting the advance of the eremy

By Captain Kenneth K · orbes

THE CANADIANS IN ACTION

Most of this gun's crew were killed but the men that remained, though wounded, carried on

AFTER THE BATTLE

The scene of some of the most intense fighting during the great German offensive of March, 1918

DETRAINING A HOWITZER

This picture gives a very good idea of the size of these guns

THE "BYNG BOYS"

The famous 22nd French-Canadian Battalion going into action with its characteristic dash and courage

By Lieut. A. Bastien

British Official

OVER THE TOP

The platoon leaving the trenches to charge.   These are British soldiers

IN THE YPRES SALIENT

Sanctuary Wood where the Canadians fought in 1915 and British and French troops advanced in 1918

By Captain Kenneth K. Forbes

FRIENDSHIP ON THE BATTLEFIELD
A French poilu bringing a wounded British Tommy to shelter and safety at the risk of his own life

CHAPTER THREE

FLANDERS—THE BATTLE OF THE LYS

I

FROM PICARDY TO FLANDERS

On the morrow of the Battle of Picardy, the strategical situation of the Germans was unsatisfactory to Ludendorff. He felt the vulnerability of the great pocket or salient which his troops had created between the Somme and the Oise. He recognized instinctively that Foch would endeavour at once to reduce this salient by an attack on the side, by exactly the manœuvre which, on August 8th, he did employ with complete success. And we know now what Ludendorff suspected, that as early as April 8th Foch was contemplating such a strike.

To preclude such a thrust Ludendorff must retain the initiative; he must compel Foch to continue to concentrate his attention on meeting, not making thrusts. He could not pursue his operations in Picardy, for his armies in their new positions lacked communications. They had advanced over the regions devastated by his own orders in 1917, and railways and roads were lacking. It would be weeks before he could bring up guns and munitions necessary to prepare a new attack. His experience of April 4–5 had demonstrated this truth: For the present Foch had the advantage of undestroyed communications behind his front, and the advantage was decisive.

Ludendorff had then to attack elsewhere, and for this eventuality he had prepared, having selected the front from La Bassée to Ypres as the field for a subsidiary effort if the Picardy venture did not realize his hopes. In the very last stages of that battle he had attempted to prepare for the new Flanders operation by assaults on the Artois front, from the Somme to the Souchez, but the troops of Byng and Horne on Vimy and the Loos Plateau above Lens had administered an instant and bloody check upon his Seventeenth and Sixth armies, and south of La Bassée nothing more could be hoped for.

In shifting his attack from south to north Ludendorff still preserved his main strategic purpose, the destruction of the British military force. He had already disposed of the British Fifth Army; he had weakened both the Third and the First, although unequally, since Horne's troops had only been slightly engaged while Byng's had undergone a terrific test. Actually all of the British reserves had been drawn into the fight and, in addition, a very considerable strain had been placed upon Petain's reserves.

An attack in Flanders would be certain to put a new and almost intolerable burden upon the weary British. The command of the Paris-Calais railway would forbid the quick arrival of French reinforcements, if, indeed, Petain would consent to spare any more of his scanty reserves for British purposes; and before French reserves could intervene, a heavy defeat might be inflicted upon the British. Ludendorff, too, was thinking of the moral as well as the military element; he was attacking the nerves of the British civilians as well as of the soldiers. Would there not be protest in Britain at the enormous expansion of British losses, while the French sacrifice was, by contrast, slight? Finally, the transfer of French divisions to Flanders would, at the very least, open the way for a successful blow at the French front a little later.

Calais and Boulogne were shining objectives, but it is essential to recognize that it was the British army which was the main objective, just as Joffre's army had been the single objective of the German High Command in the Marne time. Ludendorff had now assailed the centre and right of the British; his next attack would be upon the left flank. It might not result in decisive victory, but it would complete the task of trying out the whole British army. It would still further exhaust French reserves and it would prevent Foch from seizing the initiative by any blow at the Somme salient, delivered before the German front had become fortified, furnished with communications, "frozen."

Despite the check at the Avre, Ludendorff still had time. The appeal for American divisions had only just gone forth. He had still

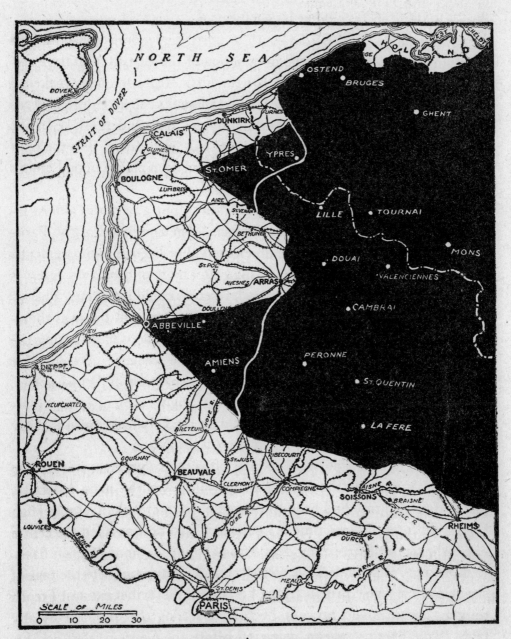

LUDENDORFF'S TWO THRUSTS

The black wedges reaching Abbeville and St. Omer indicate the German objectives in the Battles of Picardy and the Lys. The two white lines mark the front on which the two offensives were checked.

numbers and time. Heavy as his losses had been, he had inflicted heavier, while his wounded would return and the Allied loss in prisoners was a permanent loss. His vast captures in material, in artillery, and supplies were a further advantage, although guns, supplies, and material were beginning to flow across the Channel in unprecedented quantities and at an incredible pace. The Battle of Picardy had ended on April 5th. Ludendorff would begin in Flanders on April 9th, his own birthday and the anniversary of the British offensive at Arras in 1917. Pershing would celebrate his birthday at St. Mihiel in a similar fashion a few months later.

II. THE NEW BATTLEFIELD

With unerring insight Ludendorff had again selected the vulnerable spot in his enemy's armour, vulnerable alike because of the character of the country and the quality of the troops actually holding the line at this point. From Arras all the way to the La Bassée Canal, east of Bethune, the British line ran along high ground, the profit of several victories. Vimy Ridge had been captured in the Battle of Arras and retained in the recent fighting. North of Vimy the Loos Plateau had been mainly taken in 1915, although Hill 70, overlooking Lens, had only fallen to the Canadians in 1917. This much of the British front had already demonstrated that it was impregnable to direct attack.

But north of the La Bassée Canal, beginning where Smith-Dorrien had fought in October, 1914, was a country in which the natural obstacles were less considerable and the high ground mainly in German hands. In this region was Neuve-Chapelle, where Sir John French had made his first offensive in 1915, striving to take the Aubers Ridge. His failure had left the Germans on this high ground overlooking the British in the flats, which were intersected by various small streams and canals and by the Lawe and Lys rivers. These waterways were normally obstacles of some importance, but the dry weather, which had reduced the Oise and the Somme, had also abolished the customary Flanders mud.

Finally this sector was held by Portuguese troops, commanded by Portuguese officers. The material was good, but the leading notoriously bad, and the men had been kept in the line far too long, as a consequence of the strain upon British reserves to the south in Picardy. Ludendorff reports that he was worried lest the Portuguese should be relieved before he could attack and the relief was actually in process when his blow fell. The presence of a foreign contingent in the British army naturally constituted a further element of weakness, and this weakness was accentuated by the fact that the troops on either side were newly come from the furnace in Picardy, and having suffered cruel losses there now needed rest and reinforcement.

Above Armentières, that is in the region of Ypres, the British front was mainly on high ground, from "Plug Street" to "Whitesheet" Ridge, including the ground taken by Plumer in his great thrust of June, 1917, and thence by Passchendaele to the Belgian front at the Yser.

North of Armentières and south of La Bassée the British line thus rested upon admirable natural obstacles, but in the centre it was weak —and weakly held. There Ludendorff would attack, and successful penetration of this weak spot led—whither? To Hazebrouck, immediately; and Hazebrouck was the railroad centre of the north as vital as Amiens in the south. An advance of twenty-five miles—half the advance at the Somme—would reach Hazebrouck, compel the Allied retirement out of the Ypres salient and the retreat of the Belgians from the Yser they had held so long. A gain as great as that in Picardy would take Ludendorff to the edge of Calais, to the Channel. Dunkirk would fall, Calais cease to be available as a British base, and Boulogne would be in danger. British communications with England would thus be fatally compromised; what was sought in 1914 might be achieved in 1918.

The real key to the whole situation was the chain of "Mountains" extending from west to east, from Cassel to Kemmel, north of Haze-brouck and Armentières. Mont des Cats, chief summit of the central group, was just under 600 feet high, but they all rose from the Flanders Plain, looked northward over the flat ground in which Ypres was situated, surveying the roads to Calais through Poperinghe, by which the Germans had endeavoured to reach Calais in 1914. Southward they overlooked the gap between their lower slopes and the high ground beyond the La Bassée Canal, the gap between Armentières and Bethune, through which passed the canal, the Paris-Lille railway, coming east from Hazebrouck, where it sends off a spur which fed the Ypres salient. In this gap, covering Hazebrouck, was the Forest of Nieppe, thick and marshy woodland, the real barrier to Hazebrouck if the British lines on the Lawe and Lys should be broken.

Before the Germans could reach Hazebrouck they must either take the high ground north or south of the plain, back of Bethune, or back of Armentières. But if they could get Kemmel to the north and push on along the "Mountains" toward Cassel, the British and Belgian lines to the north would collapse. The mere fall of Kemmel would make the situation in Ypres precarious, if they could get Cassel they would dominate the whole plain of Flanders. They would arrive at the Channel and their Berthas could bombard Dover, sweep the Strait, open a new submarine base ten times as dangerous as Zeebrugge. Their shells might even, in no distant time, fall in London itself.

Nevertheless, the Flanders stroke was a diversion, a subsidiary incident in the general attack upon the British, and it began in a far more modest fashion. In the first hours the attack was on a front of not more than ten miles, as contrasted with sixty in Picardy, and the number of divisions employed was equally restricted. The extent of front assailed and the number of divisions used both expanded after the first day. Thus Ludendorff used only 9 divisions on the first day, and up to the 12th the number had increased to only 16; by April 16th the number had risen to 21, and by April 29th, the date of the general attack which marked the last spasm of the struggle, he had used 44 divisions, of which 35 were fresh and 9 had already been employed at the Somme.

The units used, moreover, were not comparable with Hutier's "storm troops," although there were good divisions in the two armies Ludendorff in his memoirs concedes the inferiority of training of the troops; complains bitterly of the manner in which the soldiers abandoned the battle to hunt food, and comments on the failure of the officers to preserve discipline—a new circumstance, henceforth to be familiar. This decline in the quality of the troops, traceable in a degree to the German method of skimming the cream for the storm divisions, thus lowering the value of the balance, will have grave consequences when the cream has been consumed.   But thus early the first evidences appear.   This will explain the disastrous collapse in front of the British Fourth Army on August 8th; it will explain the rapid decline in army morale, after each major effort, before July 18th.   Still, on April 9th the German divisions engaged were fresh, while the British were exhausted and the Portuguese inferior.   Therefore the German advantage was considerable.

As it began, the Battle of the Lys involved only the left flank of Horne's British First Army; as it developed it reached and passed the front of the whole of Plumer's Second Army and finally assailed the front of the Belgian army, between the Yser and the Sea.   On the German side the Sixth Army, Quast's, was first engaged; later Arnim's Fourth Army, which had fought the British all through the Flanders struggle of 1917 and at the Somme in 1916.   Bernhardi, famous for his "World Power or Downfall," forecast in his book: "Germany and the Next War," commanded a division in Arnim's army, but achieved no great thing.

III.   THE BATTLE

On the morning of April 9th all the circumstances of March 21st are reproduced on a smaller scale.   The Portuguese troops are overwhelmed by the preparatory bombardment, and their resistance collapses almost in an instant, although isolated groups still fight gallantly.   A fog, intensified by smoke shells, once more gives the Germans an additional advantage.   Before the day is over the Germans have crossed the Lawe, have passed the Lys at two points near Estaires, have thus begun to drive a wedge into the British front between Bethune and Armentières and toward Hazebrouck.

The only encouraging circumstance is the resistance along the La Bassée Canal, at the southern edge of the front now attacked.   And this Givenchy "corner" will presently have an importance almost equal to that of the Soissons "corner" in the Chemin des Dames operation. Had it given way, the Germans would have swept in behind the British centre on the high ground from Loos to Arras; there would have been a dislocation of this front, which would have prepared the way for new German operations to the south in the Somme salient. But the Givenchy corner holds and will hold.

By the next day the German pace has increased and there is an extension northward of the front assailed. The battle crosses the Belgian frontier and approaches Messines and "Whitesheet" ridges. Meantime, by the close of the same day, the Germans are approaching the Forest of Nieppe, sole barrier to Hazebrouck and its vital railways. By this time Haig has renounced his share in Foch's proposed offensive east of Amiens and is calling for French reinforcements.

On the same day Haig issues his appeal to his soldiers, an appeal as memorable as that of Joffre on the eve of the First Marne and productive of equally splendid results. Haig said:

There is no other course open to us but to fight it out. Every position must be held to the last man. There must be no retirement. With our backs to the wall, and believing in the justice of our cause, each one of us must fight to the end.

The menace of 1914 again seemed to threaten; Britain and France, London and Paris alike felt the solemnity of the words.

By April 13th the Germans had made much greater progress. Armentières had fallen on April 10th. The Germans had reached the edge of the Forest of Nieppe by the 11th. Bethune was close to the front, in extreme danger, and rapidly being reduced to ashes. The precious Bruay mines, all that remained to France of her northern coalfields, were under fire and forcibly closed. The Givenchy corner still held, but not so the Messines anchorage. By this time Messines and Wytschaete had both gone and the Germans were approaching Kemmel from the east and south and were far west of it. The next day Bailleul fell and the Germans were at the foot of the Mont des Cats. Kemmel was thus in danger and the position at Ypres already far more critical than in the evil days of 1914.

On April 16th, too, began the evacuation of the Passchendaele height, taken after so much effort and sacrifice only six months before. The lines were now drawn back upon Ypres itself, and, just as the

MARSHAL FOCH AND GENERAL WEYGAND

They are in front of the gigantic statue of Germania, in the Niederwald, keeping her Watch on the Rhine. "How did I win the war?" Foch will say chaffingly to André de Maricourt many months later. "By smoking my pipe. That is to say, by not getting excited, by reducing everything to simple terms, by avoiding useless emotions, and keeping all my strength for the job."

conquests of the Battle of the Somme in 1916 had been lost in the Picardy struggle of March, the acquisitions of the Battle of Flanders in 1917 were surrendered in the first days of the Flanders struggle. Thus the rewards of two years of sustained and terrible effort had been wiped out in less than a month.

And a new crisis was now at hand, had actually arrived by April 14th, when Foch's scanty powers were expanded and he became General-in-Chief of the Allied armies. Almost immediately he was faced by an insistent proposal made by Haig and backed by Milner. From them came what amounted to an ultimatum. Foch must agree to recognize the Flanders operation as the major battle of the Allies and divert thither a constant stream of French reserves; or agree to a British retirement, which would amount to the surrender of Ypres, the line of the Yser, the whole region north of St. Omer.

Here, again, is the old difference of opinion, which we saw at the crisis of the Battle of Picardy. Haig sees the immediate crisis developing on his front. Petain perceives the eventual danger on his front in the south. As for Foch, his first hope is for a stroke of his own at the Somme, which shall abolish the dangers on both fronts. This become impossible, he must strike a balance between the views of Petain and those of Haig. Americans may recall a similar crisis in the Civil War, when Early approached Washington, in 1864, and the capital clamoured to Grant for divisions then in Grant's hands south of Petersburg. Like Foch, Grant appreciated the fact that Early's thrust was a diversion, intended to lead him to weaken his Army of the Potomac and lessen the pressure on Richmond, and like Foch he acted with extreme deliberation, cut the thing so fine that Early arrived before Washington as the first divisions from the Army of the Potomac marched through the city streets.

Once more the enormous value of unified command is demonstrated. Without it Haig might have retired, Petain refused the necessary reinforcements! As it is, Foch strikes a just balance between the two policies. He will send more reserves north than Petain wishes, far fewer than Haig asks. He perceives that Ludendorff is seeking to exhaust French reserves, just as he is striving to smash British military strength. And he must surrender his own cherished hope of a counter-stroke. De Mitry is sent north with the first French reinforcements; more are concentrated, ready if necessary, but only if necessary. Still Petain will be disturbed; and later, on May 6th, will formally warn Foch that the limit of French contribution in the north has been reached. But by this time the Battle of the Lys will have terminated.

Meantime, as early as April 16th, the Battle of the Lys begins to die out. French troops have entered the line; the Belgians have extended their front and thereafter handsomely repulsed a German attack—"made too late" Ludendorff will comment, afterward. On April 25th the Germans do get Kemmel. The French troops cannot hold it because the position has been compromised before they take it over. Kemmel and 6,000 French prisoners are the last considerable captures of the Germans, although on April 29th they make a general attack, like that of April 4th-5th in Picardy, which is repulsed with exactly the same terrible carnage. Thus the northern corner of the salient holds; the Germans cannot advance in the centre, while the Allies from the Givenchy corner and from Mont des Cats become the northern corner—command their rear and communications. Therefore the battle descends with minor convulsions to a calm. The last German adventure "Nach Calais" has come to an end. Flanders will be quiet henceforth until Plumer and King Albert take the offensive and break out of the Ypres salient on the road to Ghent and Bruges, on the road to Lille and Mons.

"How did I win the war?" Foch will say chaffingly to André de Maricourt, many months later. "By smoking my pipe. That is to say, by not getting excited, by reducing everything to simple terms, by avoiding useless emotions, and keeping all my strength for the job." The proof of this is revealed, so far as the Flanders phase is concerned, in the testimony of General Maurice, who saw him on April 16th, when the issue of the Battle of the Lys seemed "still doubtful." To Maurice Foch said: "The Battle of Flanders is practically over, Haig will not need any more help from me."

"Not even the loss of Kemmel, a few days later, ruffled him," Maurice adds, and "Foch was right."   Foch deliberately left it to the British to bear the greater part of the burden, because he recognized that too great diversion of French reserves to the north would merely open the way for Ludendorff elsewhere.

Haig's appeal to his soldiers created a profound sensation in London, there was anxiety and even criticism at the apparent slowness of French reinforcements to arrive, but they did arrive in time.   The German was checked, and Foch repeated on the same battlefield his very great achievement of October and November, 1914, which constituted the winning of the Battle of the Yser.

IV.   THE END OF THE FIRST PHASE

April 29th is the last day of the Battle of the Lys; it is also the date which marks the close of the first phase of Ludendorff's campaign.   In these forty days, beginning on March 21st, Ludendorff delivered two blows, but in his own mind they constituted a single operation, designed to break the British will for war.   Viewed comparatively, if the Battle of Picardy resembled the breaking of a dike, the Battle of the Lys was little more than the opening of a leak and the subsequent effect of erosion.   There was no considerable rupture of the lines in Flanders, nothing to recall the Picardy experience.   The Givenchy corner had held from the outset, and except for Kemmel, the northern corner of the "Mountains" had been maintained.   The Germans had done no more than excavate a shallow salient, and if from Kemmel they dominated the Ypres salient, they were themselves equally harassed between Scherpenberg and Bethune.

Measured by British casualties, Ludendorff's achievement was more impressive.   In March the British losses—killed, wounded, captured, and missing—had amounted to approximately 175,000 of all ranks.   In April, 659 officers and 18,088 men were killed; 4,615 officers and 87,637 men were wounded; 1,285 officers and 58,018 men were reported missing or captured.   The killed for two months, all but a small fraction in the forty days of battle, totalled 39,000; the wounded, 176,000; the captured and missing, 135,000. The total loss of all ranks for the period was just under 350,000; and almost half—the dead and missing or captured—represented a total loss. The French loss can hardly have fallen below 150,000 including a considerable number of prisoners. All told, the Allied loss for the first two months of the campaign of 1918 certainly amounted to 500,000 and the cost of forty days in 1918 was as high for the British alone as the whole Verdun campaign for the French, from February to December, 1916.

Maurice asserts that in forty days Ludendorff used 141 divisions against the British and the French, and of these 109 German divisions fought 58 British, and he asserts that the British losses were greater than those in the whole of the Ypres campaign of 1917, in which the British took 24,000 prisoners and only 64 guns, whereas they lost 70,000 prisoners and upward of 1,000 guns in March and April, 1918.

Ludendorff's estimate of results in this period is also enlightening, he says:

We had achieved great successes that we must not allow later events make us forget. We had defeated the British army. Only a few British divisions were intact. Of the 59 divisions [he counts one more than the British, themselves] 53 had been engaged, 35 of them several times. The French had been obliged to engage nearly half of their divisions. The enemy had lost large quantities of stores.

On May 1st, an official German statement claimed the capture of 127,000 prisoners and 1,600 guns in their western offensive. Haig, in his official report, supplies further figures and an appraisal of the achievement of his own men. In this report, writing of "the task of the British armies," he says:

It has been seen that in the Somme battle, by the end of March, in addition to some ten German divisions engaged against the French, a total of 73 German divisions were engaged and fought to a standstill by 42 British infantry divisions and three cavalry divisions. In order to complete the comparison between the forces engaged, and to enable the nature of the task accomplished by our troops to be realized, it will be of value to give similar figures for the Battle of the Lys.

In the Lys battle prior to April 30th the enemy engaged against the British forces a total of 42 divisions, of which 33 were fresh and 9 had fought previously at the Somme. Against these 42 divisions, 25 British divisions were employed, of which 8 were fresh and 17 had taken a prominent part at the Somme.

In the six weeks of almost constant fighting, from April 21st to 30th, a total of 55 British infantry divisions and 3 cavalry divisions was employed on the battle fronts against a force of 109 different German divisions. During this period a total of 141 different German divisions were engaged against the combined British and French forces.

The splendid qualities displayed by all ranks and services throughout the Somme and Lys battles make it possible to view with confidence whatever further tests the future may bring.

On March 21st the troops of the Fifth and Third armies had the glory of sustaining the first and heaviest blow of the German offensive. Though assailed by a concentration of hostile forces which the enemy might well have considered overwhelming, they held up the German attack at all points for the greater part of two days, thereby rendering a service to their country and to the Allied cause, the value of which cannot be overestimated. Thereafter, through many days of heavy and continuous rearguard fighting, they succeeded in presenting a barrier to the enemy's advance until such time as the arrival of British and French reinforcements enabled his progress to be checked.

In the Battle of the Lys, as has been pointed out above, many of the same divisions which had just passed through the furnace of the Somme found themselves exposed to the full fury of a second great offensive by fresh German forces. Despite this disadvantage they gave evidence in many days of close and obstinate fighting that their spirit was as high as ever and their courage and determination unabated. Both by them and by the divisions freshly engaged, every yard of ground was fiercely disputed, until troops were overwhelmed or ordered to withdraw. Such withdrawals as were deemed necessary in the course of the battle were carried out successfully and in good order.

At no time, either on the Somme or on the Lys, was there anything approaching a breakdown of command or a failure of morale. Under conditions that made rest and sleep impossible for days together, and called incessantly for the greatest physical exertion and quickness of thought, officers and men remained undismayed, realizing that for the time being they must play a waiting game, and determined to make the enemy pay the full price for the success which for the moment was his.

In the course of this report it has been possible to refer to a very few of the many instances in which officers and men of all arms and services have shown courage and skill of the highest order. On countless other occasions, officers and men, of whose names there is no record, have accomplished actions of the greatest valour, while the very nature of the fighting shows that on all parts of the wide battlefront unknown deeds of heroism were performed without number.

CHAPTER FOUR

THE CHEMIN DES DAMES

I

THE PURPOSE

Ludendorff had now made two attempts to destroy the British army, one in Picardy and a lesser effort in Flanders, but, despite great incidental successes, both had failed to realize his larger purposes. The British army was badly shaken. It had suffered terrific losses, nearly one half of its strength had been put out of action, but French reserves had arrived in time to restore the situation. Thus the British troops had fulfilled their mission, they had held on until Petain's divisions could arrive and the German effort to achieve a complete rupture had failed. The logical front for a further effort was still the British, but both in Picardy and Flanders Allied concentrations and German communications alike forbade immediate attacks.

Before he could attack the British again, then, Ludendorff must do something to draw the French reserves away from the British front. He was still thinking of his original purpose, to smash the British army and thus break the British will for war; his own words demonstrate this. Accordingly he now attempted to administer the leech, the *coup de ventouse* of French military parlance. He was not thinking of Paris; the Paris circumstance does not appear in his narrative; his sole purpose was to compel Foch to withdraw French troops from Flanders and Picardy; thereafter he would resume his operations in the north, for which his preparations were never halted.

There was also the moral element. Ludendorff had always two strings to his bow. If he pressed the British hard, then there was an immediate demand from Haig for French reserves. But if he struck in the direction of Paris, even though he had no serious purpose to seek the French capital, every foot he moved toward that city would intensify the anxiety of French military and political authorities and increase their demand that French troops be withdrawn from the British front and concentrated before Paris. He had already tested the British; he would now try the French.

The Chemin-des-Dames offensive, therefore, is another step in the strategy directed against the British, and Ludendorff in the last days of May has his eyes still fixed upon Flanders. There he expects to deliver a final blow, when the French reserves have been recalled to the Paris front which he is now going to create. Actually, he will be in conference with the Crown Prince of Bavaria, putting the final touches on this operation, when Foch's counter-stroke of July 18th recalls him to his own headquarters.

But we have now to reckon with a new circumstance, which upsets all calculations. When Ludendorff planned to attack at the Chemin des Dames he set the Vesle as the limit of victorious advance. He directed his commanders to pass the Aisne and to seize the crossings of the Vesle, but he neither expected nor counted upon further advance; he makes this clear in his book. When his troops passed both the Aisne and the Vesle on the first day and the road to the Marne lay open and the roads to Paris seemingly cleared, a new situation arose.

As early as the summer of 1918 French military authorities asserted that at this crisis the Kaiser intervened—supported and perhaps persuaded by the Crown Prince—and insisted that the operation should be continued, both for dynastic and military reasons. Under compulsion, so the French believe, Ludendorff yielded; set his troops in motion again; and, as a consequence, became involved in the deep Marne salient, the Château-Thierry salient of all American accounts. Having done this and being presently checked, Ludendorff found himself in a position in which he must retire or else go on. He could not now turn his attention to Flanders because he must expect immediately a Foch stroke, so awkward was the new salient.

Accordingly, Ludendorff postponed the Flanders thrust and, in the battle of July 15th, endeavoured to exploit and expand his gains in the Marne salient in such fashion as to make possible a later and final thrust at Paris. In a word, without ever wholly surrendering the Flanders operation, without actually abandoning his determination to destroy the British army, Ludendorff momentarily substituted the Paris objective; and this substitution led to an adventure which proved fatal. It proved fatal because it gave the British time to reorganize, and, when the Marne operation had turned out badly, to attack, in their turn.

Even more than this, thanks to their long period of rest, the British can actually spare troops to support the French, in the decisive phase of the fighting in the Marne salient. This aid is small but precious, and three weeks later, before Ludendorff is able to recover his breath, after extricating his troops from the Marne mess, Haig's attack west of Amiens breaks the German lines and Ludendorff's nerve, and advertises to the world that Germany has lost the war.

The new Marne salient, then, is to prove the abyss in which all German hopes are engulfed. But it is essential to perceive that this is due to a miscalculation—whether imperial or Ludendorff's own is of small consequence—resulting from the extent of the initial success. The Chemin-des-Dames thrust was a logical circumstance in Ludendorff's main strategy, in his campaign against the British, but it was a diversion. When he permitted it to be transformed into the major operation he turned his back upon a British army, shaken but still formidable, and before he could resume his operation against it Haig was able to pass to the offensive. Napoleon made the same miscalculation in the Waterloo campaign; the result was the arrival on the field of Waterloo of the Prussian army, which had been beaten but not destroyed at Ligny.

Again; the Marne adventure consumed six weeks, and at the end of that time American troops, now rushing to the Continent at the rate of 300,000 a month, were able to intervene. Only one American division was available as a combat unit in April or May, but in June Ludendorff had to deal with three, and in July with eight.

During the war there was a natural tendency to see, in the Picardy and Marne operations, deliberate attempts to get to Paris, but in both cases the obvious strategical objective was something else, although both in Picardy and Champagne German successes resulted in marked advances in the direction of Paris. This was but a repetition of the campaign of 1914. In both instances the German was seeking the destruction of armies, not the capture of cities; and in July, 1918, as in September, 1914, the Germans actually turned their backs upon Paris.

II. FOCH'S MISCALCULATION

And now it is necessary to face the fact that at the Chemin des Dames Ludendorff, for the first and only time, outguessed Foch. The Battle of Picardy had been engaged before the Conference of Doullens called the "Coördinator." The Battle of the Lys followed before Foch could grasp the reins, and it was only during that contest that he became, in fact, generalissimo.

By the opening of the offensive of May 27th, on the contrary, Foch was firmly established, and his authority had been expanded to the necessary limits. He had begun to build his own plans. His mind had instinctively turned to the offensive as the only possible policy, and we have seen that he had considered a thrust east of Amiens. But his situation remained gravely compromised by the divergent views of Haig and Petain, and Ludendorff's attack in Flanders had forced him to postpone his own project.

The development of this operation had compelled him to transfer French divisions to the north, despite Petain's frequent warnings. He had, moreover, concentrated the balance of his scanty reserves, all French, back of the Somme front—not only because they would there be best placed if Ludendorff resumed his attack in the north, but also because he expected the thrust on the front between Noyon and Montdidier. Ludendorff did strike on this front in the final phase of his second offensive and Foch was able to parry the stroke, because of his preparations; but this was not the main blow.

Foch was still dreadfully handicapped by inferior numbers. It was impossible to be strong on all fronts. May was the dead low water of Allied numerical strength, while German strength reached its maximum. American divisions were becoming available, but not yet in sufficient strength to replace wastage, to fill the vacancies created by the actual elimination of ten British divisions, incident to the recent battles.

It may also be reasoned that Foch was, after all, right as to the front on which the German should have struck, since the blow at the Chemin des Dames proved so fatal to German purposes, at the end. Still, it must be conceded that, had he accurately divined the purpose of Ludendorff, he would have given far more attention to the Chemin-des-Dames sector and would not have left seven or eight weary and relatively inferior French and British divisions squarely across the track of an approaching cyclone. Foch's error here was Joffre's at Verdun in February, 1916. So disastrous to the German was the Verdun affair, in its later stages, that there has sprung up a legend that the Germans fell into a "trap." Not impossibly we shall presently have a Marne legend, but neither can have the smallest warrant in fact.

Thus, when Ludendorff did strike at the Chemin des Dames, he encountered tired British divisions—filled with raw levies and transferred to a "quiet" sector for rest and refit—and French troops in about the same condition. As a result, he broke through easily, swept down to the Marne again. Paris was crowded with a new horde of refugees, again heard the guns approaching the city, and for a number of days actually expected to see the enemy arrive. Foch's prestige was thus terribly wounded. So much so, that Paris believed, and believes, that he placed his resignation in Clemenceau's hands, only to be met by the answer, worthy of Roman times:

The greatest soldier in the world can afford to make *one* mistake.

Foch would not make another, and the consequences of this blunder would be fatal not to him but to Ludendorff. Yet, viewing the struggle as a duel between two great soldiers, one must perceive that in May it was Ludendorff who scored. But if Foch was momentarily at fault in failing to foresee the direction of the May thrust, his real greatness never revealed itself more impressively than in the manner in which he set about to repair the damage incident to the defeat at the Chemin des Dames. Henceforth the miscalculation is all Ludendorff's, who will misunderstand the extent of his victory and be either deceived himself or overborne by the Kaiser and the Crown Prince—will repeat all the blunders of the First Marne and pay the price Joffre could not exact from Moltke four years earlier.

"On the whole, between the strategy of Foch and that of the German High Command," writes Colonel Requin, "lies an essential difference. On the one hand an exquisite sense of proportion, an exactness of measure, essentially French traits, controlled by a superior intelligence and an inflexible will; on the other hand pride, which hurls states as well as military chiefs to perdition when it seeks to erect colossal plans on psychological errors."

III. THE CHEMIN DES DAMES

For his new front of attack Ludendorff selected the Chemin des Dames. It was old fighting ground before the present war. Napoleon and Cæsar had campaigned over it. The Craonne Plateau, along whose crest the Chemin des Dames runs, had been the first objective of Nivelle in the costly offensive of April, 1917. French and British pursuit after the First Marne had been halted on the southern slopes of the ridge in September, 1914, when Kluck dug in north of the Aisne and, sweeping the crossings of the river, opened what was to be a new and almost interminable phase: the war of positions.

Nivelle had made meagre gains at great costs in April, 1917. Later in the year Petain had made large gains at small costs, and as a result the French had taken and held all the high ground south of the tiny Ailette Brook, from the point where the Paris-Laon highway crosses it eastward to the foot of the eastern crest of the plateau. Thence it ran out into the plain, crossing the Laon-Soissons highway, and then, turning south and passing the Aisne at Berry-au-Bac, Cæsar's battleground, it reached the outskirts of Rheims.

There were three quite distinct sectors on this front. There was first the Craonne Plateau itself, a magnificent bulwark extending from west to east, dominating the marsh through which the Ailette Brook, expanded into a well-nigh impassable swamp by shell fire, trickled westward toward the Oise.   Seen from the north, this plateau seems almost like an artificial wall, so even against the skyline are the crests, so steep the northern slopes.   As a consequence, this sector was held impregnable to assault, the fundamental miscalculation of the whole Allied estimate.   But impregnable it had proven to all German assaults in the summer of 1917 before the arrival of the Hutier method and the consequent demolition of all the calculations of nearly four years of war.

Between the eastern end of the Craonne Plateau and the hills on the south bank of the Aisne was the second sector, a stretch of low land through which the Aisne flows westward.   This was manifestly the weak joint in the French armour.   Nivelle, in his calculations a year before, had planned to use this gap, once his troops were over the Craonne Plateau—to thrust forward his cavalry, which would encircle the plateau from the north and arrive before the walls of Laon on the morning of the second day of the battle.

But Nivelle had neither been able to get over nor to get through.   As a consequence this gateway by which the Aisne breaks through the high ground on its way to the Oise remained a danger point even after Craonne Plateau was well within the French lines.   The French merely occupied trench systems between Craonne and Berry-au-Bac, which had been elaborately constructed first by the Germans and then by the French, who had first taken the German systems in 1917 and later expanded them.   Still there was danger here.

South of the Aisne the forward French lines lay at the foot of the Sapigneul Heights, crowned by Fort Brimont, which Nivelle had endeavoured to take in April and May with terrific losses and ultimate failure.   Indeed, it was his insistence on renewing his sterile assaults on Brimont which led to his summary removal.   But although the French front lines ran in the low ground, through which also passed the Rheims-Laon highway and the Vesle-Aisne canal, the French support lines were solidly seated upon high ground all the way from the Aisne to the Vesle. Actually, therefore, the French position consisted of two stretches of high ground, separated by a three- or four-mile reach of low ground, traversed by the Aisne. This low ground is described in French military accounts as the *Trouée* or Gap of Juvincourt.

Ludendorff in his reminiscences recognizes the strength of the position occupied by the enemy, but he correctly remarks that if the artillery preparation were properly made, the defenders, particularly on the Craonne Plateau, would be paralyzed by shell fire and gas and that there would remain only the difficulties of the ground itself to be dealt with.

If the Germans should take the Craonne Plateau, they would still have before them the deep and difficult Aisne from Berry-au-Bac to Soissons; and even if they got across the Aisne they would still have the Vesle to force, and south of the Vesle, as south of the Aisne, the ground was high and thus favourable to the French defenders.

Even south of the Vesle there was still another obstacle, slight but backed by high ground, the tiny Ourcq, which, rising in the Tardenois Plateau, flows first west and then south into the Marne. But if the Ourcq were passed, then the pathway to the Marne would be open. Moreover, in pushing to the Marne, the Germans would be following paths trodden by their comrades in the days of the First Marne Campaign.

For his third offensive thrust Ludendorff concentrated 42 divisions, constituting the German Seventh Army, and commanded by Boehn, between the Soissons-Laon railway, which parallels the highway and the Aisne east of Berry-au-Bac. South of the Aisne 4 divisions belonging to Below's First Army would coöperate. The principal shock would be delivered by 28 divisions. Most of these, moreover, were storm troops; had participated in the Picardy but not in the Flanders fighting; and had been withdrawn for rest, refit, and training early in April. It was a far more powerful blow than Ludendorff had delivered in Flanders, although it was much lighter than that with which he had opened the campaign.

In front of this huge concentration the French had on the Craonne Plateau the Sixth Army, commanded by Duchesne, one corps of which, the 11th, commanded by Maud'huy, was actually on the front to be assailed and consisted of two weak divisions. Between the Craonne Plateau and Rheims stood the French Third Army, commanded by

Micheler, who had under his orders 4 British divisions, 3 of which were actually in line covering the Gap of Juvincourt, on either side of the Aisne. Actually the French and British were now going to oppose rather less than seven divisions of weary troops, which had fought in all stages of the Flanders and Picardy combats, to 28 fresh German divisions, each numerically stronger than French or British divisions and composed of the best material in the German army, supported by an enormous concentration of artillery and fortified by the Hutier tactic.

Even in the case of Gough's Fifth Army the odds had not been immediately as great and the explanation must of course be found in the fact that the Allied commanders, threatened with ruin elsewhere, had drawn off their best troops from the Chemin des Dames, mistakenly convinced that the position itself was impregnable. Even the lessons of Picardy and Flanders had not yet sufficed to emphasize the fact that the real secret of German success must be sought in the Hutier method. Strong as were the positions before him, Ludendorff ironically remarks they were not as strong as these Alpine heights, forced by his victorious troops at Caporetto in the preceding autumn.

Another circumstance contributed to the completeness of the disaster on the Chemin des Dames. The surprise was absolute. As late as the preceding afternoon Maud'huy learned for the first time from prisoners that an attack was coming and warned his commander, Duchesne, who in turn reserved to himself the right to order the destruction of the bridges across the Aisne, while warning his troops to be ready. But this reservation proved fatal, for, when the attack came, the German advance was so rapid that Duchesne ordered the destruction of the bridges after it was too late and the Germans were able to pass this barrier as they had been successful in getting across the Somme and Crozat Canal before the British could destroy the bridges in April.

Thus whatever information was derived from prisoners on May 26th, it did not give any adequate warning. The Allied commanders had not the smallest inkling of the amount of artillery concentrated on their front; they had no suspicion of the number of infantry divisions which had been brought up by those secret and night marches which were such an essential detail in the Ludendorff offensive. Actually the attack was in all larger aspects a complete surprise because no proper preparation had been made against it.

Moreover, as Ludendorff was now using the Hutier method for the third time and as Foch had not yet developed his answer, it was only natural that experience should have brought with it approximate perfection. Beyond all question the attack of May 27th was, on the professional military side, the best prepared and the best executed of the whole war. In it was disclosed German system working at its highest stage of efficiency. Even in defeat Allied military students and critics alike could not refuse their admiration for the new system; and the fashion in which it revealed itself at the Chemin des Dames contributed, even more than lost ground, to shake Allied confidence by raising the pressing question: Can any "parade" be found to parry the Hutier thrust? Have the Germans actually found the key, the secret of modern war, the method for breaking the trench deadlock, for which all soldiers have been seeking for nearly four years? Shall we be destroyed before we can devise an answer?

One further detail is worthy of note. On April 24th, at Villers-Bretonneux, German tanks appeared for the first time and were used with some effect, although the Germans were still new to the management of the engines and their tanks were too unwieldy. At the Chemin des Dames, on the contrary, the handling was good, and something like a hundred tanks were reported to have been used by the assailants. They were without exception too heavy and too large and they were only in a small degree responsible for a shining success attributable mainly to the Hutier system itself.

IV. LUDENDORFF'S PLAN

For the Chemin-des-Dames offensive Ludendorff had made the following plans: He would attack on a front from the Soissons-Laon highway on the west to the heights of Sapigneul on the east. His main operation would be a duplicate of that attempted by Nivelle in 1917 but delivered, of course, in the reverse direction.   One mass of troops would seek to hack their way straight across the Craonne Plateau from end to end, passing the Chemin des Dames and reaching the north bank of the Aisne; a second mass would endeavour to break through the Gap of Juvincourt, advancing from east to west astride the Aisne.   These two masses would be commanded by Boehn.   Still a third, much smaller, would be under Fritz von Below and would push west from Fort Brimont.

Given this arrangement, Ludendorff might calculate that, even if his frontal attack failed, he would take the Craonne Plateau by the blow directed, through the Juvincourt Gap, at the rear of the French and British actually on the Craonne Plateau, while if the frontal attack succeeded, then the enemy troops held in line across the Gap of Juvincourt would be similarly menaced in their rear.   Actually this amounted to attacks on front and flank.   As it turned out, both were successful, with the result that the credit for victory was divided.

But it was not enough merely to force the Craonne barrier.   To be held up immediately at the Aisne might not sufficiently shake Foch to lead him to divert troops from the British front.   It was necessary to go at least to the Vesle, and this was the limit first fixed by Ludendorff in his plans.   Once the Vesle had been reached and bridgeheads established to the south, he would transfer his operations to the old "Paris front" between Noyon and Montdidier and, seeking to push across the Lassigny Heights where he had been halted in the last days of March, menace Paris and open all roads running down to the French capital from the north.   Hutier himself would be called upon to make this attack, but it could not be timed to synchronize with the Chemin-des-Dames blow, because Ludendorff lacked the artillery to demolish both positions at once, and with the Nivelle episode in mind, recognized that any failure to make adequate artillery preparation at the Chemin des Dames would involve stupendous losses and incalculable German depression.   He therefore planned to attack at the Chemin des Dames on May 27th and beyond the Oise on June 7th, but he had finally to postpone the second blow until June 9th.

V. THE ERUPTION

At one o'clock on the morning of May 27th the artillery storm begins on all the doomed front. It is, on the whole, more terrible than all preceding bombardments; the German artillerymen have learned much in the two earlier experiments. More gas is used and the result is the approximate stupefaction of large numbers of their enemy. In truth, the artillery preparation itself this time practically disposes of the defence. The thing which Falkenhayn hoped for at Verdun, Haig and Foch at the Somme, Nivelle before the Craonne Plateau; the thing which Petain had several times achieved on a narrow front, was now accomplished upon a very wide front. Ludendorff has much praise for Colonel Bruchmüller, the German artillery officer who superintended all of the artillery preparations during the campaign.

Before four o'clock the German infantry is on the move. On the eastern end of the Craonne Plateau, on the ground where the French had maintained themselves in the terrific fighting of the preceding summer, the British garrisons are assailed almost without warning. So rapid is the German advance that the Plateau of Californie, the "Winterberg" of German battle reports, is lost in less than half an hour. The attack extends along the British front eastward and southward, and in a few hours one British general is killed, another wounded, and a third captured.

While the morning is still young the British line north of the Aisne has collapsed, the Germans have come over the eastern end of the Craonne Plateau and through the Gap of Juvincourt; they have arrived at the Aisne bridges west of Berry-au-Bac, and the bridges have not been destroyed in time. They will thus be able to cross the Aisne and menace the British and French troops holding the line from the Aisne to Rheims and threaten the French positions north of the river on the western half of the Chemin des Dames.

That is, Boehn's advance by the left flank would threaten the western positions, had they not already fallen; for the French, resistance is no more successful or sustained than the British. On this part of the front the gas effects are even more disastrous and the infantry well nigh paralyzed. At 4:15 A. M., with a single bound the Germans pass the little Ailette, they push up the heights on either side of the Fort de Malmaison won by Petain in the preceding autumn. Before noon they are streaming down the south side of the Craonne Plateau toward the crossings from Soissons eastward, while the Kaiser, having mounted the Plateau of Californie, is surveying the battle, now gone south, with emotions which a travelling biographer will promptly give to the world. "Fritz was one of the first to cross the Aisne" the Kaiser triumphantly telegraphed the Empress.

The Allied line had now collapsed all the way from Berry-au-Bac to the Crouy region, immediately north of Soissons. Worse; from Vailly, east of Soissons, to Berry-au-Bac the Germans are actually across the Aisne and this line of defence has gone. Before night comes, the advance has crossed the Vesle also, to the west of Fismes, at the point of the German wedge, and thus the line of the Vesle, also, has fallen. Even in the unfortunate first day of the Battle of Picardy there was nothing approximating this collapse. As a consequence of the disaster there is now a sag in the Allied lines all the way from Rheims to Soissons, and both of these cities are in imminent danger. Soissons will fall the next evening, while north of the Aisne, in the angle between the Aisne and the Oise, French lines are recoiling and it is still probable that they will have to be withdrawn behind the Aisne, in upon Compiègne, which will, in turn, necessitate the abandonment of the French positions on the Lassigny Hills west of the Oise.

The first day was marked by a drive at the centre; on the second follows the logical expansion of the attack, the effort to break down the sides of the breach which has been opened. Rheims and Soissons are equally enemy objectives. Meantime, the thrust into the centre of the open gap in the Allied lines continues; the advance dips far below the Vesle.

And on this second day, at a conference held in the evening—attended by the Kaiser, the Crown Prince, Hindenburg, and Ludendorff—a momentous decision is taken and announced to the armies in a terse bulletin signed by the Emperor and Hindenburg. "The attack will be pressed." This means—Ludendorff's narrative hints as much—that the Germans, surprised by the extent of their victory, are now going to transform what had been a diversion into a principal operation. They will postpone the Flanders offensive and exploit their victory toward the Marne. The French front has proven incredibly weak. It may be possible to approach Paris before the offensive reaches its term; the stain of the defeat at the Marne in 1914 may be wiped out by a victory on this river four years later. The calculation was mistaken, the consequences of the change of objective in mid-battle would prove fatal, but the situation on May 28th, in the evening, gave no sign of such a conclusion to the most successful stroke in four years of war.

VI. FOCH RESTORES THE SITUATION

On May 27th the German success was still regarded in Paris with calm. Its real magnitude was hardly appreciated except in military quarters, on the following day, when Petain undertook to deal with the problem. It is only on May 29th that Foch takes a hand, and this is the day on which, as a result of the decision approved by the Kaiser and published to his troops, the Germans had decided to transform the operation from a diversion to a major affair and, abandoning the limits Ludendorff had set for the advance, would seek the most distant objectives; in a word, would strive to exploit the preliminary success to the uttermost.

In examining the second phase of this operation, which unrolled between the Vesle and the Marne, it is essential at the outset to grasp a single fact. The military circumstances were quite different from those which arrested the attention of the civilian public and filled the press of the world. A failure to grasp the military aspects as contrasted with the civilian estimates has served to disguise the actual significance of what happened in the next few days and to give an entirely mistaken interpretation to the part played by American troops, glorious as that part actually was.

We have seen in the two earlier offensives of Ludendorff that the hoped-for subsequent profit was not realized because in each case the Germans were unable to expand their original break through. In Picardy the resistance of Byng's troops north of the Somme promptly restricted the gap to the south bank of the Somme, while the Oise River and the Lassigny Hills precluded extension southward. Thus the German advance was first canalized between the Oise and the Somme and then actually arrested before it could break out of the western end of this Oise-Somme corridor west of Montdidier and east of Amiens.

In Flanders the same thing had happened. At the outset the British on the southern side of the break about Givenchy had held firm and stopped any widening of the gap toward the south. On the north there had been a preliminary widening, due to German progress on the Messines Ridge and as far as Kemmel. But although Kemmel was taken, the balance of the "Mountains" were firmly held and the German advance thus paused on the eastern edge of the Forest of Nieppe.

Both operations had created salients, or pockets, and the obvious truth about a salient is that the narrower the mouth of the pocket the greater the difficulty in supplying the troops within it, since the communications will be under fire from both sides and the whole rear of the troops in the bulge under enemy bombardment. Moreover, the deeper the salient is, the graver the menace to the troops within it, because they will be farther from their own bases and more exposed to any attack from the sides of the salient, which, if successful, would cut them off and force them to surrender.

This simple military fact explained the failure of many previous offensives which had made initial gains but, in the end, had to be abandoned because the original break was not widened and therefore advance through the gap became perilous. To risk large numbers of troops within a salient was to invite disaster. The subsequent developments of the fighting between the Marne and the Aisne in July will supply a good illustration, even more simply complete is the example supplied by Pershing's successful attack on the sides of the St. Mihiel salient in September, which resulted in the capture of many thousand troops and nearly five hundred guns caught in the pocket.

On May 29th and the succeeding days then, while the Allied and German publics were thinking of Paris, Foch and Ludendorff were directing their attention to something quite different.   Ludendorff was seeking to expand his break through on both sides.   Foch was endeavouring to prevent the expansion.   The success or failure of the new German venture would depend, not upon the depth of the penetration made in the pocket, but on the success or failure of the effort to widen the pocket on either corner, toward Rheims and toward Soissons.   In the case of the present field of operations, moreover, unless there were a very considerable and swift widening of the salient on its western side, the southward push would have to stop, because the roads which served this region ran close to this side and both roads and railways were unavailable until Soissons was taken.

Beginning on May 29th, then, the whole problem centred on the resistance of the two corners of the pocket, or the two gateposts of the door which the Germans had suddenly cut in the Allied lines.   If the gateposts were maintained, the door was, as yet, too narrow to permit German hosts to get through in numbers which would constitute a menace to Paris.   In fact—and the point is capital—if the door were not widened, the Germans in the new pocket would presently find themselves in a dangerous predicament.

Rheims and Soissons were thus the gateposts, or "corners," in military phrase.   But neither city was itself of great military value.   The Rheims corner actually consisted of the high ground, the "Mountain of Rheims" to the south.   As to the Soissons corner, it derived importance immediately from the high ground, also to the south, where the Americans would fight on July 18th, but chiefly from the Forest of Villers-Cotterets, south and west.   Unless the Germans could take this, their advance toward Paris would be impossible, while if they captured it, then the whole French line north of the Aisne would collapse and the French would have to quit the Lassigny Hills west of the Oise.   This would mean the dislocation of all the French front between the Somme pocket and the new Marne salient and the creation of a real Paris front.

Foch, accordingly, sets out at once to maintain himself in the

Forest of Villers-Cotterets. He will even strive unsuccessfully to hold the heights just southwest of Soissons itself. Thither he will direct his scanty reserve, while smaller reinforcements will be sent to hold the Mountain of Rheims. As for the German wedge rushing toward the Marne, he will neglect this; he will assume the arrival of the Germans at the Marne and leave the fragments of the divisions swept off the Chemin des Dames to retard it as well as may be. Real German success will be measured not by the depth but by the width of the Marne pocket.

In the following days Ludendorff storms at Soissons and Rheims. He will take the latter city and the heights above it. Rheims will be encircled on three sides. The Germans will come up to the edge of the houses; they will see the Roman arch which looks north along the Laon road; new bombardments will complete the ruin of the city, but it will not fall, held by a French colonial regiment called up from rest quarters and arriving "*gentil comme ça*," as observers say afterward.

Ludendorff will have bitter words to say about the failure to get forward more promptly at Soissons when the road was opened—a failure due, after all, it would seem, to the arrival of the offending division at the limit fixed for its progress by Ludendorff himself, before the operation was transformed.

The Germans do get to the edge of the Forest of Villers-Cotterets, penetrate the first woodlands. But there they stick, will stick, and, having been pushed back ever so little in the next weeks, will suddenly be assailed by a storm coming out of the same woodlands, an American storm, six weeks hence. They do no better toward the Mountain of Rheims. Only to the south is their progress considerable. They reach the Marne at Jaulgonne on May 30th, Decoration Day in the United States. The same day the 2nd Division of Americans near Beauvais will receive an order long awaited. On the next the German effort is directed against the whole western side of the pocket between the Aisne and the Marne. Again there is small progress in the north; the progress to the south, between the Ourcq and the Marne, is more considerable, but the check is in sight.

On June 1st the Germans are in Château-Thierry and the American

3rd Division, a motorized machine-gun unit, does good service at
the Marne Bridge.   The 2nd Division has taken root across the Paris-
Metz road, west of Château-Thierry, is taking its first full look at
Belleau Wood, soon to be known as the Bois de la Brigade de Marine.
The Germans will get no farther toward Paris in this offensive or any
other, along the Paris-Metz road.

But what happens at the bottom of the pocket is always unimportant
by comparison with the events at the corners.   And both corners are

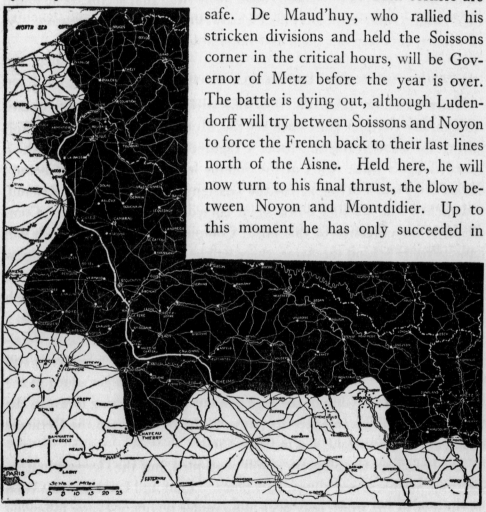

safe. De Maud'huy, who rallied his
stricken divisions and held the Soissons
corner in the critical hours, will be Governor of Metz before the year is over.
The battle is dying out, although Ludendorff will try between Soissons and Noyon
to force the French back to their last lines
north of the Aisne. Held here, he will
now turn to his final thrust, the blow between Noyon and Montdidier. Up to
this moment he has only succeeded in

LUDENDORFF'S PROFITS

Solid black shows French territory occupied by the Germans at the end of the Battle of
the Chemin des Dames.   White line shows the German front on March 21st

excavating a narrow salient, thirty-three miles deep by forty wide, at the bottom of which his guns cut the Paris-Nancy railway, almost as important as the Paris-Calais line on the Somme front, which he has also abolished. He has failed to get the Soissons corner, to smash the Rheims corner; he has been held between the Aisne and the Oise. The armies so far engaged are exhausted; Foch has brought up his reserves. Perhaps Ludendorff will find the Montdidier-Noyon front weak, since reserves have been called away from that sector, as he found the Flanders front weak after his Picardy effort, for the same reason. At all events, this step is logical and inevitable.

VII.   THE BATTLE OF THE MATZ

Once more, on June 9th, this time with all the customary circumstances, the German guns open on the Montdidier-Noyon front. Following the bombardment, Hutier's Eighteenth Army, the army which broke Gough's Fifth Army at the Somme less than two months before, assails the French in line across the Lassigny Hills, from Mont Renaud, a detached hill, looking down upon ruined Noyon, westward. Compiègne is the objective of this push; Compiègne taken, the French will have to retire behind the Aisne; there will be an extension of the dislocation of the French front from Rheims to Amiens.

But on this June 9th the Hutier tactic encounters something which suggests a counter-tactic. Imperfect still, is this answer, at which Foch— with Petain and every other French staff officer—has been working for almost three months, but a sign of progress. The German advance is still unmistakable. The Lassigny Hills fall. The Germans get south to the little Matz brook, rising in the high ground and wandering down to the Oise, a brook which will give its name to the battle, since the Germans do not get to Compiègne, nor in sight of it.

On June 10th the progress is still continued, but the German marching front has narrowed almost to a point. First and last there has been no rupture of the front, only a yielding under terrific pressure following intolerable artillery punishment. More progress on June 10th, in the morning, but in the afternoon Foch throws Mangin upon the western

U. S. Official Photo

SENDING A MESSAGE TO AN AIRPLANE

The signallers seem to enjoy this strange Chautauqua salute

THE AMERICANS IN ACTION

From the collection of war pictures at the National Museum, Washington

By H. C. Murphy

BREAKING THROUGH THE HINDENBURG LINE

The 27th New York Division penetrating the "impenetrable"

FOLLOWING THE TRACK OF A TANK

U. S. Official Photo

ADVANCING THROUGH A SMOKE SCREEN
American infantrymen in action, Meuse-Argonne. October 27, 1918

U. S. Official Photo

U. S. Official Photo

WATCHING THE ENEMY FROM A CAPTURED POST

Two American officers observing the German lines from the famous Montfaucon observatory. The made-in-Germany
binoculars serve American eyes well

U. S. Official Photo

THE MORNING ATTACK

In the haze of the dawn an American battery shells the retreating Germans. This battery works in the desolation of
what was No Man's Land in the Argonne

AMERICANS ADVANCING UNDER COVER OF BUSH TO LAY WIRE.   NEAR CHÂTEAU–THIERRY

ACROSS THE FIELDS NEAR MONT SEC

This machine-gun company is passing through a regiment of doughboys and a supply train.   The picture was taken by a
signalman of the 1st Division during the Battle of St. Mihiel

U. S. Official Photo

FRENCH CHILDREN OF SOULOSSE

Watching an American ammunition train on the way to the front. April 10, 1918

U. S. Official Photo

A GERMAN STRONGHOLD NEAR GRANDPRÉ

From this hill, studded with machine guns and protected by pits, the Americans drove the Boche after three attacks.
The camouflage and brush screen have been removed to present a hazy view of the town and swampy valley

By Captain Harvey Dunn   U. S. Official Photo

THE BOCHE LOOTER

COLD BREAKFAST ON THE MARCH

The artist has caught the feeling of that cold gray morning in the ruined village

YANKEE SOLDIER AND FRENCH CHILDREN

No wonder the American soldiers were popular in France. The little chap on the bench seems to be enjoying the Sergeant's story

U. S. Official Photo

AMERICAN PIES AT THE FRONT

Salvation Army girls at work, gas masks hanging from their necks, making fighting food at their dugouts

SERGEANT LEADING MOPPING UP SQUAD   It was taken in the Argonne Forest where the 77th Division fought

This picture gives an idea of the difficulty of cleaning out machine-gun nests in a dense thicket.

AN ILLUMINATION BOMB LIGHTS THE WAY

This is not an exhibition of fireworks but the grim business of war

ON THE ROAD TO SEDAN

Doughboys following the retreating Germans. The open formation is designed to minimize the effect of bursting shells

TAKING MOVING PICTURES UNDER FIRE

These men are in the front-line trenches at Chaussers

TANKS OF THE YANKS

Here is a procession of them going through the Argonne Forest

ATTACKING FROM BEHIND A TANK

These are men of the 107th Infantry, 27th Division, working toward the Hindenburg Line without the protection of a smoke screen

U. S. Official Photo

By Captain Harvey Dunn

THE ENGINEER—FULLY EQUIPPED

FRENCH AND AMERICAN COMRADES IN ARMS

They are watching the effect of shell fire from the scanty shelter of a ruined stable

THE HINDENBURG LINE NEAR LE CATELET

At this point, where the Scheldt Canal goes underground, American troops broke through on September 28th Lut suffered terrible losses when the Germans

STREET FIGHTING IN A VILLAGE ALONG THE MARNE

Taking such shelter as was afforded by the corners of houses and broken walls, the Americans drove the Germans out. They found it impossible to withstand the determination of our men to win an objective

"FOX HOLES" IN THE ARGONNE

This picture of men of the 18th Regiment, 1st Division, was taken just one month before the Armistice was signed

SMOKE POTS IN THE ARGONNE

An American officer setting off a smoke producer, forming part of a screen through which the attackers advance

MACHINE-GUN CREW IN ACTION

These men appear to be simply drilling but they are actually creeping toward the enemy lines in the Meuse-Argonne

ATTACKING A MACHINE-GUN NEST

The enemy guns are concealed in the woods beyond the end of the street. Approaching the venomous things, the American sharpshooters take advantage of the protection of the shattered houses

PUMPING LEAD INTO THE GERMAN LINES

Two Americans with French automatic rifles early in the morning of the first day of General Pershing's assault upon the salient of St. Mihiel

© By Committee on Public Information

THE ALLIED GENERALS AT METZ

When the Baton of Marshal was bestowed upon General Petain. The guard of honour behind Marshal Petain is composed of Marshal Joffre, Marshal Foch, of France; Field Marshal Haig, of Great Britain; General Pershing, of the United States; General Gillian of Belgium; General Albricci, of Italy; and General Haller, of Poland

U. S. Official Photo

CLEANING OUT A VILLAGE

Imagine the feeling of these men in the open street with Germans lurking at the doorways and building corners

THE HAND GRENADE

Thrown into a shelter from which the Germans are vainly trying to escape.   The smoking grenade can be seen in the left centre of the picture

By John R. Sargent, R.A.

GASSED

© Imperial War Museum, London

TO VICTORY—ON THE RUN

Through the openings blown up by the engineers in the barbed wire. the infantrymen advance to the attack

U. S. Official Photo

"KAMERAD"

A German sniper crying for the quarter he would not give

THE HOME COMING

The Frenchman returns to what the retreating Germans have left of his home

A CITY OF THE DEAD

The great American cemetery at Romagne in the Meuse-Argonne—30,000 are buried here in the heart of America's greatest battlefields

flank of the German wedge, coming out of the forest land toward Rollot, south of Mondidier, and Mangin crumples up the flank, takes prisoners, hundreds of them, and a few guns. German reserves are rushed up; the thrust is parried, but Ludendorff breaks off the battle. Mangin has been in disgrace since the failure at the Aisne a year ago, but he has been marked as a leader of attack ever since he retook Douaumont—for a moment in the spring and for ever in the autumn of 1916. He will now get back his army and do wonders with it. Two American divisions under his command will help break the last German offensive five weeks hence. An interesting man, first remembered in the French army by his advocacy of the use of France's colonies in Africa as a reservoir for the French army. One day he will command the first French army to cross the middle Rhine since Napoleon's retreat after Leipzig.

In the Battle of the Matz the Germans got forward some five or six miles on a narrow front, took the Lassigny Hills—a success that might conceivably profit them later, if they could exploit it. But after the first hours, even during them, they encountered unexpected resistance. The charm of their method seemed to have diminished. There was nothing suggesting a rupture of the French front, and with little delay the fighting took on the character remembered from the Verdun time, body to body, bayonet and grenade. Last of all there was a counter-offensive, a swift, sharp thrust not encountered at the Somme, the Lys, nor the Aisne. And the losses, which were terrific, made a lasting impression upon the minds of the German soldiers.

As for Ludendorff, his position at the Marne is not improved by his operation across the Matz. The Villers-Cotterets pivot is not broken, the Soissons corner holds, the French across the Aisne stand unshaken. He can do no more now. Still he seeks to bolster German morale by publishing his bulletins of victory. He has taken 55,000 prisoners in the Chemin-des-Dames operation; by the end of June his captures amount to 208,000 prisoners and 2,500 guns.

But the promise of May 28th, like that of March 25th, has not been realized. He has thrust his neck into a noose at the Marne. He can retire and transfer his efforts to Flanders, come back to the Vesle, as

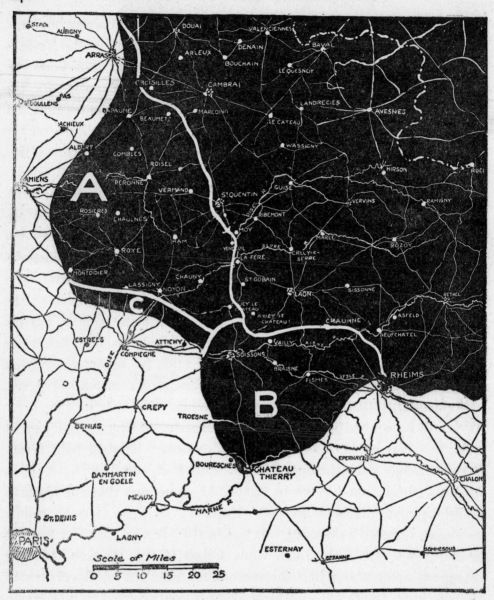

PARIS MENACED

A—Ground gained by the Germans in the Battle of Picardy.   B—In the Battle of the Chemin des Dames.   C—In the Battle of the Matz

Paris believed he wanted to do.   But if he remains in the salient on the Marne he must concentrate his attention in the south; he must hasten to strike again and abolish his inconveniences, for if he goes north or waits too long, Foch will be upon him.

But before he can strike again he must crank up his machine and this will take nearly seven weeks. And if retirement to the Vesle is possible militarily, it is morally inconceivable. After four years the German General Staff has found no satisfactory explanation for the first retreat from the Marne and the German people are in no mood for another, when, after four years, they are again looking at Paris on the map. And on the map Paris is little more than forty miles from Ribecourt, from Château-Thierry.

Paris, too, and all Allied cities and towns, are looking at the map. Paris is going through the same preparations which marked the approach of Kluck to the forts in August, 1914. There was a brief discussion as to whether Paris should be defended or evacuated, since the bombardment would destroy it. Guillaumat, a Verdun general, who had drafted the plans Franchet d'Esperey will soon use to destroy the Bulgarians, arrives to take Gallieni's place. Gallieni is dead, but his spirit lives in Paris. Life in the French capital has now become a nightmare: *Grosse Bertha* by day, Gotha raids by night, while fresh refugees steadily arrive. It is 1914 over again, after four years of agony.

Ludendorff is watching this circumstance. He tells us that after May 27th he studied the French papers eagerly, seeking the first sign of collapse. Instead he read Clemenceau's words: "I shall fight before Paris, through Paris, behind Paris." And Ludendorff does not withhold his admiration. Even in victory he complains that the German public opinion displays no such firmness. In fact, German public opinion is notably weakening. It has heard "*Nach Calais*" in April, it hears "*Nach Paris*" in June, while Calais is still untaken, and the whisper is going about that the submarines have not wholly prevented the coming of Americans—a whisper angrily controverted by all German official agents but not silenced now and soon to become a charge unanswerable.

Clemenceau had once said that the victory would go to the contestant who could stay through the last quarter of an hour. We are now entering this final quarter of an hour, it is represented by the period from May 27th to July 18th. It is the supreme agony for all Allied publics;

for France first, for Paris most of all, for the Parisians who saw the sky aflame and heard the guns each night, who knew that the barbarian was literally at the gate. But in the darkness Foch worked silently; for him the dawn was already in sight. America had bridged the gap between his numbers and those of Ludendorff. If Allied governments and publics would sustain him for a few more weeks, if the civilians would only "hold," he would be worthy of their confidence. And they would hold.

CHAPTER FIVE

THE PEACE STORM—SECOND MARNE

I
LUDENDORFF'S STRATEGY

Ludendorff was now chained to his victory. He had not lost the initiative but he had lost freedom of action. He could not conceal his next stroke, since an attack in Champagne was imposed upon him and the element of surprise would be lacking altogether.

Meantime, in June, he had pushed the Austrians into a new effort along the Piave, and this effort, momentarily successful, had ended in a colossal disaster produced alike by Italian resistance and by an Alpine flood. This terrific defeat had abolished what little was left of the Austrian will for war and had similarly banished all chance of the transfer of Austrian divisions in any number to the German front. On the contrary, Italian troops were beginning to appear on the Champagne front and would perform useful service in the next battle.

The American circumstance was even more distressing. By July Ludendorff concedes that America had become the decisive factor in the war. He counts twenty American divisions in France and fifteen in the fighting strength of Foch; and, numerically, fifteen American divisions had the strength of thirty German. He does not reckon the American division a match for the German since ours was still lacking in training, but he recognizes that American troops are fit for service in quiet sectors, thus releasing British and French.

Finally, Ludendorff at this stage of his narrative devotes far more space to the decline in the morale of his own army than to the military circumstances in the decisive battle of the campaign. Obviously he is seeking to find outside of military events an explanation for his defeat, but despite the unmistakable fact that German morale, civilian and military, was breaking down; despite the expansion of American num-

bers; despite the Italian reverse, Ludendorff's blunder in passing the
Vesle and becoming enmeshed in the Marne salient was a sufficient
explanation for his later reverse. And he was now to make a further
and equally great miscalculation. Foch, whose baton now awaited him
at the Marne, was not the soldier to permit his enemy to blunder twice
without exacting terrible payment.

For this third offensive, which in advance the German people
named the "peace storm"—significant evidence of their fondest hopes—
Ludendorff prepared a double thrust,
wholly comparable to that delivered in
Picardy in March. Then he had struck
north and south of the Cambrai salient,
planning to pinch it out by his advance.
Now he contemplated pinching out the
Rheims salient by similar attacks on
either side.

Between the Argonne and Rheims,
where he conceived the Allied lines were
weak because of the concentration in front
of Paris, Ludendorff prepared to make his

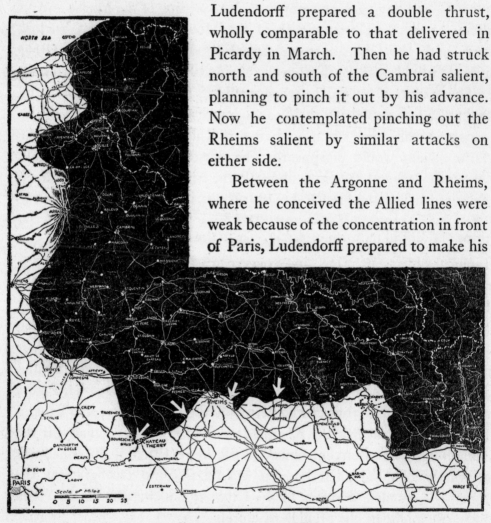

"THE PEACE STORM"

Arrows show main directions of German attack on July 15th

main thrust. He would throw not less than 52 divisions against the French Fourth Army, commanded by Gouraud. His objective would be the Marne from Épernay eastward to Châlons. This attack would uncover the rear of all the French positions on the heights of the Meuse from Verdun southward to the St. Mihiel salient. But its chief effect would be to open the eastern side of the Mountain of Rheims.

At the same time Ludendorff would attack west of Rheims, on a front between the city and the Marne at Château-Thierry, using 30 divisions, and having for his objectives the passing of the Marne and an advance toward Épernay, south of the Mountain of Rheims, to join hands with the German troops attacking on the other side. Other divisions would push south from the Marne to the Morin at Montmirail.

The operation toward Épernay would insure the elimination of the Rheims salient, and with the disappearance of this, all the difficulties incident to his own situation between Rheims and Soissons in the Marne salient would disappear. The advance to Montmirail would still further expand the circle about Paris, from which he might launch another attack if the French should still consent to a prolongation of the war.

But it will be clear that in this offensive Ludendorff had fixed geographical objectives. His first concern was to clear the whole of the north bank of the Marne from Château-Thierry to Châlons and seize the crossings of the Marne on all this front. Until he had accomplished this he would not regain his freedom of action. He could hope that a success as great as that in Picardy would open all the eastern gateways of France, abolish the Verdun positions, accomplish all that the Verdun offensive of 1916 had failed to do. He could calculate that even a more modest success, like that in Flanders, would give him the north bank of the Marne and abolish the Rheims threat to his rear. Finally, if the Chemin-des-Dames circumstances should be repeated, if the Allied line anywhere collapsed as it had on May 27th—and nowhere was the front to be assailed as strong as the Craonne positions had been—then the battle might be the prelude to supreme victory, the "Peace Storm" for which the German people clamoured.

But there was a danger, a very real danger in the new operation. To attack out of the Marne salient was a wise venture only if the western side of the salient, skirting the Villers-Cotterets Forest, were assured against a y thrust coming out of the woods and reaching the roads and railways running along the side of the salient, which were the main lines of communication of the troops to the south, whose mission it was to pass the Marne.

No success south of the Marne and west of the Rheims salient which did not amount to instant and supreme triumph, the obliteration of the salient itself, would be of lasting benefit—of any benefit if an Allied blow cut the lines of communication of the troops making the thrust. In a word, it did not matter how much Ludendorff deepened the Marne pocket, he would still have to get out of it, provided that Foch was able to narrow the entrance into the pocket between the Forest of Villers-Cotterets and the Mountain of Rheims; and to make the salient untenable Foch had but to push a force eastward five or six miles from the Villers-Cotterets Forest.

Such a thrust could be made only if Foch still had an abundance of reserves. And the basis of Ludendorff's whole reckoning was that French and British reserves had been exhausted and that American were not yet ready. He assumed that it was safe to neglect the possible attack from the west, because he calculated Foch had not the troops to make it. This was the fatal miscalculation, he underestimated his enemies' resources, while recognizing the peril incident to any such miscalculation. Here lies the key to the whole military situation.

Also, Ludendorff failed to attach sufficient importance to the events which had just occurred in the Battle of the Matz; he failed to perceive that the Hutier method was in that conflict partially checkmated by a new method of defence, which was sure to be still further elaborated between June 9th and July 15th.

II. THE TWO BATTLES OF THE MARNE

History was now to repeat itself in an amazing fashion. In the last days of August, 1914, after great preliminary victories, the Germans had pushed south between Paris and Verdun, and in the first days of September Kluck's army, ignoring Paris, had marched southeast and crossed the Marne from Château-Thierry to Meaux.   At the same time the other German armies to the eastward had conformed to this southward push and also driven across the Marne or struck at Bar-le-Duc, seeking to cut off the French troops in what had now become the Verdun salient.

This deflection of Kluck from Paris was one of the historic manœuvres of the whole conflict.   It was a logical operation, since the objective of the Germans was the French army, not any single geographical detail, not even Paris itself.   The French capital would be the prize of victory, if the French army were defeated, while possession of Paris before the French army was disposed of would be a liability.

But if this march across the front of Paris was logical, it was hazardous in the extreme, unless the Germans could be sure that there was in the fortified area no force capable of making a sortie from the forts. For if any considerable French army should be concealed in Paris and were flung against the flank and rear of Kluck's army, which had adventured south of the Marne, then only rapid retreat could save it; and even if this retreat were skilfully and successfully conducted the whole German campaign would be upset and the retreat of Kluck would draw with it the several armies stretched from Sézanne to Vitry-le-François.

We know that the French did have a force in Paris—that this force, Maunoury's army—collected by Joffre against just such an emergency— did issue from Paris, strike Kluck's flank north of the Marne and west of the Ourcq, and compel that general to rush his corps north, away from the front of the British and of the French Fifth Army, drawing Bülow's army back, too, and producing a dislocation of the whole German front south of the Marne.

Unhappily Maunoury's army had been too weak to push its initial advantage to the limit, and the British had failed to move with the speed which had been hoped for.   As a result Kluck not only escaped, but gave Maunoury three terrible days of battle and almost forced him back upon Paris.   Still in the end the dislocation produced all along the German front south of the Marne by the Maunoury thrust had opened a

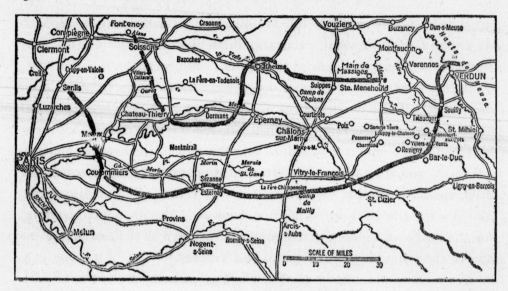

THE TWO MARNE BATTLEFIELDS

The lower black line shows the front of the first Battle of the Marne in September, 1914.
The upper that of July, 1918

gap between Bülow and Hausen, a gap which Foch had perceived and exploited. Thus the end had been a German retreat, the failure of the first blow, which was to conquer France in six weeks, and the beginning of the war of positions.

Now in July, 1918, Ludendorff was going to repeat the venture of Kluck in August and September, 1914. He was going to attempt to advance on a wide front, between the French positions covering Paris and those defending Verdun and—the point is capital—he was going to ignore the possible peril of a thrust coming from the Paris position, this time the Forest of Villers-Cotteret, not the immediate environs of the city. He was going to do this because he calculated, just as his predecessor had calculated in 1914, that the enemy was incapable of any offensive thrust.

To be sure, both Ludendorff and Kluck took some pains to cover their exposed flank—Ludendorff more than Kluck; but the important fact is that neither took care enough. Kluck has told us that on the afternoon of September 5, 1914, while he was advancing upon the British and French south of the Marne, he was suddenly informed that his Paris flank was in deadly peril.   An army of which he had no suspicion had struck outward from Paris and the First Battle of the Ourcq, the initial phase of the first Battle of the Marne, had begun.

On July 15, 1918, the German hosts were occupying a front parallel to but north of the battlefield of 1914.   They were advancing to and across the Marne, seeking to crush all the French armies between Château-Thierry and the Verdun salient.   Their lines were curving southward, and they had again left open, toward Paris and toward the Ourcq, their right flank, which between the Marne and the Aisne was charged with the mission of holding back any thrust, which, coming from the Forest of Villers-Cotterets, would threaten all their communications for the armies between Rheims and Villers-Cotterets if it made any progress, and would totally abolish all hope of success or even of permanent occupation south of the Marne if it could reach the Soissons–Château-Thierry highway, hardly more than six miles from its present front.

All the conditions of the First Marne, even to the Ourcq detail, were then reproduced in what was henceforth to be known as the Second Battle of the Marne.

III.   FOCH'S CONCEPTION

Now, at last, Foch was able to plan, not compelled to improvise. He divined the direction of the next German stroke as early as the middle of June and, divining it, he began to prepare, not merely to parry it, but to meet an offensive by an offensive.   He had advised attack before he was called to command at all, before the campaign had opened.   He had been developing an offensive on the flank of the Somme salient immediately at the close of the Battle of Picardy, when the Battle of the Lys broke and drew his attention elsewhere.

After the Battle of the Lys he had returned to his Somme offensive and he was getting this in shape when the blow at the Chemin des Dames had fallen.   Always he remained convinced that he must wrest the offensive from his opponent or fall under the succession of enemy blows.   But until July he had been unable to do more than parry blows which fell too rapidly to give him time to launch a counter-stroke and were so heavy as to exhaust his scanty reserves.

But in July he saw that Ludendorff must attack in Champagne. To be sure, Haig thought otherwise and continued to send to Foch statements of the reports of his intelligence officers indicating what was a fact, testified to again and again by Ludendorff, that the Crown Prince of Bavaria was busy at preparations for a new blow between the Oise and the Lys. But Petain's reports became clearer and clearer and the military situation convinced Foch that Ludendorff had no choice of fronts this time.

Accordingly, Foch set out to build his battle, his ideas being daily clarified as the indications of German purpose became more and more unmistakable. First of all, since the main German thrust would be between Rheims and the Argonne, it was essential to prepare a perfect answer to the Hutier tactic. This answer, Foch, Petain, and the commander of the French Fourth Army would discover. Then, on the assumption that the German would be held between Rheims and the Argonne, it was necessary to construct a counter-offensive which would overwhelm him in his weakest quarter, namely, between the Aisne and the Marne.

Foch had to insure a successful defence of the Rheims-Argonne front and the Rheims-Marne front; this was the foundation of his battle. But if these two circumstances were assured, then he could view with calm a German push from the bottom of the Marne pocket across the river. The more troops the German risked in the bottom of the pocket the more danger to him if the sides of the pocket were not abolished, if, instead, the neck of the pocket were suddenly narrowed. Only it was necessary that the Germans who passed the Marne should not be able to reach Épernay and thus break down the Rheims salient.

Accordingly Foch, in consultation with Petain and Gouraud, arranged that at the last moment before the Germans attacked between Rheims and the Argonne, the Fourth Army should draw back its main forces from all this front, leaving behind them only a small but resolute garrison to maintain a series of concrete defences and strong points.

Behind this line there would be three or four miles of entirely empty territory, then the mass of the French troops would be organized in fixed defensive positions

Thus, when the German bombardment opened, it would fail upon little more than a thin façade of French defence.   When the advance began it would encounter only the surviving remnant in the first positions, who would by wireless telegraph and by rockets signal the start and the circumstance of the attack and supply all useful information. Meantime the enemy, having broken through this thin outpost line, would enter the empty region and there they would be suddenly assailed by a storm of French artillery fire quite as destructive as that which had been sufficient to smash the troops facing Ludendorff in Picardy, in Flanders, and on the Chemin des Dames.   Such infantry as survived this storm would at last arrive on the French fixed positions, which were outside the area of the intense artillery preparation of the German tactic and would thus remain unshaken.   As for tanks, of which the Germans were correctly suspected of having a considerable number, they would be disposed of by a series of mines fixed along the routes which they must travel.

This answer to the Hutier method was worked out with exactly the same meticulous regard for detail as the German tactic itself.   It was the result of a study which approximated vivisection and had been carried on ceaselessly by the French ever since the first disasters.   It included a resource for each circumstance in the Hutier tactic, and, as the event was to prove, disposed of the tactic once and for all

When the German attack east of Rheims had failed, and always provided that the defence of the front between Rheims and the Marne had been reasonably successful, and it was organized in the same manner, then Foch would be ready to launch his counter-stroke.   For this he would concentrate in the Forest of Villers-Cotterets a force capable of delivering a crushing blow.   In constituting this force he turned to the Americans for assistance and borrowed for the blow their two finest divisions, the 1st and the 2nd, which at Cantigny and Belleau Wood had proven that they were actually combat troops.   To them he would add a number of French shock divisions, including the famous Moroccans. This force would be commanded by Mangin, who had just come back to favour in the Battle of the Matz, by reason of his successful flank attack, but had proven his offensive value in two attacks at Verdun, which in two days had turned the Germans out of all the important gains made in eight months of battle.

South of Mangin, that is between the Ourcq and the Marne, still another army, that of Degoutte, would attack; and in this army, also, there were American divisions: the 26th, in Belleau Wood, and the 3rd, south of the Marne. A portion of the 4th also served in this army, but not as a unit. For this thrust Foch amassed not less than 21 divisions, reckoning each American division as having the numerical value of two European divisions, which was the case. In addition he reinforced Gouraud both with infantry and artillery and marked other troops for use, if the events justified his expectations.

For the whole operation Foch planned to use British, Italian, and American troops, but only two British divisions were actually employed, because of the standing threat in Flanders. Still, despite the fact that eight American divisions—having the value of sixteen British or French—were employed, together with two Italian and two British, the main force actually engaged between the Argonne and Villers-Cotterets was French. Moreover, the leading was entirely French, because the Allied contingents served under French army commanders.

In the calculation, the blow of the Tenth Army, Mangin's, was to be decisive. Foch hoped for a surprise. The forest of Villers-Cotterets was an admirable cover for a concentration, a cover which proved entirely adequate, and he borrowed the Hutier device of moving his troops up secretly by night. But in addition to surprise, Foch planned to employ a new weapon, the small "whippet" tank, which was fast and offered no such target as the old unwieldy monster. Nearly three hundred and fifty of these had been assembled behind the Tenth Army and more than one hundred and fifty behind Degoutte's Sixth Army.

And for this tank arm a new tactic had been developed. There would be no preliminary artillery preparation whatever, since the

Germans occupied newly taken positions, which they had not been able to organize as they had organized the famous lines of the Somme and the Hindenburg system. But the tanks, backed by a mighty rolling barrage, which would support them all the time, would push suddenly forward, followed by the infantry, which would penetrate the enemy line through the gaps opened by the tanks and rely upon these engines to demolish any strong points and machine-gun nests which did not surrender promptly. Artillery and infantry had been trained to coöperate with the tank. Above all, the light artillery was pushed forward with the machines and thus protected them measurably against such a destruction as certain German batteries of light artillery had achieved at Cambrai.

On the morning of July 14th a lucky raid by Gouraud's troops brought back 127 prisoners, from whom it was learned that the German attack would begin at one o'clock the following morning. Therefore, every step was taken in accordance with plans. The first phase of the Second Marne was now to open. If Ludendorff's plans were successfully carried out, the Germans would reach and pass the Marne from Châlons to Château-Thierry and at the same time still further extend the "encirclement" of Paris, by reaching Montmirail and thus drawing a curve about the French capital from Montmirail to Montdidier.

Ludendorff in his memoirs maintains stoutly that after this thrust, which was merely to improve his situation between Soissons and Rheims, he intended to return to Flanders. He does not talk about any Paris drive, but it is not less clear that had he succeeded as he had planned, Paris would have been necessarily a later objective. Failure in the enterprise between the Argonne and Rheims led him to revert to the Flanders scheme, but collapse between Soissons and Villers-Cotterets quite as promptly recalled him from a future offensive to a present and difficult defensive.

IV. LUDENDORFF LOSES HIS BATTLE

At one o'clock on the morning of July 16th, three days later than Ludendorff had first planned, the German guns were to open the usual preliminary bombardment on a sixty-mile front from Château-Thierry to the Argonne. So badly had the secret been kept that even in Paris it was known that the decisive struggle was at hand, and the celebration of the national holiday had been overshadowed by a sense of what was coming. This was the story of Nivelle's misfortune of 1917. Ludendorff was now to pay a penalty as great as Nivelle, and France was to have sweet revenge.

One hour before the German was to open his battle the French guns began their overture. Upon the masses of German troops concentrated in the forward trenches for their leap forward at the "zero" hour there fell suddenly a storm of shell fire which wrought terrible havoc. And as far away as Paris the sky was red with the flame of this bombardment, while the roar of the guns was clearly heard. The most terrific night of the whole war, so all those who lived through it testify.

Still the German adhered to his programme. His bombardment continued for several hours, and then the infantry set out upon its advance. It encountered the line of advanced posts, held by officers and men who had accepted death as an inevitable consequence of their mission, and met the enemy with no other purpose than to delay him as long as possible and make his progress as costly as their time and weapons permitted. And as the German wave reached them they warned their comrades far behind of the phases of the storm under their observation.

Inevitably the wave submerged the slight barrier, although not all the strong points were taken before afternoon, and, having submerged it, entered the vacant space beyond, while the vast masses of infantry, whose mission it was to exploit the success once the Allied lines were passed, swept forward in their turn. The Hutier machine began to function with all its accustomed efficiency.

But almost immediately the German troops came under the storm which, from the opposing artillery, swept the vacant area. Appalling casualties resulted, while the tanks, advancing in their turn, were destroyed by the mines which had been left in their pathway. The gigantic blow had been delivered in space; the enemy had been thrown off his balance by the very weight of the blow, which, encountering nothing, reacted.

In the afternoon the German infantry actually reached the French fixed positions, in a very few cases penetrated them, but in every instance was promptly expelled. The next day Gouraud's troops were actually able to reoccupy the empty zone, which they had evacuated, at certain useful points, notably on the famous Main de Massiges, which had been the scene of desperate fighting on September 25, 1915, and the succeeding days. Actually a German offensive had been broken on exactly the ground which saw Joffre's first tremendous offensive checked after far more considerable initial success, in 1915.

Ludendorff says that he broke off the battle on this front on the second day, July 16th. He conceals the magnitude of his disaster, although conceding the actual check, by reference to valuable local gains, which were, of course, merely the sacrifices of territory incidental to the application of the French tactic. After this check he starts off to the north to see Crown Prince Rupprecht and launch the long-postponed Flanders operation. But he will soon be recalled to more immediate duties.

This victory of the French Fourth Army of Gouraud, hero of Gallipoli, a famous colonial fighter in the days before the present war, is one of the far-shining episodes of the war. Gouraud, a fragment of a man mutilated by previous wounds, is one of the war's most striking and impressive figures. He will share with Mangin the glory of the final phase of the conflict on the French side and fight beside Pershing on the western flank of the Argonne in September and October. He will retake Sedan at the moment when the curtain of the Armistice falls on the war drama.

The measure of the general and of the man is discoverable in the order of the day issued to his soldiers on July 7th and quoted by Babin in his account of the battle:

TO THE FRENCH AND AMERICAN SOLDIERS OF THE FOURTH ARMY:

We may be attacked at any moment. You know that no defensive battle has ever been engaged under more favourable conditions. We are forewarned and on our guard. We have been strongly reinforced in infantry and in artillery.

You will fight on a field which you have transformed by your labour and your tirelessness into a redoubtable fortress. This fortress will be impregnable if all the entrances are well guarded.

The bombardment will be terrible. You will endure it without weakening. The assault will be heavy, made in a·cloud of smoke, of dust and of gas, but your position and your arms are formidable.

In your breasts beat brave and strong hearts belonging to free men.

No one will look backward. No one will retire a single step. Everyone will have just one thought: to kill many of them up to the moment when they shall have had enough.

That is why your general tells you that you will break this assault and that it will be a glorious day.

(Signed) GOURAUD.

The companion piece of the Order of the Day of July 16th—the day of victory—follows:

In the day of July 15th you broke the effort of fifteen German divisions supported by ten others.

In accordance with their orders they were to reach the Marne in the evening. You stopped them exactly where we had decided to fight and win the battle.

You have a right to be proud, gallant infantrymen and machine gunners of the outposts, you who signalled ·the attack, you aviators who have flown above it, you battalions and batteries who have broken it, you staff officers who have so meticulously prepared the field of battle.

It is a heavy blow for the enemy. It is a glorious day for France.

I count on you to do the same every time that he dares to attack you, and from my heart as a soldier I thank you.

Babin asserts that the Kaiser watched this attack as he had observed the German repulse before Nancy four years before, and this is Babin's account of what the Emperor saw at the moment when the assault began:

While "storm troops" were arriving before the outpost line, all the wheels behind them continued to turn according to the schedule based on the hypothesis of a victorious march. The barrage rolled rhythmically forward far in advance of the waves beating against the dike which resisted them. And the divisions of the second line, perfectly satisfied that those of the first line would carry out their regular advance like the point on a dial, were launched behind them at the appointed hour; then the automobile convoys, supply wagons, horse batteries, all in columns of march. Our artillerymen fired over open sights into that mass—pounded it, ground it without respite—and helter-skelter went the men, the heavy cars, and the horses. No one ever saw more beautiful slaughter. At the source of the Ain, on that little knoll which General Marchand once liked and called "the Place de l' Opéra," seventy bodies were stretched in a confused heap. But it was perhaps in the region of the "mountains" which we abandoned at night, in conformity with plans of the command, that the carnage was most beautiful of all. One saw "them" appearing over the crests, and where no cover concealed them from view at all, then coming down the slopes, magnificent targets. "We shoot into the heap," said the gunners.

The 42nd, the Rainbow Division, had a share in this achievement, and Babin says:

It had the honour of rivalling its French comrades in courage and daring. Its men went under fire as if to a football game, in shirt sleeves, rolled up over sinewy biceps. In one trench where they worked with our chasseurs one could count sixty bodies in less than 750 feet. Ah! the Germans who have seen them at work can't any longer doubt that they are here, or even as our soldiers say, "quite a bit here."

Another American division, the 2nd, will achieve further glory on this field some weeks hence, even capturing the hill from which the Kaiser saw his machine broken.

This is Gouraud's Battle of Champagne, a famous battle on famous fighting ground. Not far way Attila's hosts were broken. On July 15th, German shells fell in Valmy, also a name that lives. Joffre's greatest offensive, that of September 25, 1915, failed gloriously in that vacant area where Gouraud smashed the Hutier machine.

By July 16th, Foch's first concern was abolished. His defence on the main front of enemy activity had been successful. He could now turn to the consideration of his counter-thrust with relative calm. Still it was necessary that the line between Rheims and the Marne should hold, and here the Germans had been more successful. The French lines between Rheims and the Marne were the creation of a few weeks as contrasted with nearly four years of effort on Gouraud's front. The Hutier tactic, therefore, was more effective, and all through July 16th the Germans made some progress west of the Mountain of Rheims, just as on July 15th they had made even more material gains.

But Foch can now reinforce this front from Gouraud's army, which has won its battle with little expense in men and is now secure from all German attack. By July 17th, Foch's mind is at rest on this second point also. The Mountain of Rheims will be held until he has had time to launch his own blow, and this blow will recall the Germans from all sides of the Marne salient. The two important elements in his defensive have now been accounted for.

South of the Marne, to be sure, the Germans have made material progress. Checked in front of the Americans, the 3rd Division facing Château-Thierry, they have penetrated beyond the Marne Hills, east of the little Surmelin stream. What would under certain circumstances be even serious is the fact that the Germans, having won across the Marne, are now advancing upon Épernay, astride the Marne, and are rather less than seven miles from the town. If they can reach it, then they will, after all, reduce the Rheims salient. To this limited objective, the German grandiose conception has already been reduced.

But Foch is bringing up a new army, to reinforce that of Berthelot, and De Mitry who led the French troops in Flanders, three months before, will soon assume all responsibility for the Germans south of the Marne. Foch is able now, also, to reassure Haig. The German effort in the south forbids any major enemy effort in the north for a considerable time, and the same is true as to the front between the Oise and the Somme. The enemy is pinned down now to the Marne sector. Foch can dispose of his own reserves as he chooses.

Wherefore, on July 17th Mangin is warned that he will be expected to attack the next morning. Degoutte is similarly advised. The two American divisions which are to share in the honour of delivering what will be the decisive stroke not merely of the battle but of the war, the 1st and 2nd, are put in motion; the last of the American troops will arrive for the battle only by double-quicking for the last miles. And tanks, artillery, shock troops, all, arrive without German discovery.

A hurried and somewhat confused operation, this attack on the Soissons corner necessarily is. Foreseen by Foch weeks in advance, it had always to wait upon victory by Gouraud, a successful defence of the Mountain of Rheims by Berthelot. General Summerall, commander of the 1st Division, who presently will have grim and bitter memories of this confusion, will continue to marvel at the success issuing from chaos.

Ludendorff will marvel also. He will have much to say about high corn covering the field of fire, of German carelessness and lack of entrenchments. He declares that he warned his subordinates, that they had expected attack, but had looked for it a week earlier and dismissed it when it failed to conform to the German time table. But the French say that the Germans withdrew several batteries on the eve of the attack, which hardly suggests expectation of an offensive; and when it came, the noise of the final preparation silenced by a terrific thunder shower, the German army revealed the first authentic sign of crumbling. Ludendorff says:

> Our infantry had not stood firm at all points, and in particular the division southwest of Soissons, that had been considered so reliable, had given way. The gap rapidly widened, especially toward Soissons.

In the next few days the German strategic situation was to Ludendorff's mind "critical"; and a new attack on Rheims "seemed hopeless."

V. FOCH BEGINS HIS CAMPAIGN

On the morning of July 18th Foch, like Joffre on the morning of the First Marne, was outnumbered by the enemy in front of him between Paris and Verdun. He was not so heavily outnumbered as he had been some weeks before. Eight American divisions were at his hands and would be used in the fight—200,000 fresh troops of unmistakable combat value, of peculiar value in the present form of attack. More than this, 1,000,000 Americans were in France and more were now arriving at the rate of 300,000 a month. He could afford to use his own and the British troops without stint because he was building up a reserve which would become available when necessary. And before large numbers of the Americans were available for combat they were sufficiently good to take over the line in quiet sectors and release French and British divisions.

Thus on July 18th Allied conditions were far different from what they had been on March 21st, on April 9th, or even on May 27th. Before the month was out Foch would have the advantage of numbers. But he had now the even greater advantage provided by his foes' mistakes and his own success in finding an answer to the Hutier tactic. His enemy was in a fatally defective position. A huge army, which was only making unimportant progress south of the Marne, had presented him with an open flank between the Marne and the Aisne and particularly between the Aisne and the Ourcq.   If he could push Mangin forward six miles at the Soissons corner of the Marne pocket, he would cut the highways, command the railroad, which alone maintained the vast host to the southward.   Ludendorff would have to quit the Marne pocket altogether.

At the time the world talked glibly about a German Sedan; it expected to see all the vast host involved in the pocket enveloped and captured. Joffre's strategy had inspired the same hope in the First Marne.   But in neither case was this possible, because in both instances the Germans possessed sufficient numbers to postpone envelopment until they were able to extricate their imperilled masses to the southward.

Foch was not playing for a Sedan; this was still a matter for the future.   But he was now taking full advantage of his own labours as far back as the Chemin-des-Dames time.   He had promptly foreseen the value of the Soissons corner, Petain had recognized it even sooner. Together both had reinforced De Maud'huy, who had just barely held on long enough to permit the Forest of Villers-Cotterets to be retained. Thus in the last days of May the victory of July 18th was made possible.

And between four and five o'clock on the morning of July 18th, France and America, the picked troops of both nations, after a brief but cyclonic artillery blast, step out between the Ourcq and the Aisne.   The surprise is complete.   Before noon the American 1st Division is well established on the open plateau within three miles of Soissons.   These troops would have advanced farther had not the French between them and the Aisne been held up in the difficult Missy-aux-Bois ravine.   But Missy-aux-Bois they hold; south of them the French Moroccans have been equally successful; southward again the 2nd Division has done marvels, it has reached Vierzy and approached the Soissons-Château-Thierry highroad, while Allied artillery is bombarding the railway line east of Soissons, which is the single rail artery feeding the whole salient. The Americans alone have taken 4,000 prisoners.

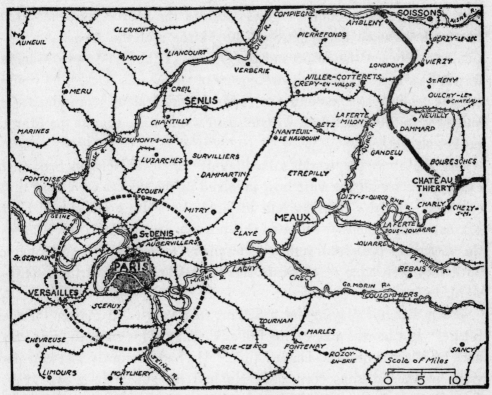

THE SOISSONS "CORNER"

Black line shows the front on July 18th between the Aisne and the Marne. Mangin's attack in which the Americans participated was between the Ourcq and the Aisne. Our 1st Division took Berzy-le-Sec and our 2nd went beyond Vierzy.

Before this first rush the German defence collapsed. Ludendorff in his memoirs complains bitterly of the failure. To him it is inexplicable—as inexplicable as the collapse of the French and British on the Chemin-des-Dames Ridge was to Foch less than two months before. Boehn's troops have been as completely overrun as were Gough's in March. A French commentator compares the effect produced upon the Germans by the tank attack to that produced upon the Romans by the first appearance of Hannibal's elephants. In any event, to their check—to the repulse in Champagne—there is now added actual defeat between the Aisne and the Marne.

Following Mangin's attack, Degoutte launches his between the Marne and the Ourcq. Here the surprise is less complete, the advance less rapid; still the whole German line retires, and French and American troops—portions of the 4th Division and the entire Yankee 26th (which, with the 42nd, participant in Gouraud's army east of Rheims, will be the first Guard troops to take part in a major engagement)—begin to go forward. The whole western side of the Marne pocket is swaying and Ludendorff's Soissons corner is cracking.

On July 19th Foch attacks all around the sides of the pocket from Rheims to the Soissons corner. The armies of Berthelot, De Mitry, Degoutte, and Mangin are all engaged. At the east, on the Rheims corner, he tries to repeat his success at the Soissons corner. There he undertakes to extend his gains, to clear the whole plateau above Soissons and across the tiny Crise brook which enters the Aisne at Soissons itself. In a word, from both sides he is trying to narrow the exit of the pocket still farther, while occupying all the host still encompassed in it.

But in this latter phase he will be less successful. Ludendorff has heard the news and is hastening back to his headquarters, sending all available troops to the scene of the disaster at once. His first concern will be to hold back the enemy at the Rheims and Soissons corners. He will have to quit the Marne pocket; he realizes this at once; his vital railway is under enemy artillery fire. But in order to get his vast accumulation of men, guns, and material out, he will have to keep the exit as wide as possible and instantly check all further attacks about Soissons and about Rheims.

Still on July 19th, and even on July 20th, Mangin's troops get forward. They reach the Soissons-Château-Thierry highway and even pass it. The American 1st Division takes Berzy-le-Sec, magnificently, before its work is completed, and Berzy-le-Sec commands the Crise Valley as well as the Soissons-Château-Thierry highway. But thenceforward the gains will be inconsiderable; the Germans will hold open their pocket while they evacuate it.

And in this retreat the Germans will show the same skill which they revealed in the First Marne. Once the sides, the corners of the pocket, are assured, they will conduct an orderly retreat—first from the south bank of the Marne, then behind the Ourcq, finally behind the Vesle, losing relatively few prisoners, surprisingly few guns.   Four American divisions—the 3rd, the 28th, the 32nd, and the 42nd—will share gloriously in the pursuit in addition to the 4th, 26th, 1st, and 2nd, which have participated in the opening phases.

By July 21st, however, the strategic consequences of the manœuvre on the Soissons corner are fully foreshadowed.   Ludendorff will get his beaten armies back behind the Vesle in good order, although he will have to call upon the armies in the north for reserves and thus use up the resources accumulated against a Flanders offensive.   To himself he concedes that the offensive has been lost (Foch will call the next tune), but on the whole his armies, save for the momentary collapse at the Soissons corner on the morning of July 18th, have done well.   Nothing suggests that he will be unable to maintain a successful defensive.

The latter phases of the Marne fighting are of little more than calendar importance.   The Germans recross the Marne on July 20th. The next day Ludendorff clears Château-Thierry; he will empty the Château-Thierry angle of the pocket first, maintaining his hold on the other Marne corner to the last possible moment.   But by August 1st he is back behind the Ourcq, in a position which he can hold for some time—will hold, in bloody and long-continued fighting with American divisions.   Nevertheless, the pressure at the Soissons corner continues; is presently redoubled by a new Mangin thrust, to which Soissons falls on August 2nd.   Between the Ourcq and the Vesle the enemy again quickens his pace.   He destroys his ammunition, burns material, and pillages and burns villages.   By August 4th he is behind the Vesle and the Aisne; the Marne pocket is emptied.   If he still holds the ground between the Aisne and the Vesle, taken on May 27th, it has no further offensive value; the defeat on the Chemin des Dames has been liquidated.

In prisoners the German lost more than 35,000; in guns, above 700. The French recovered more than 200 villages and towns, including Soissons and Château-Thierry, and reopened the Paris-Nancy railway. Ludendorff had to throw in a large portion of the reserves left to him and marked for a Flanders offensive; he was, therefore, at the end of his offensive possibilities.   He must now accept the defensive rôle, which had been accepted by the Allies at the outset of the campaign and for four months thereafter imposed upon Foch. His "peace storm" had been as unsuccessful as the parade to Paris in 1914. "You will be French, as a result of to-day," an Alsatian soldier reports that his German comrades said to him on July 18th. The German army recognized that the war had been lost. The German public was not less quick to grasp the meaning. As for the Austrian, the Bulgarian, the Turk—they were likewise informed.

On the Allied side the appreciation of the meaning of the Second Marne was not less general. On August 6th Foch became a marshal of France; Petain received the Military Medal; Pershing, the Grand Cross of the Legion of Honour. Paris could celebrate a second deliverance after a peril even graver than that of 1914, for German artillery had expanded its range, and in 1918 Paris was already under bombardment and might expect ruin if the Germans were able to approach much nearer.

VI. THE CONSEQUENCES

Like the First Battle of the Marne, the Second was one of the few decisive conflicts in human history. Only the Battle of the Dunajec, which destroyed the Russian Empire and opened the pathway to incalculable developments, can be reckoned beside the two Marne struggles in the World War. But the Second Marne, quite as much as the First, was not a Waterloo or a Sedan; it was, like Joffre's triumph four years earlier, a battle of arrest. The enemy had been checked and turned back; he had not been crushed or submitted to anything more than a local defeat, which did not deprive him of resources sufficient to restore the situation.

The actual parallel for the Second Marne is Napoleon's defeat at Leipsic. The struggle of 1918, like that of 1813, was also a Battle of the Nations. French, British, American, and Italian troops had shared in the struggle, although, of the total, 80 per cent. were French. Leipsic achieved the deliverance of Germany; it led directly to the ruin of Napoleon, since he failed to make peace after defeat and before his army was gravely shaken.

But it is in the moral consequences of the Second Marne that one is most reminded of Leipsic. Ludendorff's defeat on the Marne was the most considerable German defeat in the west since September, 1914, and it was Ludendorff's first reverse. It was clear, even on the morrow of the conflict, that the German soldier had met his master. Amidst all the confusion incident to civilian estimates of military affairs, the fact was inescapable that Ludendorff had been outgeneralled.

Nor was the stroke of Foch a matter of happy improvisation. He had begun to prepare for the victory in the hour of defeat at the Chemin des Dames when he had instantly recognized that Rheims and the Soissons corner must be held; and Petain had shared his clarity of vision, had indeed taken the first steps to achieve that end. After the battle had ended Foch recognized that Ludendorff was involved and must direct his next blow on the Marne front. Accordingly, he had begun in June to prepare his answer, to organize the Mangin stroke, the fame of which filled the world just four weeks later. Joffre had been equally clairvoyant in August, 1914, after the early disasters and during the great retreat, when he had created Maunoury's army, which on September 5th opened the First Marne.

But having won the First Marne, Joffre was less lucky in the matter of reserves than was Foch four years later. His army had been terribly exhausted by its early defeats and its superhuman efforts at the Marne. His effort to turn the Germans out of France by his operation between the Oise and the Somme was transformed into a desperate defensive, after the "race to the sea," by the rush of German reserve formations to Flanders. Therefore Joffre was unable to exploit his success.

Foch was going to be more fortunate. The British army, which had finished the Battle of the Lys in unmistakably bad shape, had thereafter been resting and refitting from May to August. It was now fresh, strong, eager to wipe out the bitter memories of Picardy and Flanders. Therefore, having gained the initiative at the Marne, Foch would be able to employ it at the Somme. The next blow would be his to deliver, his would be the right to choose the time, the place, and the character of the next operation. It would be for Ludendorff to conform to Foch's actions, as had Foch been compelled from March to July to conform to those of the German.

By contrast, Ludendorff had failed to accomplish the task set for him. It had been beyond his skill, or beyond the strength of the German armies under his command, to defeat the British and the French before the American masses had arrived and become the decisive factor in the contest. Decisive because they enabled Foch first to avoid defeat, then to take the offensive, and thereafter to expend British and French troops without concern for the diminishing man-power of both because all deficits would be made good by the American numbers which were pouring over the seas and would continue to pour for many weeks. He could count on a larger American army for the campaign of 1919 than Ludendorff could hope to engage in the same campaign.

Moreover, success had brought him freedom from the last restraint coming from soldiers or civilians among the Allied governments and armies. His prestige, enhanced in April and early May, had been for a moment shaken at the Chemin des Dames, but the victory of the Second Marne had reëstablished it. He was now to fight with hands as free as those of Ludendorff had been in March and April. Unity of command, exercised by a man now accepted as a supreme soldier, was becoming one of the chief assets of the Allied armies—won through disaster, but won beyond gainsaying.

The military events of the four months which separate the launching of Ludendorff's blow in Picardy from the delivery of Foch's counter-stroke between the Aisne and the Marne remain an open book for all future historians; but who, save those who actually lived through the terrible period, can ever appreciate the agonies, the fears, and the disappointed hopes of those months? Who can quite appreciate in the abstract the horror of the western nations as they saw one German victory after another, perceived Ludendorff's lines inexorably draw nearer and nearer to Paris and to Calais, beheld one Allied defence system after another collapse in a fashion and with a swiftness which suggested that at last the Germans had found the all-sufficing secret of victory?

Who also will forget the sound of the bells of victory, which rang from sea to sea, from Paris to Melbourne, and in America were heard from the Atlantic to the Pacific, when the glad message arrived that, after four months of defeat, there had been an authentic victory, and the defeated German hosts were once more turning their backs to Paris? And for Americans there came with joy the consciousness that the worst humiliation, become acute in recent months—the danger that America would arrive too late—had been escaped. At the critical hour and at the decisive point American troops had fought, shared in the charge that won the day—by the mere force of their numbers made that charge possible; by the magnificence of their courage helped to make it irresistible.

Since that far-off hour when the watch announced midnight and the taking of Cornwallis, a whole country had known no such joy and pride as—north and south, east and west—were evoked by reports of the events of July 18th and the following days. The fall of Richmond had been at most a sectional success; the recapture of the Marne salient was, in its American phase, the achievement of soldiers of a united nation, in which North and South were alike honourably represented.

But considerable as was the American contribution, the real effort and the great glory were French. Destiny had willed that the fate of civilization should a second time be decided at the Marne; and, a second time, French military genius and the devotion of French soldiers had been responsible for the issue of the struggle.

CHAPTER SIX

AMERICA FROM CANTIGNY TO ST. MIHIEL

I

THE FIRST DIVISIONS

The moment has now arrived when it is possible to interrupt the narration of the larger events in the campaign, and examine America's contribution in the period that extends from the opening attack of March 21st to the final retirement of Ludendorff behind the Vesle where he made good his positions for the time being on August 6th. As we shall see, the American part in the war divides itself simply into three periods: that between March and August when we fought under French command at Cantigny and between the Aisne and the Marne; that between August 6th and September 15th when Pershing organized the American First Army and led it to battle at St. Mihiel; and, finally, that period between St. Mihiel and the Armistice occupied by the campaign in the Meuse-Argonne.

Between April and August American troops fought exclusively under the direction of French commanders, generally in divisional units, but not infrequently regiments were intercalated between French units. This first period is the period of testing. The achievement of the 1st Division at Cantigny and of the 2nd at Belleau Wood demonstrated the value of American troops as combat elements. As a consequence of this demonstration, Foch built his counter-offensive of July 18th upon the foundation of American contribution. Had the 1st or the 2nd failed at Cantigny or Belleau Wood this counter-offensive could not have been risked. What eight American divisions did in this counter-offensive led directly to the creation of the American First Army. The triumph of that army at St. Mihiel satisfied Foch that the war could be won in 1918 and persuaded him to undertake the assault on the Hindenburg Line which led directly to the German surrender.

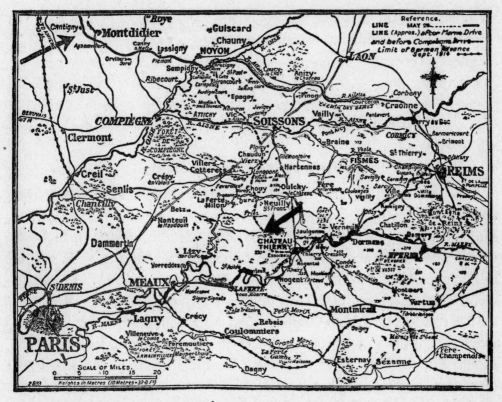

AMERICA'S FIRST BATTLEFIELD

Upper arrow indicates Cantigny, where the 1st Division fought. The lower arrow indicates Belleau Wood, where the 2nd fought. The 3rd Division went into action first just across the river from Château-Thierry.

When the campaign opened, Allied strategy was comprehended in the purpose to hold the Germans in 1918 and, employing American masses in 1919, win the war. The first German successes in March and April drove the British and French governments to make an almost despairing appeal to President Wilson to rush untrained American troops to France to fill the gaps in Allied ranks created by enormous losses in Picardy and Flanders. The divisions thus hurriedly dispatched to Europe did not arrive in time to contribute materially to checking the German assault although two which arrived in May were actually engaged in detachments on July 15th. By contrast, seven of the eight divisions which were in France before the end of March played a conspicuous part in the Second Battle of the Marne, and the eighth, serving as a replacement division, made good the losses in the other seven. To put the thing simply, the American troops who were in France when Ludendorff began his great·offensive lent Foch just the necessary weight to turn the tide after the British and French armies had halted the flood. But it was the great mass of American troops arriving after May 1st which enabled Foch to take the offensive on a gigantic scale and get a decision in 1918.

The first American troops to reach France arrived in May and June, 1917. They consisted of the small contingent which followed Pershing, and were sent at the urgent request of Marshal Joffre and Mr. Balfour who visited America after the failure of the French offensive of April, 1917, and convinced the President that the moral effect of even a small American contingent would be very great. Substantially all of the 1st Division was in Europe by June, and on Bastille Day American troops took part in the parade of the Allies, which marked the French national holiday. Exactly a year later, the 1st Division, with other American divisions which had arrived subsequently, was preparing for the first considerable American action—that known to the French as the Second Battle of the Marne but described in American official documents as the Aisne-Marne.

It was not until August, 1917, that the 2nd Division followed the 1st. September saw the arrival of the 26th, the "Yankee" Division; November brought the 42nd, the "Rainbow"; in December came the 41st, which would serve only as a replacement unit; February brings the 32nd, Michigan and Wisconsin troops; March sees the arrival of the 3rd and 5th, both Regular divisions. This is the situation when the campaign opens: eight American divisions are in France, seven fighting units and one replacement division. In April, the time of great stress in Flanders, the 77th, the "Liberty" Division, is the only addition. Eight active divisions have arrived by May 1st. Two more, arriving in May —the 4th Regular and the 28th, the "Iron" Division, Pennsylvania guardsmen—will by the very gravity of the crisis in July be drawn into the firing line.

When on March 28th Pershing placed all his scanty resources at

AMERICA'S SCIENTIFIC CON-
TRIBUTIONS TO VICTORY

WITH THE ENGINEERS IN BORDEAUX

THE LARGEST POWDER MILL IN FRANCE
Docks are shown in the foreground

"NEW WORLD WORK ON OLD WORLD SOIL"
American Army Transport Service at Bassers Docks, Bordeaux

MOBILE ANTI-AIRCRAFT SEARCHLIGHTS
In operation at Washington Barracks, Washington, D. C.

CONSTRUCTING THE AMERICAN FLYERS' ASSEMBLY PLANT

PLANES FOR AMERICAN FLYERS
Assembly Plant at Romorantin, France

GETTING READY TO FLY

Men of the 96th Aero Squadron testing a Lewis machine gun before putting it on a plane

IN A YANKEE AIRDROME IN FRANCE

The Lewis gun shown in this picture is adjustable to any angle, vertical or horizontal, that may be required to get a bead upon Boche airmen

ASSEMBLING RAILWAY GUNS IN FRANCE

The men are lifting into place one of the big 14-inch guns which later wrought so much havoc in the German trenches

ALL AMERICAN!

This 14-inch railway gun is ready to go into the shop to be disassembled and shipped back to the United States

READY TO FIRE

This picture shows the Browning automatic rifle which was used by the infantry.   It weighs 15½ pounds

BATTLE PRACTICE

These machine gunners are not in France, but in the woods near Fort Sill, Oklahoma.   Their rifles fire 400 shots a minute

Foch's disposition they actually amounted to two regular divisions: the 1st and 2nd, whose training was practically complete, and two Guard divisions, the 26th and the 42nd, which were capable of entering the line in a quiet sector; four American divisions having the value numerically of eight French or German. In April, in the Toul sector, the 26th would engage in the first considerable American skirmish at Seicheprey, a ruined village in the Woëvre Plain which will see American troops starting out for the first American victory in Europe in the following September. This first skirmish is a score for the Germans but a credit to the fighting spirit of the Yankees.

In April, Foch calls upon Pershing for the 1st Division. It will go into action on the ridge north of Montdidier covering the Paris-Calais railway, along the dike where Foch dammed the German flood a few weeks before. This is a post of honour, a position which must be held at all costs, but the 1st Division, Bullard commanding, will do more than hold. It goes into line on April 25th; four weeks later it will leave its trenches and take Cantigny, a swift and splendid achievement, America's real baptism of fire and the first milestone for Pershing's army. This is on May 26th, one day before the Chemin-des-Dames disaster, and France after the disaster will find solace in the promise of Cantigny. Foch, observing the 1st Division at Cantigny, will dare to entrust the 2nd with an even more considerable responsibility at Belleau Wood five days later. Even the 3rd, which has never yet had even its practice period in the trenches, will be rushed to Château-Thierry—Ludendorff compelling—at the same hour.

As for the 26th and the 42nd, the former in this April crisis relieved the 1st in the Toul sector, freeing it for the Cantigny task; the 42nd relieved two French divisions in the Vosges, whither the 32nd will go to free other French divisions, while the 77th and the 28th will settle behind the British, potential reserves if Ludendorff should attack again in the north. Thither will go many more divisions in the next months, aiding Haig mightily in his task of refitting and rebuilding his army.

Cantigny was a slight but promising experiment; a far severer test was now to come.

II. BELLEAU AND CHÂTEAU-THIERRY

On Decoration Day, May 30th, the 2nd Division was in billets south of Beauvais and under orders to proceed to the Somme area and take over a portion of the front adjoining the 1st Division.   This is the fourth day of the German offensive on the Chemin des Dames and the Germans already have reached the Marne.   Later in the day the orders are changed and the 2nd is ordered to the Marne area by way of Meaux—infantry to march, artillery to follow by rail.

The line of march will cross the battlefield of the First Marne.   As the troops approach the Ourcq they encounter the lamentable tide of refugees, the hundreds and even thousands of women and children fleeing before the invader.   They also meet the débris of the French divisions retiring after defeat—the stragglers and the fugitives, for most of the survivors of the disaster are still fighting.   The Americans, officers and men, have the impression of those who saw the similar exodus from Verdun in the first hours of the attack of 1916 and of others who witnessed the flight from the Somme area after the British lines collapsed in March, 1918.   The roads are jammed, there is a confusion of orders.   Harbord, commanding the Marines, will halt his troops along the highway, he will sleep in May-en-Multien, a place frequently mentioned in the days of the First Marne.

In June, the Marine brigade will reach Montreuil-aux-Lions on the Paris-Metz road, a dozen miles west of Château-Thierry.   One infantry regiment, the 23rd, will be detached to stop a gap in the French line farther north; the other is on its way.   Bundy commands the division, Harbord the Marines; the latter will get the division as a result of the present operation.   The expectation is that the men will rest from their forced marches, but at one o'clock in the afternoon General Degoutte, commanding the French corps in this region, sends an urgent appeal for help and the 6th Marines presently move out and take a position astride the Paris-Metz highway and near Clarembaut Woods.   The village of Vaux is just under the forward slope, before them, but no American soldier will get there until July.   The 6th Machine Gun Battalion will be in action on this day; will do good service; but the French are still in line ahead and Harbord is in reserve.

In the following days the whole division gets up and into position—the Marines north of the road, the infantry regiments south. The French retire upon the Americans and then through them, withdrawn from the sector on June 4th, on which day the 2nd Division faces the Germans. Their line extends northward from the national highway and then bends westward; it encircles the little village of Lucy-le-Bocage, henceforth the centre of the American sector.

Stretching before the larger portion of the American front is the Bois de Belleau, a considerable area of dense woods, which extends from the little brook just east of Lucy-le-Bocage northward to the highway coming east from Torcy and forking just outside of the village of Belleau. Beyond the fork one branch climbs the hills east of Belleau Wood and continues to Château-Thierry, the other turns south and runs along the eastern edge of the woods through the village of Bouresches and joins the Paris-Metz highway at Vaux. These two roads fairly outline the extreme of American advance in the following days; from Lucy-le-Bocage to Bouresches is less than two miles by the road which follows the brook on the southern edge of the forest. The first Marines to fall are buried where this road crosses the brook a thousand yards east of Lucy.

The Belleau Wood area constitutes a tangle of hills and undergrowth which the 26th, the New England Division, will find reminiscent of their home country, when at last they take over this sector from the 2nd. The western slope, facing the Marines, is gradual, the first portion open, compelling the assailants to move under direct observation and thus to suffer heavy losses. The highest point of the wood is in the northeast corner, looking over the ruined village of Belleau and the cross roads, and crowned by a little stone tower.

For machine-gun cover no more satisfactory circumstances could be imagined, and in among the ledges and rocks the Germans will dig many curious and clever protecting "fox holes," but they will have no real trench system. From the hills to the eastward, hills dominating the whole surrounding country, they will be supported presently by heavy artillery. Belleau Wood is actually an advanced position, useful as a cover if the offensive is to be resumed, but accepted by the Germans as the natural limit to their advance begun on May 27th and now ending as a consequence of the exhaustion of the troops and the difficulties of getting up supplies, guns, and munitions.

But the Marines do not accept it as the limit of their own front, and on June 6th, at daylight, that is on the second day of their exclusive occupation of this front, they attack. Their objective is the whole of Belleau Wood and their front and that of the French troops north and west of them is outlined by the road coming from Torcy and forking at Belleau, together with the branch which goes south to Bouresches.

The attack is by no means a complete success. The village of Bouresches is taken and the southwest corner of the woods is penetrated. Thereafter it becomes a matter of hacking one's way through the forest. The losses are heavy, the gains restricted but continuous, while the Germans are compelled to reinforce their troops. The contest has no more than local importance; there is no larger strategic purpose served by the capture of the whole area; but since American soldiers are engaged in their second offensive, it is a matter of pride for the Germans to check it.

But check it they cannot. On June 25th, three weeks after they relieved the French, the 2nd Division, with the Marine Brigade assigned to the task, has the whole of the forest, while a few days later the 9th Infantry takes Vaux, after a very brilliant little affair, marked by splendid artillery preparation superintended by a former resident of Vaux, who knew both the surface and the subsurface of the village. Before the middle of July the 2nd Division can surrender its front to the New England troops. It has done its work well; it has advanced on its whole front; it has confirmed the impression created by the 1st Division at Cantigny, after a far ruder test. At least two American divisions may be reckoned as shock troops; even the Germans, in a captured comment, concede this. And it would be a mistake to overlook the part of the 9th and 23rd Infantry. The glory has gone to the Marines, but the infantry did its equal share.

For this achievement the 2nd Division paid heavily.   Forty-eight officers and 1,176 men were killed, 196 officers and 4,879 men were wounded, 17 officers and 1,528 men missing.   The total casualties were 285 officers and 7,585 men, 7,860 of all ranks, materially more than the traditional 25 per cent. loss, which was reckoned the maximum to be demanded of any unit before it must be withdrawn.   And it was withdrawn on July 10th, only to be thrown into another battle, where it would suffer further heavy losses.   In revenge the 2nd took 1,654 prisoners and 24 guns and it advanced several miles along its whole front.   Belleau Wood, a skirmish in the World War, was for the United States the biggest battle since Appomattox and the most considerable engagement American troops had ever had with a foreign enemy.   Not in the Revolution, the Mexican War, or the Spanish conflict had as many soldiers participated in a single engagement.

It remains to mention the service of the 3rd Division.   It had been occupying an area south of the Marne and had not yet been subjected to its test of trench-training when, on May 29th, it was warned to move north to the Marne.   Its 7th Machine Gun Battalion, which was motorized, arrived opposite Château-Thierry at the moment the Marines went into line on the Paris-Metz highway.   But at Château-Thierry the emergency was greater, and in the following hours the detachment of the 3rd Division contributed, probably decisively, to checking the German rush at the river, holding the south bank while the French infantry retired.   It was a splendid service.

In the next days the infantry arrived; certain elements were used to aid the French in their unsuccessful effort to hold Hill 204, north of the river, and then the 3rd went into line south of the river facing Château-Thierry, extending as far east as the mouth of the little Surmelin stream, which comes down from the south.   On this new front they would presently be heard from and they would have a rôle in both phases of the Second Marne.

Still the glory of the June fighting rests with the 2nd Division. To claim for it that it saved Paris seems extravagant, despite the fact that its sector lay across the Paris-Metz highway, for almost as it went into line the German advance had reached its inevitable term, because the effort to break the Soissons corner had failed. Its real achievement was its offensive, the taking of Belleau Wood, still surrounded a year later by a circle of military cemeteries, testifying to the cost of the victory.

The following is the tribute contained in a German bulletin:

The Second Division must be reckoned a very good one and may even, perhaps, be counted as a storm unit. The different attacks on Belleau Wood were carried out with bravery and dash. The moral effect of our gunfire cannot seriously impede the advance of the American infantry. The American nerves are not yet worn out. They lack only training to become formidable adversaries. The men are in fine spirits and are filled with naïve assurance. The words of a prisoner are characteristic— "WE KILL OR GET KILLED."

From the enemy this is the highest praise conceivable.

III.   AISNE-MARNE

The fighting from July 15th to August 6th—the Second Battle of the Marne for the French and British, the Aisne-Marne in American official reports—saw engaged eight American divisions, the 1st, 2nd, 3rd, and 4th Regular and the 26th, 28th, 32nd, and 42nd Guard divisions. The 1st and 2nd fought as a corps under the command of Bullard, but actually as units of Mangin's army. In the first phase during the German attack, the 3rd with a fraction of the 28th was engaged south of the Marne; the 42nd, in Gouraud's army east of Rheims. On July 18th, the 1st and 2nd attacked with Mangin's army south of Soissons, the 26th with Degoutte's army north of Château-Thierry. After the German retreat began the 26th, 3rd, 32nd, and 42nd figured conspicuously in the pursuit; the 28th was in action for two glorious days on the Ourcq; and the 4th rendered brilliant service between the Ourcq and the Vesle. At the close of the battle, the 77th relieved the 4th and the 28th, the 32nd at the Vesle, and the 3rd reappeared briefly at Fismes.

The service of the 1st and 2nd at the Soissons corner was an essential circumstance in the great battle which has already been described. It is one of the finest pages in American military history as it was a decisive factor in the battle itself.   Other divisions won deserved glory afterward, but the achievement of the 1st and 2nd remains preëminent both because of the actual deeds done and because as pioneer units they established the value of the American army in France.   Every man who fought in these two divisions from April 25th to July 20th realized that America was on trial, and more than all else, this explains the devotion and the fortitude disclosed at Cantigny, Belleau Wood, and the Soissons corner.

Briefly, now, we may review the services of the other six divisions in the Aisne-Marne engagement.   In Château-Thierry the services of the machine gunners of the 3rd, on the last days of the Ludendorff drive, will never be forgotten.   Sweeping the bridge over the Marne—facing the quay, on which the statue of La Fontaine, the fabulist, native of Château-Thierry, looked out placidly upon the scene of destruction— they covered the French retreat, held on when the Germans mounted a machine gun in the clock face of a tower commanding the main street— Avenue du Maréchal Petain, *now*—and poured down upon them a stream of lead.   "One of the finest feats in the whole war," Babin says at the time.

Even more distinguished was the performance on July 15th, when the Germans crossed the Marne east of Château-Thierry and, in the bend of the Surmelin, assailed the 38th Regiment on front and flank.   But even thus assailed, the men of the 3rd held on, fought back, broke the attack, and resumed their original front—not a German left south of the Marne in their area, save for 600 prisoners.   Of this deed of the 38th, Pershing, chary of praise, wrote:

On this occasion a single regiment of the Third Division wrote one of the most brilliant pages in our military annals.

Of the milit`a divisions, the 26th, attacking on July 18th, stormed the villages of Torcy and Belleau, swept the heights, crowned by Gonetrie Farm, from which German artillery had pounded the Marines in Belleau Wood.   Halted a moment by the check administered to the French on their left, they resumed the advance, pressed through Epieds, reached the Bois de Châtelet, in whose thickets the

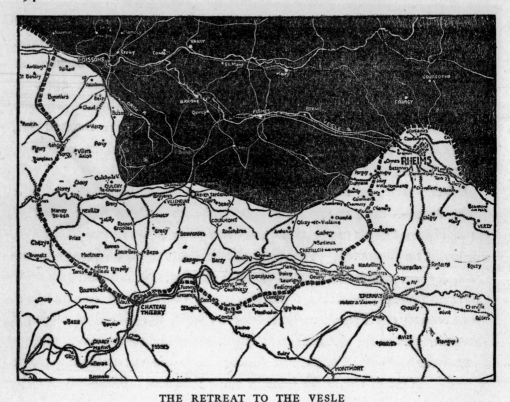

THE RETREAT TO THE VESLE

Dotted line shows the Marne salient on July 18th.   Solid black indicates the German lines in the last days of July

Germans had hidden another *Grosse Bertha* almost ready to open on Paris.

Even more fortunate were the 32nd and the 42nd, the latter brought round from Gouraud's front.   At the crossing of the Ourcq, about the villages of Seringes, Sergy, and Cierges, they crossed bayonets with Prussian and Bavarian Guard troops, militia against élite, literally crossed bayonets.   One village was taken and retaken nine times.   But the National Guard broke the Prussian Guard and pushed on.   This region is dotted with American graveyards, testifying to the bitterness of the battle.   And the 4th, relieving the 42nd, pushed the pursuit through the forests of the Nesles and Dôle, actually forced the passage of the Vesle at Bazoches, where many of their comrades sleep on the field of achievement.

THE WAR IN THE AIR

By C. R. W. Nevinson

This phase is significant, too, as the time of the testing of the second line, the militia. The 1st, 2nd, 3rd, were Regulars; one might expect much of them, but their numbers were scanty. First, before the grand march began, one must know of the new troops, the civilian-soldiers, what they could do. The answer was had at the passage of the Ourcq, also a memorable day in American history.

This July fighting, moreover, removes the last argument urged by Foch and Petain against the creation of an American army. A review of that long debate would be sterile now. In the beginning all Allied commanders felt the emergency too great for an experiment. Pershing was not convinced but yielded to the logic of events. Our men served under French officers in the time when the task was to check and turn the flood, but by the close of the Aisne-Marne the German check had become absolute. The time had come for the British army to pass to the offensive and Pershing would have time to organize an army. Moreover, the prize for which he had long contended had been won for Pershing by his soldiers; the second milestone was passed.

More American soldiers had fought in the Aisne-Marne battle than in any previous army in the history of the United States. Rather more than 175,000 were engaged, a number in excess of the armies of Lee and Meade combined at Gettysburg; and the losses, approximately 45,000, were about those of Lee and Meade together in the great struggle of fifty-five years before. In the battle American divisions captured 9,000 prisoners and 138 guns.

The heaviest loss was that of the 1st Division, 7,870, while it also led in the number of prisoners taken, 3,500. The losses of the 2nd amounted to 3,792 for twenty-four hours of action, but it took 3,000 prisoners and 75 guns against 63 for the 1st. Between June 1st when it went into action at Belleau Wood and July 19th when it went out of action at Vierzy, the 2nd Division had suffered casualties amounting to 12,000, just short of 50 per cent., but it had taken 4,700 German prisoners and nearly a hundred guns. The 3rd between June 1st and July 30th lost 7,966 and captured 8 officers and 1,112 men. The 4th between July 17th and August 12th had total casualties amounting to

6,154. Thus between April and the first days of August, four Regular divisions with a nominal strength of 108,000 had suffered a loss of 36,000, a full third.

Of the militia divisions the 26th had lost 5,300; the 32nd, 4,770; and the 42nd, between July 25th and August 4th, 5,500. Serving with Mangin's army between August 28th and September 3rd, the 32nd would take Juvigny and 1,000 prisoners with a loss of 3,819. These were all very severe losses for militia units still in the training stage. By the close of the Aisne-Marne operation Pershing's army had suffered considerably more than 50,000 casualties, but it had taken more than 10,000 prisoners and more than 150 guns.

Meantime, American divisions had begun to flow to Europe in impressive numbers. Before May 1st, nine had come in all; in May, nine more arrived; in June, seven; in July, four; in August, six; in September, four; in October, three. Such is the amazing record. By the end of October, 42 divisions had arrived, 33 of them between April and November. This represented, roughly speaking, a total of 1,200,000 men, and 29 of the 42 divisions got into action. These 29 had a numerical strength equal to that of the 58 divisions under Haig's command when the Battle of Picardy opened. On Armistice Day, Pershing commanded more troops than Haig and held a longer stretch of line.

With August the scene shifted to Chaumont, American General Headquarters henceforth, as Montreuil was the British and Chantilly had been the French. The greatest experiment in military history was now to be undertaken, an American army was to be organized on a European scale and would fight its first battle five weeks after the close of the Aisne-Marne operation.

One day before Ludendorff attacked in Champagne on July 14th, in the very heart of what was then the Marne salient, Quentin Roosevelt, flying over the enemy lines, seeking information of the coming attack, was brought down to his death near the little village of Chamery. His grave is upon a gentle eminence, overlooking the road by which the Wisconsin and Michigan troops, having taken Cierges, would come charging up a few weeks later. A country which had known the soldier as a boy, when his father was President, and his youthful pranks had nationwide currency, was moved by this willing sacrifice, and turned a sympathetic glance toward the great American whose day was already drawing to a close, but whose spirit was flaming forth in France wherever American soldiers fought.

One further circumstance. When our troops went into action at Cantigny, Europe—friend and foe alike—waited with the phrase, "too proud too fight" still fixed in mind. The German had said we would not come; he had proclaimed that we would not fight. The men of the first eight divisions knew this: and, knowing, answered what was at once an insult and a challenge.

The fact that the Battle of St. Mihiel was fought under an American commander and by an almost exclusively American army has contributed to divert attention from the Aisne-Marne operation, but the truth is that the Aisne-Marne was an infinitely severer conflict. American casualties of 45,000 in it, as contrasted with 7,000 in the St. Mihiel attack, supply an accurate standard of measurement. Moreover, in July the situation was still far from that of September, and whatever estimate America places upon its three major engagements, there is little reason to doubt that our European associates will continue to regard the Aisne-Marne effort as not only the most hopeful to the common cause but in many ways the most remarkable American performance. And however men may debate the particular sector in which the war was won—and British, French, and American critics may be pardoned their differences on this score—it is not less clear, beyond all debate, that the war was lost in the Marne salient—lost in the early morning hours of July 18th. By contrast the events in the St. Mihiel salient were no more than a "side show," and the far more significant drama between the Meuse and the Argonne only a circumstance in the exploitation of the victory obtained between the Aisne and the Marne.

CHAPTER SEVEN

FOCH MANŒUVRES

I
THE NEW STRATEGY

Between July 18th, when he regained the initiative, and November 11th, when the enemy surrendered on his terms, Foch sought three definite ends. In the fighting between the Marne and the Vesle he undertook to exact from Ludendorff the highest possible price for the German commander's miscalculations and subsequent defeat. He knew that Ludendorff still possessed sufficient reserves to cover his retirement from the Marne salient. But he also recognized that by compelling Ludendorff to employ these reserves in getting out of the Marne mess he would abolish all chance of a German offensive in Flanders and also draw away from the British front, where he meant to strike next, Ludendorff's reserves still available there.

Despite popular belief at the moment, Foch did not expect or strive for a grandiose Sedan between Rheims and Soissons. What he did aim at and accomplish was the consumption of German reserves, and he spared his own troops largely, contenting himself with brief strokes at propitious moments. In a measure he left it to American troops to get their training while shepherding Ludendorff out of the Aisne-Marne area.

Foch's second operation was the logical extension of the first. He undertook to drive the Germans out of all the country west of the Hindenburg Line which they had occupied as a consequence of their March victory and compel them to retire behind the Hindenburg system. But the underlying purpose was so to punish the Germans between their August front and that from which they had emerged on March 21st—so to use up their reserves—that they would be unable to hold these formidable positions when they had reëntered them. Foch's reasoning was that the strength of the Hindenburg Line would amount to the strength of the men holding it. His conclusion was that if the morale of the men had been smashed in the fighting between Montdidier and St. Quentin the Hindenburg Line could not be held by the enemy. If, in addition, their reserves were consumed in the struggle to defend it, the victory was assured.

In Foch's third step, his final purpose was, patently, to reap the harvest prepared by the preceding efforts. Somewhere along the road which the German had now entered, the moment would arrive when, his reserves exhausted, Ludendorff would be helpless to resist the final attack. The coming of the hour would wait upon the exhaustion of the reserves. General Buat, a distinguished lieutenant of Foch and later Chief of Staff of the French army, in commenting upon the memoirs of Ludendorff has supplied a lucid and brilliant exposition of the French strategy which won the war, an exposition contained in the examination of the Ludendorff method and the causes of its failure. Thus, the General writes, in the last weeks of 1919, when every reason for secrecy has disappeared:

Ludendorff launched heavy attacks upon the French front, but his attempts were only made successively and at intervals so widely separated that the effects of the first no longer influenced the course of the second. That is to say: French divisions that were engaged in repelling the first attempt were capable, after rest and replacement, of resisting the second. This is glaring weakness of Ludendorff's method. Ludendorff himself says: "We have not been able, either in the east or the west, once during the whole war, to carry any great break through to its logical conclusion."

Now the principle which dominates and explains all the successful and futile efforts, throughout the war—and, as a consequence, cannot too frequently be emphasized— is that no single attack, however powerful, could lead to anything decisive on the western front. The reason is that the railroads and highways are so numerous in France as to make it absolutely impossible to prevent Allied reserves, accumulated behind the front, from arriving and damming the flood wherever the enemy penetrated our lines.

The obstacle to decisive victory in France did not lie in the difficulty of achieving a break through on an organized front. That was always possible. The trouble was in exploiting that break through. Having smashed down the door, it was necessary to get well into the house. And this explains why, whenever a decision was sought, the dangerous adversary was not the man in the trenches, but the army which would come at top speed to stop the attack at a greater or less distance from the trenches that had been taken.

In other words, the first step was necessarily the annihilation or dispersal of the enemy reserves and the real break through could only come afterward. And to annihilate, disperse, exhaust the enemy reserves there was but one method; namely, to make partial attacks at many points and at short intervals, finishing by piling them one on top of the other, and, by thus compelling the enemy to keep up replacements and reinforcements, continually, suck in all his available resources.

These attacks of usury—or, better, this process of absorption of the enemy reserves—could not lead to a lack of man-power. Aside from other considerations, man is a commodity in which neither combatant is likely to be much richer than the other; hence the objective sought must be to produce a shortage of material. Economy of infantry, prodigality of artillery and other engines of war, prodigality without limit; such ought to be the characteristics of these preliminary operations.

One consequence follows logically. With little infantry one cannot get very far. Therefore, without fixing in advance the absolute limits to these attacks—for it is never wise to leave out the element of luck—one should proceed systematically, one jump after another, under the protection of artillery, keeping the enemy under constant threat.

When, as a consequence of a number of operations of this sort, all the enemy reserves have been absorbed on the front, then, only then, the hour for the break through has arrived. Then, with absolute certainty a final attack, greater than all previous attacks and designed to produce a larger breach, can be launched, provided with the maximum of material, better equipped than before with divisions, organized in depth. And nothing will check the exploitation of this break through, since nothing, or next to nothing, is left to the enemy with which to dam the flood. Then no expectation can be unwarranted.

In other words, it is putting the cart before the horse, before you have exhausted or absorbed the enemy's reserves. Once Ludendorff put us in just the hole I have described. It was in the beginning of June, 1918, on the single occasion when two German attacks came so close together that, to meet them, we were reduced to a condition in which we had no reserve divisions left. If the Germans had been able, at that moment, to make an attack anywhere on our front, no man can say what might have happened.

Exactly in the same fashion, at the beginning of November, 1918, we had successfully absorbed all of the German divisions and brought Ludendorff to the edge of that precipice over which our attack of November 14th would have tumbled him.

It is not difficult to believe that Ludendorff didn't understand this style of warfare. Perhaps he couldn't employ it because it requires an enormous equipment of artillery, airplanes, tanks, and munitions, which he did not possess. But it is less easy to understand why he should have believed that we were incapable of using it in our turn. It is harder to understand, for at this time the German front was marked by a series of salients which literally begged to be attacked.

To meet this attack, Buat insists—to parry this sort of offensive—Ludendorff's sole resource was to find new divisions. But there was only one way to find the divisions, and this was: to shorten his front.

The French general recognizes that such a retreat as was thus forecast was a hard thing to order; still, Ludendorff had ordered it in 1917, at the time of the Hindenburg Retreat, and in any event it was only French territory that was to be surrendered. "When your life is in danger, you can't afford to reject any proper means of surviving," he observes. Then he continues:

Ludendorff should have ordered such a retreat before July 15th. Closing his eyes to the real situation, he chose to repeat the experiments of March 21st and May 27th, which had turned out badly in the end. Now there are some experiments one cannot repeat in the face of an enemy even a little observant, and thus forewarned, and get off scot-free. Therefore Ludendorff's new assault not only failed of itself, but revealed the utter failure of the German method of headlong attack. His "Peace Storm" collapsed miserably on our Champagne Plains.

Then, the smallest vision of the future ought to have driven Ludendorff to order a retreat to a shorter line without a moment's delay. He could still have saved himself, at least for a time. But in his proud obstinacy he could not bring himself to do it; and in this was his ruin. Gripped on all his fronts by our attacks, he saw his reserves disappear like snow before the sun. Thenceforth we had him.

Thus, the real meaning of the operations from August 8th to the middle of September must be sought, not on the map, not in the record of ground gained, but in the capture of men and guns and in the reports of how the Germans fought. Foch's objective is the German machine; he will undertake to smash it. If he succeeds, lines and forts are nothing.

On the morning of August 6th, when the retirement to the Vesle terminates, the German army is still a formidable machine. It has suffered a sharp reverse, but nothing like Allied defeats in Picardy and in Champagne. After initial defeat the retreat has been conducted in brilliant fashion, will remain a marvel of efficiency in military annals henceforth, and the Germans still hold vast areas of recently conquered territory. Their purpose now is to maintain a successful defensive until winter terminates the campaign and gives diplomacy a chance. If the German army holds out before or behind the Hindenburg Line, German diplomats will have much Allied territory to barter with, and after the strain of a campaign like that of 1918 Allied publics and Allied statesmen are hardly likely to stand out for extravagant terms. Germany cannot expect now such a peace as she hoped for in March, but the future is not yet dark provided the German army and the German people hold out.

Ludendorff in his comments frequently talks of breaking the Allied will for war; Foch must now break the German will for war. He will not succeed if, in his forthcoming offensives, he gains restricted areas at terrific costs; another Somme, a second campaign like that of Flanders in the previous year, will be more likely to exhaust Allied endurance than German. Foch has the offensive; he must attack, but his attacks must show swift and indubitable successes or the war may end in a draw.

In solving his problem we shall see that Foch from the outset follows a totally different course from that of Ludendorff. The German sought to achieve his end by a series of brutal and terrific blows, so heavy that between each there had to be a period of rest for the assailant quite as much as for the assailed, and in the respite the vanquished regained his strength. Foch will give his enemy no respite, his blows will be short and sharp. No unit will be exhausted before it is withdrawn, no rest will be allowed the enemy. The moment one sector on the front has been shaken the next will be attacked. The dislocation will extend in all directions, the strain upon enemy reserves will be incessant. German High Command will be confused by the rain of blows, but nothing will be attempted beyond the possibilities of the situation.

The intellectual character of Foch's strategy will be disclosed in the nicety with which he calculates and the care which he manifests in avoiding the immediate pursuit of too remote an end. He is steadily striving to reduce the German reserves to that condition in which a general attack without limit can succeed, but he is far too wise to risk the blow before the preparation is complete.

In a word; if Foch is to break the Hindenburg Line in October —if he is to reduce it to impotence in early November—he must wear the German army out in August and September. What takes place between the Avre and the Scheldt will determine the future of the Hindenburg Line.

Thus, in viewing the battles of the next months between the Scarpe and the Oise, it is a mistake to lay too much stress upon the confused and bewildering phases, to attach supreme significance to the capture of this or that town. The operations, too enormous to be followed exactly, are comprehensible only when they are regarded as details in a general scheme, in a manœuvre directed at the reserves rather than the strategic centres of the enemy. At Waterloo, Napoleon fought all day to reduce Wellington's army to a condition in which it would be helpless to resist the Old Guard when at last he put it in, but, failing to accomplish this end, he saw the Guard broken by the still-unshaken British and recognized his defeat. Foch will be more fortunate, since he will be able to complete his preparation before he makes his final attack. His misfortune will be that the enemy will surrender before the final blow falls, but the surrender itself will tell the full story.

II. THE BATTLE OF AMIENS

From the moment when he had been called to command on March 26th, Foch's mind had always been concentrated upon an offensive from the Amiens front which had become a corner of the Somme salient wholly comparable with the Soissons corner of the later Marne salient. He was preparing for it in April when Ludendorff struck in Flanders, he was still considering it when the offensive on the Chemin des Dames called his attention to the new danger point. At last, with the victory at the Marne achieved, he would be able to carry out his purpose.

This purpose was to throw Haig's Fourth Army, commanded by Rawlinson and in position astride the Somme, against the German line where it was weakest, both by reason of the nature of the country and because of the insufficiency of German defences hurriedly constructed since April. On this plateau a little to the eastward Fayolle had made his sweeping advance to the Somme in the opening day of the battle of 1916, and there was admirable opportunity for employing tanks. An advance of ten or a dozen miles here would be almost as fatal to German communications in the Somme salient as an advance of half that distance had been in the Marne salient, and any considerable advance would compel the Germans to empty the bottom of the Somme pocket as they had been compelled to evacuate the Château-Thierry salient.

In the new operation Rawlinson's army would play the part of Mangin's in July. South of Rawlinson, about Montdidier, Debeney's French army under Haig's command would imitate the rôle of Degoutte's between the Ourcq and the Marne, while Humbert's French army would follow the example of De Mitry's, clearing the Lassigny Heights as De Mitry had cleared the banks of the Marne.

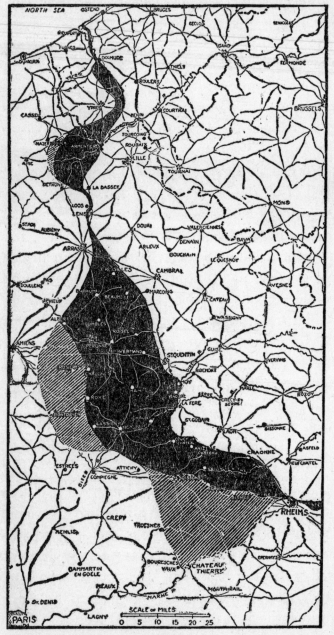

Finally, Mangin's army between the Aisne and the Oise, that is at the other corner of the salient, would have something of the mission of Berthelot's army on the Mountain of Rheims. But at the Somme, as in the Marne operation, the decisive thrust would be at the northwest corner. Ludendorff's failure at the Somme, like that at the Marne,

"PICKING LUDENDORFF'S POCKETS"

Solid black shows ground gained by the Germans between March 21st and July 18th. Diagonal white lines indicate ground regained by Foch in his blows at the Marne and the Somme.

had involved him in an awkward situation, if Foch should gain the initiative. And Foch, having the initiative, was now going to collect the damages. Speaking colloquially, he was now going to "pick the Somme pocket" as he had already "picked" the Marne "pocket." The strategy would be the same, the earlier stages of the operation identical. But later he would expand the Somme operation.

Rawlinson, who commands the Fourth Army, is one of the "old men" of the war. He commanded the "immortal" 7th Division, which was almost exterminated in heroic action in the First Battle of Ypres. He had led the Fourth Army in all the terrible days of the First Somme. Returning to his old field of battle, he would now achieve far greater laurels—would, with the valuable assistance of two splendid American divisions, break the Hindenburg Line at the strongest point a few weeks hence. He commanded, in the present battle, thirteen British infantry divisions, three cavalry, and a regiment from the American 33rd Division, which would do valiant service at Chipilly Ridge, north of the Somme, before the battle terminated. In front of Rawlinson were twenty German divisions, but nothing to compare with the defence system he faced on July 1st, two years before. German soldiers had lost their enthusiasm for trench digging, and this was a relatively new front.

In the period between April 29th, when Ludendorff made his last desperate assault in Flanders, and August 8th, when Rawlinson attacked, the British armies had enjoyed a period of profound quiet. They had been reinforced from the east; their losses in men and material had been made good; and Haig had put his troops through an intensive training, aided in this by the presence of American divisions, which acted as a potential reserve. The British army of August was a totally different thing from that of March or April; it had a new spirit and it had a score to settle. Canadian and Australian divisions were among the shock troops—brought up, Hutier fashion, at the last moment.

Of the completeness of the surprise of the Germans at Amiens there is abundant testimony. The British had prepared a feint to the north, and Maurice mentions an amusing detail—proof of the way the secret was kept—that King Albert, hearing that a "big show" was coming off in Flanders, near his own front, indignantly demanded why he had not been informed.   But as to the nature of the surprise, Ludendorff is the all-sufficient witness.   And in the surprise, tanks, as at the Marne, are to prove a potent factor, the chief factor—now and henceforth to the end—in Allied tactics, infantry and artillery learning closer coördination with them in each trial.   The disappointment of Cambrai will prove fruitful after all, since there the tank was "discovered."

Quiet as has been the British sector, however, Rawlinson on July 4th had treated the Australians to a "full-dress rehearsal" of a tank attack, whereby the village of Hamel, between Villers-Bretonneux and the Somme, was taken in shining fashion—a promise of what was to come on August 8th—and in the first days of the month Ludendorff began to draw back both in the Somme and the Flanders salients, and quit the west bank of the Ancre, evidently suspecting attack in this region—suspecting it correctly and there making adequate preparations.   Rawlinson will make little progress north of the Somme on August 8th.

Ludendorff reports that he had expected the attack; regrouped the armies between Amiens and Noyon—the Second, Eighteenth, and Ninth; placed them under the command of Boehn, a specialist in retreats, the man who had extricated the beaten troops from the Marne pocket in such brilliant fashion.   Boehn had not yet taken command. Ludendorff had hoped to turn over to him a well-established line. Foch would prevent this.

August 8th was a foggy morning.   Nature would give to Haig the same advantage she had bestowed upon Ludendorff in March.   At daylight 2,000 British guns opened on the German front and, as on July 18th, the infantry following the tanks went into action with the guns.   This time the German line collapsed far more quickly than had the British Fifth Army on March 21st.   Before noon the British had advanced south of the Somme to Framerville; they had captured not only thousands of prisoners but whole staffs.   Buchan relates that the Canadian cavalry captured a railroad train on the line near Chaulnes.   There was a total and almost instantaneous collapse south of the Somme.   The victory was not only complete but cheap. One Canadian division in the thick of the battle counted only a hundred casualties.

This date, August 8th, was in Ludendorff's account:

The black day of the German army in the history of this war. This was the worst experience that I had to go through. Six or seven divisions that were quite fairly to be described as effective had been completely broken.

And of the moral effect he says:

We had to resign ourselves now to the prospect of a continuation of the enemy's offensive. Their success had been too easily gained. Their wireless was jubilant, and announced—and with truth—that the morale of the German army was no longer what it had been.

Ludendorff investigates the disaster and finds things he had not believed possible in a German army. He learns that whole bodies of his men had surrendered to single troopers or isolated squadrons. He hears of retreating troops who hailed fresh divisions going into battle with the epithet: "Blacklegs!" and the allegation: "You are prolonging the war."

In short, Ludendorff admits it, the Battle of Amiens brought him to the conclusion that the war must be ended. It opened his eyes, and he discovered later that it opened those of Foch. He even tendered his resignation to the Kaiser, who declined it but would accept it some weeks later. From the dilemma in which he was now involved Ludendorff had no hope of finding a strategic expedient whereby to turn the situation to his own advantage. Even in passing, one cannot help contrasting the mood of Ludendorff now with that of Foch after Picardy, after Flanders, after the Chemin des Dames. The German commander complains of the decline of morale in his army but in his comment he discloses the collapse of his own morale.

To return to the battle: the army of Debeney attacks along the Avre an hour after Rawlinson begins astride the Somme. His gains are smaller, but the next day Humbert's troops are at work on the Lassigny Plateau. On August 10th the German troops in Montdidier surrender. By August 12th Rawlinson's troops have been checked before the old Somme defences held by the enemy before July 1, 1916. Debeney's army is close to Roye; Humbert's army has partially cleared the Lassigny Hills. The German has lost the use of the Roye-Chaulnes railway line; the British have captured 22,000 prisoners and more than 400 guns; Debeney has taken 8,000 more Germans. By a single blow 30,000 prisoners have been captured, Amiens has been unblocked, the Paris-Calais railway has been reopened.

But these are minor details. Foch has disclosed the crumbling morale of the German army. For the first time in the war on the western front the German soldier, and by the thousand, has refused to fight. Perhaps, after all, even the Hindenburg Line will not avail to halt the victor.

After the Battle of Amiens, Ludendorff advised his government to make peace. To the present writer Marshal Foch once remarked that after this day Ludendorff's single resource was an immediate retreat, a far-swinging retreat like that of March, 1917. "Had he done that," said the Marshal, "he would have made me a great deal of trouble. But when he chose instead to go back little by little"—and the Marshal waved his hand back and forth rapidly—"I had him."

Ludendorff had now to subordinate strategic to political considerations. Napoleon did the same in 1813 with equally fatal results. Napoleon was dominated by his anxiety to preserve his German allies; Ludendorff, as he indicates, was equally controlled by his apprehensions as to the effect—in Vienna, in Sofia, in Constantinople—of German defeats and retreats. As early as August 9th Vienna telephoned to know the truth. Ludendorff thinks the Battle of Amiens finished Bulgaria.

The British and French armies north of the Oise were checked by August 16th. The enemy had reacted strongly; further attacks meant additional casualties out of proportion to the profit. Accordingly, Foch now pushes Mangin into action between the Oise and the Aisne on August 18th, and in the next three days Mangin makes a quick advance and takes 8,000 prisoners and 200 guns. August 20th, date of Mangin's greatest progress, is another "black day" for Ludendorff. Thus the whole German front from the Somme to the Aisne has been dislocated, but all the armies engaged on the Allied side have made their advances at small cost—have captured 40,000 prisoners and more than

700 guns, and are still ready for action in a few days.   This is a beautiful illustration of the Foch method, of the use of a series of short, quick blows to produce a large result without so exhausting the assailant as to compel him to give his adversary a respite.   Now Foch is ready to expand the front, extend the dislocation, and deliver still another swift and painful blow.

Meantime, August 13th and 14th, while Boehn is painfully stopping the gaps between the Somme and the Oise, Ludendorff sees the German Chancellor summoned posthaste to Spa, and tells him that "it is no longer possible by an offensive to force the enemy to sue for peace. Defence alone can hardly achieve the object, and so the determination of the war will have to be brought about by diplomacy."   This on August 14th, not quite a month since the stroke at the Soissons corner, the fifth day of Foch's offensive campaign!   It is three months, almost exactly, before the Armistice, but even now the enemy concedes that he cannot win.   Foch's campaign is directed to prove that Ludendorff must lose.   Four years ago, on the day and hour of this Spa Conference, Liége was falling—memorable anniversary.

III.   THE BATTLE OF BAPAUME

The next phase of Foch's manœuvre will cover all the battlefield of the First Somme.   It will even expand to the southern half of the battlefield of Arras.   Foch is going to expand the area of dislocation. The Germans have taken root on their old Somme positions between the Somme and the Oise.   Foch will turn them out of this position by a flank thrust from the north.   First, Byng's army—the part of it north of the bend of the Ancre in the region where Haig's troops were so badly punished between Serre and Gommecourt on July 1, 1916— will advance toward Bapaume and the high ground about it.   Two years before, Haig had struck upward over the famous ridge from Albert, and could not get from Ovillers to Bapaume in six months.   Byng will get there shortly.   When Bapaume has fallen the Germans between the Somme and the Oise will be in danger; if Byng gets beyond Bapaume they will have to retire.

But the operation is still more forward-looking. On March 21st, Ludendorff's advance north of the Somme was to have been his principal effort, the ground being favourable. Now, with the fall of the old Somme line, he will try to stand behind the Somme from Péronne to Ham, and thence to the Oise behind the Crozat Canal—the barrier that Gough could not maintain in March. North of Péronne he will try to hold the line of the Tortille brook, but if Byng passes the Tortille he will turn the Somme line and Ludendorff will find no other way-station west of the Hindenburg Line.

August 21st, just as Mangin's thrust between the Oise and the Aisne is slowing down, Byng steps out, advances until he reaches the Arras-Albert railroad at Moyenneville—a moderate gain made by severe fighting, but it releases the left flank of Rawlinson's army which the next day takes Albert—and occupies between the Ancre and the Somme substantially the line of July 1, 1916. August 23rd, Byng's troops do better and cross the Arras-Bapaume highway. August 24th, Rawlinson and Byng both move straight across the old Somme battlefield. Byng closes in on Bapaume; Rawlinson takes all of the famous ridge where Haig fought from July to September, and, south of the river, commences to push in on the old Somme line. The pressure at the north begins to alarm Boehn, who retires from Lassigny on the 21st and clears Roye, on Debeney's front, on the 27th. Two days later Byng is in Bapaume and Rawlinson retakes Combles, a name memorable from the Somme days.

August 31st the Australians make a sudden dash forward and take Mont St. Quentin looking down on Péronne. The next day they take Péronne. Ludendorff will not be able to halt on the Péronne-Ham line. One of the finest exploits of the war was this taking of Mont St. Quentin, and on this same day, September 1st, Byng and Rawlinson emerge at the eastern side of the old Somme battlefield. They have covered in twelve days the distance which it took Haig from July to March to traverse in the First Somme operation.

But already there has been a new extension of front. On August 26th, Horne's First Army, last in action at the Battle of the Lys in April, thrusts forward on either side of the Scarpe eastward of Arras, re-

covers all the ground taken in April and May, 1917, and surrendered in the face of Ludendorff's attack in March of the current year, and begins to approach the famous Drocourt-Quéant "switch" line, before which Ludendorff rallied his troops after the first terrible days of April, 1917.

By September 1st, the date when the Australians made their brilliant dash, Foch could make his first report. Between July 15th and September 1st his armies had taken 128,302 prisoners, 2,069 guns, 3,783 machine guns. September 1st is Australia's day; September 2nd is Canada's. On this day Horne's right wing, two Canadian divisions ahead, go straight through the Drocourt-Quéant line,

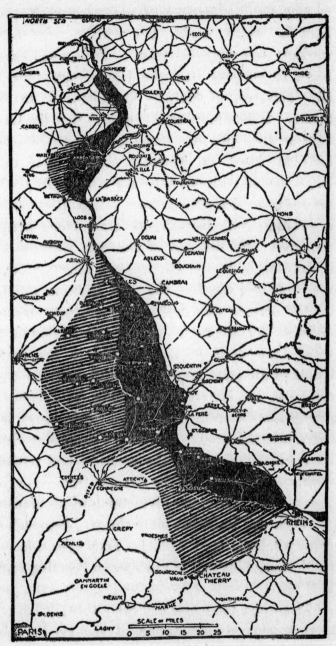

BACK TO THE HINDENBURG LINE

Solid black shows what was left of the Ludendorff gains in the first week of September. Diagonal lines indicate territory regained by the Allies between July 18th and September 2nd.

one of the most astonishing achievements of the campaign. Here at last the British have to do, not with the hastily constructed lines of recent weeks, but with a solid system established and worked over several years. Foch, analyzing this incident, will begin to perceive that the Hindenburg Line may be broken after all. This feat of Horne's Canadians is an authentic sign for the future. It has been clear for days that the Germans could no longer fight in the open nor long hold improvised defences. The Australians at Mont St. Quentin showed that the Germans could no longer defend positions naturally strong, and the Canadians at Drocourt demonstrate that they cannot retain fixed works. Foch's manœuvre is bearing fruit; Horne's operation alone nets 16,000 prisoners and 200 guns. By the end of the first week in September, Ludendorff is drawing in to the Hindenburg Line. At the same time he quits the Vesle and the Lys, the 77th Division will pursue from the Vesle to the Aisne, the 27th will reoccupy Kemmel—two New York divisions for whom far greater distinction is at hand. September 10th, Ludendorff is substantially in the position from which he launched his great attack of March 21st, but the army which has returned to its fortress is something far different from the host which emerged in the springtime. In a single month it has lost 100,000 prisoners, been defeated in ten battles surpassing Gravelotte in magnitude. Its reserves are failing, the ceaseless and terrible strain has done its work, the dislocation of the German front has extended from Rheims to Ypres. Before he closes his manœuvre, his preparation for the final battle, Foch will make one more thrust. September 12th America's First Army will begin at St. Mihiel. Foch's decision as to an attack upon the Hindenburg Line will be made when Pershing's troops have passed their final test.

Meantime, the whole of Foch's strategy lies crystal clear in even the most summary examination of the events between July 15th and September 14th. In this time he has checked a victorious German army, first halted it, then turned it back, and swept it rearward with ever-increasing speed. He has produced in two months the moral and the military effect that Ludendorff failed to produce in four. He will do nothing new in his final battle. The breaking of the Hindenburg Line is only the logical extension of the method of July 18th and the following days. The manœuvre between the Avre and the Hindenburg Line is no more than a development and a perfection of the method of the Marne salient.

Looking backward to the Marne we see on July 18th, first the attack of Mangin which upsets all the enemy's calculations and imposes upon him the necessity of retreat. The same day Degoutte attacks between the Ourcq and the Marne, then De Mitry below the Marne, while Berthelot is pushing west from the Mountain of Rheims. From July 18th to August 6th blow after blow, until the "pocket" is empty and Ludendorff has saved his divisions but strained his reserves.

The Marne operation is over August 6th. August 8th Rawlinson attacks, Debeney the same day, Humbert the next. All three exploit their successes until the 16th. Two days later Mangin strikes between the Oise and the Aisne. His blow is finished August 21st, and on the same day Byng attacks. The next day Rawlinson resumes while Humbert is active again. August 26th, Debeney strikes once more and Horne comes into action for the first time. September 1st, the Australians take Mont St. Quentin, the credit going to Rawlinson's army. The next day Horne's Canadians take Drocourt. Meantime, between the Oise and the Somme, Humbert, Debeney, Rawlinson, are crowding the Germans, now retiring in haste because of the menace to the north, and Mangin is at work again between the Aisne and the Oise. September 10th, the Somme salient is liquidated. Two days later Pershing is thrown in at St. Mihiel, carrying a new threat after a swift success.

It is by such a summary of events that Foch's strategy is best appreciated, that the strain upon the German army and command, and above all on German reserves, is most clearly set forth.

With the method must go the mind to comprehend exactly the enemy situation. Moltke was defeated at the Marne in 1914 and Ludendorff in 1918 because both of them misunderstood the extent of their success in the fighting which preceded the decisive engagement; both calculated that the enemy was already incapable of reacting, yet each time their enemy struck back powerfully and unexpectedly. The greatest quality in Foch was his correct appraisal of his opponent's condition. In the last days of September his campaign would have been completely wrecked if he had suffered a check, but he had succeeded where Moltke and Ludendorff had failed, and his foe would fall beneath his stroke.

"Victory," said Marshal Foch at the end of November, 1918—and Requin who quotes this phase adds that Foch was very fond of the comparison—"Victory is the inclined plane down which the ball rolls, very slowly at first, then faster and faster until there is no stopping it." September 13th, when he faced the Hindenburg Line, he recognized that the stopping point had been passed.

The narrative of Ludendorff is the most amazing single document in this period. His lines are broken, his divisions refuse to fight, panic seizes his soldiers when tanks appear, his allies fall away, his own nerve crumbles; the German machine, his machine, breaks down utterly, and he is to the end unconscious of the explanation. He berates the civil authorities, the German people; he scolds everybody and everything; but the fact that his army is disintegrating under attacks which he cannot foresee, forestall, or parry—that his own impotence is at last appreciated by the German soldier and the German public alike—that the failure is at the top, he never suspects. Beaten; he ascribes defeat, not to the general or the strategy which overwhelms him, but to the shortcomings of statesmen and civilians. He believes that the German army is invincible, and when it is beaten, he does not accept the fact. In exactly the same way when he believed the French army was destroyed, beaten beyond possible reaction, he followed his conviction to the disaster at the Marne. Reading Ludendorff, one perceives why in the end Foch must win. "The man is all of one sort," says Buat, "a monolith."

CHAPTER EIGHT

ST. MIHIEL

I
AMERICA'S FIRST ARMY

In the vast manœuvre between the German front of August 8th and the Hindenburg Line, the Battle of St. Mihiel is the final circumstance. Between August 22nd and September 9th, Maurice reports that the British, in driving the enemy back over the ground taken in the Battle of Picardy, had captured 53,000 prisoners and 470 guns. The French to the south had captured not less than 50,000 prisoners while the struggle between the Aisne and the Marne in July had resulted in the capture of 35,000 Germans. From September 9th to September 26th British and French armies between the Aisne and the Scarpe were driving the Germans from their last advanced positions into the Hindenburg Line itself.

Americans will find in this phase and in the next an admirable parallel in the campaign of 1864 in the Civil War. The relation of Haig, Petain, and Pershing to Foch accurately reproduces that of Sherman, Meade, and Thomas to Grant. Moreover, Americans should find an accurate estimate of the value of unified, as contrasted with divided, command by comparing the experiences of the Northern armies before 1864 with the subsequent progress of events when Grant came east and coördinated the operations of the several great armies for the first time in the war, and began a sustained attack upon the Confederacy. Between May, 1864, and the opening of the brief campaign of the following year, Grant had prepared his victory as Foch was now preparing his.

In the final phases of the war Pershing's relation to Foch was thus the relation of Sherman or of Thomas to Grant, and just as Sherman operated in the rear of the main forces of the Confederacy, Pershing was now to strike toward the rear and communications of the Germans. Had Foch's plans been completely executed, Ludendorff would have been caught between Haig and Pershing as Lee and Johnston were substantially encircled by the armies of Meade and Sherman in April, 1865. The geographical details of the two campaigns are very different, but the main circumstances are the same, and the strategy of Foch, like that of Grant, had always as its main objective the destruction of the hostile armies rather than any more limited geographical end. We shall see, too, why the armies of Haig and Pershing, like those of Meade and of Sherman, will each be convinced that its was the "knockout" blow.

The constitution of the American First Army was finally resolved upon while the Second Battle of the Marne was still in progress, although Pershing reports that an agreement in principle had been reached as early as May 19th when he conferred with Petain over the sector to be assigned to the new army; but the disaster of the Chemin des Dames postponed the realization of Pershing's dream. The desperate state of Allied fortunes from June 1st to July 18th compelled Pershing to assent to the dispersal of his division amongst French armies, first to check and then to turn back the German hordes.

The Second Marne being won, however, it was plain that the Germans had lost the initiative, and on July 24th, at a conference of all the Allied commanders, held at Foch's headquarters at Bombom, the decision was reached to continue the Allied offensive "emphatically determined," says Pershing, and the first American operation was planned against the St. Mihiel salient. Scattered American divisions were now to be concentrated and the organization of the American First Army under Pershing's personal command was fixed for August 10th.

But as late as August 30th Pershing had to fight for his army. On that day Foch came to the headquarters of the new American army at Ligny-en-Barrois, De Langle de Cary's headquarters in the First Marne, and urged a new dispersal of American divisions among Allied armies as a detail in his scheme for a general Allied offensive. This offensive will be the final stroke at the Hindenburg Line. September 2nd there is a new conference at Foch's headquarters, with Petain and Pershing both present. After further discussion Pershing's contention is established, henceforth there will be no further debate over the existence of an American army. But now it is agreed that the American army shall make only a limited offensive at St. Mihiel and then transfer its activities to the Meuse-Argonne. Foch's conception of a general offensive from Ypres to Verdun is rapidly taking form. Here already is the skeleton of the plan for the grand concentric attack to open on September 26th.

One detail of this conference worth remembering is noted by Pershing, who says that not even on this day was there any suggestion from any one present that the war could be successfully terminated in the current year. But what Horne was accomplishing on this very day at Drocourt, what Pershing himself would do ten days later, would convince Foch that the hour had arrived. The same conviction came to Grant in the first hours of the campaign of 1865 when Sheridan's success at Five Forks at last disclosed the internal crumbling of Lee's army.

II. THE HISTORY OF THE ST. MIHIEL SALIENT

The history of the St. Mihiel salient is interesting. Like all salients, it represented an incomplete operation. In 1914, after the Marne, the Germans had undertaken a double attack upon Verdun, the Crown Prince had endeavoured to push south between the Argonne and the Meuse and cut the Paris-Châlons-Verdun railway, thus isolating Verdun from the west. At the same time an army coming out of Metz had pushed up the valley of the little Rupt-de-Mad stream and sought to reach the Meuse and cut the Toul-Verdun railway, the only other considerable rail line into Verdun. Together, these operations were designed to isolate Verdun and, ultimately, by joining hands to the south of it, the two armies were to envelop and capture it.

The Crown Prince's expedition was stopped promptly, but the operation from Metz reached the Meuse at St. Mihiel and took Fort Camp des Romains, the only one of the forts of the whole eastern dike of France destined to be a German captive for any length of time, although Douaumont and Vaux were in German hands for most of 1916. The

Crown Prince also established a bridgehead at Chauvoncourt, across the Meuse, and threatened to advance upon Bar-le-Duc and turn the whole French system of defences from St. Mihiel northward.　But Joffre's turning movement in the Santerre, also the scene subsequently of the decisive phase of the Battle of Picardy, demanded German attention, and operations about St. Mihiel stopped abruptly.

In the next winter, when their hands were freer, the French attempted to abolish the salient by an attack at its northern corner, not far from the scene of the attack of the 26th Division in the American battle.　In this operation the French took Les Éparges, but were subsequently checked with bitter losses.　Les Éparges was long a name of evil omen in the French army and was one of the counts in the indictment subsequently pressed against Joffre.　The next summer, Joffre tried again on the other corner, on the heights above Pont-à-Mousson on the Moselle, at Bois-le-Prêtre, and thence westward to the Forest of Apremont, south of St. Mihiel.　But again he was checked. Such gains as were acquired in two months of severe fighting were swept away in one disastrous July day, and the salient still stood.　In the Verdun campaign of 1916, the St. Mihiel salient played a great, if passive, rôle.　It enabled the Germans to control the Commercy-Verdun railway and prevented munitioning Verdun by the Meuse Valley road and railway.　On the other side of Verdun, the German heavy artillery commanded the Paris-Verdun railway and Verdun was thus without adequate rail communications.　It was saved by motor transport, but not until the French built a new railway straight up from Bar-le-Duc and out of range of German cannon was the situation as to communications reëstablished.　This railway served a useful purpose later, in the American campaign in the Meuse-Argonne, and was materially extended. The sight of huge American Mogul locomotives operating on this remote and commercially insignificant line was one of the amusing details of later days.

The construction of the new line to Verdun reduced the value of the St. Mihiel salient to the Germans, but they still cut the main Paris-Nancy railway at Commercy by artillery fire and compelled the French to use a détour line by Gondrecourt, which added twenty miles to the distance between Paris and Nancy, but served all necessary purposes. Since the profit accruing from any operation to pinch out the salient between 1916 and the autumn of 1918 would not have been commensurate with the expense, and as the Allies had other uses for their reserves, the St. Mihiel salient became a quiet sector, and, on the Woëvre side, between the Meuse and the Moselle, a training front for American troops.

St. Mihiel itself is a town of just short of ten thousand inhabitants, a garrison place of much importance, as witnessed by the many barracks, now in ruins at Chauvoncourt, across the Meuse, scene of French repulse in the first fighting about St. Mihiel. It has public buildings of some note and in the Church of St. Étienne there is a *chef d'œuvre* of French sculpture, executed in the middle of the Sixteenth Century by Ligier Richier, one of the glorious figures of the French Renaissance and himself a "Sammiellois"; that is, a native of St. Mihiel. American soldiers will also find near the town, after the capture, a huge and hideous German cemetery, literally weighing down the side hill with its burden of German monstrosities in stone. St. Mihiel had a place in history, as the ruins of the Roman camp above it indicate. It played a conspicuous part in the French Renaissance, and it is altogether an interesting place, as the guide-books testify—too charming to remain in German hands, aside from all military considerations. But German it has been since September, 1914, four long years, and not a few of its inhabitants have remained there, compelling the French from the hills across the river to desist from all artillery practice. Comparatively intact the town was before the battle and it remained in reasonably good shape after it.

III. THE BATTLEFIELD

While the name "St. Mihiel" has been applied to the contest of September 12th, the actual battleground was east and north of the city, which fell as a result of operations which did not extend to the immediate vicinity of the town itself. To understand the situation it is necessary to grasp the simple topographic circumstances of the region.   On the east bank of the Meuse southward from Dun-sur-Meuse, soon to appear in the reports of another American battle, all the way upstream to Commercy, beyond St. Mihiel, the ground slopes upward rapidly to a ridge, rarely more than two or three miles from the river at its highest point.   Beyond the crest the high ground falls away much more abruptly to the Plain of the Woëvre.   This ridge, the Côtes-de-Meuse, or Heights of the Meuse, in the region about Verdun was the site of the famous forts, Vaux and Douaumont, to name the best known, and the Germans sought in the great struggle to capture all of these forts.

The Woëvre Plain, east of the ridge, extends for thirty or forty miles north and south and for approximately twenty due east to the Moselle.   As it approaches the Moselle, the country begins to rise again and dominates that river from another crest, comparable to that of the Heights of the Meuse above the Meuse River.   This Woëvre Plain is very flat and marshy, filled with little lakes and ponds at the southern end, where the Americans attacked; and across it, from south-west to northeast, runs the little Rupt-de-Mad, hardly more than a brook, which falls into the Moselle, not many miles south of the outlying fortifications of the German stronghold of Metz.

On the morning of September 12th the German line ran westward from the Moselle Hills, north of Pont-à-Mousson—hills which were heavily wooded—straight out across the open Woëvre Plain until it reached the foot of the Meuse Hills at Apremont.   At this point it turned a little south and reached the Meuse itself, just south of the commanding elevation on which stood the old French fort, Camp des Romains, which, in turn, occupied the site of a Roman camp.

Beyond the fort the line turned north, crossed the river in front of St. Mihiel, to take in the little peninsula on which was situated the ruined town of Chauvoncourt, then recrossed the river and ran north-eastward, cutting the Heights of the Meuse diagonally and coming back to the Woëvre Plain east of Les Éparges, the scene of the French operation of 1915.   Thence the line ran along the foot of the Meuse Hills in the Verdun sector.

There was thus created a fairly deep and narrow pocket, recalling that excavated by the German success at the Chemin des Dames but rather deeper, which had at its point, corresponding to Château-Thierry in the Marne salient, the little town of St. Mihiel. The vulnerable side of the salient was that between Apremont and the wooded hills west of Pont-à-Mousson, where the country is open and, in the main, level. An American advance of a few miles north on this front would cut off all the enemy troops to the westward in the nose of the salient, provided they did not retreat in time. If the operation were combined with a push from the Les Éparges corner, the Germans in the salient would be enveloped, exactly as the world incorrectly believed the German Crown Prince's hordes had been caught in the hours following Mangin's thrust at the Soissons corner of the Marne salient.

It was not possible to attack the salient from the west, near St. Mihiel, owing to the strength of the position on which Fort Camp des Romains stands. From this vantage point, the view up and down the Meuse Valley is one of the most extensive and impressive on the whole battle front. The attack from the Les Éparges corner could not be expected to do more than clear the enemy off the Meuse Heights, for the country was very heavily wooded and was to prove, in its difficult character, a very fair forecast of what was to come in the Argonne.

On the east side of the Meuse Hills the enemy had two striking vantage points, from which his sweep was almost as good as from Fort Camp des Romains. One of his far-reaching views was had from the village of Hattonchatel, from the church tower of which the view extends over all the plain of the Woëvre and as far as the hills in front of Metz: the other was from Mont Sec, one of the most interesting and important circumstances in the military geography of the region, already familiar to all American divisions which had been trained in the Toul sector.

Mont Sec is a detached hill, rising out of the Woëvre Plain a mile or two east of the Meuse Hills and completely separated from them. It was a mile or two inside the German lines, and it surveyed and dominated the whole plain; from it observers were able to mark every interesting detail in the life of the Allied troops in the lines to the south. The hill had been marvellously "organized" by the Germans. From the ruined village of Mont Sec, just at its foot—itself provided with an admirable example of the German pill box, where the main street turned—a carefully built brick sidewalk led back to a series of magnificent cement caves, excavated from the side of the mountain, to provide shelter for the infantry, and proudly decorated with "iron crosses" worked into the masonry. Beyond these, cement steps led to a tunnel driven into the heart of the mountain; from this tunnel staircases led up to a number of observation posts, from which the Germans could survey the whole Woëvre Plain. These observation posts were totally invisible to the enemy, who could take the air there with full security, except for chance shots, and no chance shot seems ever to have molested them.

Mont Sec could not be taken by direct attack, it was too strong, and in Pershing's scheme of things the troops who attacked would attack on a front just east of the hill and cover their flank toward it with a smoke screen. Actually the 1st Division marched right past the hill, suffering severely from its fire and only partially covered by their smoke screen; but, once it was passed, Mont Sec fell, like St. Mihiel, because the Germans left in it were caught like rats in a trap.

In Pershing's plan of operations the 1st Division, advancing east of the Meuse Hills and their outlying spur, Mont Sec, would join hand with the 26th Division, coming southeast from the Les Éparges Corner, and the meeting place would be the village of Vigneulles, just south of the Hattonchatel Hill, which is the highest summit of the whole Meuse Heights. Meantime, the rest of Pershing's operative force between Pont-à-Mousson and the 1st Division front would keep step. Thus not only would the St. Mihiel salient be pinched out and the Germans encompassed captured when the 1st and 26th divisions joined hands at Vigneulles, but the front would be pushed out eastward toward Metz, beyond the considerable town of Thiaucourt, where the Rupt-de-Mad brook assumes the dignity of a river. This new front would carry a threat both for Metz and for the Briey iron works and mines far to the north.

But the main advantages of a successful attack at this point would be comprehended in releasing the Verdun-Commercy railway and the Paris-Nancy line and establishing solidly the flank which would cover the later advance in the Meuse-Argonne. As long as the Germans held St. Mihiel they held a threat over any force operating in what was still the Verdun salient. Haig had recourse necessarily to a similar operation at the Messines Ridge, before he made his attack in Flanders, from Ypres north and eastward in 1917. It was Byng's failure to establish his left flank toward the Scheldt Canal, in the Cambrai attack of 1917, which opened the way for the counter-stroke of Marwitz. Once the line of the Meuse Heights was solidly held by the Allies from the Verdun forts southward to the Toul area, Pershing could turn his attention to his operations between the Meuse and the Argonne without any misgivings as to flank or rear.

The secondary purpose was to try out his army. The achievement of the 1st and 2nd divisions at Cantigny and Belleau Wood had led directly to the Mangin counter-thrust at the Soissons corner and the use of eight American divisions in meeting and breaking the last German offensive. This performance had persuaded Foch and Petain to consent to the organization of an independent American army. On the performance of the American army in its first "full-dress show" would depend the decision already taking shape in Foch's mind, but opposed by the British Government, by Lloyd George, to risk everything in a general offensive designed to end the war in 1918.

Pershing had already demanded for his army the honour of fighting in the most difficult of all sectors on the whole operative front, that of the Meuse-Argonne. The Battle of St. Mihiel was to demonstrate whether his eyes had been beyond his appetite. America now had an army of its own, but was the army available for serious work in 1918?— or must the decision be sought in another campaign? Foch was going ahead with his preparations for the general offensive; Pershing and Haig had lent valuable support in council; British success in Picardy and Artois was disclosing a growing weakness, actual demoralization in the German ranks; but the German would still be able to last, if he had only

French and British armies to deal with, given their sacrifices and exertions in the earlier months of the campaign. St. Mihiel was a final examination of the American soldier, of the American machine. Cantigny, Belleau Wood, the Aisne-Marne had been no more than preliminary tests; the real trial was now to be faced.

IV.　THE ATTACK

On the night of September 11th, Pershing's army was in place. The concentration had been made secretly, by night marches; the Hutier method was finding Allied application. The German was getting anxious about the St. Mihiel salient. He had begun to get his heavy guns out, but he was taking his time about it and he had no suspicion of the imminence of a major blow. His anxiety was due exclusively to an

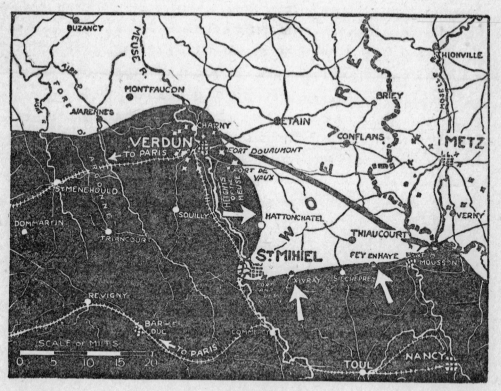

THE BATTLE OF ST. MIHIEL

Solid black shows Allied territory on September 11th. The black line from Verdun to Pont-à-Mousson indicates the front reached by the Americans as a result of the victory. Arrows mark directions of main attack.

abstract estimate of the general situation, he was now to have a concrete example.

On the south side of the salient, where the main activity was to be, Pershing thus ranged his forces: From the Moselle westward, the First Corps, Hunter Liggett commanding, with the 82nd, 90th, 5th, and 2nd in line—four divisions, of which only one, the 2nd, is in any sense a veteran unit. Its commander will presently lead the American First Army, now under the orders of the Commander-in-Chief. On the left the Fourth Corps, commanded by Dickman, who will also get his army presently. This consists of the 89th, 42nd, and 1st, the two last-named veteran divisions, and the last looking obliquely at Mont Sec.

Thence all the way round to the northeast corner of the salient are French troops, whose mission is merely to occupy the front and pluck the fruit when it has ripened. On the corner is the Fifth Corps, George H. Cameron in command. It consists of the 26th American, the 15th French Colonial, and the 4th American. But only the 26th is to participate; its mission will be to get across the mouth of the pocket or salient until it meets the 1st Division in the town of Vigneulles. Nine American divisions, then, are actually on the front. Only seven of them will be called upon for great exertions, but three more are in reserve. Counting Americans, then, the force is rather less than 300,000 strong; with the French and reserve American divisions it amounts to 500,000, of which 70,000 are French. It is the greatest American army that has yet entered battle; it is the first American army to fight in Europe. September 12th is also Pershing's birthday. It will be appropriately observed.

The bombardment which preceded the attack and lasted four hours was one of the heaviest on record. Thanks to his allies, Pershing also profited by the greatest aviation concentration which had yet been seen during the war. A certain number of tanks also participated. At dawn on September 12th the American troops crossed the trenches and advanced in the open following the rolling barrage of their guns. The Fifth Corps did not start until 8 A.M. Dawn the next morning saw the 1st and

26th in contact in Vigneulles, the honour of actual capture of the town going to the "Yankee" Division. The salient had been abolished. The line now extended from Les Éparges into the plain, passed east of Thiaucourt, and rejoined the Moselle below Pont-à-Mousson. All objectives had been reached, many of them passed; there had been no serious hitch.

The prisoners taken on this day numbered 16,000; the guns, 443; and in addition a vast accumulation of material. The captures of men and cannon are an evidence of the completeness of the surprise. Certain Austrian units in the rear were called upon to save their German comrades, one of the instances of the use of Austrians on the western front and a new evidence of the mounting exhaustion of German cannon-fodder. The total American loss was little more than 7,000, an amazingly low price to pay for such a success. Indeed St. Mihiel was one of the cheapest victories of any size in the whole war. In any other war the capture of 16,000 prisoners and 443 guns would have indicated a major disaster for the vanquished.

But the German still had reserves and he had prepared a line behind the salient—the Michael Line, on which he stopped, undisturbed, for the American objective had been rigidly limited. To be sure, Metz was not far distant, our shells were falling on the railroad station. The battlefields of Gravelotte and Mars-la-Tour, where the war of 1870 had been thrown away by Bazaine, were still nearer, but Pershing was not considering Metz; his task lay on the other side of the Meuse and thither his troops were soon moving. St. Mihiel was, after all, only a curtain raiser, but it had convinced the audience, the examination had been triumphantly passed. Foch could count on American assistance if he should decide to seek victory in the current campaign. And his decision was made. Two months—lacking a day—after St. Mihiel, Germany would surrender.

Our three battlefields in Europe, scenes of really considerable engagements in which large numbers of Americans were engaged, Aisne-Marne, St. Mihiel, and Meuse-Argonne are singularly unlike each other. In our first engagement in July our troops were scattered amongst the

French. It is impossible to see any considerable front between the Marne and the Vesle where our troops were in line and the battlefield itself is separated into numerous compartments. Only at the Soissons corner and again where our troops forced the passage of the Ourcq is it possible to get any comprehensive idea of the action. For the rest one must follow the tracks of the several divisions, tracks which lead through dense forests, filled with machine-gun emplacements, tracks along which American field cemeteries testify to the gallantry of our men. Only at the Vesle does one at last come to a front where American divisions stood in line and even passed the river in the face of terribly concentrated fire raining down from the hills above.

But in the St. Mihiel area the whole battlefield is spread before the feet of any visitor who will climb Mont Sec or Hattonchatel. Lookout Mountain does not give a better survey of the battlefields of Chattanooga, and Mont Sec adds to the view one of the most admirable examples of German protective military engineering. At its feet and stretching monotonously eastward are the ruined villages, Rechicourt, Seicheprey, where the 26th met initial reverse, Xivray, Beaumont, Essey, and Flirey. Passing through these ruins, over the tracks, which were once roads and through the débris which was once a coherent part of human habitation, one appreciates the conditions under which our troops were trained and in which our army began.

On the horizon, too, looking from Mont Sec, one sees the Bois-le-Prêtre, above the town of Pont-à-Mousson, where exactly American participation in the war began. There all through the bloody summer of 1915 American ambulance drivers brought back the wounded by Fey-en-Heye, using roads which would be later trodden by thousands of American soldiers come to pay the debt of Lafayette, the first instalment of which was receipted by the gallantry of the American ambulance drivers, two years before the majority of Americans awakened to the meaning for them of the European struggle. Forgotten now in the press of larger events, the achievements of this Ambulance Corps remains one of the finest in the history of American youth.

We shall see in the Meuse-Argonne a country far more savage, presenting infinitely graver obstacles to military operations, but not outside of Flanders was there along the whole front a more depressing stretch of shell-worked, devastated, flood-invaded territory than that which American divisions passed through and over on September 12th and 13th, a country destitute of all life, of all evidences of human residence, torn by four years of cannonading, presenting to the traveller, long months after the war had passed by and ended in other fields, something of the horror of the rotting fragments of human bodies protruding from the shallow graves along the front of every considerable struggle during the war.

One of the military consequences of Pershing's victory was to excite German anxiety as to the safety of the Briey iron fields to the northeastward, now exposed to attack both from Verdun and from the new Woëvre front of the Americans. This anxiety was due to the fact that these iron fields had become an essential detail in German economic organization, since without the iron, Germany could not continue the struggle, and it led to a miscalculation of the direction of the next American thrust. Ludendorff was expecting a blow east of the Meuse two weeks later, when Pershing attacked west of that stream; and the absence of German reserves, diverted to the Briey sector, contributed to the initial success of the Americans.

Critics of the St. Mihiel operation have justly pointed out that following the attack there was an approximate breakdown of transport behind the line. This seems to have been the case, but in this instance there were no serious consequences, because the American advance was relatively short; a similar failure in the Meuse-Argonne, however, had far more unfortunate consequences. The answer to the criticism is that such a breakdown was an inevitable circumstance of an operation as hastily prepared as either that of St. Mihiel or of the Meuse-Argonne. It was to be expected in a new army. Ours was an emergency army. For it there was no question of doing a technically perfect job, the one question was whether it could do it well enough to turn the scale. Pershing had to make brute strength a substitute for finished performance. His army had to sacrifice itself to make up for lack of time, lack of training, lack of everything save courage and devotion. And now, despite all the handicaps, it was going to accomplish just that.

In the battles of St. Mihiel and of the Meuse-Argonne our army was about in the stage of the British army at Loos; and at Loos, despite the fact that the British officers had themselves had far more experience than any of ours, not only was there a failure of transport after the battle, but the reserves, which were counted upon to win a battle which had opened with a striking success, did not arrive until the Germans, perceiving the failure of Sir John French to follow up his advantage, stopped their withdrawal from Lens and presently retook Hill No. 70. Loos cost the British 66,000 casualties in little more than a week, with only a two-mile advance on a narrow front. We got through to Sedan, more than thirty miles, with only twice as heavy a butcher's bill.

This is not to say that Pershing's army would have done better than Sir John French's had it tackled Loos under the same circumstances. It is merely to point out that the American army at St. Mihiel was still necessarily at that point in its development when certain limitations were ineluctably imposed upon it. In the St. Mihiel and Meuse-Argonne battles the American army was not a perfect military machine, moving like clockwork. It was a vast, incoherent aggregation of brave men, many of them highly efficient, seeking in eighty days to overcome the consequences of fifty-odd years of systematic neglect of military considerations by the American people and the American Government.

What was actually accomplished was little less than a miracle. The real pity is that, since that time, there has been too much effort to create the impression that we accomplished things which were in truth beyond human accomplishment, and too little appreciation of the fraction of the impossible which was actually achieved. Compared with the German or the French army, compared with the armies of Grant or Lee in 1864, Pershing's army was still a training establishment. But as a fighting aggregation it was beyond praise. It was a young army with the ignorance of youth, possibly, but with the enthusiasm, the courage, the strength of youth, and its spirit availed to surmount all handicaps and to supply Foch with just that additional power which made victory in 1918 first conceivable and then possible. And St. Mihiel was the sign manual of its capacity; on this victory Foch constructed his Battle of the Hindenburg Line. However disorganized our rear, the Germans on the American front would have a busy time.

V. AFTERMATH

Pershing saw the Battle of St. Mihiel from the heights of the Meuse, and Secretary of War Baker was with him. Side by side with Petain, Pershing entered St. Mihiel the next day. Poincaré would come soon after to see one more fragment of the Department of the Meuse, his own department, redeemed.

On all sides congratulations rained upon the victor. On the evening of the battle Foch sent this message:

The American First Army under your command has achieved in this first day a magnificent victory by a manœuvre which was as skilfully prepared as it was valiantly executed.

Everything happened exactly as planned and all the results hoped for were achieved, this was the verdict of Madelin, of Maurice, of all military critics then and since on the Allied side.

Only Ludendorff minimized the episode, came pretty close to lying about it at the time, and, in his memoirs, enters into a long defence of this inveracity, necessary to keep up the morale of the German people, he maintains stoutly: necessary, too, one may conjecture to preserve the fiction, growing pretty thin, that Americans wouldn't come, wouldn't fight, and couldn't fight even if they came and tried to—the last line of defence in the matter of these Americans. Still Ludendorff concedes that his losses were severe, while protesting that local commanders were over-confident and slow in obeying his order to evacuate the whole salient. He confesses that the Americans broke through a Prussian division on the south side, nevertheless, despite local failures, and that an Austrian division "might have done better." Ludendorff is dissatisfied with himself and discovers later that his official report to the public was too favourable. But just about this time Bulgaria is beginning to cause him more worry than Pershing.

On the human side, the St. Mihiel affair remains interesting. Photographs of the time disclose American soldiers triumphantly affixing the sign "Wilson, U. S. A." beneath the German legend "Hindenburgstrasse" at Thiaucourt, showing a youthful enthusiasm, not unattractive, over their first conquest, to which they were welcomed by the inhabitants who had been slaves rather than prisoners for four years.

Babin, who "made the campaign," writes at the time: "As for the soldiers of General Pershing, there is only one description. They have been prodigious in courage and in daring."

The Marquis de Chambrun, who was also there, has many words of praise, and adds the detail: "'The Grande Rue', in olden days, the name of the principal street of St. Mihiel, now bears the title 'Rue du General Pershing'."

Captain Arthur W. Page, the best critic of American military operations in France, quotes the following comment of the intelligence officer of the German High Command, reporting on St. Mihiel:

The artillery operation, prior to the attack, was well carried out. The objectives were bombarded with good effect, and they were able to switch from one target to another in the minimum of time and with remarkable accuracy. The coördination between the infantry and the artillery was faultless. If the infantry ran up against a machine-gun nest they would immediately fall back, and very soon new artillery preparation would be directed on that point. A great many tanks were in readiness for the attack, but they were only used in very small numbers, as the masses of infantry accomplished the victory.

Captain Page calls attention to the use of the word "victory." Ludendorff had only recently announced the German retirement was "according to plan."

Pershing, in his final report, says:

The material results of the victory achieved were very important. An American army was an accomplished fact, and the enemy had felt its power. No form of propaganda could overcome the depressing effect on the morale of the enemy of this demonstration of our ability to organize a large American force and drive it successfully through his defences. It gave our troops implicit confidence in their superiority and raised their morale to the highest pitch. For the first time wire entanglements ceased to be regarded as impassable barriers, and open-warfare training, which had been so urgently insisted upon, proved to be the correct doctrine. Our divisions concluded the attack with such small losses and in such high spirits that without the usual rest they were immediately available for employment in heavy fighting in a new theatre of operations. The strength of the First Army in this battle totalled approximately 500,000 men, of whom about 70,000 were French.

"The first successes of the American Army," writes Colonel Requin, "did not merely mark an important date in the history of the war. They represented the result on which the respective governments had staked their hopes, and were the deserved recompense of those who had collaborated for a whole year in this work." Again, later, he says of this St. Mihiel affair: "The test was conclusive. Henceforward the American forces were free to undertake army operations."

After all, St. Mihiel was America's answer at the roll call of the Nations on the eve of the final battle of the World War. Foch had already uncovered the weakness of the enemy in the manœuvre between August 8th and September 10th. The Battle of St. Mihiel revealed that new strength which would be a warrant for joining battle and an essential element in achieving victory.

CHAPTER NINE

THE BATTLE OF THE HINDENBURG LINE

I
FOCH'S SCOPE AND PURPOSE

The Battle of St. Mihiel was the final episode in Foch's manœuvre—
"manœuvre of usury," says De Thomasson in a prescient analysis
published close to the event. "The process of absorption" Buat described in an analysis previously quoted. Ludendorff's reserves are
becoming exhausted. He is beginning to break up some divisions to
keep the rest up to strength. His whole number of divisions has fallen
from 207 to 185, regiments are melting away; worse than all else, the
morale is declining even faster. The victory is ripening.

Moreover, in other fields, the same progress toward the end is
discernible. While Pershing's army was cleaning up after its victory,
the Army of the Orient was smashing Bulgarian resistance. At the
moment when Pershing would attack near Verdun, Allenby would
dispose of the Turk; Diaz was already maturing his plans for finishing off
the crumbling Austro-Hungarian force; Germany's defeats had reacted
upon her allies, and her allies' disasters would now contribute to her own.

This last battle—Armageddon, Maurice calls it, the Battle of France
in Madelin's account, more exactly the Battle of the Hindenburg Line—
will extend from Ypres to Verdun, from the Yser to the Meuse, would
have expanded east of Metz to the scene of French defeat at Morhange
in August, 1914, if the German had not surrendered when he did. No
battlefront, save that of the First Marne, was ever comparably as vast.

So vast, indeed, is the extent of this new battle that it is easy to be
lost in the details. The British, looking at their area, will see it as a
contest between St. Quentin and Ypres, designed to break the Hindenburg Line. The Americans will see it as a struggle between the Meuse
and the Argonne to reach and cut the all-important Metz-Maubeuge

railway. The French will see it as a kaleidoscopic contest in which French soldiers, now beside the British, now with the Belgians, and now beside the Americans, do heroic service at crucial moments. Even the Belgians, participating considerably and nobly, will describe it as the Battle of their Liberation.

But enormous as is the battle, and Foch will use nearly 4,000,000 men in it, the main facts are still simple; the old laws and lessons of war remain unchanged, remain as they were when Napoleon and Wellington fought all day on a front of less than five miles. Foch, after two months of manœuvre, has brought his enemy to battle under the conditions which he has foreseen. The enemy still occupies strong positions, but he has now neither the moral nor the physical power to hold these positions, and the development of the tank tactic has incalculably diminished the value of all positions.

To grasp this battle of the Hindenburg Line it is only essential to see the thing in terms of previous battles. One may divide both the hosts as of old, thus: Facing east between the sea and the Oise is Foch's left flank, consisting of the Belgian army, four British armies, and one French army. There will presently be a new British Fifth Army, Birdwood of Australia commanding. Between the Oise and Rheims is Foch's centre, held by French armies exclusively, those of Mangin and Berthelot. Between Rheims and Verdun is Foch's right flank, held by Gouraud's Fourth Army west of the Argonne, and Pershing's First Army east of it.

Between the Oise and Rheims the character of the country forbids direct attack. The Forest of St. Gobain has all along been the keystone of the German arch in France while the Chemin des Dames, although no longer to be considered impregnable, does not invite new attack. His centre being unavailable, Foch will therefore attack on both flanks.

The German position in France and Belgium is, after all, a salient—a deep and wide salient, the neck of it between Pershing's lines at Verdun and the Dutch frontier north of Liége, far narrower than the depth of it, between Liége and Ostend. Pershing's thrust northward will steadily narrow the neck of the pocket, just as Mangin's push from the Soissons

THE ENEMY IN RETREAT

Brown Brothers

GERMAN SOLDIERS ON THE WAY BACK TO THE FATHERLAND

Brown Brothers

GERMAN FOOD SUPPLIES IN BELGIUM

THIS IS WHAT THE GERMANS DID IN VALENCIENNES BEFORE THE CANADIANS CAME

U. S. Official Photo

WHAT THE VANDALS LEFT

A bridge over the Meuse after the German retreat

A SALVO TO THE ENEMY

A battery of American field artillery firing at the retreating German columns. The river at the bottom of the picture is the Aire, the road above runs from Varennes to Grandpré and was one of the main lines of American advance in the Meuse-Argonne

A SHELL HOLE IN THE GERMAN TRENCHES

This is why "Fritz" was in such a hurry to get back home

THE ENEMY IN RETREAT

German machine-gun sections established in shell craters are covering a retirement from the Hindenburg Line

BACK TO GERMANY

The beaten army, tired of war, and dejected, turn their footsteps homeward, hoping to find the peace which they were driven to violate

By Edward H. Potthast

From the collection of war pictures at the National Museum, Washington

THE ARGONNE

corner narrowed the neck of the Marne salient. Moreover, just as the vital railroad for Ludendorff in the Marne salient ran close to the Soissons corner, one of the two railroad systems serving Ludendorff's enormous salient between Holland and the Allied line runs close to Pershing's front. If Pershing, advancing to Sedan, can cut the German communications, the railroad line from Metz to Maubeuge, Ludendorff will have to come out of this last salient just as he had to retire from the Marne salient.

But such a retreat will be next to impossible, given the enormous concentration of men and of material in France and Belgium, which will have to be moved by the railroad line crossing the Meuse at Liége and along the few roads which cross the Ardennes between the Dutch frontier and the Chiers. Using his right wing, the Americans, and Gouraud's Fourth Army, Foch will strike for Sedan. To meet this thrust Ludendorff will need to make tremendous calls upon his reserves, but while his reserves are limited, those of Pershing, steadily growing, are almost without limit.

Meantime, on his left, Foch will throw the whole British army, aided by French and Belgians and presently by Americans, straight against all that enormous system of entrenchments between the Oise and the sea. If these are broken, if the German is driven out of them, if he is driven out of them at the same time that Pershing cuts the Metz-Maubeuge railway, a beaten German army will, at one time, have to meet attack in the open, in front, and on the flank. Moreover, to prevent Haig from smashing the Hindenburg Line, Ludendorff will have to pour reserves to this front also, and he no longer possesses a reservoir of reserves adequate to nourish both fronts. We shall see that in the end, lacking the necessary support, the German front before Pershing will collapse entirely and be followed by that swift pursuit which reached Sedan and would have continued without any visible limit but for the Armistice. Actually Foch will use Pershing for his right hand and Haig for his left while Petain's force will furnish the kick, the *savate* permissible in French boxing.

Ludendorff's single problem is to hang on where he is for the few weeks until the autumn rains make further campaigning impossible.   If he can do this, German diplomacy may be expected to find an honourable and not unprofitable peace by negotiation.   Even if this resource fails he can, during the winter, repeat the achievement of the Hindenburg Retreat in 1917 and draw back behind the Meuse and the Scheldt, devastating the country behind him, shortening his front and thus in- creasing his reserves and, what is at least as important, placing the water barriers of the Meuse and the Scheldt in the pathway of the terrible tanks.   Ludendorff is fighting for time and Foch's time is patently short.

But once more geographical and strategic objectives are but in- cidental; Foch has driven the German army into the Hindenburg Line and in a condition which he calculates will make German defence of the line impossible.   He is now going to try to drive the German army out of that line and, in doing this, so absorb German reserves that further resistance will be impossible, while also seeking at all times to seize any positions which will further reduce the German chance of resistance.

For four years, as a consequence of the development of modern weapons and the expansion of modern armies, the world has been thinking about positions and has well nigh forgotten that the single purpose of war and of battle must be to destroy the enemy's power to resist.   September 26th, Foch will undertake to do this.   Such is the real objective sought by Foch.   To escape the ultimate disaster, Luden- dorff fights vainly, and thereafter his government surrenders swiftly to escape the rout otherwise inevitable.

II.   THE HINDENBURG LINE

We have now to examine briefly that monstrous defence system which four years of German industry had stretched from Metz to the North Sea, the Hindenburg Line of history, subdivided in German nomenclature into sections each bearing a name drawn from Teutonic mythology.   Actually, the Hindenburg Line was neither a line nor a single system of fortifications; it was a defensive zone varying in width from three to a dozen miles, making use of every hill, ravine, river, natural obstacle, but in the main deriving its strength from the successive fields of wire entanglements backed by trenches, block-houses, concrete emplacements. Each point of cover was a machine-gun nest, and every art of modern engineering, of ancient and modern military method, was employed to increase the obstacle.

The theory of the Hindenburg Line was not that the enemy attack would be broken before it, but that the force of such an attack would be lost in the encounter with one or with another of the series of obstacles which would be encountered, and that the enemy, checked in the tangle, would be slaughtered by the concentrated fire from all sides before material progress had been made, or thrown back by a well-timed counter-attack.

Seen at close hand there was seldom anything impressive or imposing about the Hindenburg Line system.

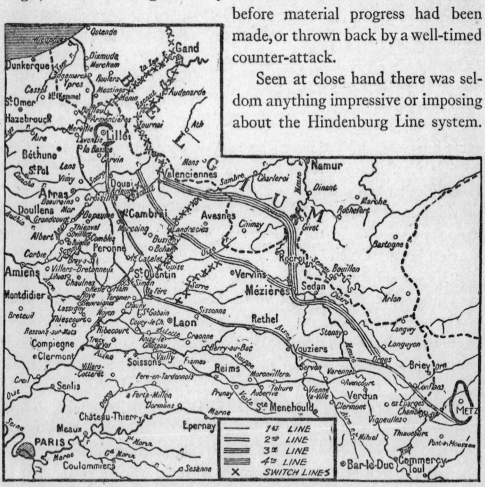

GERMAN DEFENCE SYSTEMS IN FRANCE

The fields of rusting barbed wire; the trenches following the rearward slope of the ground, indiscoverable from in front; the concrete emplacements, rarely discoverable at all, so cunningly were they hidden in the folds of the ground; all these circumstances were designedly well nigh invisible. Seen from the front, from one of the bare Artois hillsides, the Hindenburg system hardly appeared more than an area of desolation curiously furnished with barbed-wire hedges and strangely worked by shell fire.

Before the Hindenburg Line the country had been rigorously cleared; every house, tree, bush had been removed; in Picardy a glacis of devastation stretched before it, a detail in the preparation of 1917. "Between Cambrai and St. Quentin," says Maurice, "the Siegfried system from the outpost positions near Epehy to the rearmost lines near Beaurevoir was as much as ten miles deep. The most elaborate wire entanglements were provided in front of each line of trenches. Standing, after the great battle had been won and the Siegfried system had been pierced, on the ridges east of the St. Quentin Canal, in the heart of the system, one looked over miles of dense entanglements running in every direction, and was filled with amazement that it should have been possible for flesh and blood to storm a way through such obstacles. Heavily concreted shelters for the infantry and machine gunners were provided in the fire trenches, while farther back great underground barracks were constructed at a depth to make them proof against the heaviest bombardment."

"If the assailant were fortunate enough to break through the Hindenburg rampart in all its depth," writes Madelin, "he would find himself face to face with a new system. There are two lines, less continuous to be sure, resting, on one side on the entrenched camp of Lille, which was powerfully organized, and on the other on the fortified area of Metz-Thionville.

"The first of these lines is indicated by Douai, Cambrai, Guise, Rethel, Vouziers, Dun-sur-Meuse, Pagny-sur-Moselle. Still north of these was a series of detached positions: Hunding, Brunhilde, Kriemhilde, Michael." The last two will be well known to Americans, who broke the first in the Meuse-Argonne and reached the second after St. Mihiel.

"The history of war makes no mention of a similar defensive system," thinks Madelin. The reports of this period are filled to overflowing with descriptions of these defences, difficult to recognize on the spot, impossible to describe afterward, constituting a sort of labyrinth of chaos, trenches, caves, rabbit warrens, buttressed with railroad iron, sown with cement structures—monstrous turtles with a single aperture, left for machine-gun barrels. Difficult, well nigh impossible to pass when the battle had gone beyond, was this wilderness, filled then with the débris of conflict, with half-buried bodies, rotting equipment, broken guns; crammed with hand-grenades, with every conceivable engine fatal to touch; having an order, a plan, a method, but revealing it nowhere; concealing an underground world, stretching endlessly like the Catacombs, old quarries newly organized, vast warrens capable of sheltering platoons, whole companies, and reached by stairways going down to the very nethermost depths.

Strongest, this system was most elaborate, most carefully and consistently prepared between Cambrai and St. Quentin, lying in the folds of the hills, before and behind the St. Quentin Canal, borrowing the tunnel of the canal itself for an enormous shelter for troops, a shelter from which they could emerge when the enemy wave has passed forward—a circumstance which will cost the New York Division dearly when it goes straight through the whole infernal system—with Rawlinson's Australians "leap-frogging it," in the first stages of the battle, having on their flank the American 30th, which will be more fortunate and go yet farther.

All that four years of a war of positions has taught, the Germans have applied on this line: art, science, military resource can do no more. "Impregnable," the German organs announce at this moment, "a wall like to nothing that ever was before in history." "A fact conceded," Madelin responds, "but Foch has 'the trumpet of Jericho'." And with all its strength, the Hindenburg Line is, after all, the enemy's last resource. If it falls, all falls. Beaten there, even he will not long hope to hold the relatively insignificant although honorifically named lines behind. In truth, despite its magnificence, the Hindenburg Line is no more than "the last ditch"—no stronger in its time than Lee's lines before Petersburg, which fell swiftly at the end.

III. PERSHING OPENS THE BATTLE

On September 26th the honour of opening Foch's final battle falls to Pershing, who attacks between the Meuse and the Argonne, Gouraud following suit west of the Argonne. We shall examine the American operations later. It is enough to recall now that on this date Pershing and Gouraud—constituting, together, the right flank of Foch's forces—set out for Sedan. Pershing is the more fortunate; gets forward four miles and encircles Montfaucon, which will fall the next day; clears all the Hindenburg Line, but falls short of the Kriemhilde. A remarkable achievement is this first attack, not quite as good as Foch and Pershing hoped for, but something totally beyond Ludendorff's remotest expectation.

West of the Argonne, Gouraud advances more slowly. He has first to win clear of the shell-torn area demolished by the preparation for Joffre's offensive of 1915, torn again by Ludendorff's preparation and Gouraud's performance on July 15th of the current year. He does this, but no more. Ludendorff rushes up reserves and the operation on the right flank enters into a second phase in which advances are slow, costly, but the drain upon German reserves is tremendous.

One day after Pershing, Haig attacks, three armies in line: Horne to the north, Byng in the centre, Rawlinson to the south. This day and those which follow immediately are the most splendid in the history of the British army, and a modest share in the achievement belongs to the American 27th and 30th divisions with Rawlinson, the former from New York, the latter composed of southerners, mainly from Tennessee, North Carolina, and South Carolina. No unit in Lee's army of northern Virginia fought with more distinction or success than these sons of the new South.

On September 27th, Cambrai is the direction of the advance and the passage of the Canal du Nord the immediate task, one of the greatest military obstacles on the whole front an unfinished ditch thirty or forty

feet deep in places, a hundred wide, the spoil-banks—that is, the piles of
the earth which has been excavated—furnishing posts for machine guns,
notably south of Havrincourt.   A magnificent exploit was the taking of
the canal, which enabled the tanks to get across, and very briefly Byng's
army is fighting in the old Cambrai salient, the scene of its success and
disappointment a year ago.   Ten villages, 10,000 prisoners, 200 cannon,
are taken on this day, and the British call the action the Second Battle
of Cambrai in revenge for the first.   Pershing and Gouraud had taken
another 10,000 prisoners on the previous day.

While Byng and Horne fight toward Cambrai, Rawlinson aims for
Le Catelet.   He has before him the canal between the Scheldt and the
Oise, impassable for tanks save only on the narrow front where the canal
goes under ground.   Therefore Haig turns back to the old method of
artillery preparation and pounds the German lines all through September
27th and 28th.   On the 29th Rawlinson assails the Hindenburg Line on
a front of twelve miles, the Second Corps—American, comprising the
27th and 30th divisions, Major General G. W. Read commanding—in
line facing the point where the canal passes underground.   On this day
Rawlinson opens the breach in the Hindenburg Line where it is strongest,
and on the same day Debeney, about St. Quentin, also moves.   Three
British armies and one French, most but not quite all of Foch's left wing,
are in action.   By October 1st, St. Quentin has fallen, Rawlinson's
Fourth Army is approaching the last barrier in the Hindenburg system.
By October 3rd, the Hindenburg Line was smashed; 36,500 prisoners and
380 guns were the British booty.   The Germans would continue to hold
certain elements in it, but the line and the legend had gone together.

Nor was this all.   On the 28th of September, from Dixmude to
Armentières, Plumer's British First Army, with King Albert's Belgians,
suddenly breaks out of the Ypres salient, which now disappears for ever.
Again, supported this time by material aid from Degoutte's French
army, there begins that march for Roulers and Menin which Sir John
French undertook just four years ago, the march which Haig strove to
make one year ago.   As for Degoutte, he has travelled far and fast since
Harbord's Marines met him conducting a despairing defensive astride

the Paris-Metz road on June 1st. September 28th is a notable day in Flanders, it sees the Germans swept out of all the famous fighting ground of four years of war. Once more, as in the recent fighting at the Somme, ground which once took months to conquer is now cleared in hours and even in minutes.

By the 29th the limits of the old battlefield are everywhere passed. Already the German hold upon the Belgian seacoast is crumbling, Lille is menaced, all German defence between the sea and the Deule is disintegrating. Another 10,000 prisoners are taken. This series of attacks fulfils Buat's formula of accelerating the pace by piling one attack upon another and the consequent absorption of German reserves is correspondingly hastened.

IV. OCTOBER 10TH

The battle of the Hindenburg Line ends on October 10th. Military writers, including Ludendorff himself, indicate this day as the termination of a distinct phase, although to the civilian mind the transition is almost imperceptible. Let us now analyze Foch's battle, successful, decisively successful on this October 10th, fifteen days after Pershing opened it between the Meuse and the Argonne, 85 days since Foch seized the initiative at the Soissons corner, a month and a day before the end of the fighting, before the Germans surrendered. The world now knows that Bulgaria has surrendered. Turkey is conquered. Diaz has not yet delivered his final blow at the Piave, but Austria-Hungary's appeals for peace indicate what the result will be two weeks hence. Finally, Germany's first peace proposal addressed to President Wilson has been issued five days earlier, sent forward just as Haig's troops are emerging in the open country beyond the Hindenburg Line, agreed upon in the last days of September, the very last days after Pershing and Haig had delivered their first terrible blow.

Foch's strategy lies clearly unrolled on the map. As we have seen, his attack was to have two principal directions followed by his two flanks: Haig on the north with the Hindenburg Line in front of him, and Valenciennes, Maubeuge, Mons as his goals; Pershing on the other flank with the Meuse-Argonne defence lines, Hindenburg, Hagen, and Kriemhilde Stellungs before him, and Montmédy, Sedan, and the all-important Maubeuge-Metz railway as his goals. In military language (Requin's) this is described as choosing, "as principal directions of attack, those where the most important strategical results are to be expected; in other words, the directions which threaten the enemy communication lines and a tireless pursuit of the offensive along these main lines."

These main lines of communication are all the important railways serving the German front between the Oise and the sea, so far as Haig is concerned; the Maubeuge-Metz railway, on Pershing's side. Up to October 10th and for many days thereafter Pershing and Gouraud to the west of him are substantially checked. The reason is twofold: the nature of the country in which they are fighting and the importance to Ludendorff of the railroad line they are aiming at. The more badly things go in the west and the more unmistakable becomes the certainty that he must draw his armies back from the coast, the more vital to him is the Maubeuge-Metz railway, one of the two lines open for his retirement. You may put the thing simply by saying: Haig is pounding in through the front door, Pershing is trying to close the back door, Ludendorff must strive to hold both doors, but the less successful he is in keeping Haig out, the more imperative for him it is to keep Pershing from closing the back door by which he must get out himself. Ludendorff is being defeated by the Allied left flank, but he is striving to avert disaster by holding up Pershing. His success so far is due in the main to the stream of reserves he is pouring into the Meuse-Argonne battle, but since his reserves are limited, diminishing very rapidly, he is weakening himself before Haig to check Pershing, and he will find in the end that his reserves are inadequate even to do this. In Buat's phrase, Ludendorff's reserves are being "sucked in."

Now the second controlling purpose of Foch, again outlined by Requin, is "to form weak points in the adversary's positions along the rest of the front and cause the successive fall of all these weak points (salients) by encircling them, and thus gradually to bring about the collapse of the western front." Accepting the fact that Foch's right,

Pershing's army, has been checked after material but not yet decisive progress, we may now apply the foregoing principle of strategy to the left between the Oise and the sea.   By October 10th, the developments are these: three British armies, Horne's First, Byng's Third, and Rawlinson's Fourth, have attacked between September 27th and 29th from Cambrai to the outskirts of St. Quentin.   By October 10th they have penetrated—Rawlinson's army farthest ahead—the whole Hindenburg system, and British troops are on this day advancing in the open country within sight of that battlefield on which Smith-Dorrien made his despairing stand on August 26, 1914, a memorable day in the history of the "Old Contemptibles."

The result of this advance, which has already produced the fall of Cambrai and St. Quentin, has been to drive a deep wedge in the German line between the Oise and the sea.   The effect of this wedge is beginning to be felt on either side.   To the north the Germans in the great cluster of fortifications about Lille, finding their communications threatened from the rear as a result of Rawlinson's advance, are getting ready to retire.   This retirement is hastened by Plumer's pressure to the north, which we will examine in a moment.

At the same time, the German centre, impregnable to direct attack, likewise finds itself menaced as to its rear and communications, and has begun to go back.   To put it succinctly, Haig's push has now had the result of turning the Germans to the north of it out of all their splendid system of defences from Cambrai to the sea, and to the south of it out of all that bastion between the Oise and Rheims.   This is what Requin means by his phrase "choosing as principal directions of attack those where the most important strategical results are to be expected."

The results are now indicated by the fall of Laon, the evacuation of the heights from which the Germans have for four years pounded Rheims, and the preparations for the approaching retirement from Lille and from the Belgian sea coast.

In addition Foch has created weak points elsewhere in the German line.   To meet Haig's mighty thrust south of Lille, Ludendorff drew heavily on the Ypres sector for reserves. Thereupon Foch threw King Albert's army group—the Belgians, Plumer's British, and Degoutte's French—against the thinned line, and it collapsed exactly as the Allied line on the Chemin des Dames collapsed after Foch had drawn off all the reserves to meet the thrust he wrongly expected west of the Oise. This success has gravely compromised Ludendorff's position because even with the reserves drawn from Ypres he has failed to check Haig while the withdrawal of the reserves has produced a collapse to the north.

In the same way, on a reduced scale, Foch has created a weak point near Rheims. East of that city, in the region where Gouraud checked Ludendorff on July 15th, the German line rests on high ground—"the Mountains" captured by the French in May, 1917, evacuated by Gouraud as a circumstance in his defence in Champagne in July. Ludendorff, who boasted about the capture of this high ground, relied upon it and drew off reserves to face Gouraud and Pershing to the east, whereupon Foch borrows two American divisions, the famous 2nd and the 36th, and the former, in line with the French, storms the crest of these mountains in a magnificent dash while the 36th exploits the success. This is the final circumstance in compelling Ludendorff to retire from before Rheims.

V. LUDENDORFF *vs.* FOCH

We may now contrast the method of Ludendorff with that of Foch. Attacking with stupendous force, on March 21st, Ludendorff ruptured the Allied front between the Somme and the Oise over an extent of more than thirty miles. Into the gap he poured more than eighty divisions, but despite his colossal effort, he was checked before April 1st, decisively and permanently, while the forces which he had employed in the rush were exhausted. His efforts to extend the dislocation of the Allied front, first by attacks before Arras and then in Flanders, were unsuccessful; he had then to pause from April 29th to May 27th; then he exactly repeated his experience of March and April. He again ruptured the Allied front for an extent of forty miles along the Chemin des Dames and again pushed division after division into the gap he had opened, but by the first days of June he is once more checked and his effort to extend the dislocation by his operation at the Matz is halted briefly and far more completely than his similar thrust in Flanders.

He then has to pause again, this time until July 15th, when his attack fails instantly and he loses the initiative. His ruin is accomplished in the periods between his several efforts, as a result of the time allowed to his opponents, whom he has beaten and punished severely, to recover—to transport reserves from America and to choose a single commander to direct their policies. In a military way the failure of Ludendorff is disclosed in the fact that in his first two offensives he made only restricted breaches in the Allied front, was unable to expand the dislocation or disorganize the whole of the Allied armies and completely consume their reserves.

Now, by contrast, Foch wins the initiative on July 18th, and between that date and August 6th, when Ludendorff retires behind the Vesle, occupies his enemy and forces him to consume his reserves in covering the retreat from the Marne. Then on August 8th he throws Haig's Fourth Army against the German line at the Somme, achieves local success, and for a whole month exploits this success, expanding the extent of the dislocation of the enemy front until it stretches from the Scarpe before Arras to the Vesle near Rheims. So far from having a breathing spell, Ludendorff is compelled to fling division after division of reserves into the furnace, while all his armies from the Scarpe to the Aisne are subjected to local defeats, inevitable disorganization, and, finally, all of them begin to disclose evidences of demoralization.

Foch, himself, thus describes the matter to Babin:

You see it's a question of shouldering one's way through—one army advances, another follows, a third makes a push. In order to parry our blows the Germans needed to gain time, to be able to pull themselves together somewhere. But we did not give them a chance. They had to fight to save their necks. They had no end of material stored in a chain of work shops all ready for an advance to Paris, but we upset their programme on July 18th and now we're taking their workshops one after another and they're falling back all the time, which means progressive confusion and disorganization. They need to get away from us, but they can't shake us off. They have no reserves and we are at their heels, allowing them no respite.

This was after the event but General Maurice records that before March 21st, one of the Allied statesmen who had assembled at Versailles, asked Foch point blank:

"But if the Germans do make their great attack, what is your plan?" To this interrogation Foch responded: "By striking out three rapid blows, with his right, with his left, and again with his right, following these by landing out a vigorous kick."

September 10th Ludendorff gets his battered armies back to the Hindenburg Line, but instead of a respite he has a new problem set for him by Pershing's sudden and swift victory at St. Mihiel, a victory which is not only locally costly, since it smashes six divisions, but, by carrying a threat to Briey with its invaluable iron mines, compels Ludendorff to concentrate more reserves in the east; that is, outside the area in which he is now going to be attacked by a tremendous Allied force.

Before Ludendorff can adjust himself to this new condition, to the threat in the east—a threat deriving its real importance from the disclosure at St. Mihiel that the American army will henceforth have an importance hitherto unsuspected—Foch starts his general offensive on September 26th on either side of the Argonne, extends it the next day to the region between the Oise and the Scarpe and, on the next, to the region about Ypres.

More than two months have now passed since the opening of the Second Battle of the Marne, and during that time not one single moment of rest has been allowed Ludendorff, the strain upon his reserves has never been relaxed. Foch's local ruptures of the German front have in all cases been swiftly extended and by this time every one of his armies from the sea to the Moselle, from Ypres to Metz, has suffered disorganizing defeat, and this embraces every effective German army on the western front. In a word, Foch has not only expanded local dislocation of the enemy front, but the disorganization incident to local defeat. It is not positions or battles which he has won that weigh chiefly—Ludendorff counted an impressive number of these between March and July— it is the fashion in which Foch has exploited these successes. It is the result which he has produced by them which is important. Ludendorff has never been able to realize on his investments, and one unfortunate speculation has not only deprived him of the profits of two ventures, but has also impaired his credit to such an extent that he cannot now discharge the obligations which have come due.

The thing that one feels about the Foch campaign is the apparent ease, the marvellous smoothness with which one success leads to another and each local triumph seems somehow to merge into a second and greater. The drama moves so simply, naturally, logically, that the most astounding developments lack the quality of surprise when they arrive. But the reason, for there is no accident anywhere, must be found in the mind and method of the man. Ludendorff was at least as fortunate, had quite as much luck in the beginning. For him the division of Allied command was an advantage greater than any single card ever put in Foch's hand. The collapse of the Portuguese at the Lys was for him a piece of good fortune quite as great as was for Foch the refusal of a Prussian division to fight on August 8th. The tank tactic was no more effective, unexpected, potent than the Hutier tactic in its own time. The German machine in March was incomparably superior to the Allied machine in July. Ludendorff's superiority in trained troops in March was far more decisive than that of Foch in trained and untrained troops combined in August and September. Foch has said that the German machine was an express locomotive in the hands of a stage-coach driver. This conclusion is inescapable when one reviews the history of the campaign. At the outset Ludendorff had all the cards. He lost because he could neither make the most of good fortune nor survive a run of bad luck.

VI. THE END OF THE BATTLE

And now, on October 10th, the day which sees the end of the battle of the Hindenburg Line, what exactly is the situation? At the north of Lille, the army group of King Albert—containing the Belgian army, Plumer's British Second Army, and Degoutte's French army, and presently to include two American divisions, the 37th and the 91st—is advancing, is approaching Roulers, and has already made such progress that it is only a matter of hours until the Germans will have to retire from the Belgian coast and from all of Belgium west of the Scheldt. This army group also constitutes a threat to the Germans in Lille which would compel the evacuation of this city and the enormous tangle of fortifications about it which makes it the western anchorage of the whole German front even if it were not similarly threatened to the south and east.   Facing Lille and approaching it is Birdwood's new British Fifth Army, whose mission it is to move in conformity with the armies north and south and exert such pressure as it may upon the Germans in front of it.

South, between Lens and the Oise, are the British armies which have smashed the Hindenburg Line: first is Horne's British First Army, which is closing in on Douai and threatening Lille from the south.   It is already setting its feet on the roads trodden by the immortal Expeditionary Army and its troops will see Mons victoriously a month hence after taking Valenciennes.   Thanks to it and to King Albert's group, Birdwood's army will enter Lille a few days later.   South of Horne's army is Byng's which has just taken Cambrai, is through the Hindenburg Line, and passing Bavay, French's headquarters at Mons.   Byng will take Maubeuge before the end.

South again is Rawlinson's Fourth Army, which includes the 27th and 30th American divisions, Read's Second Corps, which has shared with distinction in the breaking of the Hindenburg Line.   This army is on the edge of Le Cateau, where Smith-Dorrien fought in August, 1914; will pass through Landrecies, where Haig's corps stood briefly in the Retreat; and before November 11th, will pass Avesnes, where Ludendorff and the Kaiser had their headquarters at the time of the Battle of Picardy.

Astride the Oise, Debeney's French First Army, which held the gap on the Avre in the terrible days of March when Foch arrived, has just taken St. Quentin and is aiming at Guise, where Joffre won his brilliant little battle in August, 1914.   Debeney will soon take Guise and be in Belgium before the war is over.   South of the Oise is Mangin's Tenth Army, in which Bullard's corps fought at the Soissons corner.   It has already passed La Fère and Laon; it will soon give way to the French

Third Army, commanded by Humbert, hero of the Lassigny Hills in March, hero of the Château of Mondement in Foch's army in the First Marne: and Mangin will go to Lorraine to organize the troops destined to make the thrust east of Metz if the enemy continues. Many American divisions will be marked for this adventure, but the enemy will not continue.

East of the Tenth Army is the French Fifth Army, Guillaumat, a Verdun general, replacing Berthelot, who has been called to Roumania on pressing invitation to continue his task begun before the Roumanian surrender was forced by Russian desertion. Guillaumat has passed the Craonne Plateau, reoccupied Rheims, emerged from the Gap of Juvincourt, of evil memory, and is pushing forward north of the Aisne. Mangin and Guillaumat are pushing frontally against the Hunding Stellung, one of the rearward German defence lines between the Oise and the Aisne, the westward extension of the unforgettable Kriemhilde Stellung against which Pershing is beating. Debeney's advance west of the Oise will presently turn this Hunding position. To the east again, Gouraud's Fourth Army is pounding at the Brunhilde Stellung along the Aisne from Rethel to Vouziers and Pershing's First Army is storming the Kriemhilde between the Argonne and the Meuse, with Hunter Liggett commanding. East of the Meuse, Bullard's American Second Army is just coming into line before the Michael Stellung from Verdun to Metz. The French armies between Haig and Pershing are organized in two groups, those to the west commanded by Fayolle, who saved the day in Picardy; those to the east by De Maistre, who did the same at the Second Marne. Both are under the supreme command of Petain.

The military situation at the same moment is as follows: the Germans are under orders to retreat out of all the Hindenburg Line. Their defeat is absolute. Ludendorff hopes to rally his beaten army behind a line running along a canal from the Dutch frontier to Ghent, thence behind the Scheldt to Denain, and thence behind the little Selle to the point west of the Sambre, where begins his last system of defences—the Hermann Stellung, extending to the Meuse below Sedan. But he will still strive to hold back Gouraud and Pershing on the Aisne and at the bend of the

Aire to protect the vital railway, become infinitely more precious as the retreat grows more imminent, the retreat which already looks toward-Germany.   Still farther to the east is the French group of Castelnau, last survivor of Joffre's lieutenants at the Marne left in command in France—Foch alone excepted—but Franchet d'Esperey, another, has just conquered Bulgaria.

In a word, at the close of the Battle of the Hindenburg Line, and as a consequence of decisive defeat, Ludendorff, on the night of October 9th, orders a retirement of his left and centre, a far-swinging retreat to be halted behind the Scheldt, the Selle, and the Hermann Line. This retreat calls for the evacuation of the Belgian coast, of Bruges, and of Lille, and will carry Foch's left and centre far into Belgium and close to the French frontier. But at the same time, Ludendorff orders his right to hold on in front of Gouraud and Pershing; demands of it, now that the front door is broken in and the enemy is actually in his house, that it hold open one of the two back doors by which alone Ludendorff's armies can escape from the house—and they will need both doors.

The Battle of the Hindenburg Line is over.   Foch's problem is now that of Grant after the latter had forced Lee out of his lines about Richmond.   Lee's purpose was to escape with his army from the net flung about him and stand again, Grant's problem was to destroy Lee's army before it could escape from the consequences of Five Forks and the subsequent disasters.

In the words of Requin:

The German staff proposes to establish itself upon the Antwerp-Scheldt-Maubeuge-Mézières-Metz Line, but for that purpose they need a respite, for a new defensive front can not be occupied under good condition unless it is, first, organized ahead, second, occupied by reserve troops, ready to collect the forces engaged and retreating.

The situation of the German army is in fact without an outlet. Their reserves have melted away in the gigantic battle. From sixty-seven divisions back of the front on September 26th they have fallen to forty-six on September 30th, to twenty-six by October 15th, of which only nine are considered fresh. The necessary proportion between the fighting and replacement effectives no longer exists.   In order to supply the front, it became necessary to disband twenty divisions. Also in July, the German reduced the fighting effective of all their battalions.

Ludendorff's narrative of this same period becomes one long complaint over the failure of his numbers. The vast captures of Foch's armies, more than a quarter of a million prisoners before the Battle of the Hindenburg Line is over, constituted a drain totally unforeseen. He has gathered the last dregs from Russia, he has swept up all that is left of German man-power, and it has proven woefully insufficient. Pershing's attack in the Argonne has consumed or will consume forty-seven divisions, a quarter of the whole number of German divisions available. Germany is now, as her soldiers and propagandists have proclaimed France for three years, "bled white." The hour has arrived which Bernhardi in his unforgettable book described with prescient accuracy. All Germany's foes have succeeded in putting their full strength into the field at one time; the result will be as he foresaw.

VII. "APPOMATTOX"

The moment has now arrived for the final effort. Ludendorff's broken and beaten army is staggering back to the line on which it will seek to make a final stand. Foch must now break the last semblance of a power to resist. He will do it by continuing his two main thrusts: Haig's drive toward Mons and Maubeuge, Pershing's drive with Gouraud toward Sedan and the Metz railway. The other operations are by comparison minor.

Once more the chief effort will be made by Haig and Pershing. Haig will seek to break through between the Sambre and the bend of the Scheldt below Valenciennes. He will strike the German line occupying in the main the east bank of the little Selle. If he can break through here, Ludendorff can maintain neither the line of the Scheldt to the north nor the Hermann Stellung to the south. Haig's engagement, the Battle of the Selle, begins on October 17th. It lasts until October 23rd, and Byng, Horne, and Rawlinson are engaged; two American divisions, the 27th and the 30th, fight with twenty-four British against thirty-one German divisions.

In this Battle of the Selle the Germans fight with a determination

not shown in recent engagements.   There has been a distinct and impressive rally, but even this rally comes too late and too weakly.   At
the Selle, 20,000 prisoners and 475 guns are taken, and by October 25th
the British armies are far forward.   And the next day, the Kaiser,
receiving Ludendorff coldly, will accept his resignation.

Haig is breaking his way through the gap between the Sambre and
the Scheldt.   The Selle was his first barrier.   The tiny Rhônelle,
which parallels the Selle a few miles to the north, is his last.   November
1st he breaks through; the fighting is severe but the result is decisive.
The line of the Scheldt to the north and the Hermann Stellung to the
south are turned.   Haig can now push down the valleys of the Sambre

BREAKING THE HINDENBURG LINE

Diagonal lines indicate the territory regained between July 18th and September 26th. Solid
black marks the territory taken in breaking the Hindenburg Line between September 26th and
October 23rd.

and of the Meuse; there is no system of defence in front of him, there is no sufficient natural obstacle to check him.   His road is open to Namur and to Liége.   As he advances through Maubeuge and Mons, which he will reach promptly, he is narrowing the gap between his front and the Dutch frontier through which all the German armies north of the Sambre must pass if they are to escape envelopment and the choice between surrender to the British and internment in Holland.

Here is the ultimate revelation of Foch's strategy which consisted in making two major thrusts at the points where the largest gains would result.   British advances between September 26th and November 1st have already dragged with them the Germans to the north from Cambrai to the sea, and to the south from the Oise to the Aisne.   Now Haig's armies are so placed that much and perhaps all of Ludendorff's forces north of the Sambre will be surrounded and have to surrender, and there is left to all the army group of the enemy's centre only a single exit: that part of the Metz-Maubeuge railway from Mézières eastward. If Pershing can realize Foch's conception for his second major thrust, this remaining avenue of escape will be closed.

And Pershing has realized Foch's purpose.   The last days of October have seen the American troops bite into the few remaining fragments of the Kriemhilde Line.   They have consumed the last reserves the Germans had to put in here and accordingly, on November 1st, while Haig is forcing the passage of the Rhônelle and taking Valenciennes, Pershing's First Army breaks out into the open and begins its amazing rush to Sedan and Montmédy, the rush that will take Liggett squarely across the Mézières-Metz railway, last avenue of escape for the German centre.   It will be before Sedan and in sight of Montmédy, with its mission fulfilled, on November 11th; and on this final day, when Haig's army is closing the line of retreat of the German right, Pershing, with Gouraud's assistance as always, has closed the pathway of the retreat of the German centre.

And at this same moment Mangin is in command of a great army containing six American divisions scheduled to break out between Metz and Strassburg on November 14th.   On Mangin's front the Germans have not a single division of reserves left. Mangin's attack would carry him straight through the German left wing across its rear and line of retreat, and this would in a few days have to submit to exactly the same fate already overhanging the right and the centre, while the American army, Bullard's Second Army, would encircle Metz from the northwest and repeat the events of 1870 with a German in Bazaine's place.

But all speculation as to future developments is at once idle and unnecessary. The Germans who met the Allied representatives on their mission to ask an armistice may or may not have said, "The German army is in Marshal Foch's hands," but such was the fact. Haig was master of the fate of the German right; Pershing, of the line of retreat of the centre; Mangin's blow, fast ripening, must dispose of the left, north of the Vosges. And the German surrender, to avoid this supreme disaster, was an unconditional surrender; Ludendorff asserts it, the terms of the Armistice prove it. The final battle and its immediate consequences, the liquidation of the results of the first days, began on September 26th; the last German resistance was broken on November 1st, thirty-seven days in all. From Ludendorff's attack in Picardy to his final check in Flanders was forty days. The master had been well served by his lieutenants, Petain, Haig, and Pershing; they had been well seconded by their subordinates, Fayolle, De Maistre, Gouraud, Mangin, Debeney, Humbert, Berthelot, Guillaumat, Plumer, Horne, Byng, Rawlinson, Liggett and Bullard; but the master was Foch, he was as preëminent among his generals as Napoleon among his marshals. No campaign of Napoleon had been as stupendous in its circumstances, no termination more fortunate, more decisive. Neither at Jena nor at Waterloo were the battlefield results more conclusive; neither in the capitulation at Metz nor at Sedan had the submission been more absolute than that of the German army on November 11th.

As to the legend, that piece of impudent propaganda invented by the German High Command, put forth by Ludendorff—that the German army had been unconquered and was unconquerable, remained capable of saving Germany right up to the moment when the country collapsed behind it—the facts themselves are adequate to refute this final attempt of the German High Command to preserve its ancient reputation. On this subject General Buat writes with authority in words carrying conviction:

It is a legend which should be demolished, the claim that the German army was unconquered. When it obtained an armistice, that formidable host, which on July 18th counted not less than eighty divisions of reserves, had sunk under the repeated blows of the Allies to a point where it no longer possessed more than fifteen divisions behind its battlefront; and even of these, only two were ready to engage immediately. At the same hour the Allies had a hundred. A Franco-American attack by thirty divisions, followed immediately by thirty more, was just to be launched east of Metz on November 14th and to march straight to the Sarre and the Rhine. Nothing could have stopped it.

So convinced was the German General Staff of this fact that it had ordered the evacuation of Metz and Thionville, the two boulevards of the Rhineland. More than one hundred and sixty German divisions—sadly reduced in numbers, to be sure—were going to be obliged to retreat, with our bayonets at their backs and with their southern flank uncovered, through the gap between the Moselle below Thionville and Dutch Limburg. After the Armistice, unpursued and employing all the roads between Switzerland and Holland, these one hundred and sixty divisions were unable to get away, except by sacrificing the greater part of their material. What would have happened but for the Armistice? In point of fact, it is by the hundreds of thousands of men and thousands on thousands of guns that we should have reckoned our captures, if the Germans had not decided to sign the humiliating document of November 11th.

The statistics of the victory are as follows: Between July 18th and November 11th, Foch's armies had captured 385,000 prisoners—as many as Bazaine surrendered at Metz and Napoleon III at Sedan in 1870—and 6,615 guns. The division of the captures was: British, 188,000 prisoners and 2,880 guns; French, 139,000 prisoners and 1,880 guns; American, 44,000 prisoners and 1,421 guns; Belgian, 14,500 prisoners and 474 guns. The American total is above 50,000, reckoning in it the prisoners taken by the Second Corps, with the British, and the five divisions which fought in Flanders, at Juvigny, and east of Rheims—the captures of the Second Corps alone exceeding 6,000. The number stands against 208,000, Ludendorff's count of the prisoners taken by him between March 21st and June 15th, his total of cannon was 2,500. Even more than the disparity in men, that in guns indicates the difference between the two operations.

CHAPTER TEN

THE MEUSE–ARGONNE

I
PERSHING'S TASK

Having examined the progress of the battle which won the war, it remains now to consider in some detail the part played in this battle by Pershing's forces. The general place of the American participation in the struggle has been outlined. Pershing's First Army in conjunction with the smaller force of Gouraud constituting Foch's right flank, was to deliver one of the two major thrusts. While Haig's armies were advancing through the Hindenburg Line, through the line of the Scheldt and the Hermann Stellung, through Maubeuge toward Namur and Liége, Pershing was to push down the Meuse and cut the Mézières-Metz railway from Sedan to Montmédy, closing one of the two exits of the German army between the Dutch frontier and the Allied front at Verdun, not only closing one but threatening the other. Haig and Pershing, from widely separated fronts, were thus moving toward the same point, were the essential factors in the great converging attack in the general assault all along the half circle from Ypres to the outskirts of Metz.

In his final report Pershing has set forth the history of the development of the idea for this attack. In the discussion of August 30th Marshal Foch had proposed to the American general operations which were unacceptable to him because they would require the immediate separation of the recently formed American First Army into groups to assist several French armies. This would have rendered useless all the enormous preparations already made for the new army. In addition Pershing asserts:

The inherent disinclination of our troops to serve under Allied commanders would have grown, and American morale would have suffered. My position was stated quite clearly, that the strategical employment of the First Army as a unit would be undertaken where desired, but its disruption to carry out these proposals would not be entertained.

On September 2nd, at a new conference attended by Petain, Pershing was offered the choice between two sectors: that in Champagne, where Gouraud subsequently attacked, and that in the Meuse-Argonne, where the American army actually fought. At this conference Pershing heard outlined the plan for the great converging attack which later became a reality, but records that no one present even hinted that the end was at hand. In discussing the proposed Meuse-Argonne operation, the French High Command indicated its view "that the Meuse-Argonne attack could not be pushed much beyond Montfaucon before the arrival of winter would force the cessation of operations." This estimate proved incorrect, but the month of fighting necessary to get forward from Montfaucon to Landres-et-Saint-Georges demonstrated the reasonableness of the French view. As between the Argonne Forest and the Champagne sector, Pershing chose the former because: "In my opinion no other Allied troops had the morale or the offensive spirit to overcome successfully the difficulties to be met in the Meuse-Argonne sector, and our plans and installations had been prepared for an expansion of operations in that direction. So the Meuse-Argonne front was chosen. The entire sector of 150 kilometres of front (just under a hundred miles) was accordingly placed under my command, including all French divisions then in that zone."

At first, however, the St. Mihiel operation was to be pushed, and September 12th saw it carried to triumphant conclusion. What this victory meant to the new American army, Pershing indicates thus:

The material results of the victory achieved were very important. An American army was an accomplished fact, and the enemy had felt its power. No form of propaganda could overcome the depressing effect on the morale of the enemy of this demonstration of our ability to organize a large American force and drive it successfully through his defences. It gave our troops implicit confidence in their superiority and raised their morale to the highest pitch. For the first time wire entanglements ceased to be regarded as impassable barriers and open-warfare training, which had been so urgently insisted upon, proved to be the correct doctrine. Our divisions concluded the attack with such small losses and in such high spirits that without the usual rest they were immediately available for employment in heavy fighting in a new theatre of operations.

What the moral effect of St. Mihiel was, we have seen already. It not only won for Pershing the opportunity to play one of the leading rôles in the forthcoming Allied convergent attack, already foreshadowed on September 2nd, but it also placed an enormous, an impossible burden upon the newly constituted staff of an army just organized. Within a period of two weeks the American First Army had to fight a major engagement at St. Mihiel and then transfer its front to the north, take over new lines, a totally new sector, and deliver an even greater battle. In addition, practically all the veteran divisions used at St. Mihiel, having had no adequate time to rest and refit, were unavailable at the moment and Pershing had to begin the greatest battle in American history with an army composed mainly of green troops, newly come from the United States, lacking in all the essentials of adequate preparation.

Recognizing the magnificence of the actual achievement of these troops on September 26th, it is not unreasonable to believe that, had Pershing been able to employ his veterans, he might have realized his expectation and Foch's hope and broken clear through in the first two days of the Battle of the Meuse-Argonne. It is worth recording also that, despite his own difficulties, Pershing had to spare six divisions, three of them certainly among the best in France, during the course of the operation: the 27th and 30th, which served with Haig throughout, and broke through the Hindenburg Line; the 2nd and the 36th, which were lent to Gouraud where they performed remarkable services, and the 37th and 91st, withdrawn in full battle and despatched to Flanders to serve with Degoutte, where the 37th forced the crossing of the Scheldt and took Oudenarde. Thus the measure of Pershing's achievement must be sought in the examination of his difficulties, and his achievement must be put down to the obstinate and dogged determination of his troops and of their commander-in-chief, nor can one restrain admiration at the manner in which the General, confident of his army, undertook the impossible and actually performed an incredible part of it.

He had to train a huge army on the field of battle and, unlike Haig, whose position at the First Somme was otherwise comparable, Pershing did not have adequate mechanical resources, sufficient lines of communication, or any considerable number of trained staff officers.

II. THE BATTLEFIELD

No battle area on the western front is more difficult to describe than the Meuse-Argonne sector. The Argonne itself, with its densely wooded regions, recalls vividly the circumstances of the Wilderness campaign in the Civil War, and the country over which the New York City Division advanced would have awakened many memories in the minds of the veterans of Grant and Lee. The area between the Aire and the Meuse, with its high and wooded hills and its deep and marshy valleys, bounded on the east by the Meuse, strikingly recalls that country where Gates's army first halted, then broke and captured Burgoyne's army in the campaign which led to the surrender at Saratoga. And in this region between the Aire and the Meuse there is much which recalls the woods and hills of eastern Massachusetts and the points of cover from which the "Minute Men" assailed the British "Redcoats" on their retreat from Concord and Lexington on April 19, 1775.

In advancing from south to north, Pershing's army moved through a corridor rather more than 20 miles wide at the start and narrowing as the Meuse inclined westward to a point which was exactly at Donchery, where, in the Château de Bellevue, Napoleon III capitulated in 1870 after the disaster at Sedan. In this corridor the American difficulties were these: from the west they were assailed by a flank fire delivered by the Germans from the heights and forests of the Argonne which were impregnable to direct attack; a similar fire was delivered from the east, from the Heights of the Meuse on the right bank of that stream; in front they were faced by an enemy posted in an indescribable tangle of wooded hills, marshy bottoms, and deep ravines.

Literally, in all the early stages of the battle, the Americans in the corridor between the Argonne and the Meuse Heights were assailed by a frontal fire and at the same time pounded on both flanks, in their rear, and along their communications, by the enemy who dominated them from the Argonne and from the Meuse Hills. It had been the expectation of their commander that the advance of the French on the west and of the Americans on the east of the Argonne would compel the Germans to retire at once, but so strong was the position that the enemy held on long after Gouraud and Pershing had passed them on either side and continued to sweep the Americans between the Argonne and the Meuse with a deadly cross fire.

To the difficulties inherent in the character of the country was added still another, produced by the absence of roads. The single good highway from the south to the north travelled down the valley of the Aire which was open and was exposed to direct observation and fire from the

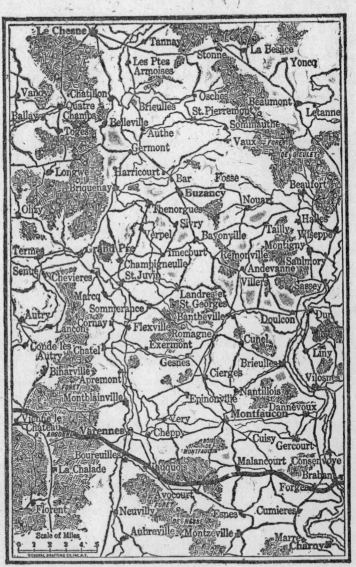

THE WOODS OF THE ARGONNE—MEUSE BATTLEFIELD

The Argonne Forest gave the Germans a strong protection for one flank and the Meuse River similarly protected the other. The numerous smaller woods gave fine protection for defensive measures between as did the hills both at Montfaucon and farther back along the line Romagne, Landres-et-Saint-Georges, Grandpré.

Germans in the Forest of the Argonne all the way from Varennes to Grandpré; that is, to the point where the Germans made their last stand. The only other passable road was that which followed the Meuse Valley from the American front northward, and this was even more completely dominated by the Germans on the Meuse Heights than was the Aire road from the Argonne. A single other road half way between the two rivers wound in and out among the hills from the American front through Montfaucon to the ultimate German position, and this road was a mere country highway totally unsuited to motor traffic, and promptly ruined by shell fire. The greatest single element in delaying the American advance was the question of communications. An army always in excess of a quarter of a million, requiring enormous supplies and munitions, needing stupendous concentration of artillery to open its difficult way, evacuating thousands of wounded daily, engaged in fighting so intense that divisions had to be relieved frequently and replacements hurried up hourly, was condemned to depend upon three roads, one of which, the Meuse route, was totally unavailable; another, that in the Aire Valley, for a long time almost equally forbidden; and what amounted to a rough country lane, already wrecked by four years of bombardment and now torn up anew.

One more circumstance added enormously to the problem of communications. When the Americans "jumped off" on September 26th, they advanced out of lines which were just within the area of the great battle of Verdun in 1916. Dead Man's Hill and Hill 304, the extreme limits of German advance, were their points of departure, and for three miles in front of them was the indescribable chaos of one of the greatest battlefields of the war, which had been subjected to intense artillery fire for months at a time and, in addition, for four years to the intermittent bombardment exchanged between fixed fronts even in quiet sectors.

No pen and no photograph can adequately describe or portray the actual devastation and destruction of the guns in the whole Verdun area, and in no section was this devastation more complete than on the left bank of the Meuse where Petain and the German Crown Prince had fought in March and April of 1916.

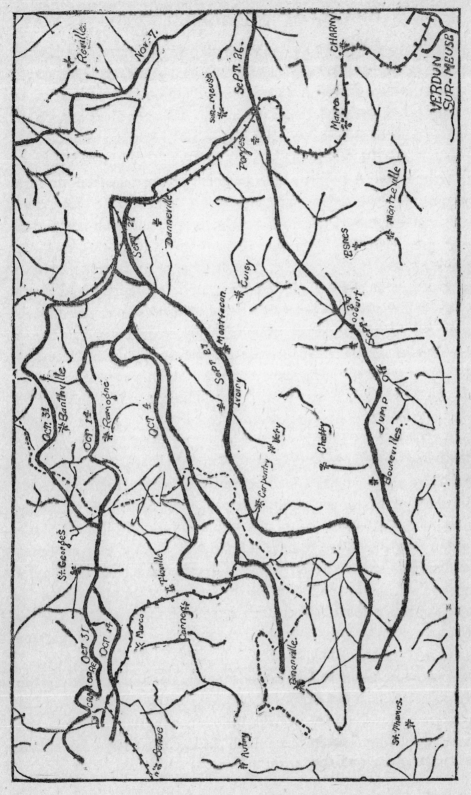

THE AMERICAN ARGONNE-MEUSE DRIVE

This final operation of the war was carried out in three phases: I. Driving forward on September 26, 1918, our First Army penetrated to a distance of from three to seven miles, taking about 10,000 prisoners. II. From October 4th to 14th the direct advance being checked the effort was directed toward the flanks. III. Between October 15th and 31st, the Kriemhilde Line was penetrated and on November 1st the First Army pushed northward continuing in pursuit of the disorganized enemy.

And the same devastation extended to the Argonne, in which there had been terrific fighting in the winter of 1914-15. The Argonne Forest itself, a long clay eminence with a crest line some 800 feet above the general level of the country, was ten miles wide, heavily wooded, its steep soft sides cut and eroded by many little brooks. But for five miles in depth before the American front of September 26th, the natural difficulties had been a thousand-fold magnified by four years of conflict, and there extended northward a region of incredible desolation most closely recalling a mountain forest which has been swept by fire. And all this chaos was intensified by a vast glacis of barbed wire miles and miles deep.

East of the Argonne and of the little Aire River was the real Verdun sector, and here directly in front of the Americans was a region comparable only with the Valley of the Ailette north of the Craonne Plateau and with that of the Ypres salient itself. Villages, orchards, trees, every living thing and every circumstance of human life, had long disappeared. Through a narrow valley flowed the tiny Forges brook going eastward to the Meuse, and the shell fire of four years had transformed its valley into an impassable marsh filled with enormous shell craters which had become deep and dangerous ponds, forbidding the passage not merely of transport but even of men. Again and again in the Verdun time soldiers had been drowned in these shell craters, and on the similar front east of the Meuse the French had long relied upon sure-footed donkeys as the sole method of transport.

Thus it will be seen that not only were highways lacking, but that when the Americans advanced they had first to pass over a deep belt of country in which there was no possibility of moving guns or supplies forward until this moat of destruction had been bridged. Men could and did get forward on September 26th, although how they did it will always remain a puzzle to those who know the country; but guns and motor vehicles could not follow, and the check after the first onrush was a consequence. When our waves had penetrated and passed all the first German lines "prepared" by the American artillery, when they had advanced beyond the effective range of their own guns, they encountered other German divisions armed with machine guns, fortified with concrete emplacements, protected by German artillery firing upon the assailant from the front and from the flanks. They were forced to halt to wait for the guns which could not come until the moat had been bridged and roads constructed; and in that time the German was able to get up reserves and the battle became one of "usury"—a repetition of the Somme, of Flanders, and, indeed, of the First Verdun itself.

This was what the French High Command foresaw when it warned Pershing that he would not get far beyond Montfaucon before winter came, and the forecast would have been accurate had it not been for the sheer fighting capacity of the green American troops, who, suffering casualties heavier than those which sufficed to break the fighting spirit of Nivelle's armies at the Craonne Plateau in April and May, 1917, wore the German out and ultimately broke through his defence line.

A satisfactory description of the various details in the topography of the country between the Meuse and the Argonne is then quite impossible. It is necessary to think of the country in which our young soldiers fought, in which they pushed forward after their first great dash, as a tangle of wooded hills, separated by marshy valleys, having no ordered system, no central ridge, no dominant hill stretching from west to east in the pathway of Pershing's troops as Vimy Ridge and the Craonne Plateau barred sectors of the Aisne and Scarpe fronts. There was no line of hills blocking our advance from south to north as the Meuse Hills or the Argonne Hills would have blocked an enemy coming from the east westward. Between October 1st, when our first rush came to a halt as a result of the failure of communications, and November 1st, when the remnants of the German army gave it up and took to their heels, our troops simply fought from hill to hill, and the capture of one hill left them with a hill on either side and one in front to negotiate. They struggled through woodland after woodland only to find fresh forests on all sides. They fought a battle of extermination with an enemy who knew the country, who had organized it for defence; whose artillery had marked down every road, every cleared space, every point of assembly, and, on signal from his aviators, deluged it with perfectly aimed shots.

In a word, the Battle of the Meuse-Argonne between October 1st and November 1st resembled Indian fighting in the earliest colonial days to a surprising extent, despite the use of all the weapons of contemporary warfare. It was not a battle of clever manœuvre, a conflict between two brilliant strategies; it was above all a conflict of men, fought at close range, fought with the bayonet, the machine gun, the hand grenade, fought to extermination under conditions of country, weather, and communications which defied comprehension.

III. THE GERMAN DEFENCE SYSTEMS

There is a very simple figure to describe the German defence systems in the Meuse-Argonne regions. The hills of the Meuse and of the Argonne constituted two distinct ridges running north and south, at first parallel and then converging, enclosing all the region where the real battle took place. The Germans occupied both ridges, and between these ridges they stretched barriers which resembled a series of gates swung from one stone fence to another in a country lane. They were solidly hinged and bolted on either side, and the American effort was to advance north through the lane, breaking down each of the successive gates along this roadway which led to their objective, the all-important railway from Metz to Mézières. There were actually three of these gates to be forced: two were in reality circumstances in the Hindenburg system and close together; the third, which was the Kriemhilde system, was three or four miles farther north and was the final barrier.

The Americans burst through the first two gates on September 26th and 27th, but the check in front of Montfaucon, and the failure of their transport system in consequence of the character of the country, delayed their progress from the second to the third gate until the Germans were able to rush reserves up; and Pershing's army fought these reserves, pushing them slowly but surely back upon the third gate, which they finally smashed on November 1st. Keeping this figure in mind, one can follow the various stages, always remembering that the Americans in the lane were long handicapped, not merely by the opposition in front, but by the punishment they received from the enemy who occupied

THE MEUSE-ARGONNE

A HILL DEFENDED BY GERMANS: CAPTURED BY AMERICANS

AMERICAN BATTERY IN ACTION

Supporting the 1st Division.   Firing at dawn.   Note the screens looped up back of the guns

U. S. Official Photo.

DOUGHBOYS UNDER MACHINE-GUN FIRE RUSHING THROUGH A STREET OF THELONNE, FRANCE

MACHINE GUN AGAINST MACHINE GUN

The Germans are attempting to set up their machine gun in spite of the rapid fire of the Americans

ADVANCING UNDER FIRE

There is nothing of the dramatic massed attack in this open order advance under fire. The photographer who took this picture was under fire, too

U. S. Official Photo

TALKING THROUGH GAS MASKS

Receiving instructions through a field telephone from an artillery observer. The information must be passed on to the gunners, gas or no gas

ON WATCH THE DAY BEFORE THE ARMISTICE

An observation tower built of light railway tracks. Picture taken November 10, 1918

THE CHAOS OF CONCENTRATED FIRE

As many as five shell craters filled with mustard gas were found in a space 10 by 13 feet

U. S. Official Photo

BIG MINE CRATER

A good example of the way the Germans destroyed the roads during their retreat. The traffic had to go around this gap

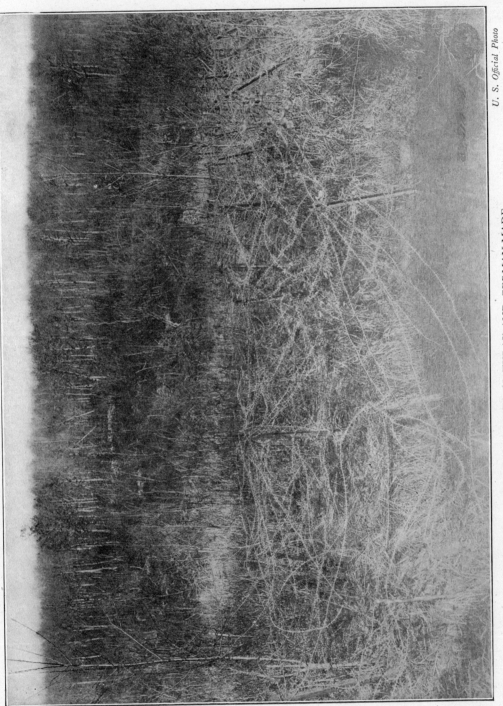

ENTANGLEMENTS, NATURAL AND GERMAN-MADE

These are the sorts of obstacles the 77th Division had to overcome in the Argonne

U. S. Official Photo

IN THE GERMANS' SECOND-LINE TRENCH

The Americans are resting in the trench they have just captured. In the Argonne

ON GUARD IN A FIRST-LINE TRENCH

A hastily dug trench along the edge of a wood. Not a posed picture. Taken October 2, 1918

"SOMEWHERE IN THE ARGONNE"

American Engineers building a temporary bridge across the Aire, northwest of Verdun

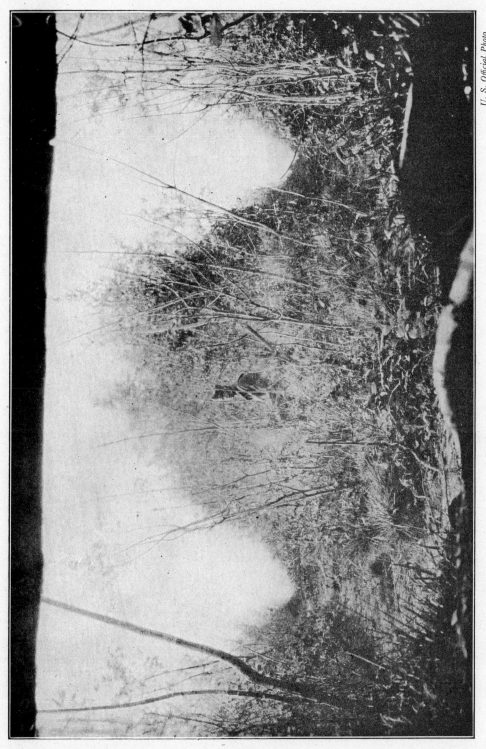

YOU ARE LOOKING THROUGH THE PORTHOLE OF A GERMAN "PILL-BOX" IN THE ARGONNE FOREST

Note the way the underbrush has been cleared to permit machine-gun fire

HAND GRENADE THROWERS IN THE MEUSE-ARGONNE

ADVANCING WITH RIFLE GRENADES

During the operations of the Argonne

AMERICAN SIGNALMEN LOOKING OVER THE ARGONNE FOREST

positions comparable with the top of the fence on either side of the lane looking down on the Americans and upon their rear and communications.

One other circumstance is worthy of note. On the British front Haig was still, on September 26th, when he attacked the Germans in the Hindenburg Line, a long way from their vital communication, and the Germans had begun to construct their reserve positions many miles back of the Hindenburg Line. The result was that Haig was able to advance rapidly for a considerable distance before he encountered the next line of German obstructions. But Pershing, when he attacked, was only a short distance from vital German communications, and therefore the Germans had constructed their second barrier in this region only a few miles behind the first. The result was that almost immediately after he broke through the Hindenburg system, the two gates of our figure, Pershing encountered the next, whereas Haig was clear through the Hindenburg Line in the first week of October and did not reach the Scheldt-Hermann Line until the last days of the month. This circumstance explains why the advances of both the British and the French were so much more extensive than those of the Americans between October 1st and November 1st. In point of fact, on this day Pershing and Haig, both of them, burst through the last German defence system, and it should be added that the section of this last line facing Pershing was far more complete and fencible than the Selle and Rhônelle defence lines which Haig surmounted.

On September 26th Pershing's army from the Argonne to the Meuse looked northward across the devastated area upon the first and second German defence systems, organized in depth for some six miles, lightly held, mainly by machine-gun detachments. At the northern edge of this fortified zone, midway between the Argonne and the Meuse, was the dominating hill on which stood the ruined village of Montfaucon, which was the point of vantage from which the Crown Prince had watched the opening of his attack upon Verdun. The hill of Montfaucon was more than a thousand feet high, rising out of much lower ground, dominating the whole front in a fashion which suggested the conning tower of a submarine. Madelin describes it as "that eagle's nest." The whole hill had been fortified by the Germans, who had provided it with a very considerable number of concrete block-houses—low structures with rounding roofs, made of reinforced concrete many feet thick, and commanding all the roads of approach to the village. Toward the Americans they showed only a narrow slit, several feet long but no more than three inches wide, through which machine guns were fired. These concrete emplacements were invisible from the air and impervious to everything except a direct hit by a heavy gun. Inside this cover three or four men could hold up a regiment and inflict terrific losses. Across the single road leading into the village, the Germans had stretched a series of concrete posts to prevent a tank attack.

It was the conception of the German command that an Allied attack between the Meuse and the Argonne would be able to get forward some three or four miles as a result of the preparation made by the artillery. But it calculated that when the assailants reached the vicinity of Montfaucon, they would have passed through the area covered by their own artillery and then, assailed by fire from Montfaucon in front and from the Meuse and Argonne hills on the flanks, the advance would be checked and would die out in front of Montfaucon. This calculation was not quite realized, for Pershing's troops did take Montfaucon on the second day of the first attack, but the town held out just long enough to enable the Germans to rush up reserves which checked Pershing's troops only a little to the north of Montfaucon itself.

Montfaucon is a conspicuous example of the extent to which the German surpassed all his opponents in protective defence works. Mont Sec, in the St. Mihiel sector, was an equally noteworthy illustration; Mont Sec and Montfaucon have furnished two of the most vivid memories American soldiers have carried away of the German defences. Since the Meuse-Argonne front covered a vital line of communication, the German defences were very elaborate. To the intricate artificial works there were added natural circumstances which made Pershing's battlefield perfectly adapted to the use of the machine gun, the Germans' favourite weapon, and the most difficult battlefield on the whole western front.

IV. FIRST PHASE

The bombardment preceding the attack on September 26th began at 2:30 A.M. and lasted for three hours. It was the usual prelude, and in these three hours more powder was burned than in the whole Civil War. A little less than 3,000 guns were in line, and thirty-five French artillery regiments reinforced the American batteries and supplied the larger part of the heavy artillery. All the guns served by American and French alike, as well as the ammunition, were of French manufacture.

The American army, in line on a 25-mile front, was divided into three corps. The order from west to east was as follows: The First Corps —comprising the 77th, 28th, and 35th divisions—was in line from La Harazee in the Argonne to Vauquois on the eastern edge of the Aire Valley. It was commanded by Hunter Liggett who would presently take over the First Army. The Fifth Corps occupied a front from east of Vauquois to the slopes of Hill 304. It was composed of the 91st, 37th, and 79th divisions, and was commanded by George H. Cameron, who was presently succeeded by Charles P. Summerall, who led the 1st Division at the Soissons corner. The front between Hill 304 and the Meuse was occupied by the Third Corps led by Robert L. Bullard, who had commanded the 1st Division at Cantigny, the American Army Corps at the Soissons corner, and would presently be succeeded by Joseph P. Dickman when Bullard took over the American Second Army. The Third Corps consisted of the 4th, 80th, and 33rd divisions. Of the nine divisions only one, the 4th, had seen severe fighting, while the 33rd had lent some of its units to the British at Chipilly Ridge in the fighting following the offensive of August 8th at the Somme.

In the scheme of things, the main advance was to be made by the Fifth Corps in the centre, which was to pass through Montfaucon and arrive at Romagne and Cunel on the edge of the Kriemhilde Stellung by nightfall. The other two corps were to cover flanks of this advance along the Meuse and astride the Aire. Gouraud's Fourth Army was attacking west of the Argonne, and it was expected that his advance and that of the American centre would lead to a prompt German evacuation of the Argonne, transformed by the two advances into a deep and narrow salient. On the west bank of the Aire the 28th Division, which had seen some fighting in the Marne salient, was expected to reach Apremont, and the 35th to take Exermont on the right bank. Arrived on this front the Americans were to halt, reorganize, and on September 27th, push through the Kriemhilde Line, north of which the German had no organized defensive system. The attack was to be a surprise. It was known that the German had but five divisions in line, only one of them first rate, and it was estimated that he could put no more than six divisions of reserves in during the first two days—four on the first, two on the second. But on the third, he would be able to put nine divisions in and these would be fully sufficient to check the American advance if it had not by that time broken the Kriemhilde Line and routed the Germans before it. Pershing's nine divisions numbered about 250,000 men and he had practically unlimited reserves to draw upon at this time. Thus he had the advantage of surprise, tremendous superiority in artillery, and numerical odds of about five to one.

We may now examine what actually took place. On the right of the line, the Third Corps almost completely fulfilled its mission, the 33rd Division crossing the Forges brook, lined the right bank of the Meuse from its point of departure to the hills north of Dannevoux in the bend of the Meuse. The 80th pushed into the woodland and hills to the westward only a little to the south of Brieulles which was its extreme objective. The 4th pushed on to the eastern edge of Nantillois which was its objective. The Third Corps had therefore substantially performed its mission, having passed through all the Hindenburg system and was in position to cover the Fifth if that corps should perform its mission and be ready to attack on the second day.

But the Fifth was less fortunate, it had the hardest mission, since the 79th Division had to take Montfaucon by direct attack supported by the 37th on its left. The 79th had the most difficult part of the front to cross, the area which had been most torn up in the 1916 fighting. As a result it "lost" its barrage, that is it did not keep up with the curtain of fire, timed to destroy obstacles and keep down resistance just in front of advancing infantry. This meant that the Germans were able to come out of their shelters after the barrage had passed, set up their machine guns, and punish the advancing infantry which was without artillery support.

As a consequence the 79th did not get to the foot of the Montfaucon Height until just before dark, and the 37th which had also passed through very difficult country was equally late. At this hour the 37th should have been far north of Montfaucon just as the 4th Division actually was. Thus threatened with envelopment, the German garrison in Montfaucon would have had to flee or surrender, and the work of the 79th would have been easy. As it was the Germans hung on, repulsed all attacks of the 79th and the 37th with heavy losses, and the 4th had to come back from Nantillois to protect its flank.

The Fifth Corps, scheduled to deliver the decisive thrust, was thus halted several miles south of its objective, and instead of being able to attack the Kriemhilde Line the next morning had to "mop up" Montfaucon instead, and it was not until night that it was able to get forward again, and even then only a short distance.

As for the First Corps and the 91st Division of the Fifth Corps, their progress had also been disappointing. The 91st had been checked in part by the reason of the failure of the 37th which had been held up in turn by the 79th. The 35th had not quite reached Baulny, while the 28th and the 77th across the Aire, after the first considerable gains, had been checked, as was to be expected by the resistance in the Argonne.

Pershing had now to face exactly the disappointments which came to Byng after his initial success at Cambrai a year before. Then a complete surprise had been partially spoiled by the success of one German battery in the town of Flesquières. This battery delayed the British advance for so many hours that the Germans were able to rush up reserves and to destroy the crossings of the Scheldt. As a result, Byng's cavalry could not get into action in time and a complete rupture of the German line was prevented.

Now the twenty-four hour delay in the American centre, caused by

Montfaucon had enabled the Germans to pour in six divisions of reserves, and nine more were available. Before he could get forward Pershing would have to wait for the guns, reorganize his communications, and evacuate his wounded. He would also have to relieve three divisions which had suffered terribly after partial check: the 79th, the 37th, and the 35th, which, after a brilliant advance on September 28th to the heights south of Exermont, had been forced to retire.

Worse even than this was the fact that the failure of his centre to reach its objectives and a similar delay suffered by the French west of the Argonne had combined to spoil the plan to pinch the Germans out of the Argonne, and they were now able to cross their fire with that of their comrades east of the Meuse, covering the flanks, the rear, and the communications of the Americans. Actually Pershing instead of rupturing the German front between the Meuse and the Argonne had merely driven a wedge, seven miles deep and less than ten miles wide at its broadest point, into the enemy front, and his men in this wedge were being punished by the Germans who occupied the high ground on both sides. In other words, Pershing had now undergone the same experience as all of his predecessors during the war of positions. The Germans when they had attacked Verdun across the Meuse on February 21, 1916, had driven a similar wedge into the French positions for an equal depth. But the fire of the French artillery from Hill 304 and Dead Man's Hill, which Pershing's troops had just passed over, paralyzed German advance until French reserves arrived, and the Germans, deprived of all the advantage of their surprise, had to halt and turn their attention to the hills across the river and clear them before they could get on.

Falkenhayn's hope of taking Verdun by a single thrust, and Pershing's design to break through the German defensives between the Meuse and the Argonne and promptly cut the Metz railroad near Sedan, were thus blocked under similar circumstances. Both at Verdun and in the Meuse-Argonne the front-line defence lasted just long enough to enable reserves to get up and prevent a rupture, and thereafter the assailants found themselves involved in a new war of positions in country admirably adapted for defence and in a posture bound to involve heavy casualties.

The enemy now had behind him good communications while Pershing's army was still separated from its bases both by the stretch of country marked by the destruction of previous battles and by the condition of the roads north of this area, wrecked by the recent battle and swept by German artillery fire alike from the front and both flanks. The result then was disappointing. An advance of seven miles had been made at the extreme point; 10,000 prisoners and 100 guns had been captured, but the enemy front was intact. Pershing was now stuck exactly where the French High Command had prophesied that he would be checked, and the German High Command had planned to halt any attack between the Meuse and the Argonne. Conceivably, had Pershing been able to use his veteran divisions, to use the 1st and 2nd against Montfaucon, his original plan might have been carried out, but both units had been heavily engaged less than two weeks before in the St. Mihiel salient; the two divisions actually engaged were totally new to offensive warfare and were literally going into their first battle.

Had Pershing been able to get to the Metz railroad in the last days of September instead of the first days of November, the effect of this triumph would have been far more disastrous than it could have been later, for between these two dates the Germans undoubtedly evacuated great masses of stores—Ludendorff asserts this. Nevertheless the ultimate arrival did carry for the enemy a deadly peril, escaped only by the Armistice. Moreover, all Allied authorities agreed that what Pershing undertook was not less than the impossible, and neither his French allies nor his German foes believed that, having thrust his army into the neck of the bottle, he would be able to push his way through before winter stopped the campaign. More than this, praise for what was actually accomplished was very generous. Madelin, who knew the Verdun area well, having made all the campaigns there from 1914 to 1917, wrote:

"Our Allies had achieved a grand success. They had taken Montfaucon, that eagle's nest reckoned impregnable, and its peak." And later he said again: "To have taken Montfaucon was a magnificent exploit, new proof of the bravery of the American soldier."

V. THE SECOND PHASE

Between September 27th and October 4th Pershing's army was occupied in straightening out its front preparatory to the resumption of a general offensive. Minor gains were made but they amounted in the main merely to liquidating the consequences of the previous attack and the line was still marked by the hills south of Brieulles, by the villages of Nantillois and Cierges and the town of Apremont just west of the Aire on the edge of the Argonne, in which the enemy still held positions in a southward salient. On October 4th Pershing undertook, despite the cross fire from the Meuse Hills and the Argonne, to force his way forward between the Meuse and the Aire. Despite some advances the attack was in the main a complete and disheartening failure. On the right and in the centre the check was immediate and absolute; on the left the 1st Division, which had replaced the 35th, reached the outskirts of Exermont; and the 28th east of the Aire advanced to the vicinity of Fléville. But the 77th, fighting magnificently in the Argonne, went through precisely the experience that the best French and German divisions had undergone in the winter of 1915 when the character of the country forbade rapid or material gain. So far from improving his position Pershing had merely accentuated the salient in which his troops suffered, and the 1st and 28th divisions on the west bank of the Aire in low ground were unmercifully pounded by the Germans in the Argonne from Cornay, opposite Fléville, to Châtel-Chehery. Until he had abolished this Argonne salient, Pershing could not hope to advance northward. Just as Falkenhayn across the river had been obliged to halt his direct advance on Verdun until he had abolished the French flank fire from the hills west of the Meuse, Pershing's next operation must be an attack on either flank to clear the Meuse Heights and the forest and hills of the Argonne. No progress toward or through the Kriemhilde Line could be hoped for until the Argonne salient was abolished; and this manœuvre consumed ten days.

The first blow was struck by the French on October 7th on the heights east of the Meuse. By October 8th the high ground had been cleared for a distance of six miles, while the 33rd Division on this latter date forced the passage of the river in brilliant style joining hands with the 29th on the Meuse Heights. This partially removed the hindrance coming from across the Meuse, but farther to the north, and particularly in the Bois de Châtillon, opposite Brieulles, the Germans hung on and, until the end of the battle, continued to punish the Americans from that flank. On October 8th, by an exceedingly clever manœuvre, Pershing threw the 28th and the 82nd across the Aire from the hills south of Fléville to Apremont, took Châtel-Chehery and Cornay, and began to march across the rear of the Germans in the Argonne salient. The result was immediate. The Germans fled northward, the resistance in front of the 77th collapsed, and by October 13th the 77th and the 82nd lined the banks of the Aire north of the Argonne Forest from Marcq to Chevieres near Grandpré. These two operations had completely abolished the flank fire from the Argonne and greatly reduced that from the Meuse Heights. West of the Argonne, Gouraud's army had made equal progress and Pershing was no longer in a pocket. The Aire Valley road, the best in the whole region, was available for his transport as far north as Fléville, while the Montfaucon road had been put in condition and a spur railroad was being pushed down the Aire Valley to Varennes from the Verdun trunk line. Meantime between the Aire and the Meuse the front had been pushed forward to the outskirts of Romagne and Cunel, and an advance had been made past Brieulles on the wooded hills to the west. In a word, Pershing was getting close to the Kriemhilde Line and Marwitz was approaching his last ditch. This was the situation when Pershing turned over the command of the First Army to Hunter Liggett, put Bullard in command of the newly organized American Second Army, and thus became chief of an army group.

Between October 13th and November 1st the Americans west of the Aire were in action against the Kriemhilde Line; between October 10th and November 1st, those between the Aire and the Meuse were wrestling with the same problem. This Kriemhilde Line from west to east was thus organized: At the southern end of the forest of Bourgogne, which was itself the extension of the Argonne north of the gap through which the Aire flows to the Aisne, the Germans occupied: Talma Farm on high ground in the midst of the forest; the considerable town of Grandpré, commanding the crossing of the river; Belle Joyeuse Farm above Grandpré, town and farm dominated by the hills of the Forest of Bourgogne; then to the eastward the steep, forest-crowned Bois-des-Loges which dominated the Aire Valley; then the village of St. Juvin and the high ground behind it extending in a well-defined ridge along the road from St. Juvin to Landres-et-Saint-Georges, thence through the Bois de Bantheville to the stretch of hills from Bantheville to the Meuse, along the north side of the little Andon brook which flows through Aincreville and Cléry-le-Petit. All advance on the west bank of the Meuse in the valley was prevented by German fire from the Bois de Châtillon across the river.

The position was exceedingly strong naturally. From Talma Farm to St. Juvin the Aire River, a deep stream flowing in a wide marshy valley, covered the German front, which was heavily wired along the river. From St. Juvin to Bantheville the hills about Landres-et-Saint-Georges dominate an open country. Eastward the Bantheville Forest was a difficult obstacle, while between Bantheville and the Meuse were high, heavily wooded forests, strong in themselves and doubly strong because of the cross fire coming from the east bank of the Meuse.

We have compared the battlefield to a lane barred by three gates. Actually the deep westward bend of the Meuse near Brieulle reduces the lane between the Aire and the Meuse to the width of a footpath, in our figure—a pass less than ten miles wide and actually a narrow gap between Bantheville Forest and the wooded hills west of the Meuse, by which the highway from the Aire Valley goes northward to Dun-sur-Meuse. This was the Thermopylæ which Marwitz attempted to hold in the last days of the Battle of the Meuse-Argonne, a solid ridge from the Forest of Bourgogne to the west bank of the Meuse with a single considerable break, that at Bantheville.

Between October 4th and November 1st, Pershing's "Second Phase," the operations fall into three distinct periods. The first occupies one day. Having regrouped his forces, he relieved the divisions most severely punished by putting in fresh and better-trained units: the 1st on the east bank of the Aire, the 32nd and the 3rd—the former proven in the passage of the Ourcq in the Marne salient, the latter at Château-Thierry. Having partially restored communications and brought up artillery, Pershing tries to repeat the effort of September 26th on October 4th. In doing this he imitates Falkenhayn at Verdun, Byng at Cambrai, Ludendorff himself before Amiens in the preceding spring; and like the other three, his attempt is an instant, complete, and bloody check. Then he has to abandon the attack in the centre, become hopeless until he has widened his front, abolished the flank fire from the Argonne, and at least reduced that from the Meuse Hills. Falkenhayn, after a similar check before Verdun in the last days of February, 1916, had to renounce the attack in the centre and devote his attention to the flanks—to fight the "Battle of the Wings" directed against Dead Man's Hill and Hill 304 on the west and Fort de Vaux on the east. Not until late April, with the hills taken and Fort de Vaux partially smothered, could he resume the direct thrust on Verdun. Before he could push this thrust home the Battle of the Somme diverted German reserves from Lorraine to Picardy. The attack on Verdun had to be abandoned.

Pershing's Second Phase was, accordingly, marked by two similar operations on his respective flanks, designed to abolish the German cross fire, which prevented the advance of his centre. On October 7th, 8th, and 9th there were attacks both across the Meuse and the Aire. That across the Meuse was only moderately fruitful, although the achievement of the 33rd, in crossing the deep river and the canal beyond it, was one of the most brilliant circumstances in the battle and a fitting climax to the operation of this division on September 26th. This crossing was made on October 8th, in conjunction with the attacks of American and French troops east of the river.

The manœuvre across the Aire was equally brilliant and wholly successful. The 77th, fighting in the Argonne Forest, performing feats of heroism and devotion which will always be memorable, was still unable to perform the impossible. Nor was the attack of the 28th, astride the Aire, capable of abolishing the deadly Argonne salient. Accordingly Pershing relieved the fraction of the 28th east of the Aire and replaced it by the 82nd, taken from corps reserve; and on October 7th, while the 77th and the 28th continued their pressure west of the Aire, the 82nd crossed the river—a feat of great daring—stormed the heights crowned by Châtel-Chehery, and reached Cornay the next day. "One of the most extraordinary feats of the whole battle," says Captain Page.

Thereupon the Germans in the Argonne, attacked frontally by the 77th and threatened on their flank and rear by the 28th and the 82nd, cleared out of the Forest and retired behind the Aire, while the 82nd, taking Marcq and repassing the Aire, took St. Juvin a few days later. In all these operations, as in the fighting north and east of the Aire, a certain number of controversies have arisen as to the credit for the taking of various towns, but however important this accurate appraisal of individual achievement may seem to the various units, it is relatively minor in the larger view. The contributions of the three divisions actually engaged in the reduction of the Argonne each possessed sufficient distinction to satisfy the most devoted partisans. The American army as a whole, moreover, can afford to be proud, both of the dogged and never-ending struggle of the 77th in the Argonne and of the dash and gallantry of the 82nd and the 33rd in the passage of the Aire and the Meuse.

By October 10th the operations in the Argonne and the Meuse Heights, corresponding to the "Battle of the Wings" in the Verdun offensive of 1916, were over, and Pershing was able to resume the thrust in the centre, which had been intended as the main attack all along but had been held up, after the first swift advance on September 26th, by the resistance of Montfaucon and again, on October 4th, by the cross fire from the Argonne and the Meuse Heights.

The Third Phase, from October 10th to November 1st, is a direct drive through the Kriemhilde Stellung from Grandpré, which the 77th approached on October 13th and 14th, to the Meuse at Brieulles.

In this last period the fighting is intense all along the line but the decisive progress is on either side of the Montfaucon-Bantheville highway which follows the little Andon brook through the Bantheville gap in the hills of the Kriemhilde Stellung.   In this advance, the 32nd takes and passes Romagne, future site of the great American cemetery, on October 14th. The 5th, to the right, takes Cunel, its crossroads, woods, and hills, on October 14th–17th.   The 42nd prolongs the advance to the left.   Then suddenly, about October 20th, a deep wedge begins to work through the Kriemhilde Line astride the Andon brook.   The 32nd enters Bantheville Forest and begins to encircle Landres-et-Saint-Georges.   The 89th takes over from the 32nd and extends the wedge, cleans up all of Bantheville Woods by October 21st and 22nd.   The 90th gets Bantheville while the 5th and 3rd clean up all the high ground between Bantheville and the Meuse Valley.   This means that by the end of October Pershing's centre is clear through the Kriemhilde system.

To the east, the progress is much slower in consequence of the even more difficult character of the country.   The 77th takes Grandpré on October 17th, but the 78th, relieving the 77th, is pushed out immediately and not until two weeks later is in possession of Taeema Farm, Grandpré, Belle Joyeuse Farm, and is still absolutely checked before the Bois-des-Loges, where it advanced into the woods after climbing the smooth slopes only to be driven out an innumerable number of times.   The 82nd is still checked along the St. Juvin-Landres-et-Saint-Georges Ridge, although it continues to hold St. Juvin, taken on October 15th.   The 42nd, fighting furiously, is held before the same ridge.

The real story of this final period from October 10th to October 31st is disclosed on the battle map whereon each day's advance is marked by a red line.   The whole story of the battle is in these lines, appropriately red because the price of the progress they reveal was paid in blood.

Looking at these successive days, the name of every hill and village will stir the memories of hundreds and thousands of men who knew in terms of sacrifice and suffering what each meant in October, 1918.   These day-by-day advances, insignificant even on the largest-scale map, are the inevitable circumstance of the war of positions. This is what the British army experienced at the Somme and in Flanders, the German army before Verdun, the French army on the Craonne Plateau in 1917. The battle is one of usury; precisely as long as both sides can continue to pour in reserves at this point of conflict the progress of the assailant will be slow and the wastage on both sides enormous. So far in the war of positions each side has been able to find reserves, and the assailant has been compelled to abandon the struggle either by weather, by losses, or by reason of an attack elsewhere. In meeting and halting the German attack at Verdun in 1916, the French used—not at once but in the aggregate—67 divisions, two thirds of their whole army, and their losses were 350,000. The Germans used fewer divisions but suffered slightly higher loss.

But, unlike all previous generals fighting on the defensive in such a contest, Marwitz cannot match division against division with his opponents. The thing that was sought at the Somme and in Flanders has at last been achieved in the Argonne. The time has come when the German can no longer find reserves to meet all three of his enemies. The result is that Pershing's attack, in his second phase, consumes all the German reserves, 47 divisions in line at one time or another during the struggle; and on October 31st, end of the Second Phase, not only has Liggett's army driven a wedge through the Kriemhilde Stellung, which is like more than one wedge the British drove through the German lines at the Somme, but the American battle has consumed all available German man-power. Positions, strong naturally if not fully prepared, are still in the German's hands, but his position is that of Lee after Five Forks. Marwitz might say, like the great Southern General, "My line has been stretched so thin that it has broken." The assault of the American First Army on November 1st was like the attack of the army of the Potomac about Petersburg on the morning following Five Forks. Positions of great strength, capable of indefinite resistance, were overrun in a few hours because Lee no longer had the troops to man them.

This, after all, is the true meaning of the Battle of the Meuse-Argonne. The effort to bring off a sudden rupture—and a rapid advance, to do the impossible—failed after preliminary success that at least justified the hope. Having missed the brilliant achievement, Pershing, like Haig after July 1st at the Somme, set to work to wear out the enemy whom he could not annihilate with a sudden blow. He did it in twenty-eight days. He succeeded where Haig failed because the Germans no longer had sufficient reserves to fight two major battles, one against the British along the Scheldt, and another with the Americans on the Meuse. It took four weeks to exhaust Germany's available resources. When they were exhausted, the road to Sedan was open.

Thus, in a very striking fashion, what Pershing did in the Meuse-Argonne and in a lesser degree at St. Mihiel—that is, in his campaign in Lorraine from September 12th to November 1st—was what Grant did in his campaign from the Rapidan to Petersburg in 1864. In each case the power for resistance of the defensive commander was broken by the weight of successive blows, no one of which of itself achieved the immediate success hoped for; but the cumulative effect of all the blows produced not merely victory, but in one case the destruction of the weaker army and, in the other, a retreat more precipitate than had yet taken place on the western front—a retreat not yet ended on Armistice Day—which had involved the surrender of one of the two vital lines of communication of the enemy.

Such was the true meaning of all those confused and confusing struggles in the Argonne Forest itself, for Côte Dame Marie, for Côte de Châtillon, Bois-des-Ognons, Bois-de-Pultierre, Bois-des-Loges, Bois-de-Cunel, and a hundred other hills and woodlands where our soldiers doggedly, obstinately, gloriously met and overcame the resistance of a desperate enemy far better trained and equipped, and, in the end, annihilated some of his finest divisions, still fighting with much of their old skill and determination. The places, after all—the trenches, the machine-gun emplacements, the lines themselves—are of minor significance. One may sum up the second and decisive phase of the Battle of the Meuse-Argonne by the simple statement that, on a front less than twenty miles wide and four miles deep, Pershing's First Army fought, wore out, and defeated decisively all the divisions Ludendorff could collect to cover his vital communications, and, when this four weeks of fighting was over, swept forward in a practically unresisted march of victory which reached and passed all the objectives indicated as the goals of the campaign.

VI.   THE FINAL PHASE

On November 1st opens the final phase.   The German Fifth Army has been fought to a standstill.   Forty-seven divisions have been used east and west of the Meuse, mainly to the west; thirteen of these have been used twice and two, three times.   Not a few of the German divisions have actually been destroyed, and the commander of at least one has been captured, with the fragments of his division.   His honourable boast it was that he had led his unit to the extreme point of penetration of the German advance both in Picardy and at the Marne.   Against this formidable concentration twenty-two American divisions and four French had fought.   Eleven of our divisions had been used twice and one, three times.

The attack of November 1st was delivered by the First Army, west of the Meuse.   Three army corps and seven divisions were employed between the Meuse and the Bourgogne Forest.   On the right the Third Corps had the 5th and the 90th divisions.   In the centre the Fifth Corps had the 2nd and the 89th and was again the wedge of attack as on September 26th.   On the left, the First Corps had the 80th, 77th, and 78th divisions.

"The general assault was preceded," says Pershing, "by two hours of violent artillery preparation.   The infantry advanced, closely followed by accompanying guns.   The artillery acquitted itself magnificently, the barrages being so well coördinated and so dense that the enemy was overwhelmed and quickly submerged by the rapid onslaught of the infantry.   By nightfall the Fifth Corps, in the centre, had realized an advance of almost nine kilometres (just short of six miles) to the Bois-de-la-Folie, and had completed the capture of the heights of Barricourt,

By Claggett Wilson

A SHELL HOLE ON THE CHEMIN DES DAMES

Claggett Wilson went to France in the ranks of the 5th Regiment of Marines in June, 1917. In the spring of 1918 he was transferred to the French Fourth Army for experience as a line officer and saw action on the Chemin des Dames, Rheims, Verdun, and later at Château-Thierry. During the winter of 1918–19 he was with the Army of Occupation in Germany. He was wounded twice and received the Croix de Guerre.

while the Third Corps, on the right, had captured Aincreville and Ande-
vanne. Our troops had broken through the enemy's last defence,
captured his artillery position, and had precipitated a retreat of the
German forces about to be isolated in the forest north of Grandpré.

"On November 2nd and 3rd we advanced rapidly against heavy fighting on the fronts of the right and centre corps; to the left the troops of the
First Corps hurried forward in pursuit, some by motor trucks; while the
artillery pressed along the country roads close behind. Our heavy artillery
was skillfully brought into position to fire upon the railroad from Carignan
to Sedan (Metz-Mézières), and the junctions at Longuyon and Conflans."

At the same time the 77th and the 80th passed on either side
of Buzancy; thenceforth the battle degenerated into a pursuit race,
and on November 7th elements of the 42nd were on the left bank
of the Meuse facing Sedan—actually astride the Metz-Mézières railroad. Officially it was the French who first entered the city, but the
citizens of Sedan testify that the first Allied troops in their town belonged to the "Rainbow" Division.

In the same period there had been a general crossing of the Meuse
by Liggett's right and centre while the left was moving on Sedan.
The 90th Division took Stenay (once the place of residence of the
German Crown Prince); on the last morning of the battle, while
the 5th passed the river at Dun, pressed through the forests which
cover the northern end of the Heights of the Meuse, and occupied
Louppy on the Loison, taking the château of the Marquis d'Imécourt
which had been Marwitz's headquarters during the battle. The 32nd
crossed the Loison at Jametz, also clearing the Heights of the Meuse.

To the southward the 79th, 26th, and 81st American divisions,
with French assistance, completed the clearing of the Meuse Heights in
the region which had seen the opening of the attack on Verdun in 1916.
At the close of the struggle, the 26th was close to the famous Twin
Hills of Ornes from which the Kaiser had watched the Verdun battle and
beneath which, in the great forest of Spincourt, the Germans had
massed their batteries for the opening phase of that struggle. There is
a hill on the Verdun-Sedan highway above Mouzon—where in 1870

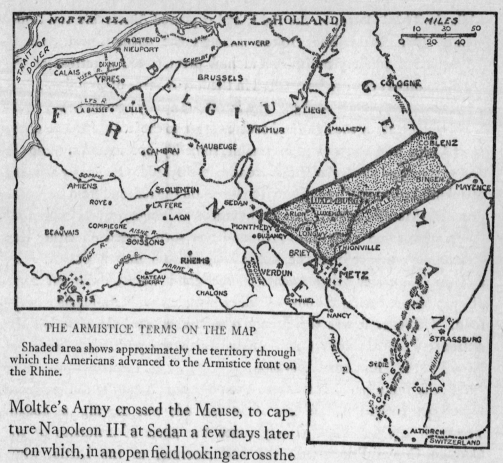

THE ARMISTICE TERMS ON THE MAP

Shaded area shows approximately the territory through which the Americans advanced to the Armistice front on the Rhine.

Moltke's Army crossed the Meuse, to capture Napoleon III at Sedan a few days later —on which, in an open field looking across the river over all its battleground, the Fifth Corps has erected a simple but satisfying monument of rough stones and of mortar with German swords, bayonets, and helmets cemented in, which marks the extreme point of advance of the American army—of the Fifth Corps, which was the centre, in the Battle of the Meuse-Argonne. Here, with the river passed and with Montmédy and the Belgian frontier in sight of the 5th Division above Louppy, is the high-water mark of America in battle in the World War, the point reached on Armistice morning.

What might have followed, had the Armistice not intervened, is only in part a matter of conjecture. The roads to Luxemburg and Briey, taken by our troops when the march to the Rhine began, were already open; the power for effective resistance of Marwitz's army was broken. Moreover, while the American Second Army was in line for operations northwest of Metz, Mangin, with six American corps, was ready for a thrust southeast of the fortress, between it and the Vosges. The evacuation of Metz had indeed begun, and American progress, already inevitable, would have hastened it. To the Americans would unquestionably have fallen the chief honour of restoring Metz to France, within a few days, had German resistance continued.

The actual fruits of American victory were measured in the capture of 26,000 prisoners, 847 guns, and 3,000 machine guns, together with a vast accumulation of war material. In its two months of existence, the American army in France had taken 42,000 prisoners, 1,290 guns, and enormous amounts of material. The American loss at the Meuse-Argonne was 117,000; 124,000 in the St. Mihiel and Meuse-Argonne conflicts combined. Twenty-two American divisions had been engaged, while at the moment of the Armistice the total of American divisions which had seen action was 29 and the number of organized divisions in France 42. Reckoning the original strength of the 22 divisions at 600,000, which is high, and the replacements at 150,000, which is also high, we had, engaged, around 750,000 men in the battle; 700,000 is probably more accurate, but our numbers actually engaged at any one moment did not exceed 300,000. Six French divisions, approximately 60,000, had also been under Pershing's command during the conflict, bringing his total up to approximately 660,000, while the Germans, using 47 divisions, certainly did not engage much more than 400,000. The theoretical strength of our 29 combat divisions in France on November 11th and already battle-trained was 1,200,000.

VII. THE ACHIEVEMENT

What individual divisions or their commanders accomplished, splendid as the deeds were, cannot be examined here. Of Pershing's subordinates, four—Bullard, Liggett, Summerall, in the fighting, and Harbord, in his brief but splendid battle service at Château-Thierry and the Soissons "corner" and his even more considerable contribution in the Service of Supplies—deserve mention in any study, however summary. Liggett, Bullard, and Dickman ultimately commanded armies,

Liggett succeeding Pershing on October 12th and carrying the Meuse-Argonne action forward to supreme success; Bullard taking over the Second Army and bringing it into shape in the brief time following his promotion and preceding the Armistice. Dickman commanded the Army of Occupation after the Armistice.

But necessarily the larger praise must fall to the Commander-in-Chief. Neither in strategy nor in tactics was he called upon or even permitted by circumstances to disclose his resources. It was not in the application of the science of war that he acquired distinction. His supreme service lay in correctly estimating the fighting capacity of his green troops, their capacity for hard, indescribably bitter, and murderous fighting under well-nigh-impossible conditions of country and of weather, coupled with their ability to endure losses, made inevitable by their lack of training and defects in equipment and in accessories. It was this spirit that drove men, again and again, armed only with the bayonet, against machine-gun nests and wired and organized positions, suffering losses very nearly approximating extermination, but losing neither confidence nor determination.

Exact appraisal of what was accomplished does not lessen the achievement of the general or of his army. The American army which fought in the Meuse-Argonne was not superior in morale to the British army which had struggled at the Somme in 1916 or in Flanders in 1917. It was not superior to the French armies, which had won the Marne, defended Verdun, entered the campaign of 1917. It was not superior in this respect to the German army which advanced to the Marne in 1914, attacked Verdun in 1916, or opened the Battle of Picardy in 1918. But, while the youth of all three of the great European contestants had disappeared in the struggle and the survivors were weary beyond words, after hideous and unforgettable disappointments following supreme effort, our men were fresh to their work, unshaken in nerve, unslackened by disappointment.

Nor was our army in any sense a perfect machine directed by a general staff comparable with those of France or Germany. It had not even reached that wholly restricted stage of progress marked by the

British at the Somme, for in 1916 Great Britain had far more trained officers, who had been trained under modern conditions. It was still in the stage of improvisation; officers and men were learning—in the most wasteful and expensive fashion in which soldiers can learn— paying the price America and England have always paid for their peace-time neglect of their armies.

And our army did not spring from the bosom of the nation fully armed and equipped. On the contrary, we were able to engage a vast army in Europe eighteen months after we entered the contest only be- cause our Allies supplied the mechanical equipment. We fought our battles with French cannon and French munitions, exclusively. The failure of an aviation programme was responsible for heavy losses in the Meuse-Argonne, which were totally unnecessary, had we begun in 1914 to put our small army on a proper basis for contemporary conflict. Even in motor transport, we depended largely upon our Allies to the end. But the fact that France could and did furnish most of the tools, covered the failure of the Government, which, in the last analysis, was the failure of the American people, to a dangerous degree, dangerous because the lessons that should have been taught were once more concealed by accidents and fortunate circumstances.

Had our young army undertaken its Meuse-Argonne campaign against a German army such as Nivelle attacked with his veterans at the Aisne in 1917, the result would have been, not mere defeat but swift, complete, and incalculable disaster. Exactly the same thing would have occurred if Pershing with his army had been asked to solve the problem of Haig in Flanders in that same year. Fortunately, when our hour came, the decline in German morale, fighting resources, the reduction of their reserves had reached a point where our superior morale, unlimited numbers, and enormous physical superiority bridged the gap created by the difference between American training and that of German.

Pershing saw that this would happen; he saw it before the Second Marne, and again and again assured Foch that American troops could be used, despite their lack of experience and incomplete training. His opinion was confirmed by the events in the Aisne-Marne fighting, by the St. Mihiel episode, and by the long, gruelling, but successful Battle of the Meuse-Argonne. The French did not believe that American troops could fight successfully under American commanders and as divisional units in the early summer, because of their lack of training. The French would have been right, had the German condition been that of any previous period of the war; but it was not.

In. the late summer the French were still convinced that the American force could not be operated as an army for exactly the same reason, and because, in addition, the training of an army staff is a matter of years, not weeks. Again they were right in theory and wrong in fact, because they were thinking of the German of the past, while Pershing's new army would have to deal with the German of the present. They accurately forecast the check of the American offensive between the Meuse and the Argonne at the precise point where the check came. But they did not foresee that, after the check, Pershing's green army could literally eat up German reserves, paying for their meal in generous and terrible costs, and, in the end, by main strength, force their way through when the German had no more reserves to throw into action. It was at this point that French calculation, eminently correct in the main, broke down and Pershing's estimate proved the more accurate. In a long war there comes a moment when weariness concedes much to be impossible, but to the untired man there is nothing impossible, and Pershing and his army were unwearied.

To compare the American army, on the scientific side, with the German, the French, or even the British which had been at the real practice of modern war a far briefer time than either, is utter nonsense. It is by measuring its accomplishment in terms of the tools it possessed, the training which it had received, the experience of its officers, that one acquires the real and just estimate of its performance. It was called upon to do what had hitherto proven impossible in the war of positions— and the Battle of the Meuse-Argonne from September 26th to November 1st was a battle of positions—it did the impossible because in the autumn of 1918 the impossible had become just possible, but only for brave, determined, absolutely self-sacrificing men.

By far the most just and generous measure of American achievement is furnished by General Maurice, of the British army, 'an accomplished soldier and in every sense the preëminent British military critic. He writes:

It is probably true that no French or British staff would, after long experience of previous failure, have advised an attack on the Meuse-Argonne front until elaborate improvements and extensions of the roads and railways behind the front of attack had been carried out and until equally elaborate preparation for prolonging those roads and railways into the territory captured from the Germans had been completed. It is probably equally true that French and British soldiers, after the bitter lessons of the past, would not have attacked with any confidence unless they had ocular evidence that everything had been done beforehand to help them forward. There are times and occasions in war when the valour of ignorance has its advantages. With greater experience the American infantry would have learned to overcome the German machine guns with less loss of life, and the services of supply would have worked more smoothly. Had the American army waited to gain that experience, the war would certainly have been prolonged by at least six months and the cost of life would have been certainly greater than it was.

Pershing must have taken all these factors into consideration when he threw in his vote for fighting the great battle which began on September 26th. He decided that the vigour and valour of his troops would more than counter-balance their lack of battle experience, and he was justified by the result.

"Did America win the War?" No. The campaign of 1918, in France, which ended in victory, was won by the supreme genius of Ferdinand Foch, who was able to direct the operations of more than 6,000,000 men who first and last fought in three great armies, the French, British, and American, with precious assistance furnished by the tiny Belgian force in such fashion that the enemy attack was broken, the enemy strength shaken, and in the final operation completely and decisively destroyed—the will to war and the capacity for resistance annihilated.

Foch could not have won the war without American forces, with anything but a huge American contribution, and he could not have won it in 1918 if the American troops had not been able, led by a man who forced his European associates to recognize the ability of his army, to do what, as late as September, 1918, no one expected it would be able to do. We were the reserves which arrived at the decisive moment, and our arrival enabled the master to repeat the achievement of Napoleon at Marengo and win a battle three times lost. And this is glory enough; to claim more is to be unworthy of our own soldiers. For behind 1918, behind July, 1918, when we began, lay the terrible years in which France had saved the war at the Marne and at Verdun and Britain had wasted the German at the Somme and in Flanders. Even in the current year, the resistance of the British and the employment of French reserves had prevented German triumph in two struggles, unexampled in all previous history of war.

Beside the Meuse-Argonne, all other American battles are insignificant, and in no one of its earlier conflicts was the nation more nobly served by an army and a commander, by officers and common soldiers, and general and officers agree in awarding the chief glory and supreme praise to the soldier, for the Meuse-Argonne was, in the very nature of things, a "soldier's battle," and the American soldier won it.

On the battlefield where Petain had said, immortally, "They shall not pass!" Pershing had said, simply, "We will go!"—and both proud prophecies were realized to the undying glory of France and the United States.

CHAPTER ELEVEN

THE ARMISTICE

I
THE CONQUEST OF LUDENDORFF

The first of the series of German proposals which led to the Armistice of November 11th was uttered by the German Government on October 5th. It saw the light of day at the precise moment when Haig had broken through the Hindenburg Line between St. Quentin and Le Catelet, when Pershing, despite temporary check, was exerting enormous pressure between the Meuse and the Argonne. But before we examine this document, it is necessary to look backward and see the origin of the German decision expressed with ever-growing clarity in the succession of documents issued prior to the final meeting at Rethondes.

It is to Ludendorff that history must turn now and hereafter for any clear explanation of the German surrender. Upon him the Government relied necessarily, as the master of the military destinies of his country, to avert defeat. When the hour arrived in which he became convinced that disaster could be avoided only by negotiation, by armistice, he notified his government: first, that the war could not be won; secondly, that it might be lost if negotiations were not pressed rapidly. The Government first did nothing; then, seized with a panic, sought to reconstruct the ministry, reorganize the electoral and political system of Prussia, and finally, revolution arriving, capitulated, while the Emperor, his heir, and the kings and kinglets of Germany fled the country.

Of the explanation for all this sudden, enormous transformation, Ludendorff from first to last betrays no comprehension, explains frankly that it passes his understanding. Still bewildered, in the closing hours his emperor dismisses him for signing an order urging that the war continue, and Ludendorff goes, sadly forecasting, quite correctly, that within a fortnight the House of Hohenzollern will cease to rule.　Yet underlying all else it is plain that the responsibility is Ludendorff's.　Germany, the dynasty, the system, everything was founded upon the rock of military invincibility; when the rock was riven, all crumbled.

The progress of the idea of defeat in Ludendorff's mind is one of the most amazing stories of the whole war, not always told truthfully by Ludendorff himself.　But in his narrative the truth is always discernible, sometimes by confession, sometimes by the manner in which, with true Prussian arrogance, he orders it from his presence, denounces it like a drill-sergeant, establishes it by denying it.　A strange psychological study is this narrative—something more than a mere memoir of Ludendorff—in truth, the revelation of the soul of the Prussian soldier, exactly the sort of document which might have issued from one of the generals of Frederick the Great, who saw the Frederickan methods collapse, when, with Frederick in his grave, they were employed against Napoleon.

To begin at the beginning, the first chill seizes the German Chief Quartermaster after his first two efforts, March 21st and May 27th, have failed to achieve a decision.　He feels the disillusionment behind him, but neither he nor his associates share it.　Still, in June, Kühlmann blurts out his prophetic words that military victory is henceforth impossible, impossible for Germany, but the truth finishes Kühlmann and he is no longer Secretary of State.　Hintze, the successor, pleases Ludendorff who regards the home front as restored.

But time marches.　Foch strikes back between the Aisne and the Marne and Ludendorff recognizes at once that the thing he undertook to do in March is no longer possible in July, he cannot crush the Allies before the Americans arrive in Europe; they have arrived and the situation is serious.　He stops his attack and assumes the defensive but— significant circumstance for the psychologist—the Second Battle of the Marne lost, he writes of the desire and need for rest: "Whether the enemy would let us have it was the question!"　Now Clausewitz and all his German soldier followers down to Bernhardi have asserted that the ultimate purpose of war is to make the enemy submit to your will,

and, the Second Battle of the Marne lost, Ludendorff's words suggest—
his "let" confesses—whose will is now in subjection.

Still Ludendorff hopes for a successful defensive. He prevented
Allied victory by his operations in 1916 at the Somme, in 1917 at
the Aisne and in Flanders. Recalling these stupendous assaults is there
any reason to believe that he will be less successful now? Early in
August he can still decide that his army will be able to defeat the coming
offensives. Since he has always found a strategical remedy, Ludendorff
sees no reason to doubt that he will be equally fortunate now. His army,
on the whole, satisfies him, even after the first defeat.

But on August 8th the light suddenly breaks in upon him. Haig
smashes his line by the Somme; his troops run away, refuse to fight,
curse their officers and their government. Nothing like this has been
seen in Prussian ranks since Iena and Auerstädt in 1806, never expected
again in German quarters. A "black day," the first of many black days
to come! And it brings Ludendorff briefly to the decision, memorable
henceforth, that the war must be ended.

Instinctively one turns back four years—almost exactly—to the
days when Foch was fighting at Fère-Champenoise, when, after defeat
and retreat for four days, on the morning of the fifth he reports to
Joffre: "My centre is retiring, my right is broken, impossible to
manœuvre. *The situation is excellent. I attack.*" A hard situation,
Foch later explains to André de Maricourt; hard because the soldiers are
weary. The old orders, like an old tune, no longer enthuse them. They
say: "We have been beaten to that tune and we will march to it no
more." Then Foch explains. The great test arrives; one must hit upon
something new—something that seems new, for the problem does not
change, cannot change—something which will lead the soldier to say:
"Ha, we haven't tried that before, have we?" And he does try that,
perhaps successfully, perhaps not; but time is gained until the moment
arrives, the moment at Fère-Champenoise when the blow could be
delivered.

Now Ludendorff has no "new tune"; he has no "new mantle to wrap
round the old, threadbare costume"—another figure that Foch employed.

He says quite frankly that the war must end.   August 13th–14th he explains his views to a conference held at Spa, attended by the Emperor and Hintze.   This interview is prolonged by reports furnished by Arz, Austrian general, the Austrian Emperor, Charles, also being in attendance.   There is great talk about a Polish arrangement, about all sorts of things.   Then Hintze goes home to talk to party leaders, to tell them what Ludendorff says—that the enemy cannot be forced by an offensive to sue for peace, that the defensive cannot bring peace; that the army is showing signs of collapse, on August 8th, and now again on August 20th—this time in front of Mangin, "another black day for Germany."   Out of this conference there proceeds exactly nothing: a few vague words spoken in the Reichstag, a general expansion of the wave of depression, but of action, nothing.   Meantime, the situation becomes worse, daily. The Allies advance, the retreat to the Hindenburg Line is enforced, the German armies reach the line in bad condition, having suffered enormously.   On September 26th—the date is memorable—Pershing breaks the Hindenburg Line in the Argonne; and in the next two days the British break it in Picardy, the Anglo-Franco-Belgian group, in Flanders.

II.   LUDENDORFF'S DECISION

Thereupon, Ludendorff acts—goes into Hindenburg's office at six o'clock on the afternoon of September 28th—a busy afternoon for Pershing, now north of Montfaucon, and for Rawlinson, entering the Hindenburg Line victoriously at the Scheldt Tunnel—and declares that there must be a request for an armistice; that the situation can only grow worse.   To all of which the old Hindenburg nods his massive head, will continue to the end to have faith in the old German God and hope for a miracle, but never omits to nod when Ludendorff speaks.   Armistice means evacuation of all occupied territory; to Ludendorff it means something worse, an admission of defeat; but the admission has to be made, and Ludendorff and Hindenburg shake hands over it, "as men burying their dearest hopes!"   Hintze wept when Ludendorff told him the worst in August.

In a new conference, on September 29th—for which Foch's orchestra plays disconcerting music in Flanders, in Picardy, in Lorraine—Ludendorff suddenly discovers that before there can be action there must be a change of government. These politicians, so he reveals his thought, talk of a change of government at the moment when the German army is crumbling. Will a new ministry affect Foch? But it has to be, Ludendorff agrees. Hindenburg nods once more, but the note, the demand for an armistice, must issue on October 1st; the date is furnished by Hintze, who wept and will weep, but cannot hurry the politicians or achieve a change of government in three days, not even if these three days are filled with reports of the collapse of the Hindenburg Line, of the Siegfried system, gone with the Wotan the Brunhilde crumbling, a true *Gotterdämmerung*.

Ludendorff is still dissatisfied, therefore he has recourse to a new device: he sends one of his best-informed subordinates up to Berlin with a carefully prepared statement of the exact military situation, to be read to the Reichstag leaders. This is on the night of October 2nd, the news from all the battle fronts continues evil; Bulgaria conquered and surrendered; Turkey conquered and soon to surrender; Austria awaiting the last blow, now in sight; Pershing only just checked, no one can see for how long, Haig unchecked, just beginning to emerge on the German side of the Hindenburg Line; King Albert on the outskirts of Roulers, Bruges, Ghent; the Belgian "pawn" losing its value for the bargain German diplomacy has always had in mind, if worst comes to worst.

Ludendorff's lieutenant, Major Baron von dem Busche, despite his name a direct sort of person, performs his duty; he tells the Reichstag that wastage can no longer be replaced; battalions are shrinking; the "absorption of reserves," lucidly explained by General Buat, proceeding at an unbelievable rate—Allied attacks now piling one on top of the other as Buat indicated; the morale worsening in due proportion; that it is time to make up their minds that the war is "hopeless." He tells them that what is bad will be worse, will grow worse with every twenty-four hours—that the enemy is getting nearer and nearer to the realization of his aim; in substance, that the situation is desperate, the armistice must be sought immediately, but there must be no outward disclosure of the weakness inwardly manifest.

The result of this exposition of Major Baron von dem Busche might have been foreseen. It produced a panic. Ludendorff had been a little too successful in his effort to hasten things. Instead of being hurried, the whole audience, the whole legislative branch of the German Government, succumbs to the panic. Its world has crumbled suddenly; it has never suspected the truth, despite outward evidences of less fortunate days. It has left everything to the army, and now the army announces with brutally frank words that the war is lost; that High Command, army, everything will collapse in irremediable ruin if the civil government does not get an armistice at once; calls upon it to act, and to act with the appearance of strength. Napoleon made similar demands upon the French legislature in his last days, after having kept it in utter ignorance and servile attitude for years—and with the same result.

Compare this performance with that of the first days of June, when the Germans were at the Marne, forty miles from Paris, their shells falling in the city, their Gothas sowing destruction in the boulevards. Then Clemenceau had told the people how dangerous were the days in which they lived, but he had also told them—Ludendorff read the speech and admired it: "I will fight before Paris, through Paris, behind Paris." But no one speaks this word now in Germany. Ludendorff has succumbed to that moral test, which Foch triumphantly passed at Fère-Champenoise as far back as September, 1914. German leadership is failing now.

In all the history of this World War, to me there seems nothing more tragically satisfying than these next few days. The German structure rested upon the single foundation-stone of force, physical force, embodied by the army. The force begins to crumble; the hour arrives when there is required moral strength, not more than was asked of the Allied leaders in March and in June, but without moral strength all is lost. And in this hour, while the war is still ten times as far from Berlin as it was from Paris in June and not an inch of German territory involved, leaders, civil and military alike, are seized with paralysis. Their universe has crumbled and they, unlike Foch, cannot improvise; their people and their armies will no longer march to the old tune, they have been beaten marching to it—and the new tune cannot be found. Gambetta found it in 1870. After Sedan, after Metz, there was still France left, and men who could vitalize the conception; but now the German mass is sinking, the granite is becoming clay, the clay softens with each hour.

Ludendorff does not understand the panic he has produced, examines Major Baron von dem Busche with great care but no result. Discovers that a Pole was present at the session, and, as a Pole would—having known Prussia as arrogant and mighty for a century and a half, beholding it shaken and shaking—rushes out and tells the world. And the whole world shortly hears that Germany is in a panic, a circumstance which will contribute to the interpretation that Paris and London, even Washington, will put upon the request for an armistice when it does come, as it must come now.

But meantime there must be the inevitable political manœuvre, a new cabinet. Germany cannot change the tune, to revert again to Foch's figure, so it will seek to change the instruments on which the old tune has been played—a futile performance, Ludendorff correctly asserts. Then, on October 3rd, Ludendorff absent but Hindenburg present, the new cabinet meets and hears from Hindenburg a recapitulation of the Ludendorff view—"there appears to be now no possibility, to the best of human judgment, of winning peace from our enemies by force of arms." Hindenburg adds a pencil note to the effect that Great Headquarters, in advocating an armistice, as the statement indicates, is solely influenced by a desire to obtain an honourable peace. A thoughtful qualification, useful in the future when responsibilities come to be fixed, but a codicil in a last will and testament, becoming valid only after death.

The next day, the new ministry established, the business of the note disposed of, the action is at last taken, seven days after Ludendorff advised it as of immediate necessity. And, in consequence, on the morning of October 5th, the people of Paris, London, Washington, of the whole Allied world, read headlines arranged to meet the conditions of national interest: "Pershing victorious in a new attack." "Haig is through the Hindenburg Line." "Petain surrounds Laon." "Prisoners taken since September 1st, 123,000; since July 15th, 250,000." "Czar of Bulgaria abdicates." "Panic in Berlin as Allies Advance from Ypres to Verdun." And finally: "The new German Chancellor, Maximilian of Baden, requests the President of the United States to Undertake the Restoration of Peace, Germany Asking an Immediate Armistice." The basis of this peace is to be the Reichstag proposal of July, 1917, before the Russian collapse, before the Treaty of Brest-Litovsk, before the Treaty of Bukharest: "No annexations and no indemnities." But Foch's figure still stands; this is an old tune, too; the world is marching to Foch's music. And the fact, witnessed by all the yellowing newspapers of that hour, is that the proposal falls flat; newspaper readers glance at it impatiently, and then back at the reports from the fronts, official reports of towns liberated, positions taken, prisoners and guns captured. Allied publics are, in truth, at the beginning of the most satisfying month ever lived by the newspaper readers of nations at war. "Leave it to Foch," begins to be heard from one end of the world to the other.

III. "UNCONDITIONAL SURRENDER"

The first German note, which cost so much in labour and resulted in so little—little that was advantageous to the German—had incalculable consequences in the Allied world, where it was the first authentic sign of the dawn, after four long years of ineffable darkness. It read:

The German Government requests the President of the United States to take in hand the restoration of peace, acquaint all the belligerent states of this request, and invite them to send plenipotentiaries for the purpose of opening peace negotiations.

It accepts the programme set forth by the President of the United States in his message to Congress on January 8th and in his later pronouncements, especially in his speech of September 28th, as a basis for peace negotiations.

With a view to avoiding further bloodshed, the German Government requests the immediate conclusion of an armistice on land and sea.

The speech of January 8th, the message to Congress, was, in fact, the Fourteen Points; that of September 28th, spoken at the

THE LAST DAYS OF FIGHTING

U. S. Official Photo

AT THE BRIDGEHEAD BOUNDARY LINE

One of the many American machine guns covering the neutral zone. The German towns of Frickhofen and Durndorf are within range

AN AMERICAN SENTRY ON GUARD ON NOVEMBER 11th

Brown Brothers

He is standing on the line of the farthest American advance before the fighting stopped. At his feet is a shell hole
from a German gun

THE AMERICANS ON THE MARCH TO THE RHINE

Before the ladders could be taken down from the arch of welcome erected in Mersch, Luxembourg, to greet the American army on the march to the Rhine, troops of the 2nd Division were pouring through the city in motor trucks, and the work of building and decorating the arch had to be completed while the Americans were actually marching beneath it.

THE AMERICAN WATCH ON THE RHINE
Sentries from the Rainbow Division on the water front

IN AN OUTPOST IN ALSACE

Two doughboys ready for action with an automatic rifle

U. S. *Official Photo*

IN HONOUR OF ROOSEVELT

These American soldiers in Germany are firing a 21-gun salute two days after the Colonel's death at his home in Oyster Bay

SUNSET

American sentries guarding a road near Otzingen, Germany

THE AMERICAN FLAG ENTERING A TOWN IN GERMANY

U. S. Official Photo

A VICTORY LOAN POSTER IN GERMANY, APRIL, 1919

U. S. Official Photo

ALL ABOARD

Showing how the 85,000 German helmets were loaded on the train for transportation from Metternich, Germany, to the United States for the Fifth Liberty Loan

ON THE RHINE

Provost guards of the city of Coblentz in the foreground. Fortress of Ehrenbreitstein in the background

opening of the campaign for the Fourth Liberty Loan in New York City, memorable for the assertion: "Militarism must go, root and branch."

Two references damned the German document, two references to peace by negotiation. Neither the nations of Europe nor America, engaged in war with Germany, longer thought of peace by negotiation—the hour for that, thank God, had passed. Across America like wildfire ran the unforgettable words of Grant at Donelson: "Unconditional surrender; I propose to move upon your works at once." And in Europe and America, German bad faith in the past forbade belief in German good faith now, if there were yet good faith.

Accordingly, the President replied on October 6th—no delay necessary on his side of the debate—by three questions:

What does the German Chancellor mean by accepting the two utterances of January 8th and September 28th? Does he mean that the negotiations will be no more than discussions of their application in detail?

Is Germany ready to retire from the invaded regions? If not, of course the President would not feel at liberty to recommend a cessation of hostilities to his associates, without such an evidence of good faith.

Finally, for whom is the Chancellor speaking? The "Old Gang"? The actual text of the note follows:

Does the Imperial Chancellor mean that the Imperial German Government accepts the terms laid down by the President in his address to the Congress of the United States of the 8th of January last, and any subsequent addresses, and that its object in entering into a discussion would be to agree on the practical details of their application?

The President feels bound to say with regard to the suggestion of an armistice that he would not feel at liberty to propose a cessation of hostilities to the governments with which the Government of the United States is associated against the Central Powers so long as the armies of those powers are upon their soil. The good faith of any discussion would manifestly depend on the consent of the Central Powers immediately to withdraw their forces everywhere from invaded territory.

The President also feels that he is justified in asking whether the Imperial Chancellor was speaking merely for the constituted authorities of the Empire who have so far conducted the war. He deems the answer to these questions vital from every point of view.

A moderate and non-committal response, calculated to cause the Germans many misgivings and getting them nowhere, but widely criticised at the moment because the President consented to talk with the Germans at all! "More note-writing," harsher critics said—a criticism no longer valid. The benefit derived from the President's conversations may be exaggerated, but of harm there was not the least. Foch was continuing; he was doing more, he was quickening the pace.

Four days later, the new German Secretary of State for the Foreign Office, Doctor Solf, replies by informing the President that the new Ministry is supported by the great majority of the Reichstag, and that, thus supported, the new chancellor speaks for the great mass of the German people. All that Doctor Solf or anybody else could say under the circumstances, but it proves new cause for protest in Allied countries, particularly in the United States, still clinging to the Wattersonian war cry, "To hell with the Hohenzollerns and the Hapsburgs!" repeated perfectly reverently.

And at just this moment a German submarine must sink a British passenger boat in the Irish Sea; of 150 women and children only seventeen are saved. Still another puts under a Japanese steamer with more women and children similarly murdered. A worse disaster for the German peace offensive than the loss of the Hindenburg Line itself was this new submarine activity! On the heels of this, with both events in mind, the President writes his second reply:

The President acknowledges Germany's acceptance of his terms, without apparent qualification, reminds her that evacuation and armistice are military matters, things that military men must look after.

"See Foch about those," is the direct implication.
Then he continues:

No arrangement can be accepted by the Government of the United States which does not provide absolutely satisfactory safeguards and guarantees of the present military supremacy of the armies of the United States and the Allies in the field.

This means, can mean only, disarmament.
Then the President calls attention to "illegal and inhumane"

methods of German soldiers and sailors. He is thinking of the *Leinster* on water and the still-continuing devastations of the German armies in the region they are evacuating: Lens, Cambrai, Douai—the first destroyed, the other two partially ruined—of St. Quentin, with its cathedral pillars undermined for dynamite, destruction only prevented by the swiftness of the entrance of Debeney. While these offences persist, all thought of armistice is useless. Then the President continues:

The destruction of every arbitrary power anywhere that can separately, secretly, and of its single choice disturb the peace of the world, or if it cannot be presently destroyed, at least its reduction to virtual impotency.

The power which has hitherto controlled the German nation is of the sort here described. It is within the choice of the German nation to alter it.

The President feels bound to say that the whole process of peace will, in his judgment, depend upon the definiteness and the satisfactory character of the guarantees which can be given in this fundamental matter. It is indispensable that the governments associated against Germany should know beyond a peradventure with whom they are dealing.

Now it is time to turn back to Ludendorff. On the military side the situation is this: Pershing is still checked, it is costing incredible effort to hold him, but he is being held, will be held for two more weeks. Haig is through the Hindenburg Line, but the Germans from the sea to the Meuse are getting back, crippled but unbroken as to front, to the Hermann Line, line of the Scheldt; there is preparing behind them the line of the Meuse-Antwerp. Most important of all, the German army is fighting, on the whole, better than before, not giving the smallest basis for any hope of victory, but holding out the prospect, rather slim but still discoverable, of keeping together until winter stops the fighting. Prince Max, the new chancellor, ministers, and newspapers generally, are at this moment uttering brave words, calling upon each other and the army to stand firm; and the army is standing relatively firm, firmer than before.

Wilson's second note comes to Ludendorff in this situation as the unmistakable proof of the determination of the enemy to demand unconditional surrender. The determination to "destroy Germany" was, for him, instinct in the President's letter to Solf. Whether Wilson was sincere in seeking peace by understanding and was overborne by Clemenceau and Lloyd George, Ludendorff does not know, but now there was left but one thing to do: to fight it out, to rouse the country, to appeal to the people. The peace manœuvre had served only to reveal the true state of Allied purpose. Now the hour was come, too, for Prince Max and everyone else to translate their brave words into deeds. Ludendorff had advised peace; if it could be had by negotiation. He was willing to consent to evacuate occupied territories, the military circumstances warranted so much, but he insisted that the armies should stand ready to fight, within their own frontiers, against the possibility of the failure of negotiations.

But Foch believed he could destroy the German army before it reached the frontiers; the Allied publics believed it; soldiers and civilians in Allied countries believed that the German peace manœuvre was, after all, intended solely to save the army, caught now in the vise between Pershing and Haig, doomed to supreme military disaster if the fighting continued. The peace manœuvre had failed, there was nothing left but to resume the fighting. Ludendorff was ready. He was ready, but, unfortunately for him, the situation, momentarily better, was now worsening again, would grow worse henceforth rapidly to the end.

Wilson's second note causes more conferences in Berlin. Ludendorff attends and is asked more questions. Can the war be won? Same answer: No. Not unless the luck of Tannenberg returns. There is one more careful, sorrowful examination of the situation, search for some possible avenue of escape, examination of questions of reserves, of the transfer of troops from the Ukraine. No hope here. As for the western front, Ludendorff believes a break through possible but not probable, does not expect it "on my conscience." But the fighting might grow worse any moment.

This amounts to an effort of the civil government, the new ministry come to power at this awful moment, to take account of stock. It examines the army commander, puts him through one rigorous test after another, submits a formal questionnaire, containing the old questions in a fresh form. But the answer is always the same. Ludendorff does not want to break off with Wilson, he wants to continue. On the other hand, bad as the situation is, it seems better to fight than to consent to dishonour, to destruction, implied in the suggestion of disarmament.

In the face of this testimony the civil government, weak perhaps, did a thoroughly human thing: it consented to abandon the submarine campaign, issued orders to that effect. For Ludendorff this is capitulation, the supreme confession of weakness, the first long step toward the abyss. There is a new exchange of notes, Germany speaking on October 20th, the President on the 23rd. The German note is immaterial, the President's noteworthy because of the emphasis laid upon the proposal to render Germany incapable of further military effort. The note also contains more than a hint of the suspicion that the "Old Gang" is still in charge in Berlin. "A strong answer to our cowardly note," Ludendorff thinks, received by the German Government on October 24th. The next day Ludendorff tells the Kaiser, Hindenburg nodding approval, that "we must fight on." The Kaiser decides nothing but is still friendly—for the last time—to Ludendorff. And the same day there comes to light an address to the German army, signed by Hindenburg, directed to the German army, containing the declaration:

Wilson's answer is a demand for unconditional surrender. It is thus unacceptable to us soldiers.

October 25th Berlin is aflame with this Hindenburg note, Ludendorff held responsible by all. The Reichstag is shaken. The general who cannot win the battle, who has lost the victory, who has confessed that the line may be broken at any moment, declares against peace. How will this message strike the Allied governments—President Wilson, who has just suggested that militarism must disappear, if peace is to be contemplated? In a word; suddenly, completely, the line does break, but it is the home front which collapses. Ludendorff must go.

The same day, having listened to this storm, Ludendorff meets two members of his faithful staff outside the Ministry of the Interior and tells them, "Germany is lost!" He sees the Kaiser the next morning, the final interview, recalling how many memories—recalling the interview in

February when he told the Supreme War Lord that the battle would be hard but that victory was to be attained. The Kaiser listens to his captain's words, his manner changed; refers to the offending order bitterly, accepts the resignation proffered again. On his way out Ludendorff tells a friend that in a fortnight there will no longer be an emperor in Germany. A correct prophecy, for on November 9th Germany was a republic. And so, exit Ludendorff.

In reality it is something more, the German system itself has broken down. The idea of emperor, state, civil government, all founded upon force, has broken down. The hour has come for the nation to rise as France rose in 1792 and again in 1870, in despair the latter time, but Germany does not rise. What happens is the same phenomenon visible in 1814, when Napoleon called upon France to rise, the legislature to rally to the throne, the people to the nation, and on the heels of the appeal the Allied armies occupied Paris, only the soldiers making a gallant but hopeless fight, the people standing quite apart, rather welcoming the invaders. The moment arrives when the nation sees its fate as something totally different from that of its recent master. In the case of Napoleon it was a man. In the German case it is something rather different. The largest man, the Kaiser, Ludendorff, or the imaginary, legendary Hindenburg, derives his stature from the idea he embodies, and crumbles so much the more easily to dust when the idea falls. What is now taking place in Germany is like a rout in a great, disciplined army, when all discipline breaks down with defeat, the "*Sauve qui peut!*" of Waterloo.

IV. THE END

October 26, 1918, is, then, an ever-memorable date. The departure of Ludendorff is the sign to all the world that Germany has turned in rage upon all her gods. Ludendorff gone, the others, as he foresaw, will follow fast. On this same day, anniversary of the Caporetto disaster a year ago, the Italian army has crossed the Piave, sweeping the ruined Austrian army before it, and the Hapsburg Monarchy has a new prime minister taking office under pledge to make a separate peace. The Upper House of Prussia has passed three electoral reform measures,

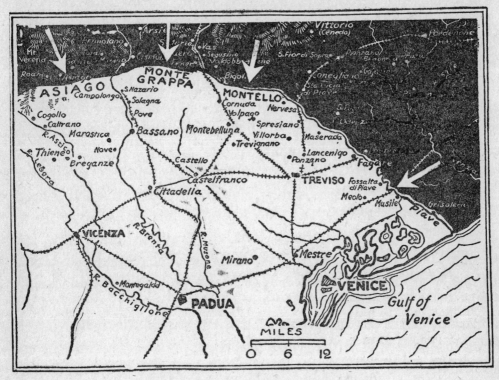

THE SECOND BATTLE OF THE PIAVE
Arrows show the direction of the main Austrian attacks

interesting as disclosing panic passion for democracy, but unimpressive to Foch. The British cavalry has occupied Aleppo in Syria, and shortly Turkey will leave the war. The next day, October 27th, Germany replies to the President's letter of October 23rd, giving new assurances, becoming increasingly valid, that the people are in charge of the German Government, which will be wholly true a few days later when the mob appears in Berlin. In Vienna a solemn assurance is given that the rights of the Czecho-Slovaks and the Jugo-Slavs are recognized, given by the new foreign minister, Count Julius Andrassy, who tells President Wilson no obstacle is now in the way of peace negotiations. Two days later Vienna will appeal to the President, its army now in full flight, to intervene in the name of humanity. October 31st, Turkey does withdraw unconditionally and the Inter-Allied War Council meets at Versailles: Clemenceau, Lloyd George, Colonel House for President Wilson, and Marshal Foch.

The next day Pershing starts for Sedan, Haig for Mons; the German front is at last broken and Vienna and Budapest report revolutions. Count Tisza, Hungarian prime minister when the fatal ultimatum was sent to Serbia four years ago, is shot by a common soldier. Bohemia sets up a new government, the first since the far-off time of the Winter King and the Thirty Years' War. Two new republics, Jugoslavia and Czechoslovakia, appear November 1st, and then on November 3rd the Kaiser approves of an act amending the constitution by "transferring fundamental rights of the Kaiser's person to the people." On the same day the Serbians reënter Belgrade.

And now, November 3rd, the first authentic rumour of revolution in Germany comes from Kiel: the German navy mutinies on rumour of an order to make a final, foredoomed sortie, such as Cervera made at Santiago. The men begin to organize soldiers' and sailors' councils, more than an echo of Russian bolshevism; and on the same day Austria signs a capitulation covering everything, an abject surrender without condition, a document signed for an empire already defunct. At Versailles the Interallied Conference has decided on the terms Germany can have by asking Marshal Foch for them. Meantime Germany has told President Wilson that it has stopped air raids, and is grieved that Allied planes are still spreading panic in the Rhine Valley.

Now at last President Wilson informs Germany on November 1st that, having referred German communications to the Allied cause, he is able to state that the Allied Powers are willing to make peace with Germany on the basis of the Fourteen Points, England reserving liberty of action in the matter of freedom of the seas; France, in the matter of compensation for damages done to the civil population and property.

Two days later German Headquarters asks and receives permission to send representatives through the Allied lines to get Marshal Foch's terms, and as these representatives set out on their penitential progress, Germany suddenly flames up in revolution. November 9th the Chancellor announces the abdication of the Kaiser, who will appear inside the Dutch frontier the next morning, the Crown Prince following by another route. "The cascade of thrones" has begun. In the next few days Switzerland will be filled to overflowing with German kinglets, grand dukes, Austrian archdukes, the Austrian Emperor fleeing as well. King Constantine of Greece need be lonely no longer. Friedrich Ebert, vice-president of the Social Democratic Party, a person of low extraction, a saddler, is the first president of the German Republic, which will seek more regular elections through a constituent national assembly later. November 12th the Austrian Kaiser imitates the German Kaiser and the House of Hapsburg, like that of Hozenzollern, has ceased to rule or reign. In Berlin, in a score of other German cities, bolshevism raises its head; anarchy marches, Germans are shooting one another as Frenchmen did Frenchmen at the end of the Siege of Paris forty-seven years earlier, Bismarck looking on with cynical interest at Versailles.

In sum, in the week between November 5th and November 11th all the settled and established institutions of the Central Powers are going down in a heap. The captains and the kings are departing. The German army, driven out of Sedan, across the Meuse, out of Valenciennes, across the Scheldt, struggling back to the French frontier, is on the edge of ruin. The Austro-Hungarian army has ceased to exist. Bulgaria is in Allied hands. An Allied fleet has passed the Dardanelles, whose forts have gone silent now, and is anchored off the Golden Horn. Enver, like William II, has fled; Austria-Hungary, its emperor gone, has become a confusion of racial entities. Roumania, rising from recent ruin, has cast off old chains and is stretching out her hands to resume old aspirations.

And in the midst of all this chaos, tumult—perhaps the most terrific week in all human experience—the armies of Foch have pressed on. That western front, that black line stretched from the North Sea to Switzerland, which through four long years of agony had fixed itself upon the minds and the memories of millions, has disappeared. Its rigid and unyielding menace has been replaced by a new line which moves daily, hourly, engulfing new provinces, cities, towns in its liberating waves. The facts of this week remain for history, but who can forget or preserve the emotions of that time—the joy, the gratitude, the relief that came with the recognition at last that Justice would prevail over

Might and that the German sword had been broken and was now being dashed from the German hand.

V. ARMISTICE

And while Germany is falling into chaos, everything gone or shortly to go which for fifty years has oppressed the minds and the souls of men, there sets out from Spa, Ludendorff's headquarters, a few days before, one of the most sorrowful and satisfying processions this planet has ever seen, headed by Erzberger, one of the "turncoats" who turned in 1917. It proceeds by a long, circuitous route prescribed by Foch through Avesnes, where the Kaiser and Ludendorff heard the news of March 21st.   It is preceded by pioneers whose mission it is to patch up the roads lately destroyed by armies in retreat, to fix a path by which representatives of Germany can go to something far more humiliating than Canossa.   It is long after dark when the procession meets the first French picket line, the advance guard of Debeney, some of the men who checked the German rush at the Avre on March 26th and the succeeding days, which saw Foch begin.   A strange encounter this was, of which many picturesque descriptions have survived, flashing of lights in the dark, examination of papers, new delays to fill up trenches across the road, strange whiteness of the German faces not difficult to explain, but fixed in the minds of the witnesses out on that lonely road surrounded by the destruction wrought by other Germans not a week ago, cannon still sounding to right and to left, rifles and machine guns still going off.   For the war is continuing.

Then at last the German ambassadors are put on their road again, going southward into the wilderness of the Hindenburg Line through the ruins of St. Quentin, seen in the morning light, called to their attention by a Frenchman who says significantly, "There *was* St. Quentin."   And at last, after innumerable wanderings in this tangle of desolation—wanderings the Germans afterward allege to have been a part of French design to fix upon their minds, as a prelude to receiving the sentence awaiting them, the reality of what Germany had done—the Germans are embarked upon a special train and arrive, place unknown to them, in a forest identified later as the Forest of Compiègne, toward which Ludendorff aimed in June, through which Kluck advanced in August, 1914.

The place to which they have come, a mere railroad siding—the nearest village is Rethondes—is the place where Foch awaits them in his own car. They are greeted courteously but coldly; they will complain much of this coldness later, as will other Germans who go to Versailles on a similar errand a few months hence. Not even their passage over the Hindenburg desert can explain to them the coldness of their reception; in fact, they encounter for the first time visible evidence of what mankind thinks of them, of all Germans—has been thinking since Louvain, since the *Lusitania*—has been thinking more clearly with each successive revelation of the German soul.

November 8th, in Marshal Foch's car, they perform their mission. Their reception is as coolly correct as always: formal bows, nothing more. And then the direct question: "What is it that you wish, gentlemen?" The question which carries the supreme humiliation—which places upon the Germans the necessity to sue for peace. This is a very far cry from that final moment when Thiers made his last appeal to Bismarck in an interview preserved in a picture known to most Frenchmen and all Germans. Forty-seven years ago Marshal Foch saw the Germans in Metz, and for forty-seven years Foch, like every Frenchman, has remembered the scene at Versailles and looked longingly over Bismarck's frontier into what was once France, and has remained French.

What happened at Rethondes is little memorable in detail: hopeless protests; debates, all from the German side. The army of Foch continuing to sweep forward; the Kaiser abdicating, disappearing, and reappearing upon a Dutch railroad platform; revolution sweeping over Germany; the German ambassadors at Rethondes await the return of a courier sent to Berlin with Foch's terms, and still delayed by roads and war, returning at night, November 10th. Then, finally, at five o'clock on the morning of November 11th the Armistice is signed, and to all the army fronts there goes forth word that at eleven o'clock this morning the war will cease. The enemy has surrendered, and from one end of the

Allied world to the other the news of the victory is flashed forth.   At last there will be peace.

Most interesting of all comments on the Armistice is that of Marshal Foch, made long after the event, to his friend, André de Maricourt. The Marshal had been explaining his philosophy of war, his conviction that two things are essential to victory.   The general must "will" to conquer and he must also know how to employ his resources.   It is in this discussion that Foch said: "Yes, the Kaiser served up to us a formidable machine and some excellent foremen, but all the same the express train was confided to a stage-coach driver.   We couldn't help conquering."   And then he breaks out as follows:

And now don't talk to me about glory, beauty, enthusiasm which I know.   All these things are mere language, we must avoid these expressions in France.   They are useless, they are just so much energy wasted.   The war is over.   That is worth saying, but epithets are as worthless as phrases.   Nothing exists except the fact because, as I have said before, only the proofs are of any use.

What do I consider a useful fact, one that satisfies me?   The interview at Rethondes, that was a proof, a testament.   That testament established the disintegration of the German Empire, and when I saw Erzberger take his pen passionately and sign that testament, then I was satisfied with having "willed" the victory, and with having employed the resources, for the business was liquidated.

The actual text signed by Erzberger and his associates was as follows:

I—MILITARY CLAUSES ON WESTERN FRONT

One—Cessation of operations by land and in the air six hours after the signature of the armistice.

Two—Immediate evacuation of invaded countries: Belgium, France, Alsace-Lorraine, Luxemburg, so ordered as to be completed within fourteen days from the signature of the armistice.   German troops which have not left the above-mentioned territories within the period fixed will become prisoners of war.   Occupation by the Allied and United States forces jointly will keep pace with evacuation in these areas. All movements of evacuation and occupation will be regulated in accordance with a note annexed to the stated terms.

Three—Repatriation, beginning at once, to be completed within fifteen days, of all the inhabitants of the countries above enumerated (including hostages, persons under trial, or convicted).

Four—Surrender in good condition by the German armies of the following war material: Five thousand guns (2,500 heavy and 2,500 field), 25,000 machine guns, 3,000 minenwerfer, 1,700 airplanes (fighters, bombers—firstly, all of the D 7's and all the night bombing machines). The above to be delivered *in situ* to the Allied and United States troops in accordance with the detailed conditions laid down in the note (annexure No. 1) drawn up at the moment of the signing of the armistice.

Five—Evacuation by the German armies of the countries on the left bank of the Rhine. The countries on the left bank of the Rhine shall be administered by the local troops of occupation. The occupation of these territories will be carried out by Allied and United States garrisons holding the principal crossings of the Rhine (Mayence, Coblentz, Cologne), together with the bridgeheads at these points of a thirty-kilometre radius on the right bank and by garrisons similarly holding the strategic points of the regions. A neutral zone shall be reserved on the right bank of the Rhine between the stream and a line drawn parallel to the bridgeheads and to the stream and at a distance of ten kilometres from the frontier of Holland up to the frontier of Switzerland. The evacuation by the enemy of the Rhinelands (left and right bank) shall be so ordered as to be completed within a further period of sixteen days, in all, thirty-one days after the signing of the armistice. All the movements of evacuation or occupation are regulated by the note (annexure No. 1) drawn up at the moment of the signing of the armistice.

Six—In all territories evacuated by the enemy there shall be no evacuation of inhabitants; no damage or harm shall be done to the persons or property of the inhabitants. No person shall be prosecuted for offences of participation in war measures prior to the signing of the armistice. No destruction of any kind shall be committed. Military establishments of all kinds shall be delivered intact, as well as military stores of food, munitions, and equipment, not removed during the time fixed for evacuation. Stores of food of all kinds for the civil population, cattle, etc., shall be left *in situ*. Industrial establishments shall not be impaired in any way and their personnel shall not be removed.

Seven—Roads and means of communication of every kind, railroads, waterways, main roads, bridges, telegraphs, telephones, shall be in no manner impaired. All civil and military personnel at present employed on them shall remain. Five thousand locomotives and 150,000 wagons in good working order, with all necessary spare parts and fittings, shall be delivered to the associated powers within the period fixed in annexure No. 2, and total of which shall not exceed thirty-one days. There shall likewise be delivered 5,000 motor lorries (camione automobiles) in good order, within the period of thirty-six days. The railways of Alsace-Lorraine shall be handed over within the period of thirty-one days, together with pre-war personnel and material. Further, the material necessary for the working of railways in the countries on the left bank of the Rhine shall be left *in situ*. All stores of coal and material for the upkeep of permanent ways, signals, and repair shops shall be left *in situ*. These stores shall be maintained by Germany in so far as concerns the working of the railroads in the countries on the left bank of the Rhine. All barges taken from the Allies shall be restored to them. The note, annexure No. 2, regulates the details of these measures.

Eight—The German command shall be responsible for revealing within the period of forty-eight hours after the signing of the armistice all mines or delayed-action fuses on territory evacuated by the German troops and shall assist in their discovery and destruction. It also shall reveal all destructive measures that may have been taken

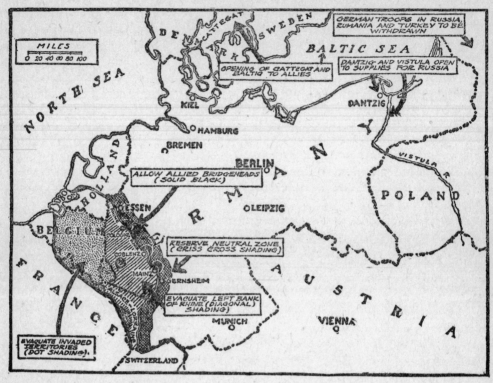

AMERICA'S ADVANCE TO THE RHINE

(such as poisoning or polluting of springs and wells, etc.). All under penalty of reprisals.

Nine—The right of requisition shall be exercised by the Allied and United States armies in all occupied territories, subject to regulation of accounts with those whom it may concern. The upkeep of the troops of occupation in the Rhineland (excluding Alsace-Lorraine) shall be charged to the German Government.

Ten—The immediate repatriation without reciprocity, according to detailed conditions which shall be fixed, of all Allied and United States prisoners of war, including persons under trial or convicted. The Allied Powers and the United States shall be able to dispose of them as they wish. This condition annuls the previous conventions on the subject of the exchange of prisoners of war, including the one of July, 1918, in course of ratification. However, the repatriation of German prisoners of war interned in Holland and in Switzerland shall continue as before. The repatriation of German prisoners of war shall be regulated at the conclusion of the preliminaries of peace.

Eleven—Sick and wounded who cannot be removed from evacuated territory will be cared for by German personnel, who will be left on the spot with the medical material required.

II.—DISPOSITION RELATIVE TO THE EASTERN FRONTIERS OF GERMANY

Twelve—All German troops at present in the territories which before belonged to

Austria-Hungary, Roumania, Turkey, shall withdraw immediately within the frontiers of Germany as they existed on August 1, 1914. All German troops at present in the territories which before the war belonged to Russia shall likewise withdraw within the frontiers of Germany, defined as above, as soon as the Allies, taking into account the internal situation of these territories, shall decide that the time for this has come.

Thirteen—Evacuation by German troops to begin at once, and all German instructors, prisoners, and civilians as well as military agents now on the territory of Russia (as defined before 1914) to be recalled.

Fourteen—German troops to cease at once all requisitions and seizures and any other undertaking with a view to obtaining supplies intended for Germany in Roumania and Russia (as defined on August 1, 1914).

Fifteen—Renunciation of the treaties of Bukharest and Brest-Litovsk and of the supplementary treaties.

Sixteen—The Allies shall have free access to the territories evacuated by the Germans on their eastern frontier, either through Danzig, or by the Vistula, in order to convey supplies to the populations of those territories and for the purpose of maintaining order.

III.—CLAUSE CONCERNING EAST AFRICA

Seventeen—Evacuation by all German forces operating in East Africa within a period to be fixed by the Allies.

IV.—GENERAL CLAUSES

Eighteen—Repatriation, without reciprocity, within a maximum period of one month in accordance with detailed conditions hereafter to be fixed, of all interned civilians, including hostages (persons?), under trial or convicted, belonging to the allied or associated powers other than those enumerated in Article Three.

Nineteen—The following financial conditions are required: Reparation for damage done. While such armistice lasts no public securities shall be removed by the enemy which can serve as a pledge to the Allies for the recovery or reparation for war losses. Immediate restitution of the cash deposit in the National Bank of Belgium, and, in general, immediate return of all documents, specie, stocks, shares, paper money, together with plant for the issue thereof, touching public or private interests in the invaded countries. Restitution of the Russian and Roumanian gold yielded to Germany or taken by that power. This gold to be delivered in trust to the Allies until the signature of peace.

V.—NAVAL CONDITIONS

Twenty—Immediate cessation of all hostilities at sea and definite information to be given as to the location and movements of all German ships. Notification to be given to neutrals that freedom of navigation in all territorial waters is given to the naval and mercantile marines of the allied and associated powers, all questions of neutrality being waived.

Twenty-one—All naval and mercantile marine prisoners of the allied and associated powers in German hands to be returned without reciprocity.

Twenty-two—Surrender to the Allies and United States of all submarines (including submarine cruisers and all mine-laying submarines) now existing, with their complete armament and equipment, in ports which shall be specified by the Allies and United States. Those whioh cannot take the sea shall be disarmed of the personnel and material and shall remain under the supervision of the Allies and the United States. The submarines which are ready for the sea shall be prepared to leave the German ports as soon as orders shall be received by wireless for their voyage to the port designated for their delivery, and the remainder at the earliest possible moment. The conditions of this article shall be carried into effect within the period of fourteen days after the signing of the armistice.

Twenty-three—German surface warships which shall be designated by the Allies and the United States shall be immediately disarmed and thereafter interned in neutral ports or in default of them in allied ports to be designated by the Allies and the United States. They will there remain under the supervision of the Allies and of the United States, only caretakers being left on board. The following warships are designated by the Allies: Six battle cruisers, ten battleships, eight light cruisers (including two mine layers), fifty destroyers of the most modern types. All other surface warships (including river craft) are to be concentrated in German naval bases to be designated by the Allies and the United States, and are to be completely disarmed and classed under the supervision of the Allies and the United States. The military armament of all ships of the auxiliary fleet shall be put on shore. All vessels designated to be interned shall be ready to leave the German ports seven days after the signing of the armistice. Directions for the voyage will be given by wireless.

Twenty-four—The Allies and the United States of America shall have the right to sweep up all mine fields and obstructions laid by Germany outside German territorial waters, and the positions of these are to be indicated.

Twenty-five—Freedom of access to and from the Baltic to be given to the naval and mercantile marines of the allied and associated powers. To secure this the Allies and the United States of America shall be empowered to occupy all German forts, fortifications, batteries, and defence works of all kinds in all the entrances from the Cattegat into the Baltic, and to sweep up all mines and obstructions within and without German territorial waters, without any question of neutrality being raised, and the positions of all such mines and obstructions are to be indicated.

Twenty-six—The existing blockade conditions set up by the allied and associated powers are to remain unchanged, and all German merchant ships found at sea are to remain liable to capture. The Allies and the United States shall give consideration to the provisioning of Germany during the armistice to the extent recognized as necessary.

Twenty-seven—All naval aircraft are to be concentrated and immobilized in German bases to be specified by the Allies and the United States of America.

Twenty-eight—In evacuating the Belgian coast and ports Germany shall abandon *in situ* and in fact all port and river navigation material, all merchant ships, tugs, lighters, all naval aeronautic apparatus, material and supplies, and all arms, apparatus and supplies of every kind.

Twenty-nine—All Black Sea ports are to be evacuated by Germany; all Russian war vessels of all descriptions seized by Germany in the Black Sea are to be handed over to the Allies and the United States of America; all neutral merchant vessels seized are to be released; all warlike and other materials of all kinds seized in those ports are to be returned and German materials as specified in Clause Twenty-eight are to be abandoned.

Thirty—All merchant vessels in German hands belonging to the allied and associated powers are to be restored in ports to be specified by the Allies and the United States of America without reciprocity.

Thirty-one—No destruction of ships or of materials to be permitted before evacuation, surrender, or restoration.

Thirty-two—The German Government will notify the neutral governments of the world, and particularly the governments of Norway, Sweden, Denmark, and Holland, that all restrictions placed on the trading of their vessels with the allied and associated countries, whether by the German Government or by private German interests, and whether in return for specific concessions, such as the export of shipbuilding materials, or not, are immediately cancelled.

Thirty-three—No transfers of German merchant shipping of any description to any neutral flag are to take place after signature of the armistice.

VI.—DURATION OF ARMISTICE

Thirty-four—The duration of the armistice is to be thirty-days, with option to extend.   During this period if its clauses are not carried into execution the armistice may be denounced by one of the contracting parties, which must give warning forty-eight hours in advance.   It is understood that the execution of Article III and Section Eighteen, under IV, shall not warrant the denunciation of the armistice on the ground of insufficient execution within a period fixed, except in the case of bad faith in carrying them into execution.   In order to assure the execution of this convention under the best conditions, the principle of a permanent international armistice commission is admitted.   This commission will act under the authority of the allied military and naval Commanders-in-Chief.

VII.—THE LIMIT FOR REPLY

Thirty-five—This armistice to be accepted or refused by Germany within seventy-two hours of notification.

This armistice has been signed the Eleventh of November, Nineteen Eighteen, at 5 o'clock French time.

> F. FOCH,
> R. E. WEMYSS,
> ERZBERGER,
> A. OBERNDORFF,
> WINTERFELDT,
> VON SALOW.

VI.—PREMATURE?

Since the actual signing of the Armistice of November 11, 1918, a mighty controversy has arisen and continues, a controversy turning on the question as to whether it would not have been better to pursue the fighting to the logical end. This debate has been marked by charges and counter-charges, the contestants alleging and denying that the decision to grant an armistice was premature. As the Treaty became a matter of controversy, in its turn, the indictment of the Armistice was added to the others filed against President Wilson, who was accused of having enabled the German military party to escape complete exposure, ultimate humiliation, by opening "conversations" with the Germans over the heads of the soldiers.

As to the main discussion, decision is perhaps impossible; as to the allegation against the American president, it has little foundation. It is equally untrue that his conversations conquered or saved the Prussian, and the claims of his friends and the accusations of his critics are equally outside the limits of reason. Yet even if decision in the main controversy is impossible, certain illuminating facts are spread upon the record.

Thus General Maurice, when the controversy was just beginning, on the morrow of the Armistice, went to France and talked with the soldiers, who were reported as most indignant. What he learned, he has written. From the Dutch frontier near Ghent to the Meuse, the Allied armies were approaching the limit of immediate exploitation on their successes. Behind them lay a desert, lacking in communications, needing weeks to bridge; before them the enemy was retiring, creating still another gulf of chaos. Pursuit between the Scheldt and the Meuse was destined to slow down shortly, should the combat continue.

East of the Meuse it was different. Between Metz and Strassburg the French and Americans were about to break out in a new offensive, thirty divisions in line, thirty in reserve. The country was undevastated, their communications intact. The Germans were without reserves and there was no approximate limit to the progress that might be made, after the first severe fighting, which would attend the rupture—that definitive rupture described by Buat.

But even this campaign carried with it certain obvious dangers. The Kaiser had long ago sworn that if ever the French should succeed in their determination to regain their "lost provinces" they would recover only a wilderness. To have prolonged the war meant to transform Alsace-Lorraine into another Hindenburg desert. It meant to risk a similar wasting of all of Belgium, through which the German armies would retire. The victory was certain, but the price, not merely in blood but in destruction, was sure to be colossal.

The decision to permit the Germans to sign an armistice saved Belgium and Alsace-Lorraine. It gave back to France her old lands intact, with an industrial equipment capable of making good in large measure the losses suffered in the north of France. It insured to France under the later terms of the Treaty of Versailles, the Saar Coal Basin, which would in part, at least temporarily, replace the ruined Lens Basin, until such time as the mines of the Pas-de-Calais were again in working order. If Rheims, St. Quentin, Soissons, Lens, and Arras had been destroyed, France received immune from all injuries, Strassburg, Metz, Mühl-hausen, and Colmar.

If it was an irritating and a disturbing circumstance that the German armies returning home should be welcomed as victors, greeted with arches of triumph, hailed as conquerors; if, in Germany, Ludendorff and his associates could propagate the legend that the German army had been invincible and the defeat had been the work of civilians—could allege that the nation had collapsed behind an unshaken army—this inveracity was too great to endure the test of time. The terms of the Armistice were the witness to absolute defeat and the position and condition of the German armies—facts which would stand forth more and more clearly as the years passed.

Beyond all else the sacrifice had been too great to permit the shedding of one more drop of blood unnecessarily. Europe was too near the edge of the abyss to dare risk any prolongation of the strain of war. To Foch was left the task of fixing the terms, and it is common knowledge that neither he nor his comrades could believe that any German army, however beaten, would accept such terms as he handed to Erzberger at Rethondes. The farther one was from the front on November 11, 1918, the more loudly was heard the clamour for "finishing the job." But the decision to end it by the Armistice must seem, with each succeeding year, more warranted, as the true extent of the dislocation of the machinery of government and existence is more accurately appraised.

Realizing the difficulties, the barriers in the pathway of reconstruction despite the termination of hostilities on November 11th, one may calculate what might have been the situation if the war had proceeded for a few more weeks or months and, between the Scheldt and the Meuse on the west and the Rhine on the east, a new belt of ruined provinces had been created, including all of Belgium, together with Alsace-Lorraine, Luxemburg, and the German Rhineland. A Waterloo or Sedan, however stupendous, would hardly have been an adequate compensation.

One final and memorable circumstance, preserved in millions of letters and innumerable accounts of the moment, is the testimony of the meaning to the soldiers themselves, when, on the hour, silence suddenly fell along all the front from Holland to Switzerland. At 10:59 shells were still falling, bullets were striking, all the noise of destruction which had continued for more than fifty-two months was still audible. But at eleven o'clock exactly there was silence—so abrupt, so complete as to be oppressive. Almost as in a dream men rose from the trenches for the first time, save at the moment of attack, and looked steadily across the "No Man's Land" to the enemy trenches beyond.

In a score of tongues and dialects the phrase sounded: "The war is finished!" The hour so long looked forward to, so long held almost beyond hoping for, had at last arrived and found millions of men, on either side of the firing line, so exhausted that the defeated welcomed the relief that accompanied surrender and the conquerors celebrated their triumph in a sleep at last unbroken by shells or alarums. Paris, London, New York might give way to an enthusiasm which needed expression, but for the real victors the sweetest circumstance of victory, aside from safety, was the sleep it permitted. For them the longest nightmare in human experience had ended and, remembering how great were their agonies, their sacrifices, the sum of their miseries, one may well find unconvincing the arguments of those who would have prolonged the march of victory to the Rhine or even to Berlin.

CHAPTER TWELVE

THE OTHER FRONTS

I

THE ITALIAN CONTRIBUTION

It remains now briefly, very briefly, to summarize the events on four fronts including the period from March to November in which the issue of the war was decided on the western front. These four other fields of conquest were the Italian, the Macedonian, the Turkish, and that sea front on which the submarine was fought and checked, and it is only on this last front that success exercised anything like a decisive influence upon the issue of the main conflict. Had the submarine been able to perform the task allotted to it, it would have been impossible for two millions of American soldiers to cross the ocean; starvation would have come to Britain; and the Allies would have been compelled, while the German armies were still advancing toward the Paris front, to make a peace of approximate submission.

As for the three land campaigns, only that of Italy was of real magnitude or exercised any considerable influence upon events in France. The Italian front was actually, as Allied official statements and comments of the time indicated, the right flank of Foch's single front, which thus extended from the North Sea to the Adriatic, from the Yser to the Piave; and the brief interruption of the continuity of this line, incident to the interposition of Swiss territory, did not actually separate the two fractions. At the time of Caporetto, Italian disaster had made immediate and compromising demands upon British and French reserves. To this Haig ascribed his inability to exploit the initial success at Cambrai in that year. As late as March and April, 1918, British and French divisions were in Italy and had incontinently to be recalled during the Battle of Picardy.

In June, at the moment when the Battle of the Chemin des Dames in all its peripheries had come to an end, Ludendorff called upon his Austrian allies to make a major offensive on the Piave. Success would mean the recall of Italian troops beginning to appear in Champagne; it would mean the necessity of another transfer of Allied reserves, desperately needed before Paris, to the valleys of the Adige and the Po. It might mean the collapse of Italy, and the corresponding disarray of Allied affairs.

This battle was to be delivered at the moment when Allied forces were at their lowest ebb and, following immediately upon the success at the Chemin des Dames, was to continue the moral as well as the military pressure upon Allied statesmen, public and military leaders. A second Caporetto might present to Foch the choice between (a) fatally weakening his Paris front, to reinforce the Italian, and (b) seeing the Italian army removed from the war because of the failure of Allied reinforcements to arrive and the subsequent appearance of Austro-Hungarian divisions in decisive numbers along the French front. Nor was it totally beyond calculation that the Italian armies, having been eliminated, the victorious Austrian hosts would sweep across the Valley of the Po and, by menacing France with invasion by all the Alpine passes from Mentone to Switzerland, compel Foch to divert French divisions from Champagne and from Picardy to Savoy, Dauphiné, and Provence.

The fact that with relatively insignificant Allied assistance, with only a handful of British and French troops present, Italy broke this attack at the Piave, must be reckoned an enormous contribution to Foch's victory. By the time Ludendorff was ready for his final offensive, that of July 15th, Foch could not only dismiss all anxieties as to his Italian flank but he could also count on a material Italian contribution to his resources in man-power on the French front. He could dismiss all calculation which might involve the transfer of French and British divisions to the Adige. He could, in sum, say to himself: "The next circumstance on the Italian flank will be an Italian attack; the offensive power of the Austrian army has been broken not for the moment, but for the rest of the war."

The Piave was the Italian Marne. In its relation to the general

Allied cause the Second Battle of the Piave was similar to that of Castlenau's victorious defence at Nancy, to the First Battle of the Marne, and Gouraud's equally shining resistance between Rheims and the Argonne to the Second. In the nature of things the attention of the world was concentrated upon the Paris front. Italy's triumph produced a general sense of relief but no accurate appraisal of achievement. Nevertheless, on the military side it was a very real factor in Foch's campaign. On the moral side it was the first "lift"—the first authentic victory after the opening of the terrible round of defeats on March 21st.

II. THE SECOND BATTLE OF THE PIAVE

The plans of the Austrians for their attack—which was fixed first for June 11th, the date when Ludendorff broke off the Battle of the Matz, and then postponed until June 15th—were as follows: there was to be a feint at Adamiello, just south of the Swiss frontier and looking toward the Valtelline, to distract Italian attention, and then three converging thrusts—the first on the Asiago Plateau, where Cadorna had just barely checked the Austrian offensive of 1916, and where weather and French troops had assisted Diaz in another successful defence after Caporetto; the second, directed at the Montello Heights where the Piave enters the plain and turns south toward the sea; and the third, between Montello and the sea, mainly along the Udine-Vicenza railway.

It was the purpose of Arz, the commander-in-chief of the Austrians, to turn the Italians out of the Piave line by smashing through from the mountains and coming down in the plain by the Astico and Brenta valleys exactly as his predecessors had sought to do in 1916 and 1917. If the Italians could be driven off the hills—they only held the southernmost slopes—and the success were swift and complete, then the Italian troops holding the Piave line might be enveloped and captured. If the progress were slower, ultimate success would mean a retirement behind the Adige and the Po, the surrender of Venice and Padua and the approach to Verona. But if the thrust out of the mountains failed, the capture of the Heights of Montello would involve an Italian retirement from the line of the Piave to the Brenta, and the capture of Venice.

Finally, the purpose of the third thrust, between Montello and the sea, was mainly to occupy the Italians on this front, prevent the diversion of reserves to the north, and exploit any success at Asiago or Montello. It will be seen that the largest profit which the Austrians could hope to attain would be realized by decisive success on the Asiago Plateau. Actually the conditions recall those of Caporetto, and a similar immediate and complete success, a repetition of Below's achievement with German troops, would have reproduced the terrible circumstances of the previous year.

But there was no repetition of Caporetto. First of all the Italians in the hills on the Asiago Plateau and on Monte Grappa stood firm—briefly and completely broke Arz's most dangerous thrust. This phase ended abruptly and Diaz was assured of the stability of his flank and the safety of his communications. By contrast the fighting on Montello was much more desperate and the issue for several days doubtful. The Austrians succeeded in passing the Piave, climbed the eastern and northern sides of Montello, and thus threatened the line of the Piave southward to the sea. They also succeeded in passing the river farther to the south, notably in the lagoons where the front was nearest to Venice. But Italian resistance stiffened, a small British contingent rendered valuable assistance, and presently the Austrians were pushed off the summit of Montello by counter-attacks which restored the situation. The Austrian thrust was thus checked, the advances were inconsiderable, and the line of the Piave was maintained.

But at this point there was a heavy rain in the mountains. The Piave rose suddenly and swept away many of the Austrian bridges, particularly those behind their troops on the slopes of Montello. Thereupon the Italians again counter-attacked and the Austrians were compelled to retire north and east of the Piave, to abandon all of their gains and many of their guns; many thousands of their troops were actually drowned in the flooded river. Thus the last phase of what had been termed "the hunger offensive," designed to be an impressive prelude to Ludendorff's July "peace storm," ended in a disaster of vast proportion leading directly to bitter recrimination in the Hungarian Parliament, to a confession of a loss exceeding 100,000 in killed and drowned alone, the final destruction of morale, and of the hope of victory or the willingness to continue, in the Hapsburg Monarchy. Henceforth, until the supreme disaster of the closing days of the war, the Austrian army swiftly disintegrates. Although the Italians did not follow up their advantage until three months later, the Second Battle of the Piave actually broke the Austrian military power.

Ludendorff comments bitterly on this disaster. He notes that the Austrian soldier seemed to have fought well, and he suspects the cause of defeat was to be found in the fact that the attack was made on too broad a front. But what angers him most is the disclosure in the Hungarian Parliament. On the military aspect Ludendorff says that the failure was extremely painful to him and abolished the hope that relief on the western front might be gained in Italy. He now proposed the transfer of Austrian troops to the western front. Two divisions did come after delays, arriving in July, but the condition of these was wretched and they required training before they could be put into quiet sectors. Two more came in September but proved of little use. Pershing encountered and captured some of these Austrians at St. Mihiel.

On the moral and on the military side Italy rendered a supreme service to her allies in the Second Battle of the Piave. The Italian army fought in a manner which disclosed the fact that the soldiers and the country had recovered alike from the consequences of the disaster at Caporetto and from the infection of pacifism and treason which had contributed to that earlier disaster. Not even the magnitude of the events on the northern front should obscure this service, nor can any one who recalls the state of Allied minds between the Chemin des Dames and the Second Battle of the Marne forget the encouragement and relief consequent to the realization that the Allies, thanks to Italy, had at last won a battle and abolished one front of peril.

III. IN MACEDONIA

Three months after the victory at the Piave the Army of the Orient, by a swift and brilliant victory, abolished the Macedonian front and brought Bulgaria to the point of capitulation. Sarrail had been removed from the command of the Salonica army upon the arrival of Clemenceau, who feared neither politicians nor political generals. Guillaumat, Nivelle's successor at Verdun, replaced Sarrail, reorganized the Army of the Orient, now materially reinforced by Greek troops raised by Venizelos. But before he could put into operation his plans for an offensive, Guillaumat was recalled to become Governor of Paris, again threatened by the Germans. He was succeeded by Franchet d'Esperey, one of the army commanders at the First Marne who had been in charge of the army group to which belonged the French Sixth Army, victim of the Chemin-des-Dames offensive—a circumstance which explained D'Esperey's transfer to the Army of the Orient. By an odd coincidence the two generals who were now to win amazing victories in the east, D'Esperey in Macedonia and Allenby in Palestine, had been transferred to the scene of their subsequent successes under circumstances which suggested demotion.

The Macedonia offensive opened on September 15th, three days after Pershing had abolished the St. Mihiel salient, and at the close of those actions which constituted Foch's manœuvre between Montdidier and the Hindenburg Line. Before the composite Army of the Orient—containing Italian, French, Serbian, Greek, and British contingents—stood three enemy armies, all of them composed of Bulgarian troops, but one of them still called the Eleventh German Army and commanded by a German general, although its German contingent had disappeared. The two Bulgarian armies occupied the front east of the Vardar in a semicircle from the gulf into which the Struma empties to the Vardar near the old Serbo-Greek frontier. The so-called German army occupied the front from the Vardar to Lake Ochrida and Austrian contingents prolonged the line across Albania to the Adriatic.

The decisive manœuvre in the Macedonian battle was that of the Serbs. They occupied the sector between the Vardar and the Plain of Monastir along the old frontier. In front of them was a tangle of high mountains, Sokol, Dobropolie, and Vetretnik constituting the highest peaks. While the British between the Struma and the Vardar with

Greek assistance demonstrated vigorously, the magnificent Serbian remnant pushed north, took the mountain peaks, descended into the valleys of the Cerna and the Vardar, thus separating the so-called German army from the two Bulgarian forces, and threatening the rear of the Bulgarians between the Vardar and the Struma. What followed was swift and complete. The so-called German army, pursued by the French on their front and threatened by the Serbians in their rear along the Vardar Valley, unsuccessfully endeavoured to retire upon Uskup and thus acquire a line of retreat into Bulgaria; failing, it surrendered, while the Bulgarian Government proposed an armistice and then, sending commissioners to Salonica, made an unconditional surrender and retired from the war. About 75,000 prisoners and an enormous booty in material were the immediate fruits of victory, while the Bulgarian army was forced to give up its arms and demobilize.

In his memoirs, Ludendorff has many bitter words to say about the Bulgarian episode. He regards it as merely the consequence of treachery, of a prearranged bargain with the Allies, which is hardly to be borne out by any subsequent indication of tenderness for the Bulgars. He angrily alleges that Bulgarian divisions actually refused to fight, a circumstance which alone could explain for him the Serbian success. But granted this, he has already confessed that Prussian divisions had refused to fight, as far back as the "Black Day" of August 8th, nearly six weeks before the Bulgarians are accused of following Prussian example.

The fact is that Ludendorff fails to appreciate the effect upon his allies of his own defeats. His effort to explain the disasters in the west, after September 15th, by reference to Macedonian circumstances is, as General Maurice points out, merest moonshine. But the reverse is unmistakably true. Bulgaria entered the war merely because she believed, her despicable Czar believed, that Germany would win. She continued in the war because German aid was necessary to hold the territories conquered from Serbia. She quit the war when it became clear that Germany, so far from winning, was on the point of losing the conflict and dragging her allies with her.

Ludendorff might have found ample analogy for what occurred after his August defeats by the most cursory examination of the experiences of Napoleon after his Russian reverses. Then the Prussians were the first to go over to the enemy, not merely to surrender as did the Bulgars. Later the Saxons quit him on the battlefield of Leipsic, while the Bavarians, who had profited by his prosperity, endeavoured to forbid his retreat to France. The moral effect of the Bulgarian defeat and surrender, of the swiftly following Turkish collapse, was undoubtedly felt upon the western front, but in both instances the eastern collapse had only followed Ludendorff's own defeats at the Marne, along the Somme, and his disastrous retreat to the Hindenburg Line—events which were not to be mistaken anywhere, least of all in Sofia or in Constantinople. That the Bulgarian surrender led to the Austrian collapse is more arguable, but the Austrian collapse did not come until Ludendorff had been driven out of the Hindenburg Line and had forced his government to ask an armistice, which was a confession of defeat, emphasized by the circumstances attending the German demand.

On the military side, the consequences of the Bulgarian surrender were relatively minor, because the decision of the war was had absolutely in France, before the victorious Army of the Orient was able to intervene effectively. Of course, Roumania promptly rose, threw off her German shackles, and would in the briefest time have mobilized her armies and, placing them beside the Army of the Orient, moved north to Budapest and to Vienna, to Germany beyond, reinforced by Jugo-Slavs and Czecho-Slovaks, had Austria survived or Germany held out. As it was, Roumania, although rushing her preparations, was not called upon to intervene again, and was able to occupy the districts promised her before her first entrance into the war: Transylvania, the Bukowina, ultimately the eastern half of the Banat, and, as Russian anarchy continued to march, that Bessarabian fraction of Moldavia which had been Latin since the days of Trajan and had been last stolen from the Roumanians by the Russians in sorry return for Roumanian service at Plevna.

The surrender of Bulgaria also opened the land route to Constantinople, which was being followed by British forces, when Turkey succumbed, following disasters in Palestine. But most satisfactory of all consequences of the victory was the reëntry of the Serbs into their capital after three years of absence. The actual triumph which brought them into their own had resulted from the stroke of Marshal Mishitch's survivors of that army which the gallant old Putnik had led south across the Albanian mountains in the terrible winter retreat of 1915. It contained veterans who had defeated the Turks at Kumanovo in 1912, Bulgarians at the Bregalnitza in 1913, and had twice, in 1914 and 1915, routed Austrian armies at the Jedar and Valievo.

There is no finer national page in the history of the World War than that which sets forth the Serbian struggle. No nation, not even Belgium, had known so much of hostile occupation or of enemy brutality; no people had been so ravaged by disease, so maltreated by enemies seeking their extinction. Yet at the moment when the House of Hapsburg— which had plunged the world into war to abolish the Serbian menace to the persistence of Austrian tyranny—was in exile, its monarchy in ruins, King Peter was reëntering Belgrade, and Serbia was not only intact but about to realize the age-long dream of the Southern Slavs. Poetic justice could ask no more, while contrasted with Serbian glory was Bulgarian shame; two treacherous attacks upon her neighbours had not merely gained her nothing, they had left her territorially weakened, with her Macedonian ambition unrealized and her dream of Balkan hegemony shattered.

IV. ARMAGEDDON—"SIDE SHOWS"

On September 19th, four days after the victory in Macedonia and one week before the opening of the Battle of the Hindenburg Line, Allenby struck the Turks north of Jerusalem and standing between Jaffa and the Jordan well north of Jericho. The battle taking its name from Samaria, and doubly memorable in history because the final phase terminated on the Plain of Armageddon, was fought between Allenby's British army, containing a large Indian contingent and a very small French detachment. and the Turkish Eighth and Seventh armies, which when the battle began were in line from the Mediterranean eastward. During the first stage of the battle the Turks fought well but were steadily pressed back. Presently the Turkish front between the sea and the Jordan was broken, and through the gap along the sea coast Allenby launched his cavalry, which swept first northward and thence eastward to Nazareth and the Plain of Armageddon, across the rear of the whole Turkish host. The German commander, Liman von Sanders, barely missed falling into the net by a precipitate flight northward. The balance of the two Turkish armies, more than 60,000 men and 400 guns, fell into Allenby's hands, while Sanders and the remaining Turkish army, the Fourth, fled north to Damascus and thence to Aleppo, pursued by the British and their Arab allies led by Emir Feisul, son of the Sherif of Mecca. At a single blow Turkish military power had been broken and Allenby would be a field marshal and Lord of Megiddo in recognition of his victory. On October 31st Turkey capitulated. Enver Pasha and his Germanophile associates fled eastward.

Allenby's victory brought the final ruin to the Turkish Empire, which, however it might survive in some weakened form, was now definitively deprived of its Arabian provinces. Mesopotamia passed entirely into British hands and French claims upon Syria would be presently recognized. Like Ferdinand of Bulgaria, Enver Pasha had staked his country's future upon a German victory, and German defeat had brought utter ruin.

With the victories in Palestine and Macedonia, as with the victory of Maude's army at Bagdad in a preceding campaign, the history of the so-called "side shows" terminated. Each of them was a failure in so far as it was designed, by an operation in a minor field, to produce or to influence the result in the main theatre of operations, which was always the western front. With the troops wasted at Gallipoli Sir John French might have been able to achieve considerable results in the unfortunate offensive at Loos in September, 1915. Had the Gallipoli venture not been undertaken, the Serbian army might have been saved and the Danube barrier to German expansion maintained. It was necessary to maintain troops in the east to cover Egypt and India, but the attempt to expand the useful occupation of Basra and the adjoining oil fields into a dash to Bagdad, which should counter-balance the defeat at Gallipoli, was a rash and costly venture.

The Salonica episode is less clearly to be set down as a total loss. It unquestionably prevented the delivery of Greece to the Central Powers and the use of its coast and islands for German submarine bases with fatal consequences to Britain's Mediterranean line of communications. But it no less patently represented the locking up of very considerable troops needed elsewhere, and a tremendous expansion of the strain placed upon Allied shipping. Indeed, so great was the strain that the British had resolved in the spring of 1917 to insist upon the evacuation of the whole Macedonian front, which would have led to very grave consequences.

In the end, victories were won in Mesopotamia, in Palestine, and in Macedonia, but they were won only after the results in the main field had been assured. Moreover, while Germany was never able to draw from her Turkish and Bulgarian allies those divisions she asked for to use on the western front, she was not required, save during some brief operation, to employ German troops on these fronts, while her Turkish and Bulgarian allies occupied many French and British divisions which would otherwise have been available in France. Moreover, at one great crisis, when Roumania entered the war in 1916, Bulgarian and Turkish troops, commanded by Mackensen, contributed the necessary strength to render harmless what might have been a fatal stroke.

The moment arrived in the war when Germany's allies demanded help from her. It was the hour when the German situation was gravest in the west. Failing these reinforcements, both her allies succumbed; the Turkish resistance was more considerable than the Bulgarian, but the collapse of both was prompt and beyond all remedy. Not only this, but the Bulgarian collapse opened the Hungarian frontier both to Allied and Roumanian attacks, Roumanian blows—had they been needed— to finish off the Hapsburg nation.

In sum: it is clear that the Allies wasted men and material and severely taxed their transport by endeavouring to achieve a victory in a minor field.   The Gallipoli venture was indefensible, the Salonica invest-ment one of its evil consequences.   The first Bagdad gamble was as futile as the Gallipoli affair and necessitated great subsequent investments in men and material, made necessary to retrieve lost prestige.   Nor did the capture of Bagdad lead to any useful result, since the collapse of Russia abolished all possibility of an extension of the campaign northward. Palestine was a brilliant incident, after an unfortunate beginning at Gaza, but the divisions which were locked up in this army might have saved Gough on March 21st, and the victory in France would, in any event, have brought Turkey to her knees.

The Germans, on the contrary, made no such mistakes; they kept their attention on the western and Russian fronts, using the minor fields only as scenes of brief campaigns, in which they were able to har-vest shining results at small costs—results which, notably in 1915 and in 1916, drew attention away from real reverses in other regions.

It was the German purpose to create a vast central empire, a Mittel-Europa, extending from Hamburg to Basra, including all of the Turk-ish Empire and menacing Egypt and even India.   By their conquests of Serbia and Roumania and by their alliance with Bulgaria and with Turkey, they did construct this empire and, but for Venizelos, Greece would have been enlisted by Constantine.   But the dream of Mittel-Europa was shattered at the Second Marne and at the Hindenburg Line, and could not have survived even had there been no victories in the battles in Macedonia and Palestine.

On the dramatic side, however, there is obvious satisfaction in seeing the great German Mittel-Europa crumble under blows from all sides which, falling simultaneously, demolish it.   The battles which achieved its ruin in Macedonia and in Palestine are themselves brilliant episodes in the war, which have brought justly deserved rewards to the successful commanders.

So complete were the Turkish and Bulgarian surrenders that the recapitulation of the terms of the two armistices can add little.   In sum: Bulgaria and Turkey laid down their arms; opened their territories, their railroad lines, their harbours, and their waterways to their enemies;

A SMOKE SCREEN FOR AMERICAN DESTROYERS

THE AMERICAN NAVY
IN THE WAR

A SUBMARINE'S GUN

U. S. Navy Official

Many of the smaller patrol boats were outranged by the guns carried by U-boats, but seldom did the Germans risk
an engagement, preferring to use their shells on defenceless merchantmen

AMERICAN BATTLE SQUADRON IN THE NORTH SEA

BEHIND THE GUNS ON AN AMERICAN DESTROYER

DEPTH BOMBS IN AIR
These were fired from Y-guns

A CAMOUFLAGED AMERICAN DESTROYER

BRITISH "OLYMPIC" WITH AMERICAN TROOPS ON BOARD

U. S. Navy Official

THE PERISCOPE OF AN AMERICAN SUBMARINE OFF THE IRISH COAST

A SUBMARINE "CRASH DIVE"

AMERICAN SUBMARINES ALONGSIDE MOTHER SHIP IN BANTRY BAY, IRELAND

AN AMERICAN SCHOONER ON FIRE

But the Allied vessels in the neighbourhood hesitate to go to the rescue for they think it is a German decoy ship simulating distress to bring them within torpedo distance

AMERICAN SUBCHASERS IN PORT

Though but 110 feet long they patrolled the open sea despite heavy weather

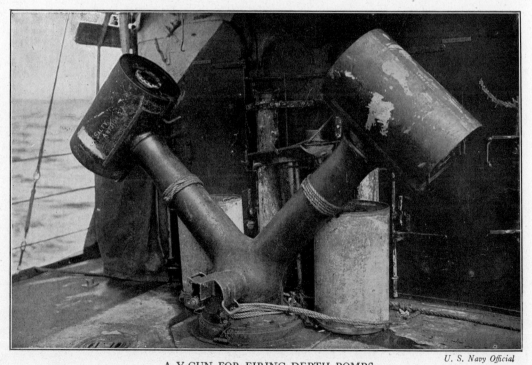

U. S. Navy Official

A Y-GUN FOR FIRING DEPTH BOMBS

It is constructed so that both sides may be discharged at once

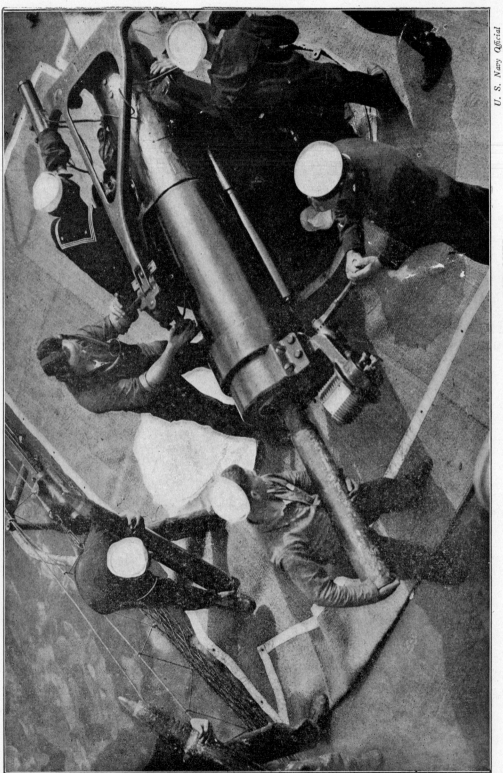

A GUN IN ACTION ON THE STERN OF A DESTROYER

In the submarine zone crews were constantly on watch at their guns, and fired at suspicious objects on the least provocation. The great amount of wreckage floating in the English Channel and the Bay of Biscay during the height of the submarine peril kept the gun crews always alert, but very seldom were submarines actually sighted

agreed to demobilize their armies, to surrender war materials and all else, including the derelict Turkish fleet, which might be required. Turkey agreed to the evacuation of Persia, Syria, Mesopotamia, the Hedjaz, and the Yemen; in fact, placed herself unreservedly and unconditionally in Allied hands.

V. THE LAST OF AUSTRIA

On October 24th the Italian army, with certain British and French contingents and an American regiment, the 332nd, passed the Piave from the mountains to the sea in the final offensive of the war. For the first days the struggle was severe, and then, in the week which saw the Caporetto disaster in the previous year, Austrian resistance collapsed. Armies were transformed into mere fleeing mobs. The rout which had come to a single Italian army in the days of Caporetto now overtook the whole Hapsburg host, and it fled eastward, disintegrating as it ran, until no army was left. Since Waterloo there had been no such battlefield collapse on the continent of Europe.

Too late to change events, and after vain appeals to the United States and to the Allies, Austria surrendered at discretion, unconditionally, abjectly. Already more than 400,000 prisoners, 7,000 cannon, 250,000 horses, booty unequalled in this or any other war, had been gathered in. During the next few days Trent and Trieste welcomed Italian armies, all that Italy had lost in the war was reclaimed, all that Italy had longed for since the fall of the Napoleonic Kingdom of Italy was seized. Before the world had grasped the true meaning of the colossal victory, Italian troops were at the summit of the Brenner Pass and Italian warships occupied Austrian ports. Italia Irredenta was redeemed and Trieste and Trent welcomed their liberators a full month before Strassburg and Metz.

Such were the consequences of the Battle of Vittorio-Veneto. Actually a nation had collapsed behind its army; had more than collapsed, it had resolved into its component racial elements. There was no more Austria, no more Hungary, in the sense in which both had existed for centuries. Italian, Roumanian, Serbian, Croatian, Slovenian, Slovakian, Czechic, and Polish tribes turned at last to their own racial and national pathways while the wretched Austrian fragment, German by language, proclaimed a republic, and Hungary, shorn of all her subject races, began that internal degeneration which would culminate in Bela Kun and the Roumanian invasion.

It was to avoid this disintegration that Austrian statesmen, encouraged by German leaders, had risked the fatal ultimatum now more than four years old. After the Balkan wars, Austria-Hungary had felt herself doomed by Slavic renaissance unless insolent and menacing Serbia were conquered and crushed. Germany had felt with the decay of Austria her own position between France and Russia would become dangerous while her dream of a Middle European empire, of a "place in the sun," would be shattered. To avoid this, Austria and Germany had risked all and now had lost all. At the moment when German armies were at the point of capitulation, the Austro-Hungarian Empire had become a memory and the Emperor of Austria would reign but a single day longer than the German Kaiser.

On the military side the Italian victory in the final struggle at the Piave is not to be compared with that of June or that of the previous year. It was a great victory, mainly an Italian victory, for Diaz had but two British and a single French division under his command. Nevertheless, if his own success in June had contributed materially to decisive Allied victories in July and August in France, the reaction of those victories and of the further triumphs in September and October had produced the moral collapse which gave to his early successes in the last battle their unlimited horizons.

The value of Italy to her allies in the war has been singularly underestimated. Her notification to France of her assured neutrality, in August, 1914, enabled Joffre to use in the north those divisions which otherwise would have been immobilized along the Alps to the utter ruin of France at and even before the Marne. Italy's entrance into the struggle in 1915 exactly coincided with Russian disaster at the Dunajec, and had Austrian troops not been drawn to the Italian front, Russia might have been completely crushed in 1915, and Germany with

Austrian assistance might have come west in 1916 before Great Britain was ready. What the blow at Verdun might have been under these circumstances is not difficult to perceive.

A year later Russian collapse did occur, and it was Italy who suffered the first blow in consequence, having inflicted heavy losses upon the Austrians and kept them fully occupied at the Isonzo until the moment when the release of German divisions on the western front and the decline of Italian morale, due to the enormous sacrifices on the Bainsizza Plateau, made Caporetto possible. The rally of Italy at the Piave is a splendid page in national history and proved as fatal to Austrian purposes as the French stand at the Marne had been to German designs.

In 1918 Italy won the first victory in a very great and desperate battle which had immediate and continuing influence upon events in the French field. And in 1918 Italy prevented the transfer of any appreciable number of Austrian troops to the western front while she sent thither splendid divisions of her own, two of which played a very real part in the defence of the Mountain of Rheims in the German phase of the Second Battle of the Marne, and continued gallantly and usefully in the subsequent fighting.

Without Italian aid it seems impossible to calculate the victory which was finally achieved. It is true that after Caporetto a certain number of British and French divisions were sent to Italy, some of which remained even to the moment of the Battle of Picardy, but they cannot be regarded as counter-balancing in any appreciable degree that whole mass of Austrian military establishment which would have been available for use on the western front after Russian collapse had Italy remained neutral or retired from the war. Further than this the Italian navy was of very great assistance in the Mediterranean, and but for Italian participation in the Balkan campaign, the Salonica operation must have been abandoned and Greece surrendered to the Central Powers.

Had Russia continued in 1917 and 1918 to fight with the determination and energy which she displayed in 1916, it is not unreasonable to suppose that Germany would have been beaten in the latter year; but, with Italy in and Russia out, the Allies were still unable to win the war, and it required the uttermost strength of all three nations to hold the line until America could arrive. Therefore, it seems simple justice to say that Italian participation was an indispensable condition not alone of victory but of the earlier escape from defeat.

VI. THE SUBMARINE

During all the period of the fighting on land until, on the eve of complete surrender, the Germans abandoned their undersea campaign, the submarine remained a grave menace, checked measurably but only measurably and, in the judgment of Tirpitz, was destined to have become more dangerous with the new craft Germany had in hand in October. One may say of the campaign waged against the submarine nothing more positive than that at the moment when it was abandoned the total of Allied building had over-passed the monthly average of sinking, and that the realization of the American shipbuilding programme, together with the acceleration of British construction, had abolished the immediate peril, while the new method of convoy, depth bombs, and the patrol, made possible by American light craft in European waters, were slowly but surely reducing the harvest of the underseas boat.

The great achievement, however, was the successful moving of more than 2,000,000 soldiers across the ocean with only one real disaster, the sinking of the *Tuscania*. Half a million were moved in the first thirteen months and 1,500,000 in the last six months. A miracle was accomplished alike in the movement of the army and of the cargoes, and the total of tons rose from 373,000 in April to 750,000 in October. In these figures is revealed the true failure of the submarine campaign. It was designed to bring Britain and France to their knees before America could effectively intervene in the war. It failed in its primary purpose, although it did bring the United Kingdom to the outer edge of starvation, and it totally failed to prevent the transportation of American masses whose total casualties due to the submarine were less than 700 in a total of more than 2,000,000 embarked.

But it is essential to remember that, although the campaign failed, the failure was by no means assured before the end of 1917, and the losses remained grave to the very end. Thus in 1917 the total sinkings were 6,200,000 tons, and for the first four months of the unlimited sinking, 2,700,000 tons. The monthly average for the eleven months of the campaign of 1917 was 530,000 tons. The measure of the success of the anti-submarine operations is revealed in the reduction of this average to 255,000 tons in the ten months of submarine warfare in 1918. The margin between the two rates represents the postponement of decisive defeat during the time when new construction could be carried forward, and it was one of the ironies of the situation that the German ships interned in American ports, and presently seized and operated by the United States Government after we entered the war, played a decisive part in the transport of American troops to France.

For the ten months of unrestricted warfare in 1917, the Germans sank 5,502,000 tons; in 1918, for a similar number of months, 2,554,000 tons. To have reduced the submarine destruction by nearly 3,000,000 tons in ten months represents the achievement of the Allied navies, but mainly of the British fleet. It was accomplished by the convoy system, by the use of depth bombs, patrols, "mystery ships"; it was facilitated in a measure by the decline in the morale of the German sailors, a consequence of increased Allied efficiency in destruction. The mutiny in the German navy in the closing hours of the war, when the orders were issued for the High Seas Fleet to go out on an adventure like that of Cervera at Santiago, represented the results of British strength as disclosed in the Battle of Jutland, and Allied success in the long battle with the submarine. Admiral Sims has reported that of the German submarines not less than 205 were sunk, 13 by Americans, a certain number by French, Italian, and Japanese ships, but the vast majority by the British navy, which in addition earned world-wide admiration by Sir Roger Keyes's brilliant exploit in bottling up the harbour of Zeebrugge on April 23rd. This venture, directly modelled upon Hobson's deed in the *Merrimac* at Santiago, but a far more considerable, dangerous, and successful achievement, for the time at least sealed up the

Zeebrugge outlet to the Bruges submarine base, while on May 10th Commodore Hubert Lynes performed a similar feat at Ostend, thus closing the other gateway to the Belgian "wet triangle."

Tirpitz believes that had the submarine campaign been pressed instead of suspended under American pressure, in 1916, it might have won the war; and he discloses the interesting circumstance that, while the world held him responsible for the first submarine blockade venture, he had in fact opposed it—for practical, not for humane, reasons—believing at that time that such a blockade was beyond German resources and that the blockade of the Thames estuary held out greater promise of profit and less risk of international complications.

But whatever else may be said of Tirpitz's conclusions, he is certainly correct in his belief that the submarine and the campaign in the first months of 1917 brought the Allies nearer to defeat than any military operation during the war, and brought Great Britain nearer to absolute surrender than at any time in her history since the Norman Conquest; but, by contrast, it brought Germany to absolute ruin by bringing America to Europe. Like Ludendorff, Tirpitz concedes that the campaign of 1917 would never have been launched had German leaders suspected the swift onset of Russian revolution. One of the great blunders of all history this submarine campaign must be reckoned, and however near it brought Germany to success, its responsibility for the ultimate collapse is unmistakable.

In truth, like the Hutier tactic in the field, the submarine campaign at sea in the end encountered a defensive tactic which deprived it of its deadliest possibilities. This was inevitable and should have been foreseen by the Germans. Napoleon's march to Moscow was no more ruinous to his empire than the submarine gamble eventually proved to be for the Empire of the Hohenzollerns. By it Germany lost the war, aroused the animosity of neutrals as well as the implacable hatred of belligerents, and found herself at the end compelled to surrender her own merchant fleet to make good in part the ravages of her undersea boats.

And despite the submarine interlude the British navy played an even greater part in the ultimate downfall of Germany than it had in the destruction of Napoleon. It not merely conveyed more than half the American army to Europe in its merchant ships, but in the first days cleared the ocean of German vessels, war and merchant alike, and held the seaward gates of the German Empire in a relentless grip from the beginning to the end. If the German people did not literally starve, a very considerable number of them suffered from hunger, and the military machine was more and more handicapped by the absence of necessary materials obtainable only from the outside world. Great as was the physical and material handicap imposed upon Germany by the British fleet, the moral blockade was almost more deadly. Germany was isolated from the world, and while both in peace and war the products of American forge and farm, mine and factory, flowed to Germany's enemies, Hamburg and Bremen became as deserted as the ancient harbour of Carthage. The German flag became unknown on the high seas or in foreign ports and all the magnificent achievement of German commercial expansion was reduced to nothing.

Yet, aside from the Battle of Jutland, the naval phase of the war was lacking in every larger element of appeal. If Beatty more than Jellicoe possessed the "Nelson touch" it revealed itself in no Trafalgar, had no opportunity to reveal itself. The war on the sea was in a sense as unromantic, as hard, as painful as the war in the trenches. Yet it had a far more shining reward. On the day on which a German admiral brought the German High Seas Fleet to Scapa Flow under its own steam, and, on Beatty's order, hauled down the German ensign, Great Britain won a greater triumph over a naval rival than had been known since the days when Rome conquered Carthage. The Kaiser had challenged British supremacy of the seas, and the end of the conflict was the scene at Scapa Flow, one of the most complete and absolute victories ever won, a victory which not alone destroyed the enemy's power to resist but shattered the tradition without which no navy can exist. Without the British navy there could have been no victory on land, and if Beatty had no victory of the Second Marne or of the Hindenburg Line to reward his labours, Foch was no more successful in reviving for the

French army the tradition of Napoleon than was Beatty in preserving for the British navy the prestige of Nelson. That the American navy served usefully and gallantly under Beatty must be a cause for national pride hereafter, not less for the navy than the Meuse-Argonne achievement for the army.

And not only had Western ideas of democracy and liberty prevailed against the Prussian conception of autocracy and of militarism but the military tradition of the French Revolution had again triumphed over that of Frederick the Great. Moltke had met Joffre at the First Marne and been defeated, Falkenhayn had met Petain at Verdun and been repulsed, Ludendorff had encountered Foch and been conquered. Not only had the defeats of Wörth, Gravelotte, and Sedan been avenged in the two Marne battles and before Verdun, but for the Prussian share in Waterloo and the German accomplishment at Sedan Foch had paid measure for measure at the Battle of the Hindenburg Line. His campaign from March 26th to July 18th, made in adversity, had been as brilliant as Napoleon's last campaign in the Marne valley in 1814, and Foch had succeeded where the Emperor failed. His campaign from July 18th to November 11th had been as successful as any one of the great Emperor's earlier campaigns which culminated at Austerlitz, Jena, or Wagram, and in the cause of Washington, Foch had revealed the genius of Napoleon.

In the cause of human liberty he had employed talents which will entitle him hereafter to rank with Cæsar and Napoleon as one of the supreme soldiers of all time, and he had employed those talents, not to achieve for himself imperial glory or world dominion, but to establish for his own country and for the democracies allied with France those liberties which the German had sought to abolish. Through him France had risen once more from the dejection of defeat to her ancient estate as the first champion of human liberty in the world. And before the splendour of Foch's achievement every other personal contribution to the greatest struggle in all human history sinks into insignificance.

CONCLUSION

The victories whose decisions were written in the several armistices settled all the issues on which the war had been fought. The German effort to dominate the Continent by force of arms was shattered at the Battle of the Hindenburg Line as that of Napoleon had been broken at Waterloo. The return of Alsace-Lorraine, determined in the document of Rethondes, righted the ancient wrong of 1871 and repealed the Treaty of Frankfort which for forty-seven years had oppressed all conceptions of justice and troubled the peace of the world. The arrival of the German fleet in Scapa Flow terminated a German challenge to British sea power which had been developing since the opening of the reign of William II.

Beyond all else, the victories of the armies of Marshal Foch at last refuted the Prussian doctrine practised by Frederick the Great in Silesia, by him and by his successors in Poland, by William I in Schleswig and in Alsace-Lorraine. The archaic conception that the necessities of the strong are sufficient warrant for the plundering and enslavement of the weak fell with the revelation that however long the evil principle may seem to prevail, in the end the concerted efforts of the weak will overthrow the strong.

Once more a nation had endeavoured to realize the ambition of Charles V and Philip II of Spain, of Louis XIV and Napoleon of France. Tempted by unmistakable superiority in numbers, organization, military and economic resources, Germany had sought a continental supremacy by arms which was to be the prelude to a revival in the world of the Roman episode. And once more the end had been as before. After shining victories and temporary successes the attempt had failed, and the failure had brought untold miseries and humiliations to the dynasty and the nation. In all essential details history had but repeated itself, the will of the separate nationalities and races for liberty had vindicated itself upon the battlefield.

And it was to vindicate this will for liberty that the several nations had taken up arms, that Belgium had resisted invasion; that Britain, seeing herself threatened, had declared war; that invaded France had borne all agonies with unflinching determination to die rather than to be conquered or enslaved.

As the German purpose and the German spirit more and more clearly revealed not only the ambition but the savagery of conquest, one nation after another was drawn into the struggle, with the conscious or unconscious instinct for self-preservation dictating its action. In the end the circle of Germany's foes extended around the world, and men of Australia, Canada, and the United States, fought beside those of Europe and of the white populations of Africa on the western battle front.

And this issue, the supreme issue of the war, however disguised in eloquent phrases or camouflaged by moral appeals, was settled in the battles which preceded the Armistice. The world fought Germany because the world saw in the German purpose a direct and deadly threat to its own liberties, to its own safety, alike to its institutions, its ideals, and its simplest and most material interests. The only solution to the struggle could be the destruction of German military power, and that power was broken by the victories from July to November, 1918.

Nor was the downfall of Germany the sole consequence of the victories. Not only did the races which had been free on August 1, 1914, retain their liberties on November 11, 1918, but other races, long held in subjection but never surrendering their national faith and their instinctive longing for liberty, escaped from bondage as an incident in German defeat. The Poles, the Czechs, the Slovaks, the Southern Slavs, the Italians of Austria and the Roumanians of Hungary were emancipated by the fact of victory. In the first eleven days of November, 1918, a new Europe emerged from chaos, and even in Asia there were far-reaching transformations.

These things, in the words of Marshal Foch, were "facts." They were enduring evidences that the issues for which the war had been fought were settled. The Peace Conference might, after long deliberation and mighty discussion, endeavour to trace lines upon the map which would express the facts of the war, the results of the victory and of the defeat, but the results themselves lay beyond the authority of the Peace Conference to modify or measurably to transform.

This had been true in 1648 after the Thirty Years' War, in 1815 after the Wars of Napoleon. In each case an attack upon the liberty of the world had been repulsed. The fall of Napoleon and the collapse of the French effort to dominate the Continent were achieved results. The efforts at Vienna to make the decision of the question immediately at issue extend to cover the questions of the future failed utterly and miserably. The defeat of Napoleon had not rendered permanent the subjection of Italy, the disunion of Germany, the damnation of the principles of the French Revolution. It had done no more than dispose of the question for which Europe had struggled toward settlement from Austerlitz to Waterloo.

The actual progress of the Conference of Paris is, perhaps, the best illustration of the truth, established in history, that peace settlements settle nothing; rather, they signal the arrival of that new set of problems, controversies, conflicts out of which is made the history of a later period. What was decided at Vienna remained a matter of controversy a century and more after the Congress had adjourned and decades after its last participant had died. But what was done at Waterloo—the result, the decision—has not changed since the evening of June 18, 1815, when, the Guard having failed, Napoleon took the road for Paris and St. Helena. In our own experience it is at Appomattox that the Civil War ends. What lies beyond is the period of Reconstruction, the development of a new phase.

Therefore this history of the World War closes with the battles of the Hindenburg Line, of Vittorio-Veneto, of Macedonia, and of Armageddon, and with the narration of their immediate consequences, which were: the surrender of Germany; the separation of Austria-Hungary into its racial fragments; the restoration to France of Alsace-Lorraine; the occupation by Italy of her Irredenta; the liberation of Belgium and Serbia, restored to national independence; the revolution in Germany and elsewhere, which temporarily or permanently removed from the hands of a few that arbitrary power which they had exercised in such fashion as to oppress millions and to menace the freedom of all mankind.

There are those to whom the victory will seem vain, if to the deliverance from the German menace there be not added security against all future war, insurance against every later international conflict. The aspiration is a great and noble dream, and any fraction of it actually realized will be of enduring benefit to all mankind. But for myself, I am content that the German attack has been repulsed. Terrible as has been the sacrifice and great as is the suffering which still continues, I cannot conceive that the existing misery approximates that which would have resulted had Foch failed to hold the line between March 26th and July 18th, or if between the Marne and the Meuse he had not broken the German army and that for which the German army stood in the sum total of human existence.

Not a few of my friends have given their lives in the struggle, and my life is the poorer because of the loss. Much of the world that I knew and loved has been turned into ruins, which I have seen in their full desolation and ugliness. I have seen the horror and the misery of battle at the front and behind the front and known the agony which comes to a whole nation when the enemy is literally at the gate.

And yet, remembering the days of September, 1914, when the German army approached Paris, when that incarnation of ruthless force which was the German army seemed about to engulf all that was beautiful and free in the world; recalling the hours of Verdun, the even more terrible hours in the spring of 1918, when German victory seemed not merely possible but probable; turning back to the moments immediately following the invasion of Belgium, the sinking of the *Lusitania*, the moments in which the character, the power, and the purpose of the German were revealed and it seemed as if all our conceptions of right, justice, of all that makes for sweetness and light in this world, were about to be shattered; I cannot but feel grateful and content at those fruits of victory which are assured, were assured at the moment when German surrender wrote the everlasting condemnation of the German idea and the German conception of human existence.

Nor can I believe that the awful sum of human misery and sacrifice this war has brought is proven vain, if the single profit be the repulse of one more monstrous effort to enslave men's spirits with the idea of force and men's bodies with the application of that force, as Germany applied it in Belgium, in France, in Poland—as Germany's allies applied it in Serbia, in Roumania, in Hapsburg Austria and Hungary.

At Verdun I saw thousands of men, in the heat of battle, marching to death which was imminent and well nigh inescapable, with a single thought in their minds, a single phrase on their lips—"They Shall Not Pass!" And if the realization of their will be all of our victory which stands the test of time, I cannot believe the benefit to mankind has been incommensurate with the sacrifice. Nor can I fail to be humbly grateful to the men of my own race, who on those same Verdun hills so wrought that the French sacrifice of 1916, which might otherwise have been sterile, became a fruitful sowing against the harvest of 1918.

THIS VOLUME CONCLUDES MR. SIMONDS'S
HISTORY OF THE WORLD WAR

EDITOR

AMERICA'S CONTRIBUTION TO VICTORY

By MARSHAL FOCH

On March 21st, Germany launched her offensive against the hinge of the allied armies in the region of Saint-Quentin. You know what its effects were. It soon reached the Scarpe, advanced up the Somme, which it crossed, and progressed down the Oise. The situation suddenly became very grave.

In those critical days, on the 28th of March, General Pershing and General Bliss generously came forward with an offer to lead their men into battle, and they both said to me: "We are here to be killed; forward then with our men."

Soon after, on the 25th of April, at Sarcus, we met the same generals; on the 2nd of May, at Abbeville, with the concurrence of the Allied governments, we asked the American Government to land in France, each month, 120,000 infantry men or machine gunners, and replacement troops.

In fact, during the month of March, the United States sent to us 69,000 men; in April, 94,000; 200,000 in May; 245,000 in June; 295,000 in July; 235,000 in August.

The strength of the American army went up from 300,000 men on the 11th of March to 954,000 in July and 1,700,000 in October.

On the 2nd of June, the Versailles Supreme War Council asked President Wilson to continue sending troops in the same way, from 200,000 to 300,000 men per month, and to have in readiness for the spring of 1919 one hundred American divisions. President Wilson answered that he agreed and that if more were needed, they would be forthcoming.

But during that time the American troops did not remain idle. As early as the month of May, two American divisions went into the fight with the French First Army in the region of Montdidier; three were in the Vosges, where they relieved the French; two were in training.

In June, two more were on the Marne, at Château-Thierry, and in the Belleau Wood, where they assumed a large share of the resistance offered to the enemy.

On July 18th, five American divisions took part in the victorious counter-offensive of the French Sixth and Tenth armies, and contributed greatly to its success.

At the same time, on the 24th of July, the American First Army was formed, under the command of General Pershing. Its appointed task was to clear the communications between Paris and Nancy by pushing the enemy back at Saint-Mihiel.

On the 12th of September, 14 American divisions, 8 in the first line and 6 in support, conquered the salient of Saint-Mihiel, capturing 200 guns and 15,000 prisoners.

Some days later, on the 26th of September, between the Aisne and the Marne, in the rough Argonne region, 14 American divisions went into a great offensive. On the second day, Montfaucon was left behind; on the 14th of October Grandpré was taken; Châtillon on the 21st, Bantheville on the 30th; on the 1st of November, Buzancy; on the 4th, Beaumont, and on the 9th the whole line of the Meuse, from Mouzon to Bazeilles, was in our possession.

In the meantime, two American divisions lent their assistance to the French Fifth Army near Romains; two others to the British armies in the region of Saint-Quentin, and still two others, jointly with the French Fourth Army, stormed the formidable positions at Orfeuil; then, two American divisions shared in the offensive of the Flanders group, on the Lys and the Scheldt. Finally, six more were getting ready, together with the French army, for the offensive of the 14th of November in Lorraine, when the Armistice of November the 11th was signed, taking our weapons from us.

Thus the American army had powerfully aided in winning the victory, for the Armistice was tantamount to a capitulation, an absolute capitulation.

Thus the American army, supported by a government firmly determined to keep up the fight to the very end, had returned to France the visit Lafayette had paid to America at the time of America's birth.

I think of those moving memories of days of anguish and days of success as I salute the American nation which so valiantly upheld us in the war.

I salute my American comrades in arms, generals, officers and soldiers, all equally glorious, thanks to whom a decisive victory has been achieved for freedom.

II

A CHRONOLOGY OF THE EVENTS OF THE WORLD WAR

1914

June 28.—The Austrian Archduke, Francis Ferdinand, is murdered at Serajevo, Bosnia, by a Serbian.

July 23.—Austria-Hungary sends an ultimatum to Serbia.

July 25.—Serbia agrees to most of the demands of Austria-Hungary, and asks arbitration of the rest.

Russia begins to mobilize.

July 28.—Austria-Hungary declares war on Serbia.

July 31.—Germany demands that Russia cease mobilization.

August 1.—Germany declares war on Russia.

August 3.—Belgium decides to defend herself against German violation.

Germany declares war on France.

August 4.—Great Britain declares war on Germany. German invasion of Belgium begins.

August 6.—Italy proclaims her neutrality.

August 7.—Germans enter Liége.

French troops cross German frontier into Alsace-Lorraine.

August 15.—Japan demands the German possessions at Kiau-chau, China.

August 15-23.—French armies are forced to retire after engagements at Morhange (Alsace-Lorraine) and at Neufchâteau and Charleroi (Belgium.)

August 19.—Germans occupy Louvain.

August 20.—Germans occupy Brussels and turn south toward Paris.

August 23.—The British at Mons (Belgium) holding left wing, are attacked by superior force and compelled to join in retreat of whole allied line. Japan declares war on Germany and begins bombardment of Tsingtau.

Germans take Namur.

August 25.—Germans destroy Louvain.

August 26.—Allied forces capture Togoland.

August 30.—Russian armies are in East Prussia and Galicia.

August 31.—Hindenburg defeats the Russian army at Tannenberg.

September 1.—French line from Verdun to the Somme is in retreat. Joffre has reorganized the army.

September 2.—Russians take Lemberg, capturing 250,000 prisoners and enormous stores of supplies.

September 4.—Great Britain, France, and Russia sign a treaty not to make peace separately.

September 5-10.—In the Battle of the Marne the French with slight aid from Great Britain break the German offensive.

September 13.—The German retreat is halted at the Aisne and trench warfare begins.

September 18.—Kluck regains some of the ground which the British and the French had taken north of the Aisne.

September 20.—The "race to the sea" between the opposing armies begins and the centre of the conflict mounts northward.

The famous cathedral at Rheims, France is destroyed by German guns.

September 27.—General Botha is successful in an invasion of German Southwest Africa.

October 3.—First contingent of Canadians, consisting of 33,000 men embarks for England.

October 9.—Antwerp is occupied by Germans after ten days' bombardment; remaining Belgian troops escape to Holland.

October 14.—First British troops reach Ypres.

October 15.—Ostend falls into the hands of the Germans.

October 16-28.—In order to block the Germans the Belgians (in the Battle of Yser) in despair open the sluices and flood the country.

October 20.—Hindenburg begins his first campaign for Warsaw in order to divert the Russians from Galicia.

October 20-November 15.—The First Battle of Ypres results in terrific losses in men and territory for the British and French. Germany fails to reach the Channel ports.

October 29.—Turkey enters the war as an ally of Germany and Austria and begins bombarding the Russian ports on the Black Sea.

November 7.—The Japanese capture Tsingtau, the fortified portion of the German possessions at Kiau-chau.

November 9.—German cruiser *Emden* is caught and destroyed at Cocos Island.

November 15.—The deadlock on the western

front begins, destined to last, with little change, until March, 1917.

November 23.—Basra is held by a small British force sent from India.

December 1.—Austria strikes Serbia with overwhelming force.

Botha has stamped out **De Wet's rebellion** in South Africa and has De Wet a prisoner.

December 6.—After six weeks of sanguinary fighting the Germans occupy Lodz, Poland, but fail to reach Warsaw.

December 8.—**British win naval victory off** Falkland Islands.

December 15.—Serbia frees herself from Austria for the time being.

December 17.—Great Britain declares Egypt a British protectorate, terminating the suzerainty of Turkey.

December 26.—United States protests to Great Britain against seizure and detention of cargoes to neutral ports.

1915

January 1.—The deadlock which is to last until May begins in Poland.

Germany's outlook is dark without being desperate; she thinks Italy will remain neutral and feels sure that Roumania will; Austria day by day becomes more of a dead weight.

January 3-4.—Russian armies defeat Turkish forces in the Caucasus.

January 7.—British Government answers protest of United States with regard to the seizure of cargoes for neutral ports.

January 16.—Russian armies begin to pass over Carpathians from Galicia into plains of Hungary.

January 24.—A naval engagement is fought in the North Sea off **Dogger Bank**, between powerful British and German fleets, ending in victory for the British.

January 26.—The German Government seizes all corn, wheat, and flour—the beginning of a rationing system.

January 30.—German submarines sink several British merchant ships.

February 2.—Great Britain decides to seize grain and flour shipments to Germany.

February 4.—**Germany declares a submarine war zone** around the British Isles, after February 18, and announces that enemy merchant ships will be destroyed; neutral vessels are warned of danger.

February 10.—The United States protests to Germany against risks created by German war zone decree—the **"strict accountability"** note.

February 15.—German troops have Russians in full retreat after desperate fighting in the Masurian Lakes region.

February 16.—Germany offers to withdraw war-zone decree if Great Britain permits

movement of foodstuffs to civil population of Germany.

February 18.—The German war-zone decree becomes effective and Germany disclaims responsibility for accidents to neutral vessels.

Kamerun is in the hands of the French and British.

February 19-20.—British and French warships bombard Turkish forts at entrance to Dardanelles but later abandon their task as impossible.

American Secretary of State sends identic note to Germany and Great Britain suggesting an agreement between these two powers respecting the conduct of naval warfare.

February 28.—Germany replies to the identic note from United States and indicates that she is willing to discuss an agreement with regard to the conduct of naval warfare.

A German cruiser sinks the *William P. Frye* in the Pacific.

March 1.—France and Great Britain announce their intention to prevent commodities of all kinds from reaching or leaving Germany.

March 10.—The British employ for the first time, massed artillery fire preliminary to an infantry advance. They capture Neuve-Chapelle but fail to win the road to Lille.

March 18.—*Irresistible* and *Ocean* are sunk by Turkish mines in the Dardanelles.

March 23.—The Austrian fortress of Przemysl is surrendered with 119,000 prisoners to the Russians after a siege which lasted 200 days.

March 28.—British passenger ship, *Falaba*, is torpedoed and sunk; an American loses his life.

April 2.—Russians are fighting desperately in the Carpathians and three days later announce gains along a 75-mile front but by the third week in April the army has come to a standstill.

April 22-May 13.—In the Second Battle of Ypres the Germans gain ground north of that gained in the first battle, but fail to break through the British line; they employ asphyxiating gas for the first time.

April 25.—Anglo-French troops are landed on both sides of the Dardanelles after suffering heavy losses and the futile Gallipoli campaign begins.

April 28.—American S. S. *Cushing* is bombed by German airplanes.

April 30.—Germans invade the Baltic provinces of Russia.

May 1.—A Russian army is destroyed in the Battle of the Dunajec (east of Cracow) and other Russians in the Carpathians are forced to retreat hastily.

American *Gulflight* is sunk off Scilly Islands. Two Americans are lost.

May 7.—The Cunard liner, *Lusitania*, is sunk without warning by a German submarine off the Old Head of Kinsale, near Queenstown

1153 persons lose their lives, including 114 Americans.

May 10.—President Wilson delivers his "too proud to fight" speech in Philadelphia.

May 13.—The United States protests to Germany against its submarine policy, culminating in the sinking of the *Lusitania* and declares that it will not omit any word or act necessary to maintain the rights of its citizens.

May 23.—American steamer, *Nebraskan*, is torpedoed off Fastnet.

Italy enters the war, against Austria-Hungary only.

May 26.—German submarine sinks battleship, *Triumph*, in Dardanelles.

May 27.—Germans sink *Majestic*. The fleet is withdrawn from the Dardanelles.

May 28.—Germany answers America's note of the 13th and makes a cowardly attempt to shift the responsibility of the sinking of the *Lusitania* to Great Britain.

June 2.—Russians evacuate Przemysl and continue to retreat in Galicia, leaving the Austrians and Germans in charge.

June 8.—William J. Bryan, Secretary of State, resigns.

June 9.—United States sends a second note to Germany with regard to the *Lusitania* massacre and demands that the Imperial Government adopt such measures as are necessary to safeguard American lives and American ships.

June 11.—The Italians advance toward Trieste.

June 22.—The Russians evacuate Lemberg which they have held since September, 1914.

July 8.—Germany offers safety to United States vessels in submarine zone under certain specified conditions.

July 15.—Germany admits that American steamer *Nebraskan* was damaged by torpedo from a German submarine and expresses regret.

Conquest of German Southwest Africa is completed and the colony passes under the control of the Union of South Africa.

July 17.—Bulgaria commits herself to the Central Powers.

July 25.—American steamer *Leelanaw*, carrying contraband, is sunk by a German submarine. Warning is given and no lives are lost.

August 4.—German troops occupy Warsaw, capital of Russian Poland, after a swift encircling advance over vast territory from north, west, and south.

August 5.—Miss Edith Cavell is arrested by the Germans and charged with helping prisoners to escape.

August 17-September 20.—Germans capture Kovno, Brest-Litovsk, Grodno, Vilna, and other fortresses on Russia's second line of defense.

August 19.—The *Arabic* is sunk by German submarine on way to New York; forty-four passengers, including several Americans are lost. Later the German Government expresses regret.

August 20.—Italy declares war on Turkey.

August 26.—German Ambassador von Bernstorff at Washington declares that hereafter liners will not be sunk by German submarines without warning.

August 29.—*Hesperian*, American steamer, is torpedoed off Fastnet.

September 5.—The Russian Grand Duke Nicholas is displaced from command of all Russian armies and the Czar takes charge.

September 25.—French undertake an offensive in Champagne region, which gains grounds but fails to break through the German line. British at Loos suffer heavy losses.

October 5.—First Allied troops land at Salonica at the invitation of the Greek Government.

October 6-December 2.—Austro-German-Bulgarian troops conquer Serbia. Monastir falls into the hands of the enemy.

October 11.—Bulgarian troops cross the Serbian frontier.

October 12.—Miss Edith Cavell, an English nurse at Brussels, is shot by the German military authorities, for assisting the enemies of Germany to escape to Belgium.

October 20.—Fighting around Ypres is intense.

October 28.—Aristide Briand (Socialist) succeeds Viviani as Premier of France.

November 7.—The Italian passenger ship *Ancona* is sunk in the Mediterranean by an Austrian submarine.

November 28.—Germany declares the campaign against Serbia at a close, practically the whole country being overrun by Austro-German-Bulgarian armies and the Serbian army being half-dispersed, half-annihilated.

December 1.—Italy joins the Allied agreement not to make separate peace.

December 3.—United States requests the recall of German military and naval attachés at Washington.

December 6.—United States protests to Austria-Hungary against the "wanton slaughter of defenceless noncombatants" on the *Ancona* and demands reparation.

December 15.—Sir John French retires from the command of the British army in France and Flanders and Sir Douglas Haig takes charge.

December 19.—Anglo-French troops withdraw from Anzac and Suvla Bay (Gallipoli Peninsula).

December 30.—British passenger steamer *Persia* is sunk in Mediterranean. Three hundred and ninety-two passengers and crew are lost.

1916

January 9.—The attempt to force the Dardanelles is abandoned and the Gallipoli Peninsula is entirely free from British and French troops.

January 13.—Cettinje, capital of Montenegro, falls before Austro-Hungarian armies, and the whole country is overrun by the victorious troops.

February 10.—Germany and Austria announce that they will treat armed merchant ships as war ships and sink them without warning.

February 16.—The Turkish fortress at Erzerum, Armenia, is captured by the Russians. Kamerun (Africa) is conquered.

February 21.—The Germans launch a great offensive at Verdun, destined to last until October 23, but fail in the attempt to break through French line.

February 25.—General Petain takes charge of the army at Verdun at midnight.

February 26.—French counter-attack at Douaumont and bring the Germans to a standstill.

March 8.—Germany declares war on Portugal for breaches of neutrality.

March 24.—French steamer *Sussex* is torpedoed without warning; about 80 passengers, including Americans are killed or wounded.

April 19.—President Wilson addresses Congress on relations with Germany, especially with regard to the submarine campaign, and sends a note to Germany stating that the United States will be compelled to sever diplomatic relations with the German Empire unless the Imperial Government immediately abandons its present method of submarine warfare.

April 21.—Sir Roger Casement, Nationalist leader, is arrested in Ireland and sent to England to meet a traitor's death.

April 24.—A revolution breaks out in Dublin, Ireland, led by members of the Sinn Fein society; casualties on both sides totalling 304 killed and 1,000 wounded; sixteen leaders are convicted of treason and shot.

April 29.—A besieged British army of 9,000, under General Townshend, surrenders to the Turks at Kut-el-Amara upon exhaustion of food; thus the first British attempt to reach Bagdad fails.

May 1.—Irish rebellion comes to an end.

May 4.—Germany informs United States that submarine commanders have been ordered not to sink merchant vessels without warning and without saving lives.

May 14.—Austrians begin preliminary bombardment of the Italians through the Trentino.

May 15.—The Austrians advance rapidly.

May 26.—The Greek garrison holding Fort Ruppel surrenders to Bulgarian forces.

May 31.—British and German fleets meet off Jutland (Denmark) in the greatest naval engagement of history, the Germans finally withdrawing. Both sides suffer heavy losses in men and ships.

June 3.—Cadorna has checked the Austrian advance and during the next ten days recovers most of the lost ground.

June 4.—A Russian offensive is begun on a front of 250 miles in Volhynia, Galicia, and Bukowina. Austrians suffer heavy losses.

June 5.—Earl Kitchener, British Minister of War, on his way to Russia is drowned by the sinking of the cruiser *Hampshire* by mine or torpedo.

July 1.—A great Allied offensive is launched by British and French at River Somme—to last until November, which gains ground but fails in its larger purpose.

July 2.—Haig decides to "fight out the line" along the Meuse.

July 9.—The German commercial submarine *Deutschland* arrives at Baltimore having crossed the Atlantic with a cargo of chemicals—returning on August 23 with gold, nickel, and rubber.

July 14.—Haig breaks through German second line on a three-mile front.

August 3.—Sir Roger Casement is hanged at London for treason in promoting the Irish rebellion.

August 6-9.—Italian troops capture Gorizia in a brilliant attack.

August 27.—Italy declares war on Germany. Roumania enters the war on the side of the Allies and begins an invasion of Transylvania, Hungary. Later she is completely crushed.

August 29.—Field Marshal von Hindenburg succeeds General von Falkenhayn as German Chief-of-Staff.

September 4.—Bulgarian and German troops invade Dobrudja, Roumania, overrunning the whole district by January.
German East Africa is surrendered to the British.

September 13.—The Army of the Orient under General Sarrail begins offensive against Monastir.

September 15.—The British use for first time (in the Somme battle) the "tank" or armoured and armed motor truck, capable of crossing trenches and demolishing obstacles.

October 1.—The third phase of the Battle of the Somme closes but bad weather prevents the British triumph, which, a short time before, seemed inevitable.

October 9.—Venizelos assumes direction of the new government at Salonica and declares war on the Central Powers.

October 24.—The French at Verdun regain important positions lost to Germans from February to June.

November 2.—Germans evacuate Vaux.

November 14.—British near Ancre capture 5,000 prisoners and numerous guns.

November 17.—First Roumanian army is decisively beaten.

November 18.—General Serrail takes Monastir.

November 19.—The Serbs are back in their own country. German armies begin an invasion of Roumania.

November 12.—Francis-Joseph, Emperor of Austria and King of Hungary, dies at Vienna; he is succeeded by his grand-nephew Charles I.

Dr. Alfred Zimmermann succeeds Von Jagow as Minister of Foreign Affairs in Germany.

December 6.—David Lloyd George becomes Premier of Great Britain, succeeding Asquith. Germans enter Bucharest.

December 12.—Germany offers to enter into peace negotiations; the offer is later declared by the ten Allies to be "empty and insincere."

General Nivelle succeeds Joffre as Commander-in-Chief of the French armies.

December 15.—Battle of Verdun ends with victory for the French.

December 18.—President Wilson sends a note to the belligerent nations, suggesting an avowal of respective views regarding peace terms.

December 24.—Joffre is appointed Marshal of France.

December 26.—Germany replies to President Wilson's note, proposing a meeting of peace delegates, but failing to state war aims or peace terms.

December 30.—The Russian monk, Rasputin, is assassinated.

1917

January 22.—President Wilson addresses United States Senate on peace: "It must be a peace without victory"; there should be an independent and autonomous Poland; outlets to sea should be neutralized and the seas should be free; military and naval armaments must be limited.

January 31.—Germany resumes unrestricted submarine war, declaring that "from February 1, 1917, sea traffic will be stopped with every available weapon and without further notice"; American passenger ships may sail once a week under prescribed conditions.

February 3.—United States breaks off diplomatic relations with Germany.

February 6.—British report a German retirement out of Grandcourt but it is not until the middle of March that the movement is well under way and the whole front from Arras to Soissons begins to go back.

February 24.—Kut-el-Amara, in Mesopotamia, is captured by the British (after a campaign begun on December 13), retrieving the surrender of April, 1916.

February 28.—A proposal from Zimmermann, German Foreign Secretary, dated Berlin, January 19, becomes known, looking to alliance with Mexico in event of war with United States, and also suggesting Japanese participation; Mexico to receive financial support and to be compensated with New Mexico, Texas, and Arizona.

March 8.—The Cossacks begin a disturbance which is a few days later to expand into a revolution.

March 11.—Bagdad, most important city of Mesopotamia, and terminus of Germany's railway project, is captured by British troops under General Maude.

March 13.—Revolution rages in Russia in Petrograd, the disturbances beginning over a shortage of food, with sympathetic strikes in munition factories and finally with mutiny of troops; the Duma assumes control of the movement.

March 15.—Czar Nicholas abdicates the throne of Russia in favour of Grand Duke Michael who abdicates the following day, and a Provisional Government is established.

March 17-19.—The Germans withdraw before the British, evacuating 1,300 square miles of French territory, from Arras to Soissons, including Bapaume. Alexandre Ribot succeeds Briand as Premier of France.

April 2.—President Wilson asks Congress in Extraordinary Session to declare that recent acts of the German Imperial Government are in fact war; the Senate adopts the war resolution, 82 to 6, on April 4; the House 373 to 50 on April 6.

April 6.—The United States declares war against Germany; ninety German vessels (600,000 tons) are seized.

April 8.—Austria-Hungary breaks off diplomatic relations with the United States.

April 9-May 15.—The British and the French under Nivelle carry on offensive against the German lines near Arras in which Vimy Ridge is carried by the Canadians and the whole German line is thrown into retreat after having suffered heavy losses. The famous Hindenburg Line is pierced.

April 10.—Bulgaria breaks off diplomatic relations with the United States.

April 14.—French launch an attack against the Craonne Plateau.

April 21.—Turkey breaks off diplomatic relations with the United States.

April 23.—Haig wins local successes on a nine-mile front from Croisilles to Gavrelle.

April 25.—The Battle of Craonne Plateau ends.

May 4.—The American navy begins active participation in the war, a destroyer flotilla coöperating with the British fleet in the war zone.

May 5.—After terrific fighting around Bullecourt the Battle of Arras begins to die out.

May 14.—Cadorna opens the great Italian offensive on Isonzo front by attacking the southern edge of the Bainsizza Plateau.

May 15.—General Petain succeeds General Nivelle as Commander-in-Chief of the French armies. Foch becomes Chief of the General Staff of the French armies.

May 17.—Russian Provisional Government is reconstructed. A. F. Kerensky, a Socialist leader, becomes Minister of War.

May 18.—President Wilson signs the Selective Service Act which creates an army of 500,000 men in addition to Regulars and National Guard.

May 23.—Italians advance on Southern Carso.

May 30.—Italians are held by a series of counter-offensives in which Austrian and Russian troops join.

June 7.—With a great mine explosion, the British blast away the top of Wytschaete-Messines Ridge (White-sheet Ridge), dominating Ypres from the south, and wipe out a German salient.

June 12-29.—Greece becomes a belligerent: King Constantine abdicates the throne on June 12, in favor of his second son, Alexander, in response to the demands of England, France, and Russia; Venizelos becomes Premier on June 25, and [diplomatic relations [are severed with Germany on June 29.

June 13.—Major-General Pershing and his staff arrive in Paris to prepare for the first American expedition.

June 15.—The First American Liberty Loan is closed, with the $2,000,000,000 over subscribed by fifty per cent.

June 26.—The first American troops arrive in France, having sailed secretly on June 14.

July 1-17.—The Russian army, led by Minister of War, Kerensky, assumes an offensive in Galicia for the first time since the revolution; Halicz is captured and 36,000 German, Austrian, and Turkish prisoners are taken.

July 4.—Bethmann-Hollweg resigns as German Chancellor.

July 14.—Dr. Georg Michaelis becomes Chancellor of Germany.

July 19.—The German Reichstag adopts a peace resolution (proposed by Socialists, Radicals, and Catholics) expressing desire of the German people for peace without forcible acquisitions of territory, and with mutual understanding and lasting consideration.

July 19-26.—The recently victorious Russian army mutinies and retreats in the face of a German counter-attack; Kerensky becomes Premier with unlimited power.

July 31.—The Battle of Flanders (Passchendaele Ridge) which is to result in success for the Franco-British forces begins.

August 15.—A peace appeal by Pope Benedict (dated August 1) is made public; he suggests disarmament, evacuation of Belgian and French territory, restitution of German colonies, and settlement of political and territorial questions in a conciliatory spirit for the general welfare.

Canadian troops in a brilliant attack capture Hill 70, dominating Lens (declared impregnable by the Germans).

August 18.—Italians under Cadorna begin the operation against the Bainsizza Plateau which is to result in one of the most brilliant military achievements of the war.

August 20-24.—A French attack along the Meuse results in the capture of important positions and 10,000 prisoners.

August 24.—Italians capture Monte Sant.

August 27.—President Wilson replies to the Pope's peace message; he condemns proposals for punitive damages, the dismemberment of empires, and the establishment of economic leagues, but declares that a peace agreement made by present German rulers must be supported by German people. American exports to neutral countries are placed under Government control.

September 3.—Riga, Russia's second most important seaport, is occupied by Germans the demoralized Russian army withdrawing. The Hutier tactic is used with great success.

September 7-10.—Premier Ribot resigns and Paul Painlevé becomes Premier of France.

September 8.—Intercepted telegrams from Luxburg, German Charge in Argentina, to Berlin, recommend that Argentine vessels, if sunk by German submarines, should be destroyed "without leaving a trace" (spurlos versenkt).

September 15.—Russia is proclaimed a republic.

September 20-October 12.—A series of British attacks in the Ypres sector are retarded by muddy ground.

September 26.—British advance in the Ypres area.

October 9.—Allied forces advance in Flanders.

October 17.—Russians are defeated by the Germans in a naval engagement in the Gulf of Riga.

October 19.—Russian Government flees to Moscow.

October 23-25.—A French offensive under Petain near Soissons results in a maximum gain of nearly four miles and the capture of 12,000 prisoners and 200 guns.

October 24- November 10.—An Austro-German army, with overwhelming artillery, breaks through the Italian lines and causes withdrawal not only from Austrian territory, but from northern Italy to the Piave River. The Italian army collapses before the Hutier tactic in the Caporetto disaster.

October 30.—The Kaiser calls Count von Hertling, a tool of the military party, to succeed Michaelis as Chancellor of Germany.

October 31.—General Allenby begins his campaign for Jerusalem by the capture of Beersheba.

November 2.—Germans retreat on the Chemin des Dames.

November 3.—First American casualties in France.

November 6.—Passchendaele Ridge is carried by the Canadians and the end of the Third Battle of "Wipers" is at hand.

November 7-14.—A second revolution in Russia, under direction of Bolsheviki (or Maximalist faction of Radical Socialists), results in overthrow of Kerensky government; the new Premier Lenin and Foreign Minister Trotsky declare for an immediate democratic peace, the handing over of land to peasants, and the convocation of a constitutional assembly.

British troops under Allenby capture Gaza.

November 16.—Georges Clemenceau becomes Premier of France upon the resignation of Painlevé.

Allenby occupies Jaffa, the port of Jerusalem.

November 18.—Sir Stanley Maude dies in Mesopotamia.

November 20.—The British at Cambrai move forward without the usual artillery preparations, gaining five miles on a wide front and capturing 8,000 Germans; "tanks" play an important part.

November 30-December 5.—German counter-attacks regain half the ground recently lost to British near Cambrai.

December 1.—German East Africa, last and largest of Germany's overseas possessions, comes under complete control of Allied forces.

December 4-7.—The United States Congress, following recommendations by President Wilson, declares war on Austria-Hungary.

December 7.—An armistice goes into effect, on the Russo-German front under the direction (on the part of Russia) of Lenin and Trotsky.

December 11.—Allenby enters Jerusalem.

December 22.—A peace conference assembles at Brest-Litovsk, German-occupied Russia, with delegates from Russia, Germany, Austria-Hungary, Bulgaria, and Turkey; the Central Powers propose a general peace without forcible annexations and indemnities, the Allies to join with Russia; Russia must recognize the demand of the peoples of Poland, Lithuania, Courland, Esthonia, and Livonia for self-government, and German troops will not be withdrawn from those territories.

1918

January 8.—President Wilson addresses Congress on America's programme of world peace, specifying fourteen "rectifications of wrong and assertions of right."

January 16.—The United States Fuel Administrator orders the closing of manufacturing industries for five days, and of all essential businesses for nine Mondays, to save fuel and relieve the railroads.

January 21.—Strikes in Austrian cities, in favor of peace, but aggravated by food shortage, cause the closing of important war industries.

January 24.—Chancellor von Hertling replies to peace terms of Premier Lloyd George and President Wilson—declining to allow interference in Russian affairs, leaving Italian matters to Austria-Hungary to answer, pledging support to Turkey against proposals affecting its territory, declaring that withdrawal from France should be agreed upon between Germany and France, that Belgian details be settled at a peace conference, and that dismemberment of Alsace-Lorraine can never be considered.

January 28-February 4.—Strikes occur in Berlin and other German cities in favour of peace without indemnities or annexations, the abolition of militarism and war industries, and participation of workmen in peace parleys.

February 9.—The first peace treaty is signed between representatives of Central Powers and the new republic of Ukraine, in southern Russia.

February 11.—President Wilson, addressing Congress, analyzes recent Austro-German peace utterances and restates four principles upon which a just and permanent peace could be founded.

The Russian Government, though refusing to sign a peace treaty, declares war with the Central Powers at an end.

February 18-19.—Germany resumes hostilities against Russia; Russian armies flee toward Petrograd, despite the appeals of Lenin and Trotsky, as the German troops approach; the Russian Government declares its willingness to sign the peace treaty dictated by the Teutons.

March 3.—A peace treaty is signed at Brest-Litovsk, between Russia and the four Central Powers. Besides territory occupied by Germans new terms compel Russia to "evacuate" Ukraine, Esthonia, Livonia, Finland, the Aland Islands, and the Transcaucasian districts of Erivan, Kars, and Batum.

March 21-23.—The Germans launch an attack against fifty miles of the British and French line in Picardy, from Arras to La Fere, gaining a maximum of thirty miles.

March 23.—Paris is bombarded by long range guns at a distance of seventy-five miles.

March 24.—Peronne and Bapaume are recaptured by the Germans.

March 25.—German troops are in Noyon and Paris is in acute danger.

March 26.—Foch is charged by the British and French governments with coördinating the action of the Allied Armies on the Western Front, and the great French strategist becomes Commander-in-Chief of the Allied forces in France—British, French, American, Italian, Belgian, and Portuguese.

Roumania signs a definitive treaty with the Central Powers at Bukharest.

March 28.—Pershing offers to lead his men into battle.

March 30.—Ludendorff makes a second effort south of the Somme. British hold their position.

April 9-16.—The German blow shifts to the north, from La Bassée to Ypres; the British evacuate portions of Messines and Passchendaele Ridges.

April 25.—Germans capture Kemmel Hill.

April 29.—The Germans make a general attack and are repulsed with frightful carnage. The Battle of the Lys ends.

May 27-June 1.—The Germans move southward along the front against French and British troops from Soissons to Rheims.

May 30.—Germans reach the Marne at Jaulgonne.

June 1.—Germans are at Château-Thierry.

June 9.—Foch employs a counter-tactic which is later to develop into a successful answer to the Hutier tactic.

June 9-11.—Germans advance toward Compiègne, between the salients created by the first and third phases.

June 10.—Mangin leads a successful attack on the western flank of the Germans.

June 15-23.—The Austrians launch a supreme effort along the whole line of the Piave River, are partly successful at first, but are thrown back in disorder across the river by an Italian counter-offensive.

June 19.—The Germans attempt to take the city of Rheims by attacks from three sides; they gain ground but fail in their main object.

July 15.—Ludendorff launches a final offensive. The Germans attack along a fifty mile front centring at Rheims, gaining ground to the west but being held in the east.

July 18.—The Allied army in France under the leadership of Foch launches a successful counter-attack against the western side of the salient in the German line from Soissons to Château-Thierry.

July 24.—First American Army is formed under General Pershing.

August 4.—The opening of the fifth year of war finds the Allies on the offensive all along the line in France, the initiative having been wrested from the Germans.

August 6.—Ludendorff retires behind the Vesle and the Aisne-Marne engagement ends. Foch becomes a Marshal of France.

August 8-10.—A new Allied drive is directed against the German salient near Amiens (Second Battle of the Somme); the attacking troops are British, French, and American, under Field-Marshal Haig, and they advance fourteen miles.

August 13-14.—Ludendorff at the conference at Spa, attended by the German Emperor, says that the war must end.

August 15.—American troops land at Vladivostok, to coöperate with the Allied army in Siberia.

August 16.—British and French armies north of the Oise are checked.

August 18-20.—A third offensive is directed against the German line by the British in the Lys salient south of Ypres.

August 20.—The Allied army's blow is shifted once again, to the region between the Oise and the Aisne; the superiority of the Allies becomes clear, and a forced evacuation of French territory is begun by the Germans—Albert is reoccupied on August 22, Noyon and Bapaume on the 29th, Péronne on September 1, St. Quentin on August 31, Lens on October 2, Cambrai on October 9, Laon and La Fere on October 13, Lille and Ostend on October 17, Valenciennes on November 2, Sedan on November 7, Tournai and Mèziéres on November 8, and Mons and Maubeuge on November 11.

September 10.—Ludendorff gets his battered armies back to the Hindenburg line.

September 12.—Americans begin the attack on the St. Mihiel salient which is to open the railway from Verdun to Toul to the Allies.

September 15.—The Macedonia offensive opens and marches toward a successful campaign, the Serbs rendering brilliant service.

September 19-20.—British forces under Allenby decisively defeat the Turks.

September 26.—Pershing opens the Battle of the Hindenburg line in which the Allied forces break through the Hindenburg line and begin the march to victory.

September 27.—British attack in front of Cambrai and take 10 villages, 10,000 prisoners, and 200 cannon.

September 28.—President Wilson declares for impartial justice at the peace table, and expresses belief in a league of nations as most essential, with no alliances within the league.

September 29.—Bulgaria withdraws from the war, accepting terms dictated by the Allies, including the evacuation of Serbian and Greek territory and the use of Bulgarian roads by Allied troops.

October 2.—The Italian fleet with the help of twelve American submarine chasers and British and French light craft penetrates the Austrian naval base of Durazzo, and destroys all the fortifications and many of the boats.

October 3.—The Hindenburg line is smashed.

October 5.—The new German Chancellor requests the President of the United States to take a hand in the restoration of peace, and accepts as a basis for negotiations the President's programme as set forth in his speeches of January 8 and September 28.

October 10.—The Battle of the Hindenburg Line ends.

October 14.—President Wilson informs Germany that no armistice can be arranged without safeguards for the military supremacy of the Allies, and calls special attention to one of the peace essentials—the destruction of arbitrary power in Germany.

October 15-31.—The Kriemhilde Line is penetrated and the First American Army pushes northward in pursuit of the disorganized German army.

October 23.—President Wilson replies to the third peace note of the Germans and says he will take up the question of armistice with his co-belligerents, refers details to field commanders, and says that if we must deal with the present Imperial Government of Germany we must demand surrender for we cannot trust it.

October 24.—The Italian Army, aided by British and French forces, opens an attack which results in the complete collapse of the Austro-Hungarians. The Battle of Vittorio-Veneto.

October 26.—The Kaiser accepts Ludendorff's resignation.

October 27.—Germany replies to the President's note of October 23 giving new assurances that the people are in charge of the government of Germany.

October 31.—Turkey withdraws from the war, accepting terms dictated by the Allies.

November 1.—President Wilson informs Germany that the Allied powers are willing to make peace on the basis of the Fourteen Points, England reserving liberty of action in the matter of freedom of the seas, France in the matter of compensation for damages done to civil population and to property.

November 4.—Austria-Hungary withdraws from the war, accepting terms dictated by the Allies.

November 9.—The Chancellor announces that Wilhelm has abdicated as German Emperor; Friedrich Ebert, Socialist, is appointed Imperial Chancellor pending establishment of a constitutional assembly. Germany becomes a republic.

November 11.—German delegates sign an armistice agreement presented by Marshal Foch and hostilities come to an end.

THE PRONUNCIATION OF WAR NAMES

By C. O. Sylvester Mawson, Litt.D., Ph.D.
(Copyright, 1918, by C. S. Hammond & Co., New York City)

KEY TO PRONUNCIATION

Vowel sounds: āle, bâre, ärm, ȧsk, senāte, ăm, organ, sofạ; ēve, ĕvent, ĕnd, novĕl, bakẽr; īce, ĭll; ōld, ôrb, ŏbey, ŏdd, cŏmbine; ūse, ûrn, ūnite, ŭp, locŭst; fōōd, fŏŏt; ou as in out: oi as in oil; ü as in menu.

Note.—u, as in French menu or German Müller, has no equivalent in English. To produce it, hold the lips rigidly in position to say ōō and attempt to say ē. ö or oe in German resembles the English u in urn; e. g., Göthe or Goethe is pronounced gû'tĕ.

Consonants: As in English. ch as in chair; g as in go; kw for qu as in queen; s as in so; sh as in she; z as in zone; zh as in azure.

Special symbols: ᴋ (small capital) for ch as in German ich or Scotch loch; ɴ (small capital) indicates nasal tone of preceding vowel, as in French bon (bôɴ); ŋ (= ng) for n before the sound of k or hard g as in bank (băŋk), finger (fĭŋ'gẽr); ' indicates the elision of a vowel, or a mere suggestion of a vowel sound, as in Ypres (ē'pr').

Accents: The principal or primary accent is indicated by a heavy mark ('), and the secondary accent by a lighter mark ('); thus, Bouvines (bōō'vēn'); Massachusetts (măs'ȧ-chōō'sĕts).

Note.—French names have the primary accent on the final full syllable, but this accent should generally be very slight. The other syllables are marked with equal stress. In German names, the principal accent is placed earlier in the word, as in English. In Hungarian and Bohemian names, the accent is on the first syllable. In Polish, as in Italian, the accent is on the penult. In Russia, the accent is capricious but very marked.

Aachen (or Aix-ᴌa-Chapelle), ä'ᴋĕᴅ
Aalst (or Alost), älst
Abbeville, ăb'vēl'
Abée, ȧ'bä'
Acheux, ȧ'shû'
Achicourt, ȧ'shĕ'kōōr'
Achiet, ȧ'shyä'
Acossée, ȧ'kŏ'sä'
Acoz, ȧ'kō'
Acq, ȧk
Adelsberg, ä'dĕls-bĕrk
Adige (river), ä'dĕ-jä
Adinkerke, ȧd'ĕn-kĕr'kĕ
Adria, ä'drē-ä
Aerschot, är'sᴋŏt
Aerseele, är'sä'lĕ
Aettfrycke, ät'frē-kĕ
Aehre, ä'rĕ
Agincourt, ȧ'zhăɴ'kōōr'; Eng. ăj'ĭn-kôrt
Agordo, ä-gôr'ōd
Ahrdorf, är'dôrf
Ahrweiler, är'vī-lẽr
Aidin, ᴌ-dēn'
Aincreville, ăɴ'kr'-vēl'
Aintab, īn'tȧb'
Aire, âr
Aisne (river), ân
Aivenne, ȧ'vĕn'
Aix-la-Chapelle (or Aachen), āks'lȧ'-shä'pĕl'
Ala, ä'lä
Albeek, äl'bāk
Albert, äl'bâr'
Albesdorf, äl'bĕz-dôrf
Albona, äl-bō'nä
Aleppo, ȧ-lĕp'ō
Alexandretta (or Iskanderun), ăl'ĕ-zăn-drĕt'ȧ
Alken, äl'kĕn
Allarmont, ȧ'lär'môɴ'
Alle, äl'ĕ
Allennes, ȧ'lĕn'
Allenstein, äl'ĕn-shtīn'
Allondrelle, ȧ'lôɴ'drĕl'
Alost (or Aalst), ä'lŏst
Alsdorf, älz'dôrf
Alsemberg, äl'zĕm-bĕrk

Althofen, ält'hō'fĕn
Altkirch, ält'kĭrᴋ'
Altzingen, ält'zĭng-ĕn
Amance, ȧ'mäns'
Amanweiler, ä'mȧn-vī'lẽr
Ambacourt, äɴ'bȧ'kōōr'
Amblimont, äɴ'blē'môɴ'
Ambresin, äɴ'br'-săɴ'
Amel, ä'mĕl
Amiens, ȧ'myăɴ'
Amohines, ȧ'mŏ'ĕn'
Amont, ȧ'môɴ'
Amougies, ȧ'mōō'zhē'
Ampezzo, äm-pĕt'sō
Ancre (river), äɴ'kr'
Anderlecht, äɴ'dĕr-lĕkt
Andenne, äɴ'dĕn'
Angres, äɴ'gr'
Anhée, äɴ'ä'
Aniches, ȧ'nēsh'
Anlier, äɴ'lyä'
Anloy, äɴ'lwä'
Anneux, ȧ'nû'
Annevois, ȧn'vwä'
Anor, ȧ'nŏr'
Anould, ȧ'nōōl'
Anoux, ȧ'nōō'
Ans, äɴs
Ansauville, äɴ'sŏ'vĕl'
Anthée, äɴ'tä'
Antheit, äɴ'tĭt
Anthelupt, äɴ'tĕ-lüp'
Antilly, äɴ'tē'yē'
Antioch, än'tĭ-ŏk
Antreppe, äɴ'trĕp'
Anvin, äɴ'văɴ'
Any, ȧ'nĕ'
Anzelin, äɴ'ză-lăɴ'
Anzin, äɴ'zăɴ'
Apilly, ȧ'pē'yĕ'
Apremont, ȧ'pr'-môɴ'
Arbe, ȧrb
Arcey, är'sĕ'
Archennes, är'shĕn'
Arches, ärsh
Arco, ar'kō, **Ardahan**, är'dȧ-hän'
Ardoye, är'dwä'
Argenteau, är'zhäɴ'tō'

Argonne, är'gŏn'
Arleux, är'lû'
Arlon, är'lôɴ'
Armentières, är'măɴ'tyâr'
Arnaville, är'nä'vĕl'
Arques, ärk
Arracourt, ȧ'rȧ'kōōr'
Arras, ȧ'räs'
Arraye, ȧ'rä'
Arry, ȧ'rē'
Ars, ärz
Arsdorf, ärz'dôrf
Artes, ärt
Artois, är'twä'
Arville, är'vĕl'
Asch, äsh
Ascq, ȧsk
Asiago, ä'zyä-gō
Asolo, ä'zŏ-lō
Assche, äs'kĕ
Assweiler, äs'vī-lẽr
Ath, ȧt
Athesans, ȧ'tĕ-säɴ'
Athies, ȧ'tē'
Athus, ȧ'tü'
Attainville, ȧ'tăɴ'vēl'
Attigny, ȧ'tē'nyĕ'
Atweiler, ät'vī-lẽr
Aube (river), ōb
Aubel, ō'bĕl'
Aubencheul, ō'băɴ'shül'
Aubenton, ō'bäɴ'tôɴ'
Auberive, ōb'rēv'
Aubers, ō'bâr'
Aubigny, ō'bē'nyĕ'
Aublain, ō'blăɴ'
Auchel, ō'shĕl'
Auchy, ō'shē'
Audenarde (or Oudenarde), ou'dĕ-när'dĕ
Audincourt, ō'dăɴ'kōōr'
Audun,ᴌō'dŭɴ'
Auge, ōzh
Augustowo, ou'gŏŏs-tō'vō
Aulnois, ōl'nwä'
Aulnoye, ōl'nwä'
Aumetz, ou'mĕtz
Auronzo, ou-rônt'sō

Autel-Bas, ō'těl'-bä'
Autoing, ō'twän'
Autrey, ō'trĕ'
Auvillers, ō'vē'lâr'
Avecapelle, äv'kà'pĕl'
Avelghem, ä'vĕl-gĕm
Avennes, à'vĕn'
Avesnes, à'vän'
Aviano, ä-vyä'nō
Avion, à'vyōn'
Avioth, à'vyŏ'
Avricourt, à'vrē'kōor'
Avril, à'vrēl'
Ay, à'ē
Ayette, à'yĕt'
Awenne, à'vĕn'
Azerailles, à'zē-râ'y'
Azoudange, ät'sou-dàng'ē

Baccarat, bà'kà'rà'
Badia, bä-dē'ä
Baelegem, bä'lē-gĕm
Baelen, bä'lĕn; bä'län'
Bagdad (or Bhagdad), bàg-däd'; Eng. bàg'dàd
Bagneux, bàn'yû'
Baileux, bä'lû'
Bailleul, bá'yûl'
Baisieux, bä'zyû'
Baku, bá-kōō'
Bâle (or Basel), bäl
Ballersdorf, bäl'ĕrz-dôrf'
Bambrugge, bäm'brōō'gē
Bannonville, bá'nôn'vĕl'
Bapaume, bá'pōm'
Barbarano, bär'bä-rä'nō
Bar-le-Duc, bár'-lē-dük'
Baroncourt, bá'rôn'kōor'
Baronville, bá'rôn'vĕl'
Baronweiler, bä'rŏn-vī'lĕr
Barst, bärst
Barvaux, bár'vō'
Bascoup, bä'kōō'
Basel (or Bâle), bä'zĕl
Basra (or Busra), bŭs'rä
Bassano, bäs-sä'nō
Bassée, La, lá' bá'sä'
Bastogne, bäs'tŏn'y'
Batilly, bá'tē'yē'
Batum, bá-tōōm'
Baudrecourt, bō'dr'-kōor'
Bauffe, bōf
Baugnies, bō'nyē'
Baulon, bō'lôn'
Bautersem, bou'tĕr-sĕm
Bavay, bá'vĕ'
Bazeilles, bá'zä'y'
Beaucourt, bō'kōor'
Beaumetz, bō'mĕs'
Beaumont, bō'môn'
Beauquesne, bō'kän'
Beauraing, bō'rän'
Beaurevoir, bō'rē-vwä'
Beauvais, bō'vĕ'
Beauval, bō'vàl'
Beauvillers, bō'vē'lâr'
Bebing, bä'bǐng
Bechy, bĕк'ē
Beckingen, bĕk'ǐng-ĕn
Becquevoort, bĕk'vôrt'
Beeringen, bä'rǐng-ĕn
Beernem, bär'nĕm
Beerst, bärst
Beine, bân
Beinheim, bīn'hīm
Beirut (or Beyrout), bä'rōōt'
Belfort, bĕl'fôr'
Belgrade, bĕl'grâd'
Bellefontaine, bĕl'fôn'tĕn'
Belleghem, bĕl'ē-gĕm
Bellem, bĕl'ĕm
Bellevaux, bĕl'vō'
Bellicourt, bĕl'ē'kōor'
Bellignies, bĕ-lē'nyē'
Belluno, bĕl-lōō'nō
Belosi, bá-lō'sē
Belval, bĕl'vàl'
Belverne, bĕl'vĕrn'
Beney, bĕ-nĕ'
Benningen, bĕn'ǐng-ĕn

Bensdorf, bĕnz'dôrf
Berchem, bĕr'кĕm
Berg, bĕгк
Berlaimont, bĕr'lĕ'môn'
Bernacourt, bĕrn'kōor'
Bernissart, bĕr'nē'sár'
Bernweiler, bĕrn'vī'lĕr
Berquette, bĕr'kĕt'
Bertincourt, bĕr'tän'kōor'
Bertogne, bĕr'tŏn'y'
Bertrichamps, bĕr'trē'shän'
Bertrix, bĕr'trē'
Berzée, bĕr'zä'
Besançon, bē'zän'sôn'
Bethonvilliers, bē-tôn'vē'yâr'
Béthune, bä'tün'
Bettainvillers, bĕ'tän'vē'lâr'
Bettemberg, bĕt'ĕm-bĕгк
Beuthen, boi'tĕn
Beverloo, bĕv'ĕr-lō'
Beverst, bĕv'ĕrst
Beyrout (or Beirut), bä'rōōt'
Bhagdad (or Bagdad), bàg-däd'
Bialystok, byä'lǐ-stŏk
Bienville, byän'vĕl'
Biesme, bē'âm'
Biestre, bē'ĕs'tr'
Bievre, bē'âv'r'
Bihain, bē'än'
Bilsen, bǐl'sĕn
Billy, bē'lē'
Binche, bänsh
Bioncourt, byôn'kōor'
Bionville, byôn'vĕl'
Bisten, bǐs'tĕn
Bitburg, bǐt'bōork
Bitschweiler, bǐt'shvī'lĕr
Biwer, bē'vä'
Blagny, blá'nyē'
Blamont, blá'môn'
Blandain, blän'dän'
Blaregnies, blá'rá'nyē'
Blaton, blá'tôn'
Bleialf, blī'àlf
Bleiburg, blī'bōork
Bleid, blīd
Blenod, blē'nŏ'
Bloemendaele, blōō'mĕn-dä'lē
Blumenthal, blōō'mĕn-täl
Bockryck, bŏk'rĕk
Boelhe, bōōl'ē
Boesinghe, bōō'sǐng-ē
Boevange, bōō'väng-ē
Bohain, bō' än'
Boisleux, bwá'lû'
Boismont, bwá'môn'
Boltweiler, bŏlt'vī-lĕr
Bomal, bō'mál'
Bomy, bō'mē'
Boncourt, bôn'kōor'
Bonhome, bō'nŏm'
Bonlez, bôn'lē'
Bonnes, bôn
Bonneville, bôn'vĕl'
Bonnevoye, bôn'vwä'
Bonviller, bôn'vē'yä'
Boom, bōm
Borg, bôгк
Borgo, bôr'gō
Borsbeke, bôrz'bä-kē
Bosphorus (or Bosporus), bŏs'pǫ-rŭs
Bosseval, bŏs'vàl'
Botoshani, bō-tǫ-shán'y'
Botzen, bŏt'sĕn
Bouchain, bōō'shän'
Bouchout, bōō'shōō'
Bouconville, bōō'kôn'vĕl'
Boucq, bōōk
Boudoir, bōō'dōor'
Bougnies, bōō'nyē'
Bouillon, bōō'yôn'
Boulers, bōō'lär'
Boulogne, bōō'lôn'y'; Eng. bōō-lōn'
Boult, bōōl
Bouquemaison, bōōk'mä'zòn'
Bourbourg, bōōr'bōor'
Bourcy, bōōr'sē'
Bourdonnay, bōōr'dŏ'nä'
Bourg-Bruche, bōōrк'-brōōк'ē
Bourg-Fidêle, bōōr'-fē'dál'

Bourgogne, bōōr'gŏn'y'
Boursies, bōōr'sē'
Boussy, bōō'sē'
Bousval, bōōs'vál'
Bouverie, bōōv'rē'
Bouvignes, bōō'vēn'y'
Bouvigny, bōō'vē'nyē'
Bouvines, bōō'vĕn'
Bouvron, bōō'vrôn'
Beuxières, bōō'zyâr'
Boves, bōv
Bovigny, bō'vē'nyē'
Bovrinnes, bō'vrǐn'
Era, brä
Brabant-le-roi, brá'bän'-lē-rwä'
Braffe, bráf
Braila, brá-ē'lä
Braine, brän
Braine-le-Comte, brän'-lē-kônt'
Braives, bráv
Branchon, brän'shôn'
Brand, bränt
Braquis, brá'kē'
Bras, brä
Bratte, brát
Braunsberg, brounz'bĕгк
Braux, brō
Bray, brē
Bray-sur-Seine, brē'-sür'-sän'
Bray-sur-Somme, brē'-sür'sŏm'
Breganze, brä-gänt'sä
Brenta (river), brĕn'tä
Brest-Litovsk, brĕst'-lyĕ-tôfsk'
Bretton, brĕt'ŏn
Brie, brē
Briey, brē'ē'
Brin, brän
Brioni, brē-ō'nē
Brixen, brǐk'sĕn
Brouay, brōō'ĕ'
Brouck, brouk
Brouckirk, brou'kǐrk
Brouveliers, brōōv'lyâr'
Bruay, brü'ē'
Bruges, brüzh
Bruly-de-Pesche, brü'lē'-dē-pâsh'
Brusa (or Brussa), brōō'sä
Brussels (or Bruxelles), brŭs'ĕlz
Bruxelles (or Brussels), brü'sĕl'
Bruyeres, brü'yâr'
Bry, brē
Bucquoy, bü'kwä'
Buczacz, bōō'chách
Buderschied, bōō'dĕr-shĕt
Budin, bōō'dǐn
Bug (river), bōog
Buhl, bōōl
Buire, bwĕr
Buironfosse, bwē'rôn'fŏs'
Bukharest (or Bucharest), bōō'kā-rĕst'
Bukowina (Bukovina), bōō'kŏ-vē'nä
Bullingen, bōōl'ǐng-ĕn
Bully, bü'yē'
Bult, bül
Burano, bōō-rä'nō
Bures, bür
Burnhaupt, bōōrn'houpt
Bursf, bōōrsf
Burtscheid, bōort'shǐt
Busendorf, bōō'zĕn-dôrf
Bushire, bōō-shēr'
Busigny, bü'sē'nyē'
Busra (or Basra), bŭs'rä
Butgenbach, bōōt'gĕn-báк
Buttia, bōōt'yä
Buzegney, bü'zâ'nyē'
Buzy, bü'zē'
Buziéres, bü'zyâr'

Caesarea (or Kaisarieh), sĕs-á-rē'á
Caeskerke, käz-kĕr'kē
Calais, ká'lĕ'; Eng. kál'ā
Callenelle, kál'nĕl'
Camblain, kän'blän'
Cambrai (or Cambray), kän'brĕ'
Cambrin, kän'brän'
Camisano, kä'mĕ-zä'nō
Canfanaro, kän'fä-nä'rō
Cantain, kän'tän'
Capelle, La, lá' ká'pĕl'

Capodistria, kä′pō-dēs′trē-ä̱
Cappet, káp′ĕt
Caprino, kä-prē′nō
Carency, kä′rän′sē′
Carignan, kä′rĕn′yäN′
Carnières, kär′nyär′
Carole, kä-rō′lä
Carvin, kär′văN′
Cassel, kás′ĕl
Casteau, kás′tō′
Castelfranco, käs-tĕl′frän̄′kō
Caster, käs′tä′
Castre, käs′tr′
Castua, käs′twä
Cateau, Le, lĕ kä′tō′
Catillon, kä′tē′yôN′
Caudry, kō′drē′
Cavalese, kä′vä-lā′zä
Cavarzere, kä-vär′dzä-rä
Cerfontaine, sĕr′fôN′tän′
Cernavoda (or Tchernavoda), chĕr′nä-vō′dä
Cernay, sĕr′nĕ′
Cetinje (or Cettinje), tsĕt′ĕn-yä
Chalons-sur-Marne, shä′lôN′-sür′-märn′
Chalon-sur-Saône, shä′lôN′-sür′-sōn′
Chambley, shän′blĕ′
Chambrey, shän′brĕ′
Champagney, shän′pä′nyĕ′
Champigny, shän′pē′nye′
Chapelle, La, lä′shä′pĕl′
Charency, shä′rän′sē′
Charey, shä′rĕ′
Charleroi (or Charleroy), shär′lĕ-rwä′
Charleville, shárl′vĕl′
Charmois, shär′mwä′
Chassart, shás′är′
Chastre, shás′tr′
Chatalja (or Tchatalja), chä-täl′jä
Château-Regnault, shä′tō′-rĕ′nyō′
Châteauroux, shä′tō′rōō′
Château-Salins, shä′tō′-sä′läN′
Château-Thierry, shä′tō′-tyĕ′rē′
Châtel, shä′tĕl′
Châtelet, shät′lĕ′
Châtillon, shä′tē′yôN′
Châtillon-sur-Marne, shä′tē′yôN′-sür′-märn′
Chaudefontaine, shōd′fôN′tän′
Chaulnes, shō′n′
Chaumont, shō′môN′
Chauny, shō′nē′
Chauvency, shō′văN′sē′
Chaux, shō
Chemin des Dames, shĕ′măN′ dä̱däm′
Chenevières, shĕn′vyär′
Chenicourt, shĕ-nē′kōōr′
Cherain, shĕ′räN′
Cherso, kĕr′sō
Chievres, shĕ′ĕ′vr′
Chimay, shē′mĕ′
Chiny, shē′nē′
Chioggia, kyōd′jä
Ciney, sē′nĕ′
Cittadella, chĕt′tä-dĕl′lä
Cividale, chē′vĕ-dä′lä
Clary, klä′rē′
Clavier, klä′vyä′
Clemency, klĕm′äN′sē′
Clerken, klĕr′kĕn
Clermont, klĕr′môN′
Clervaux, klĕr′vō′
Cleurie, klü′rē′
Clezentaine, klĕz′äN′tän′
Codroipo, kō-drō′ĕpō
Coingt, kwăN
Colroy, kŏl′rwä′
Combles, kôN′bl′
Comines, kō′mĕn′
Commercy, kō′mĕr′sē′
Compiègne, kôN′pyĕn′y′
Condé, kôN′dä′
Conegliano, kō′näl-yä′nō
Conflans, kôN′fläN′
Cons, kôNs
Conselve, kôn-sĕl′vä
Constanta (or Kustendje), kôn-stän′tsä
Corbais, kŏr′bĕ′

Corbeek Loo, kŏr′bäk lō
Corbion, kŏr′byôN′
Corceuil, kŏr′sŭ′y′
Corcieux, kŏr′syŭ′
Corcy, kŏr′sē′
Cornieville, kŏr′nē′vĕl′
Cornimont, kŏr′nē′môN′
Corravillers, kŏ′rä′vē′lär′
Cortemarck, kŏr′tĕ-märk
Cortessem, kŏr′tĕs-ĕm ‖
Cortina, kŏr-tē′nä
Coucy, kōō′sē′
Coucy-le-Château, kōō′sē′-lĕ-shä′tō′
Coulommiers, kōō′lŏ′myä′
Coulonges, kōō′lôNzh′
Courcelles-Chaussy, kōōr′sĕl′-shō′sē′
Courrières, kōō′ryär′
Courtemont, kōōrt′môN′
Courtrai, kōōr′trĕ′
Court-St.-Étienne, kōōr′-säN′-tä′-tyĕn′
Couvin, kōō′văN′
Cracow (or Krakow), krä′kō
Crajova (or Craiova), krä-yō′vä
Craonne, krä′ôn′
Crécy (or Cressy), krä′sē′; Eng. krĕs′ĭ
Crécy-sur-Serre, krä-sē′-sür′-sär′
Crevic, krĕ′vĕk′
Crimea, krĭ-mē′ä; krī-mē′ä
Croisilles, krwä′sĕl′
Croismare, krwä′mär′
Croix, krwä
Crombeke, krŏm′bä-kĕ
Crupet, krü′pĕ′
Cuesmes, kwĕm
Cuinchy, kwăN′shē
Cul-des-Sarts, kül′-dĕ-sär′
Custines, küs′tĕn′
Cysoing, sē′swăN′
Czenstochowa, chĕn′stŏ-kô′vä
Czernowitz, chĕr′nŏ-vĭts

Dagny, dä′nyĕ′
Dagonville, dä′gôN′vĕl′
Daleiden, dä-lī′dĕn
Dalheim, däl′hīm
Dalstein, däl′shtīn
Damas, dä′mä′
Damascus, dä-mäs′kŭs
Damerkirch, dä′mĕr-kĕrx
Dammartin, dän′mär′täN′
Damvillers, dän′vē′yä′
Daniele, dä-nyä′lä
Danjoutin, däN′jōō′täN′
Danne, dän′nĕ
Danzig (or Dantzic), dän′tsĭk
Dardanelles, där′dä-nĕlz′
Darhamps, där′äN′
Darmont, där′môN′
Dedeagatch (or Dedeagach), dĕ-dĕ′ä-gäch′
Deerlyck, där′lĕk
Delatyn (pass), dĕ-lä′tĭn
Delle, dĕl
Delme, dĕl′mĕ
Denain, dĕ-näN′
Dendermonde (or Termonde), dĕn′dĕr-mŏn′dĕ
Dergneau, dĕr′nyō′
Desvres, dâv′′r′
Diarbekr (or Diarbekir), dĕ-är′bĕk′′r
Dickenbusch, dĭk′ĕ-bŭs
Diedenhofen (or Thionville), dē′dĕn-hō′fĕn
Dieulouard, dyû′lōō′är′
Dieuze, dyûz
Differdingen, dĭf′ĕr-dĭng′ĕn
Dignano, dĕ-nyä′nō
Dijon, dē′zhôN′
Dinant, dē′näN′
Dippach, dĭp′äx
Dixmude, dĕ-nyä′lä; dĕ′mŭd′
Dnieper (river), nē′pĕr
Dniester (river), nēs′tĕr
Dolleren, dŏl′ĕr-ĕn
Dombasle, dôN′bäl′
Dommartin, dôN′mär′täN′
Dommary, dôN′mä′rē′
Dompaire, dôN′pär′
Don, dôN

Doncourt, dôN′kōōr′
Dongelberg, dŏng′ĕl-bĕrx
Donjoutin, dôN′jōō′täN′
Dormans, dôr′mäN′
Dornach, dŏr′näx
Douai (or Douay), dōō′ä′
Doullens, dōō′läN′
Drave (river), drä′vĕ
Drohobycz, drŏ-hŏ′bĭch
Drouville, drōō′vĕl′
Dubno, dōōb′nō
Dukla, dōōk′lä
Dunkirk, dŭn-kûrk′
Durazzo, dōō-rät′sō
Durbuy, dür′boi′
Düren, dü′rĕn

Eberstein, ä′bĕr-shtīn
Ebersweiler, ä′bĕrs-vī′lĕr
Ébly, ä′blē′
Echternach, ĕx′tĕr-näx
Ecly, ĕ′klē′
Écoivres, ä′kwä′vr′
Écossines, ä′kō′sĕn′
Ecouviez, ä′kōō′vyä′
Edeghem, ä′dĕ-gĕm
Edingen, ä′dĭng-ĕn
Eecke, ä′kĕ
Eecloo, ä-klō′
Eessen, ä′sĕn
Eglingen, ĕg′lĭng-ĕn
El Kuds (or Jerusalem), ĕl kōōds
Ellezelles, ĕl′zĕl′
Elsenborg, ĕl′zĕn-bôrx
Élouges, ä′lōōzh′
Éloyes, ä′lwä′
Elverdinghe, ĕl′vĕr-dĭng′ĕ
Embken, ĕmp′kĕn
Enghien, äN′gäN′
Enos, ä′nŏs
Entroeungt, äN′trŏ′ûN′
Épernay, ä′pĕr′nĕ′
Épinal, ä′pē′nál′
Epirus, ĕ-pī′rŭs
Eppe Sauvage, ĕp′ sō′väzh′
Erdorf, ĕr′dôrf
Eregli, ĕr′ĕ-glē′
Erivan, ĕr′ē-vän′
Ermeton, ĕr′mĕ-tôN′
Erneuville, ĕr′nû′vĕl′
Ernonheld, ĕr′nôn-hĕld
Erpent, ĕr′päN′
Erpion, ĕr′pyôN′
Erpoin, ĕr′pwäN′
Erquelinnes, ĕrk′lĕn′
Errouville, ĕr′ōō′vĕl′
Ertvelde, ĕrt′vĕl-dĕ
Ervilliers, ĕr′vē′yär′
Erzingan, ĕr′zĭn-gän′
Erzerum, ĕrz-rōōm′
Escaudain, ĕs′kō′däN′
Esch, ĕsh
Eschweiler, ĕsh′vī-lĕr
Esnes, ân
Esneux, ĕs′nû′
Espierres, ĕs′pyär′
Esqueheries, ĕs′kĕ-rē′
Essey, ĕs′ĕ′
Estaires, ĕs-tär′
Esti, ĕs′tē
Estinnes, ĕs′tĭn′
Estre Blanche, ĕs′tr′-bläNsh′
Étain, ä′täN′
Étalle, ä′täl′
Étival, ä′tē-väl′
Ettelbruck, ĕt′ĕl-brōōk
Étueffont, ä′tü′fôN′
Eulmont, ûl′môN′
Eupen, oi′pĕn
Euphrates (river), û-frä′tēs
Everbecq, ĕv′ĕr′bĕk′
Evergem, ä′vĕr-gĕm
Évette, ä′vĕt′
Eydtkuhnen, īt-kōō′nĕn
Eynatten, ī-nät′ĕn
Eyne, ī′nĕ
Eysden, īs′dĕn

Falaen, fá'län'
Falisolle, fá'lē'sŏl'
Falmagne, fál'män'y'
Famars, fá'mär'
Famillaveux, fá'mēl'á'vŭ'
Farschweiler, färsh'vī-lēr
Faulx, fō
Fauvillers, fō'vē'lär'
Fays Dillot, fĕ'dē'yō'
Feignies, fĕ'nyē'
Feltre, fĕl'trā
Feluy, fĕ-loi'
Fépin, fā'păn'
Fère, La, lá' fâr'
Fère-Champenoise, fâr'-shän'pĕ-nwäz'
Fère-en-Tardenois, fâr'-än'-tard'-nwä'
Ferrière, fĕ'ryär'
Ferté-Gaucher, La, lá'fĕr'tä'-gō'shä'
Ferté-sous-Jouarre, La, lá' fĕr'tä'-soo'-zhoo'är'
Fianona, fyä-nō'nä
Filsdorf, fēlz'dŏrf
Finnevaux, fĭn'vō'
Fins, fäns
Fiume, fyoo'mä
Flawinne, flá'vĭn'
Fleurbaix, flŭr'bĕ'
Fleurry, flŭ'rē'
Fleville, flĕ'vēl'
Fligneux, flĕ'nyŭ'
Flines, flēn
Flirey, flē'rē'
Flobecq, flō'bĕk'
Florennes, flō'rĕn'
Florenville, flō'rän'vēl'
Florée, flō'rā'
Fontaine, fôn'tĕn'
Fontenay, fônt'nē'
Fontenoy, fônt'nwä'
Fontoy, fôn'twä'
Fonzaso, fôn-tsä'zō
Forrières, fō'ryär'
Fosse, fōs
Fouchy, foo'shē'
Foucogney, foo'kôn'yĕ'
Foug, foo
Fougerolles, foozh'rŏl'
Fournies, foor'mē'
Foville, fō'vēl'
Fraire, frâr
Fraise, frâz
Fraize, frâz
Framières, frá'myâr'
Framont, frá'môn'
Frécourt, frä'koor'
Freisdorf, friz'dŏrf
Fresne, frĕn
Fresnes-en-Woëvre, frĕn'-än'-vō'ĕv'r'
Fresnoy, frĕ'nwä'
Fretin, frĕ-tän'
Freudenburg, froi'dĕn-boork
Freux, frŭ
Frévent, frä'vän'
Frévillers, frä'vē'lär'
Fribourg, frē'boork
Fricourt, frē'koor'
Friesach, frē'zäk
Frisang, frē'zän'
Froidchapelle, frwä'shá'pĕl'
Fromelles, frō'mĕl'
Frouard, froo'är'
Fumay, fü'mē'
Furnaux, für'nō'
Furnes fürn

Gaesbeek, gäz'bāk
Gail (river), gál
Galatz, gä'läts
Galicia, gá-lĭsh'ĭ-á
Gallaix, gá'lĕ'
Gallipoli, gäl-lē'pō-lē
Gammerages, gäm'räzh'
Gand (or Ghent), gän
Gargnano, gär-nyä'nō
Gavis, gä'ĭfs
Gavrelle, gá'vrĕl'
Gaza (or Ghazzeh), gä'zá
Geet Betz, gät bĕts

Gelinden, gĕl'ĭn-dĕn
Gelucourt, gä'lco-koort
Gembloux, zhän'bloo'
Gemona, jä-mō'nä
Gémonville, zhä'môn'vĕl'
Gemund, gä'moont
Genappe, zhĕ-näp'
Gérardmer, zhä'rär'mä'
Gerbetal, zhĕrb'näl'
Gerbeviller, zhĕrb'vē'yä'
Gérouville, zhä'roo'vēl'
Gesponsart, zhĕ'pôn'ä͟rt'
Ghazzeh (or Gaza), gŭz'ĕ
Ghent (or Gand), gĕnt
Ghistolles, gē'stĕl'
Ghyvelde, gē-vĕl'dĕ
Gibecq, zhē'bĕk'
Gildweiler, gĕlt'vī-lēr
Girecourt, zhēr'koor'
Giromagny, zhē'rō'má'nyĕ'
Gironville, zhē'rôn'vēl'
Givenchy, zhĕ'vän'shē'
Givet, zhĕ'vĕ'
Givry, zhĕ'vrē'
Gladbeek, gläd'bāk]
Gleiwitz, glī'vĭts
Glimes, glēm
Glons, glôn
Gmünd, g'münt
Gnesen, g'nä'zĕn
Godarville, gō'där'vĕl'
Gogney, gō'nyĕ'
Golbey, gōl'bĕ'
Gondrecourt, gôn'dr'-koor'
Gondreville, gôn'dr'-vĕl'
Gorcy, gŏr'sē'
Gorizia (or Görz), gō-rĭd'zē-ä
Gorgue, La, lá' gŏrg'
Görz (or Gorizia), gŭrts
Gosselies, gōs'lē'
Gouvy, goo'vē'
Gouy, gwē
Gradisca, grä-dĕs'kä
Grado, grä'dō
Graide, gräd
Graincourt, grän'koor'
Grammont, grá'môn'
Grandfontaine, grän'fôn'tĕn'
Grand Pré, grän' prä'
Grandvoir, grän'vwä'
Granges, gränzh
Graty, grä'tē'
Gravelines, gráv'lēn'
Gravelotte, gráv'lŏt'
Grembergen, grĕm'bĕr-gĕn
Grenay, grĕ'nĕ'
Greux, grŭ
Grevenmacher, grä'vĕn-mäk'ĕr
Grimnée, grän'nä'
Gruchten, grook'tĕn
Grupont, grü'pôn'
Gueblange, güb'läng-ĕ
Guebweiler, güb'vī-lēr
Guentrangen, gün'träng-ĕn
Guewenheim, gü'vĕn-hĭm
Guiscard, gēz'kär'
Guise, güēz'
Gulpen, gŭl'pĕn
Gumbinnen, goom-bĭn'ĕn
Gundolsheim, goon'dŏlz-hĭm
Gussainville, gü'săn'vĕl'

Labay-la-Vieille, á'bĕ'-lá'-vē'á'y'
Hablainville, á'blän'vĕl'
Habonville, á'bôn'vĕl'
Hacht, häkt
Hachy, á'shē'
Hadol, á'dō'
Hadonville, á'dôn'vĕl'
Haesdonck, häs'dônk
Hal, häl
Hallaer, hál-lär'
Hallainville, á'län'vĕl'
Halling, häl'ĭng
Halma, häl'mä
Halsdorf, hälz'dôrf
Hamah, hä'mä
Hamme, hä͟m'ĕ
Hamoir, á'mwä'
Hamonville, ám'ôn'vĕl'

Han, hän
Hannapes, á'näp'
Hanret, än'rä'
Haraucourt, á'rō'koor'
Harcigny, är'sē'nyĕ'
Hargicourt, är'zhĕ'koor'
Hargnies, är'nyĕ'
Harlebeke, här'lĕ-bä'kĕ
Harmignies, är'mĕ'nyĕ'
Harnes, ärn
Harre, är
Harville, är'vĕl'
Hary, á'rē'
Hasnon, äs'nôn'
Haspres, äs'pr'
Hastière, äs'tyär'
Hatrize, á'trēz'
Haubourdin, ō'boor'dĕn'
Haudemont, ōd'môn'
Haussy, ō'sē'
Hautchin, ō'shän'
Haut Fays, ō' fĕ'
Hautmont, ō'môn'
Havangen, ha'fäng-ĕn
Havay, á'vĕ'
Havre (Fr. Le Havre), hä'vĕr; Fr. lĕ äv'r'
Hayange (or Hayingen), á'yänzh'
Hayingen (or Hayange), hī'ĭng-ĕn
Hazebrouck, áz'brook'
Heer, här
Heiderschied, hī'dĕr-shĕt
Heimbach, hīm'bäk
Heimsbrunn, hīmz'broon
Heinerschied, hī'nĕr-shĕt
Hélène, á'lĕn'
Helgoland (or Heligoland), hĕl'gō-länt'
Hellebeeg, hĕl'ē-bāk
Hellemmes, ĕl'ĕm'
Hem, ĕn
Hénin, á'nän'
Hennemont, ĕn'môn'
Henripont, än'rē'pôn'
Herbesthal, hĕr'bĕz-täl
Herbeumont, ĕr'bŭ'môn'
Herbeviller, ĕrb'vē'lä'
Herchies, ĕr'shē'
Herent, hä'rĕnt
Herenthals, hä'rĕn-täls
Herenthout, hä'rĕnt-out
Hergarlen, hĕr'gär-lĕn
Hergenrath, hĕr'gĕn-rät
Hergnies, ĕr'nyĕ'
Héricourt, á'rē'koor'
Héristal (or Herstal), á'rē'stál'
Hermies, ĕr'mĕ'
Herrines, ō'rĕn'
Herseux, ĕr'sŭ'
Hersin, ĕr'sän'
Herstal (or Héristal), hĕr'stäl
Herzegovina, hĕr'tsĕ-gō-vē'nä
Herzheim, hĕrts'hīm
Hesdin, ĕs'dän'
Hestrud, ĕs'trü'
Heuchin, ŭ'shän'
Heudicourt, ŭ'dē'koor'
Heusweiler, hoiz'vī-lēr
Heusy, ŭ'sē'
Héverlé, á'vĕr'lä'
Heyst, hĭst
Hinckange, hĕn'käng-ĕ
Hinges, änzh
Hirson, ĕr'sôn'
Hives, ēv
Hody, ō'dē'
Hofen, hō'fĕn
Hoffeld, hō'fĕlt
Hogne, ôn'y'
Hollebeke, hŏl'ē-bä'kĕ
Hollenthal, hŏl'ĕn-täl
Hollerich, hŏl'ĕr-ĭx
Holluin, ō'lwän'
Holsbeek, hŏlz'bäk
Hombeek, hŏm'bäk
Homécourt, ō'mä'koor'
Hompre, ôn'pr'
Hon, ôn
Hondschoote, hônd'shō-tĕ
Hooglede, hō'glä-dĕ
Horodenka, hō'rō-dĕn'kä

Horpmael, hôrp′mäl
Houdain, ōō′dăn′
Houdremont, ou′dr′-môn′
Houplines, ōōp′lĕn′
Houx, ōō
Houyet, ōō′yĕ′
Huiron, wē′rôn′
Huldenberg, hōōl′dĕn-bĕrĸ
Huppaye, ü′pä′
Huy, hoi

Ichteghem, ĭĸ′tĕ-gĕm
Iddergem, ĭd′ēr-gĕm
Idria, ē′drē-ä
Igny, ē′nyē′
Illangen, ĕl′äng-ĕn
Illy, ē′yē′
Incourt, ăn′kōōr′
Indon, ĭn′dĕn
Ingolmunster, ĭŋ′gĕl-mŭn′stēr
Ire, ēr
Iseghem, ĭz′ē-gĕm
Iskanderun (or Alexandretta), ĭs-kăn′dēr-ōōn
Ismailia, ĕs′mä-ēl′yȧ
Itegem, ĭt′ē-gĕm
Itterbeek, ĭt′ēr-bāk
Ittre, ē′tr′
Ivangorod, ē-vän′gô-rŏt
Izel, ē′zĕl
Izier, ē′zyä′

Jabbeke, yȧb′ä-kē
Jallet, zhä′lĕt
Jamagne, zhä′män′y′
Jamboli (or Yamboli), yȧm′bô-lē
Jametz, zhä′mĕs′
Jamoignes, zhä′mwän′y′
Jarny, zhär′nē′
Jaroslaw (or Jaroslau), yȧ-rôs′läf
Jarvillo, zhär′vĕl′
Jassy (or Yassy), yäs′ĕ
Jaulny, zhōl′nē′
Jeandelizo, zhän′dē-lēz′
Jeanton, zhänt
Jedda (or Jidda), jĕd′ȧ
Jehay, zhē-ā′
Jemappe, zhē-mäp′
Jenlain, zhän′lăn′
Jerusalem (or El Kuds), jē-rōō′sȧ-lĕm
Jeumont, zhŭ′môn′
Jidda (or Jedda), jĭd′ȧ
Jodoigno, zhŏ′dwän′y′
Jouf, zhü′ĕf′
Joncheroy, zhôn′shē-rē′
Jonvillo, zhôn′vĕl′
Jouarre, zhōō′är′
Junglinster, yōōng′lĭn-stēr
Juniville, zhü′nē′vĕl′
Juprelle, zhü′prĕl′
Jurbiso, zhür′bēz′
Juseret, zhü′sĕ-rä′
Juvigny, zhü′vē′nyē′
Juville, zhü′vĕl′

Kain, kăn
Kaisarieh (or Kaisariyeh or Caesarea), kī′sä-rē′yĕ
Kaisersberg, kī′zĕrs-bĕrk
Kalisz, kä′lyĕsh
Kall, käl
Karahissar, kä-rä′hĭs-sär′
Kattecherberg, kät′ē-chĕr-bĕrĸ
Kattenhofen, kät′ĕn-hō′fĕn
Kedange, kä′däng-ē
Keltsy (or Kiclce), kyĕl′tsĭ
Kelz, kĕlts
Kemmel, kĕm′ĕl
Kemplich, kĕmp′lĭĸ
Kerbela, kĕr′bĕ-lä
Kerling, kĕr′lĭng
Kessel, kĕs′ĕl
Koyem, kī′ĕm
Kholm, kôlm
Khotin, kô′tyĕn
Kief (or Kiev), kē′yĕf
Kiclce (or Keltsy), kyĕl′tsē
Kishinef (or Kishinev), kē-shē-nyĕf′
Klagenfurt, klä′gĕn-fōōrt
Klausen, klou′zĕn

Kleinhau, klīn′hou
Koekelberg, kōō′kĕl-bĕrĸ
Kohlscheid, kōl′shīt
Kolomea, kō′lō-mä′ä
Kommern, kŏm′ĕrn
Königsberg, kû′nĭĸs-bĕrĸ
Kovel, kô′vĕl-y′
Kragojevatz (or Kraguyevatz), krä-gōō′yĕ-vȧts
Krainberg, krīn′bĕrĸ
Krakow (or Cracow), krä′kō
Krath, krät
Krautscheid, krout′shīt
Kremenchug (or Krementchug), krĕm′ĕn-chōōk′
Kromnitz, krĕm′nĭts
Kreuzau, kroi′tsou
Kronenberg, krō′nĕn-bĕrĸ
Kuds, El (or Jerusalem), ĕl kōōdz
Kur (or Kura, river), kōōr; kōō′rä
Kurisches Haff, kōō′rĭsh-ĕs häf
Kustendje (or Constanta), küs-tĕn′jĕ
Kut-el-Amara, kōōt′ĕl-ä-mä′rä

La Bassée, lä′ bä′sḙ′
La Capelle, lä′ kä′pĕl′
La Chapelle, lä′ shä′pĕl′
Ladeuze, lä′dûz′
La Fère, lä′ fâr′
La Fère-Champenoise, lä′ fâr′-shän′-pē-nwäz′
La Ferté-Gaucher, lä′ fĕr′tä′-gô′shä′
La Ferté-sous-Jouarre, lä′ fĕr′tä′-sōō′-zhōō′är′
Lagarde, lä′gärd′
Lagny, lä′nyē′
La Gorgue, lä′ gôrg′
Laibach, lī′bäk
Laires, lâr
Laison, lä′zôn′
Laix, lä
La Laterne, lä′lä′tĕrn′
Lamarche, lä′märsh′
Lamorteau, lä′môr′tō′
Landrecies, län′drä′sē′
Landres, län′dr′
Laneffe, lä′nĕf′
Langomarck, läŋ′gē-märk′
Langres, län′gr′
Languion, län′gē′ôn′
Lannoy, lä′nwä′
Laon, län
La Panne, lä′ pän′
La Pinte, lä′ pănt′
La Roche, lä′ rôsh′
Latakia, lä′tä-kē′ä
Laticana, lä′tē-sä′nä
La Trouche, lä′ trōōsh′
Laumesfeld, lou′mĕz-fĕlt
Lautenbach Zell, lou′tĕn-bäk tsĕl′
Lavelino, läv′lĕn′
Laventie, lä′vän′tē′
Lavoir, lä′vwä′
La Voivre, lä′ vwä′vr′
Lebbeke, lĕ-bä′kĕ
Le Cateau, lĕ kä′tō′
Ledeberg, lä′dē-bĕrĸ
Ledeghem, lä′dē-gĕm
Leeuw, lä′ōō
Legnago, lā-nyä′gō
Le Havre, lĕ äv′r′
Leidenborn, lī′dĕn-bôrn
Le Mans, lĕ män′
Lembecq, län′bĕk′
Lemberg (or Lwów), lĕm′bĕrĸ
Lendmara, länd-mä′rä
Lens, läns
Lovico, lä′vē-kō
Lo Quesnoy, lĕ kä′nwä′
Liancourt, lē′än′kōōr′
Liart, lē′är′
Libau, lē′bou
Lichtenborn, lĭĸ′tĕn-bôrn
Lichtervelde, lĭĸ′tĕr-vĕl′dĕ
Liederkerke, lē′dĕr-kĕr′kĕ
Liège, lē′ĕzh′
Lienz, lē′ĕnts′
Lierneux, lē′ĕr′nû′
Lierre, lē′är′
Liessies, lē′ĕs′ē′

Ligne, lēn′y′
Ligneville, lēn′y′-vĕl′
Ligny, lē′nyē′
Ligny-en-Barrois, lē′nyē′-än′-bä′rwä′
Lillo (or Lisle), lĕl
Lillers, lē′lär′
Limburg, lĭm′bûrĸ; Eng. lĭm′bûrg
Limey, lē′mē′
Linden, lĭn′dĕn
Linne, lĭn
Lironvillo, lē′rôn′vĕl′
Livenza (river), lē-vĕnt′sä
Liverdun, lē′vĕr′dûn′
Lixières, lē′zyär′
Locon, lô′kôn′
Lodz (or Lódz), lôdz; lōŏj
Lommer, lŏm′ĕr
Lommersweiler, lŏm′ĕrz-vī′lĕr
Lomprez, lôn′prĕ′
Lomza (or Lomzha), lôm′zhä
Longarone, lôŋ′gä-rō′nä
Longchamps, lôn′shän′
Longeville, lônzh′vĕl′
Longlier, lôn′lyä′
Longvilly, lôn′vē′yē′
Longwy, lôn′vē′
Lonny, lô′nē′
Loo, lō
Loos, lô-ôs′
Lophem, lō′pĕm
Lorentzweiler, lō′rĕnts-vī′lĕr
Lorraine (or Lothringen), lô-rän′
Lorry, lô′rē′
Losheim, lōz′hīm
Lothringen (or Lorraine), lôt′rĭng-ĕn
Lotzen, lût′sĕn
Louette St. Denis, lōō′ĕt′ săn′ dē-nē′
Louette St. Pierre, lōō′ĕt′ săn′ pyär′
Lougres, lōō′gr′
Louvaigne, lōō′vĕn′y′
Louvain, lōō′vän′
Louvignies, lōō′vē′nyē′
Lubey, lü′bĕ′
Lublin (or Lyublin), lyōō′blyĕn
Lucheux, lü′shû′
Lucy, lü′sē′
Lünebach, lü′nē-bäĸ
Lunéville, lü′nä′vĕl′
Lure, lür
Lussin, lōōs-sēn′
Luttange, lōōt′äng-ē
Lutterbach, lōōt′ĕr-bäĸ
Luttre, lü′tr′
Lutzk (or Lutsk), lōōtsk
Luxembourg, lŭk′săn′bōōr′
Luxemburg, lŭk′sĕm-bûrg; Ger. lōōks′ĕm-bōōrk
Lwów (or Lemberg), lvōōf
Lys (river), lēs

Machecourt, mäsh′kōōr′
Mâcon, mä′kôn′
Macquenoise, mäk′nwäz′
Magneux, mä′nyû′
Magnières, mä′nyär′
Magny, mä′nyē′
Mährisch-Ostrau, mä′rĭsh-ôs′trou
Mainville, măn′vĕl′
Mainz (or Mayence), mĭnts
Maisiers, mä′zyär′
Maisons-Alfort, mä′zôn′-zäl′fôr′
Maizeray, mäz′rē′
Maizeville, mäz′vĕl′
Maizy, mä′zē′
Malamocco, mä′lä-môk′kō
Malatia, mä′lä-tē′ä
Maldegem, mäl′dē-gĕm′
Malines (or Mechlin), mä′lēn′
Malo-les-Bains, mä′lô′-lä′-băn′
Malroy, mäl′rwä′
Malvaux, mäl′vō′
Mamerz, mä′mär′
Manage, mä′näzh′
Mance, mäns
Manicamp, mä′nē′kän′
Manneren, män′ē-rĕn
Manonvillers, mä′nôn′vē′lär′
Mans, Le, lĕ män′
Mantova (or Mantua), män′tô-vä
Mantua (or Mantova), măn′tū-ȧ

Marainviller, mȧ'răN've'yä'
Marbache, mȧr'bäsh'
Marche, märsh
Marchiennes, mȧr'shyĕn'
Marchin, mȧr'shăN'
Marcinelle, mȧr'sē'nĕl'
Marck, märk
Marcoing, mȧr'kwăN'
Marcq, märk
Marenne, mȧ'rĕn'
Maretz, mȧ'rĕs'
Margival, mȧr'zhē'vȧl'
Mariakerke, mȧ-rē'ȧ-kĕr'kĕ
Maricourt, mȧ'rē'kōōr'
Marienburg, mȧ'rē'ĕn-bōōrk
Marieux, mȧ'ryû'
Markirch, mär'kÍrk
Marlemont, märl'môN'
Marles, märl
Marloie, mȧr'lwä'
Marly, mȧr'lē'
Maroilles, mȧ'rwä'y'
Maron, mȧ'rôN'
Marquin, mȧr'kăN'
Marsal, mär'zȧl
Marseille (or Marseilles), mȧr'sȧ'y'
Marseilles, mär-sȧlz'
Mars-la-Tour, märs'-lȧ'-tōōr'
Martincourt, mȧr'tăN'kōōr'
Marville, ...ȧr'vēl'
Massemen, mȧs'ē-mĕn
Massigcs, mȧ'sēzh'
Maubert-Fontaine, mō'bȧr'-fôN'tĕn'
Maubeuge, mō'bûzh'
Maulde, mōld
Maxenchamp, mȧ'zăN'shäN'
Mayence (or Mainz), mȧ'yäNs'
Mazée, mȧ'zä'
Meaux, mō
Mecca (or Mekka), mĕk'ȧ
Mechlin (or Malines), mĕk'lÍn
Medernach, mä'dĕr-näk
Medina, mȧ-dē'nä
Meerssen, mär'sĕn
Mekka (or Mecca), mĕk'ȧ
Melle, mĕl
Mellier, mĕl'yä'
Melreux, mĕl'rû'
Melun, mē-lûN'
Membruggen, mĕm'brōōg-ĕn
Menil, mē-nēl'
Menin, mē-năN'
Menil-la-Tour, mē-nēl'-lȧ'-tōōr'
Merbecque, mĕr'bĕk'
Merbes, mĕrb
Merchtem, mĕrk'tĕm
Mercken, mĕr'kĕn
Mercy-le-Bas, mĕr'sē'-lĕ-bä'
Mercy-le-Haut, mĕr'sē'-lĕ-ō'
Merlemont, mĕrl'môN'
Mersch, mĕrsh
Merval, mĕr'vȧl'
Merville, mĕr'vēl'
Messancy, mē-säN'sē'
Messein, mē-săN'
Messines, mē-sēn'
Mestre, mĕs'trä
Métaires, mȧ'târ'
Metnitz, mĕt'nÍts
Metrich, mĕt'rÍk
Mettecoven, mĕt'ē-kō'fĕn
Metz, mĕts; Fr. mĕs
Metzeral, mĕt'sē-räl
Metzerwiese, mĕt'sĕr-vē'zĕ
Meulebeke, mû'lē-bä'kĕ
Meuse (river), mûz; Eng. mūz
Mézières, mȧ'zyär'
Mirwart, mĕr'värt
Mitrovicza (or Mitrovitz), mē'trō-vĕt'sa
Moerbeke, mōōr'bä-kĕ
Moerkerke, mōōr'kĕr-kĕ
Moere, mōō'rĕ
Moggio, môd'jō
Mohammera, mō'hȧ-mä'rä
Mohiville, mō'ē'vēl'
Mohon, mō'ôN'
Moircy, mwär'sē'
Moldava (river), môl-dä'vȧ
Molhain, mō'lăN'

Monastir, mŏn'ȧs-tēr'
Monceau, môN'kō'
Moncel, môN'sĕl'
Monchy, môN'shē'
Mondelange, mŏn'dē-läng'ē
Monfalcone, mŏn'fäl-kō'nä
Mons, môNs
Mons-en-Pévéle, môN'-zäN'-pä'väl'
Mont, môN
Montagnana, mŏn'tä-nyä'nä
Montbéliard, môN'bä'lyär'
Montdidier, môN'dē'dyä'
Montfaucon, môN'fō'kôN'
Montherme, môN'tĕrm'
Monthureux, môN'tü'rû'
Montigny, môN'tē'nyē'
Montjoie, môN'jwä'
Montrœdy, môN'mä'dē'
Montmirail, môN'mē'rȧ'y'
Montoise, môN'twäz'
Montreau Vieux, môN'trō'vyû'
Mont-St.-Amand, môN'-säN'-tȧ'mäN'
Mont-St.-Aubert, môN'-säN'-tō'bär'
Mont-St.-Éloy, môN'-säN'-tä'lwä'
Mont-St.-Jean, môN'-säN'-zhäN'
Mont-St.-Martin, môN'-säN'-mär'tăN'
Mont-St.-Pierre, môN'-säN'-pyär'
Mont-St.-Rémy, môN'-säN'-rä'mē'
Montsec, môN'sĕk'
Moorslede, mōrs'lä-dĕ
Moreuil, mō'rû'y'
Morey, mō'rē'
Moriville, mō'rē'vēl'
Morville, môr'vēl'
Mosul, mō'sōōl'
Mouaville, mōō'ȧ'vĕl'
Mouchin, mōō'shăN'
Moulbaix, mōōl'bä'
Moulins, mōō'lăN'
Mouscron, mōōs'krôN'
Moustier, mōōs'tyä'
Mouvaux, mōō'vō'
Mouzay, mōō'zē'
Moyen, mwä'yäN'
Moyenmoutier, mwä'yäN'mōō'tyä'
Moyenneville, mwä'yĕn'vēl'
Mozet, mō'zĕ'
Muggia, mōōd'jä
Mülhausen, mül'hou'zĕn
Münster, mün'stĕr
Murville, mür'vēl'
Mush, mōōsh
Musson, mü'zôN'
Muysen, nä'sĕn
Muzeray, mü'zē-rē'

Nadrin, nä'drăN'
Nakhitchevan, nä'kē-chĕ-väN'
Nampteuil, nä'tû'y'
Namur, nä'mür'
Nancy, näN'sē'; Eng. năn'sÍ
Nandrin, näN'drăN'
Narew (or Narev river), nä'rĕf
Nassogno, nä'sôn'y'
Nazareth, (Belgium) nä'zȧ'rĕt'
Nennig, nĕn'Ík
Nesle, näl
Neubois, nû'bwä'
Neuenburg, noi'ĕn-bōōrk
Neufchâteau, nû'shä'tō'
Neufchatel, nû'shä'tĕl'
Neufchef, nû'shĕf'
Neuilly-sur-Marne, nû'yē'-sür'-märn'
Neumarkt, noi'märkt
Neutitschein, noi'tÍt'shÍn
Neuve Chapelle, nûv' shä'pĕl'
Neuve Église, nûv ä'glēz'
Neuve Maison, nûv' mä'zôN'
Neuves Maisons, nûv mä'zôN'
Neuville, noi'vēl'
Neuweiler, noi'vÍler
Niekirchen, nē'kĕr'kĕn
Niel, nēl
Nieuport, nē'ōō-pôrt
Nikolaief (or Nikolayev), nyē'kō-lä'yĕf
Nîmes (or Nismes), nēm
Ninove, nē'nōv'
Nivelles, nē'vĕl'
Nives, nēv
Noerdange, nōōr'dáng-ē

Noirefontaine, nwär'fôN'tĕn'
Noirval, nwär'vȧl'
Noisy-le-Sec, nwä'zē'-lē-sĕk'
Noreuil, nō'rû'y'
Norroy-le-Sec, nō'rwä'-lē-sĕk'
Norvenich, nōr'fē-nÍk
Nouzon, nōō'zôN'
Novillo, nō'vēl'
Novogeorgievsk, nō'vō-gĕ-ôr'gĕ-yĕfsk
Noyelle, nwä'yĕl'
Noyen, nwä'yäN'

Obaix, ō'bä'
Oberbruck, ō'bĕr-brōōk
Obersgegen, ō'bĕrz-gä'gĕn
Ober-Weiler, ō'bĕr-vī'lĕr
Ober-Weiss, ō'bĕr-vīs'
Occoches, ō'kôsh'
Ocham, , ō'shän'
Octringen, ōk'trÍng'ĕn
Oderen, ō'dē-rĕn
Oderzo, ō-dĕrt'sō
Oedelem, ōō'dē-lĕm
Offey, ō'fē'
Ogeviller, ōzh've'yä'
Ogy, ō'zhē'
Ohain, ō'äN'
Ohey, ō'ē'
Oignies, wä'nyē'
Oise (river), wäz
Oisy, wä'zē'
Ollignies, ō'lē'nyē'
Olloy, ō'lwä'
Olmütz, ōl'müts
Olzheim, ōlts'hÍm
Omicourt, ō'mē'kōōr'
Onnaing, ō'näN'
Oombergen, ōm'bĕr-gĕn
Oostacker, ōst'äk'ĕr
Oostcamp, ōst'kämp'
Oostkerke, ōst'kĕr-kĕ
Opont, ō'pôN'
Oppy, ō'pē'
Orbey, ōr'bē'
Orchies, ōr'shē'
Orchimont, ōr'shē'môN'
Orcq, ōrk
Origny, ō'rē'nyē'
Ornel, ōr'nĕl'
Orsay, ōr'sē'
Orsera, ōr-sä'rä
Orval, ōr'vȧl'
Ossero, ōs-sä'rō
Ostiglia, ōs-tēl'yä
Ostrog, ōs-trōk'
Ostrow, ōs'trōf
Ottendorf, ōt'ĕn-dôrf
Ottignies, ō'tē'nyē'
Ottingen, ōt'Íng-ĕn
Ouchez, ōō'shä'
Oudenarde (or Audenarde), ou'dĕ-när'dĕ
Oudler, ōōd'lä'
Ouffet, ōō'fä'
Ouire, wĕr
Ourcq (river), ōōrk
Ourthe (river), ōōrt

Padova (or Padua), pä'dō-vä
Padua (or Padova), păd'û-ȧ
Pagny, pä'nyē'
Pagnies, pä'nyē'
Pago, pä'gō
Paliseul, pä'lē'sûl'
Palmanova, päl'mä-nō'vä
Pange, päng'ĕ
Panne, La, lä pän'
Pannes, pän
Parenzo, pä-rĕnt'sō
Paris, pär'Ís; Fr. pä'rē'
Parroy, pä'rwä'
Pas-de-Calais, pä'-dē-kä'lē'
Passchendaele, päs'kĕn-dä'lē
Patignies, pä'tē'nyē'
Pattingen, pät'Íng-ĕn
Pâturages, pä'tü'räzh'
Paxonne, pä'zôN'
Pecq, pĕk
Pelingen, pä'lÍng-ĕn
Pellestrina, pĕl'lĕs-trē'nä

408

Peltre, pĕl′trä
Pepinster, pĕp′ĭn-stĕr
Perck, pĕrk
Peremysl (or Przemysl), pĕ-rĕ′mĭshl-y′; pshĕ′mĭshl-y′
Perl, pĕrl
Pernes, pĕrn
Péronne, pā′rŏn′
Perthes, pĕrt
Peschiera, pā-skyä′rä
Petersbach, pā′tĕrz-bäk
Petingen, pĕt′ĭng-ĕn
Petit-Croix, pē-tē′-krwä′
Petit-Magny, pē-tē′-mä′nyē′
Petitmont, pē-tē′mŏN′
Petrokov (or Piotrków), pyĕ′trŏ-kôf′
Peuthy, pū′tē′
Peuvillers, pū′vē′lär′
Pfaffenheim, pfäf′ĕn-hĭm
Pfetterhausen, pfĕt′ĕr-hou′zĕn
Philippeville, fē′lēp′vĕl′
Phlin, flän
Piacenza, pyä-chĕnt′sä
Piave (river), pyä′vä
Picardy, pĭk′ar-dĭ
Pierrefonds, pyâr′fôN′
Pierrepont, pyâr′pôN′
Pietro, pyē′trŏ
Pieve di Cadore, pyĕ′vä dĕ kä-dô′rä
Pilken, pĭl′kĕn
Pillon, pē′yôN′
Pinte, La, lä′ pänt
Piotrków (or Petrokov), pyôtr′kŏŏf′
Piove, pyŏ′vä
Piræus, pī-rē′ŭs
Pirano, pē-rä′nŏ
Pitthem, pĭt′ĕm
Plainfaign, plän′fäN′
Plancher - les - Mines, plän′shä′-lä′-mĕn′
Plasschendaele, pläs′kĕn-dä′lĕ
Plombières, plôN′byär′
Podgórze, pŏd-gōō′zhĕ
Poelcapelle, pōōl′kä′pĕl′
Poitiers, pwä′tyä′
Poix, pwä
Poix-St.-Hubert, pwä′-säN′-tü′bâr′
Pola, pō′lä
Polleur, pŏ′lûr′
Pont-à-Celles, pôN′-tä′-sĕl′
Pont-à-Marcq, pôN′-tä′-märk′
Pont-à-Mousson, pôN′-tä′-mōō′zôN′
Pontebba, pŏn-tĕb′bä
Ponte di Piave, pôN′tä dē pyä′vä
Pontoy, pôN′toi
Pont-Pierre, pôN′-pyâr′
Pont - Ste. - Maxence, pôN′ - sänt′-mä′zäNs′
Pont-sur-Sambre, pôN′-sür′-säN′br′
Poperinghe, pŏ′pĕ-räng′
Pordenone, pŏr′dä-nŏ′nä
Portogruaro, pŏr′tŏ-grōō-ä′rŏ
Portole, pŏr′tŏ-lä
Portore, pŏr′tŏ-rä
Port Said, pŏrt sä-ēd′
Potteaux, pŏ′tŏ′
Pozières, pŏ′zyär′
Predazzo, prä-dät′sŏ
Pripet, prē′pĕt
Prisrend, prē′zrĕnt
Profondeville, prŏ′fôNd′vĕl′
Promontore (cape), prŏ′mŏn-tŏ′rä
Pronsfeld, prŏnz′fĕlt
Proskurof (or Proskurov), prŏ′skŏŏ-rôf′
Proven, prŏ′vĕn
Provenchères, prŏ′väN′shâr′
Provin, prŏ′väN′
Prum, prōōm
Pruth (river), prōōt
Przasnsyz, pshäs′nĭsh
Przemysl (or Peremysl), pshĕ′mĭshl-y′
Pulnoy, pŭl′nwä′
Pultusk, pōōl′tōōsk
Pussemange, püs′mäNzh′
Püttlingen, püt′lĭng-ĕn
Puxieux, pü′zyŭ′

Quareux, kä′rŭ′
Quarnero, kwär-nä′rŏ
Quartes, kärt

Quatre-Bras, kä′tr′-brä′
Quesnoy, Le, lĕ kä′nwä′
Quevaucamps, kĕ-vŏ′käN′
Quievrain, kē′ĕ-vräN
Quievy, kē′ĕ-vē′

Raddon, rä′dôN′
Radmaunsdorf, räd′mounz-dôrf
Radom, rä′dŏm
Radzivilov, räd′zĕ′vĕ-lôf′
Raeren, rä′rĕn
Rambervillers, räN′bĕr′vĕ′lär′
Rambruch, räm′brŏŏk
Ramecourt, räm′kŏŏr′
Ramet, rä′mä′
Ramillies, rä′mĕ′yĕ′
Ramonchamps, rä′môN′shäN′
Ramont, rä′môN′
Rance, räNs
Ranconnière, räN′kŏ′nyâr′
Raon, räN
Raon-l'Étape, räN′-lä′täp′
Rappoltsweiler, räp′ŏlts-vī′lĕr
Rastenburg, räs′tĕn-bōōrk′
Raucourt, rŏ′kŏŏr′
Raulecourt, rŏl′kŏŏr′
Raulseur, rŏl′sûr′
Rava (or Rawa), rä′vä
Raves, räv
Raville, rä′vĕl′
Ravnagora, räv′nä-gŏ′rä
Rawaruska, rä′vä-rōōs′kä
Rechingen, rĕĸ′ĭng-ĕn
Recogne, rĕ′kŏn′y′
Redu, rĕ′dü′
Regnieville, rĕ′nyĕ′vĕl′
Réhainviller, rä′äN′vĕ′yä′
Réhan, rä′äN′
Reichlange, rĭĸ′läng-ĕ
Reims (or Rheims), rēmz; Fr. räNs
Reisdorf, rīz′dôrf
Releghem, rĕl′ĕ-gĕm
Remagne, rĕ-män′y′
Rémaucourt, rä′mŏ′kŏŏr′
Remich, rä′mĭk
Remiremont, rĕ-mēr′môN′
Rémy, rä′mē′
Renaix, rĕ-nä′
Renland, räN′länt
Renlies, räN′lē′
Renwez, räN′vä′
Repaix, rĕ-pĕ′
Resteigne, rĕs′tĕn′y′
Rethel, rĕ-tĕl′
Reuland, roi′länt
Revin, rĕ-väN′
Rezonville, rĕ-zŏN′vĕl′
Rheims (or Reims), rēmz; Fr. räNs
Ribecourt, rĕb′kŏŏr′
Ribemont, rĕb′môN′
Richterich, rĭĸ′tĕ-rĭĸ
Riempst, rĕmpst
Rienne, rē′ĕn′
Riga, rē′gä
Rigny, rē′nyē′
Rimbach, rĕm′bäk
Rimogne, rē′môN′y′
Rinnthal, rĭn′täl
Rivière, rē′vyär′
Robecq, rŏ′bĕk′
Robechies, rŏb′shē′
Robelmont, rŏ′bĕl′môN′
Roche, La, lä′ rŏsh′
Rochefort, rŏsh′fôr′
Rochehaut, rŏsh′ŏ′
Rochesson, rŏsh′sôN′
Roclincourt, rŏ′kläN′kŏŏr′
Rocroi, rŏ′krwä′
Rodemachern, rŏ′dĕ-mäk′ĕrn
Roeux, rŏ′ŭ′
Roisel, rwä′zĕl′
Roly, rŏ′lē′
Rombas, rŏm′bäs
Roncq, rôNk
Roobors, rŏ′bôrs
Rorbach, rŏr′bäk
Rosée, rŏ′zä′
Rosières, rŏ′zyär′
Rosières-en-Santerre, rŏ′zyär′-säN′ säN′tär′

Rossart, rŏ′sär′
Rotgen, rŏt′gĕn
Rothau, rŏ′tou
Roubaix, rōō′bĕ
Rouen, rwäN
Rouffach, rōō′fäk
Rougemont, rōōzh′môN′
Roulers, rōō′lä′
Roupy, rōō′pē′
Rousbrugge, rous′brŏŏg-ĕ
Rouves, rōōv
Rouvres, rōō′vr′
Rouvrois, rōōv′rwä′
Rouvroy, rōōv′rwä′
Roux, rōō
Roverbella, rŏ′vĕr-bĕl′lä
Roveredo, rŏ′vä-rä′dŏ
Rovigno, rŏ-vē′nyŏ
Rovigo, rŏ-vē′gŏ
Royaumeix, rwä′yŏ′mĕ′
Roye, rwä
Rozoy-sur-Serre, rŏ′zwä′-sür′-sâr′
Rozzo, rŏd′zŏ
Ruddervoorde, rŭd′ĕr-vŏr′dĕ
Rudlin, rŭd′län′
Rulles, rül
Rumbeke, rŭm′bä-kĕ
Rumes, rüm
Rumigny, rü′mē′nyē′
Rupt, rüp
Russen, rŭs′ĕn
Rzeszow, zhĕ′shŏŏf

Saar (river), zär
Saarbrücken, zär′brük′ĕn
Saarburg, zär′bŏŏrk
Sablon, sä′blŏN′
Sachsenburg, säk′sĕn-bŏŏrk
Sacile, sä-chē′lä
Safed, sä′fĕd′
Saffelaere, säf′ĕ-lä′rĕ
Saida, sä′ĕ-dä
Sains, säN
Sains-Richmont, säN′-rĕsh′môN′
Saint-Amand, säN′tä′män′
Saint-Benoit, säN′-bĕ-nwä′
Saint-Blaize, säN′-bläz′
Saint-Bresson, säN′-brĕ-sôN′
Saint-Cyr, säN′-sēr′
Saint-Denis, säN′-dĕ-nē′
Saint-Dié, säN′-dyä′
Saint-Étienne, säN′-tä′tyĕn′
Saintes, säNt
Saint-Genest, säN′-zhĕ-nĕ′
Saint-Georges, säN′-zhôrzh′
Saint-Gérard, säN′-zhä′rär′
Saint-Germain, säN′zhĕr′män′
Saint-Ghislain, säN′-gĕs′läN′
Saint-Gilles, säN′-zhēl′
Saint-Hilaire, säN′-tĕ′lâr′
Saint-Hubert, säN′-tü′bâr′
Saint-Jean, säN′-zhäN′
Saint-Josse-ten-Noode, säN′-zhŏs′ täN′-nŏd′
Saint-Julien, säN′-zhü′lyäN′
Saint-Laurent, säN′-lŏ′räN′
Saint-Léger, säN′-la′zhä′
Saint-Léonard, säN′-lä′ŏ′nár′
Saint-Marcel, säN′-mär′sĕl′
Sainte-Marguerite, säNt′-már′gĕ-rēt′
Sainte-Marie, säNt′-mä′rē′
Saint-Martin, säN′-mär′täN′
Saint-Maurice, säN′-mŏ′rēs′
Saint-Medard, säN′-mĕ-där′
Saint-Michel, säN′-mĕ′shĕl′
Saint-Mihiel, säN′-mĕ′yĕl′
Saint-Nabord, säN′-nä′bŏr′
Saint-Nicholas, säN′-nē′kŏ′lä′
Saint-Omer, säN′-tŏ′mär′
Saint-Ouen, säN′-twäN′
Saint-Paul, säN′-pŏl′
Saint-Pierre, säN′-pyär′
Saint-Pol, säN′-pŏl′
Saint-Privat, säN′-prē′vä′
Saint-Quentin, säN′-känt′täN′
Saint-Remy, säN′-rĕ-mē′
Saint-Simon, säN′-sē′môN′
Saint-Sulpice, säN′-sül′pēs′
Saint-Trond, säN′-trôN′
Saint-Venant, säN′-vĕ-näN′

Sainville, săn'-vĕl'
Saleux, să'lû'
Saloniki (or Salonica), să'lŏ-nē'kē
Salvore, săl-vŏ'rä
Sambre (river), săn'br'
Samrée, săn'rā'
San (river), săn
Sancourt, săn'kōōr'
San Giorgio, săn jôr'jō
Santeuil, săn'tû'y'
San Pietro, săn pyä'trō
Sapogne, să'pŏn'y'
Sappois-le-Bas, să'pwá'-lĕ-bä'
Sappois-le-Haut, să'pwá'-lĕ-ō'
San Vito, săn vē'tō
Sarajevo (or Sarayevo), să'rä-yä-vŏ
Sarifa, să-rē'fä
Sart, sär
Sarthe (river), sårt
Saulnes, sōn
Saulnot, sō'nŏ'
Sauvigny, sŏ'vē'nyē'
Saulxures, sō'lür'
Save (river), säv
Saventhem, sä'vĕn-tĕm
Schaerbeek, sкär'bäk
Scheven, sкă'vĕn
Schifflingen, shĭf'lĭng-ĕn
Schio, skē'ō
Schirmeck, shĕr'mĕk
Schleiden, shlī'dĕn
Schmidtheim, shmĭt'hīm
Schoenecken, skōō'nĕk-ĕn
Schöneberg, shû'nĕ-bĕrk
Schooten, skō'tĕn
Schopp, shŏp
Schrierlach, shrēr'läk
Scutari (or Skutari), skōō'tä-rē
Seclin, sĕ-klän'
Sedan, sĕ-dän'
Segelsem, sä'gĕl-sĕm
Seicheprey, sĕsh'prĕ'
Seine (river), săn
Selbach, zäl'bäk
Seloignes, sĕ-lwán'y'
Seneffe, sĕ-nĕf'
Senlis, săn'lēs'
Sénon, sä'nŏN'
Sentheim, zänt'hīm
Seny, sĕ-nē'
Seraing, sĕ-răN'
Seres, sĕr'ĕs
Sereth (river), să-rĕt'
Serres, sâr
Servance, sĕr'väns'
Servigny, sĕr'vē'nyē'
Seuil, sû'y'
Sevran, sĕ-vräN'
Sézanne, sä'zán'
Sibret, sĕ'brä'
Sichen, sĭк'ĕn
Siedlce (or Syedlets), shĕl'tsĕ
Sierck, zĕrk
Signy-l'Abbaye, sĕ'nyĕ'-lá'bä'
Signy-le-Petit, sĕ'nyĕ'-lĕ-pĕ-tĕ'
Silenrieux, sĕ'län'ryû'
Sillegny, sĕ'lĕ'nyē'
Silly, sĕ'yä'
Simmerath, zĭm'ĕ-rät
Sin, săn
Sinay, sĕ'nĕ'
Sinob (or Sinope), sĕ-nŏb'
Sinope (or Sinob), sĭ-nŏ'pĕ
Sinsin, săn'săn'
Sinspelt, zĕnz'pĕlt
Sirault, sĕ'rō'
Sivas, sĕ'väs'
Sivry, sĕ'vrĕ'
Skoplje (or Wsküp), skŏp'lyĕ
Skutari (or Scutari), skōō'tä-rē
Sleydinge, slī'dĭŋ-gĕ
Slype, slĕp
Snaeskerke, snäs'kĕr-kĕ
Sochaux, sŏ'shŏ'
Sofia (or Sophia), sŏ'fē-á; sŏ-fē'ä
Sohier, sŏ'ā'
Soignies, swá'nyē'
Soire, swâr
Soissons, swä'sŏN'
Sokolof (or Sokolow), sŏ'kŏ-lŏf'

Solbach, zŏl'bäk
Solesmes, sŏ'läm'
Sologne, sŏ'lŏn'y'
Somain, sŏ'măN'
Sombrin, sŏN'brăN'
Somergem, sŏ'mĕr-gĕm
Somme (river, department), sŏm
Sommerviller, sŏ'mĕr've'yä'
Somzée, sŏN'zä'
Soppe, zŏp'ĕ
Sorcy, sŏr'sē'
Sotenich, zŏ'tĕ-nĭk
Sottegem, sŏt'ĕ-gĕm
Souain, sōō'ăN'
Souilly, swē'yē'
Soulosse, sōō'lŏs'
Soultzbach, zoults'bäk
Soultzmatt, zoults'mät
Soumagne, sōō'mán'y'
Soumay, sōō'mĕ'
Soupir, sōō'pēr'
Sourbrodt, zour'brŏt
Sourvoy, sōōr'vwä'
Spilimbergo, spē'lĕm-bĕr'gō
Spincourt, spăN'kōōr'
Spittal, shpĭt'äl
Spy, spē
Staple, stá'pl'
Staufen, shtou'fĕn
Steenbrugge, stän'brōōg'ĕ
Steenvoorde, stän'vōr-dē
Steige, shtī'gĕ
Sterrebeek, stĕr'ĕ-bäk
Stettin, shtĕ-tēn'
Stosswihr, shtŏs'vēr
Stoumont, stōō'mŏN'
Straimont, strĕ'mŏN'
Stralsund, shträl'zōōnt
Stree, strä
Strigno, strē'nyō
Struma (river), strōō'mä
Stryj, strē'y'
Sugny, sü'nyē'
Suippes, swēp
Suwalki, sōō-väl'kē
Sweveghem, swä'vē-gĕm
Swevezeele, swä'vē-zä'lē
Swinemünde, svē'nĕ-mün'dē
Syedlets (or Siedlce), syĕd'lyĕts

Tabriz, tä-brēz'
Tahure, tá'ür'
Taintrux, tăN'trü'
Tarcento, tär-chĕn'tŏ
Tarcienne, tär'syĕn'
Tarnopol, tär-nŏ'pŏl-y'
Tarnow, tär'nŏŏf'
Tavaux, tä'vŏ'
Tavigny, tá've'nyē'
Tchatalja (or Chatalja), chä-täl'jä
Tchernavoda (or Cernavoda), chĕr'nä-vŏ'dä
Tellancourt, tĕ-län'kōōr'
Tellin, tĕ-lăN'
Templeuve, tän'plûv'
Tentre, tän'tr'
Termes, tĕrm
Termonde(orDendermonde),tĕr'mŏnd'
Ternuay, tĕr'nû'ĕ'
Thann, tän
Thaon, tän
Thélus, tä'lü'
Thérouanne, tä'rōō'án'
Thézey, tä'zĕ'
Thiant, tĕ'äN'
Thiaucourt, tyŏ'kōōr'
Thiefosse, tyĕ-fŏs'
Thielt, tĕlt
Thiene, tyĕ'nä
Thil, tĕl
Thillot, tĕ'yŏ'
Thionville (or Diedenhofen), tyŏN'vĕl'
Thirimont, tē'rē'mŏN'
Thourout, tōō'rōō'
Thuin, tü'äN'
Tillet, tē'yä'
Tincourt, tăN'kōōr'
Tirlemont, tēr'l'mŏN'
Tolmezzo, tŏl-mĕt'sŏ
Tomasof (or Tomaszow), tŏ-mä'sŏŏf

Tongres, tôN'gr'
Tourcoing, tōōr'kwăN'
Tournay (or Tournai), tōōr'nä'
Traubach, trou'bäk
Trenchiennes, trän'shyĕn'
Trebizond, trĕb'ĭ-zŏnd'
Tregnano, trä-nyä'nŏ
Trélon, trä'lŏN'
Treviso, trä-vē'zŏ
Triaucourt, trĕ'ŏ'kōōr'
Trieste (or Triest), trĕ-ĕst'
Trieux, trĕ'û'
Trouche, La, lá' trōōsh'
Turkheim, tōōrk'hīm

Uberstrasse, ü'bĕr-shträs'ĕ
Udine, ōō'dĕ-nä
Ugny, ü'nyĕ'
Umago, ōō-mä'gŏ
Unio (or Unieh), ü-nē'ĕ
Urbach, ōōr'bäk
Urbeis, ōōr'bīs
Urfa, ōōr'fä'
Urmatt, ōōr'mät
Urmiah (or Urmia, Urumiah), ōōr'mē'ä
Urrel, ōōr'ĕl
Uruffe, ü'rüf'
Usküp (or Usküb, Skoplje), üs-küp'

Vacquerie, vá'kĕ-rē'
Vagney, vá'nyĕ'
Valenciennes, vá'län'syĕn'
Valhey, vál'ĕ'
Valjevo (or Valyevo), väl'yá-vŏ
Valmerangen, väl'mĕ-räng'ĕn
Valmy, väl'mē'
Vance, väns
Vancouleurs, văN'kōō'lûr'
Vandières, văn'dyär'
Vannes, ván
Vardar (river), vär'där'
Varennes-en-Argonne, vá'rĕn'-zăN'-är'gŏn'
Vaucourt, vŏ'kōōr'
Vaudemont, vŏd'mŏN'
Vaux, vŏ
Vécoux, vä'kōō'
Veglia, vä'lyä
Veiving, fī'fĭng
Velaines, vĕ-län'
Velasnes, vĕ-län'
Vellerois, vĕl'rwä'
Vellescot, vĕl'skŏ'
Vendée, văn'dä'
Vendegies, vänd'zhē'
Vendin, văn'dăN'
Venezia (or Venice), vä-nĕt'syä
Venice (or Venezia), vĕn'ĭs
Vennezey, vĕn'zĕ'
Ventron, văn'trôN'
Verdenal, vĕrd'nál'
Verdun, vĕr'dŭn'
Vermand, vĕr'mäN'
Verneuil, vĕr'nû'y'
Verona, vĕ-rō'ná; It. vä-rō'nä
Versailles, vĕr'sä'y'; Eng. vĕr-sälz'
Verviers, vĕr'vyär'
Vervins, vĕr'văN'
Verzy, vĕr'zĕ'
Viaden, vē'á-dĕn
Vicenza, vē-chĕnt'sä
Vigneulles, vē'nyül'
Villafranca, vĕl'lä-frän'kä
Villemontoire, vĕl'mŏN'twár'
Villers-Bretonneux, vĕ'lär'-brĕ-tŏ'nû'
Villers-Cotterets, vĕ'lär'-kŏ'tĕ-rĕ'
Villers-la-Ville, vē'lär'-lá'-vĕl'
Villerupt, vĕl'rüp'
Villiers, vē'yä'
Vilvorde, vĕl'vŏrd'
Vimy, vē'mē'
Vincey, văn'sĕ'
Vireux, vē'rû'
Vistula (or Weichsel), vĭs'tû-lá
Vitrimont, vē'trē'mŏN'
Vitry-en-Artois, vē'trē'-äN'-är'twä'
Vitry-le-François, vē'trē'-lĕ-frän'swä'
Vittorio, vĕt-tô'rē-ŏ
Voivre, La, lá' vwä'vr'
Volga, vŏl'gá; Russ. vôl'gä

Volhynia, vŏl-ĭn′ĭ-à
Volta, vŏl′tä
Voorde, vōr′dĕ
Vosges, vōzh
Vottem, vŏt′ĕm
Vouziers, vōō′zyâr′
Vy-les-Lure, vē′-lä′-lür′

Wahlesscheid, vä′lĕz-shīt′
Walcourt, vàl′kōōr′
Walheim, väl′hīm
Wallendorf, väl′ĕn-dôrf
Wallers, và′lär′
Wancennes, vän′sĕn′
Wanlin, vän′lăn′
Wardin, vár′dăn′
Warta (or Warthe), vär′tĕ
Warzée, vár′zä′
Wasigny, và′sē′nyē′
Wasmes, väm
Wasserbillig, väs′ĕr-bĭl′ĭk
Wassigny, và′sē′nyē′
Waterloo, wô′tĕr-lōō′; *Du.* wä′tĕr-lō′
Watigny, và′tē′nyē′
Watweiler, vät′vī-lĕr

Wavre, vàv′r′
Wavrin, và′vrăn′
Waxweiler, väks′vī-lĕr
Weerde, wär′dĕ
Weerf, wärf
Wehingen, vä′hĭng-ĕn
Weichsel (or Vistula), vīk′sĕl
Weismes, vīz′mĕz
Weiten, vī′tĕn
Weitersweiler, vī′tĕrz-vī′lĕr
Wembach, väm′bäk
Werlaing, vĕr′lăn′
Wervicq, vĕr′vĕk′
Weselberg, vä′zĕl-bĕrk
Wetteren, wĕt′ĕr-ĕn
Wibrin, vē′brăn′
Wignehies, vēn′yĕ-ē′
Wiltz, vēlts
Wintzenheim, vĭnt′sĕn-hīm
Wizernes, vē′zârn′
Woel, wōōl
Woëvre, vŏ′ĕv′r′
Woippy, voi′pē
Wolmeringen, vŏl′mĕr-ĭng′en
Woluwe-Saint-Lambert, wŏl′ŭ-wĕ-sĕnt-läm′bĕrt

Wörth, vûrt
Würselen, vür′zĕ-lĕn

Xammes, zàm
Xaronval, zà′rôn′vàl′
Xertigny, zĕr′tē′nyē′
Xironcourt, zĕ′rôn′kōōr′
Xivry, zē′vrē′
Xures, zür

Yassy (or Jassy), yäs′ĕ
Ypres, ē′pr′
Yser (river), ē′sä′
Yvoir, ē′vwár′

Zabern, tsä′bĕrn
Zamosk (or Zamosc), zä′mŏshch
Zeebrugge, tsä′brōōg′ĕ
Zellenburg, tsĕl′ĕn-bōōrk
Zirknitz, tsĕrk′nĭts
Zittau, tsĭt′ou
Zloczów, zlŏ′chŏŏf
Zweibrücken, tsvī′brük′ĕn

NOTE: This index covers fully the historical text written by Mr. Simonds. It omits the supplemental material with which each volume concludes, as the detailed tables of contents made the indexing of this matter superfluous.

INDEX

Reference to volume numbers are indicated by small characters (² for instance) preceding page numbers

THE COUNTRY LIFE PRESS, GARDEN CITY, NEW YORK